CW01021869

85136458

Explore the World

GREEK ISLANDS

Author:
Anne Midgette

An Up-to-date travel guide
with 129 color photos
and 47 maps

Dear Reader: Being up-to-date is the main goal of the Nelles series. Our correspondents help keep us abreast of the latest developments in the travel scene, while our cartographers see to it that maps are also kept completely current. However, as the travel world is constantly changing, we cannot guarantee that all the information contained in our books is always valid. Should you come across a discrepancy, please contact us at: Nelles Verlag, Schleissheimer Str. 371 b, 80935 Munich, Germany, tel. (089) 3571940, fax. (089) 35719430, e-mail: Nelles.Verlag@t-online.de

Note: Distances and measurements, including temperatures, used in this guide are metric. For conversion information, please see the *Guidelines* section of this book.

LEGEND

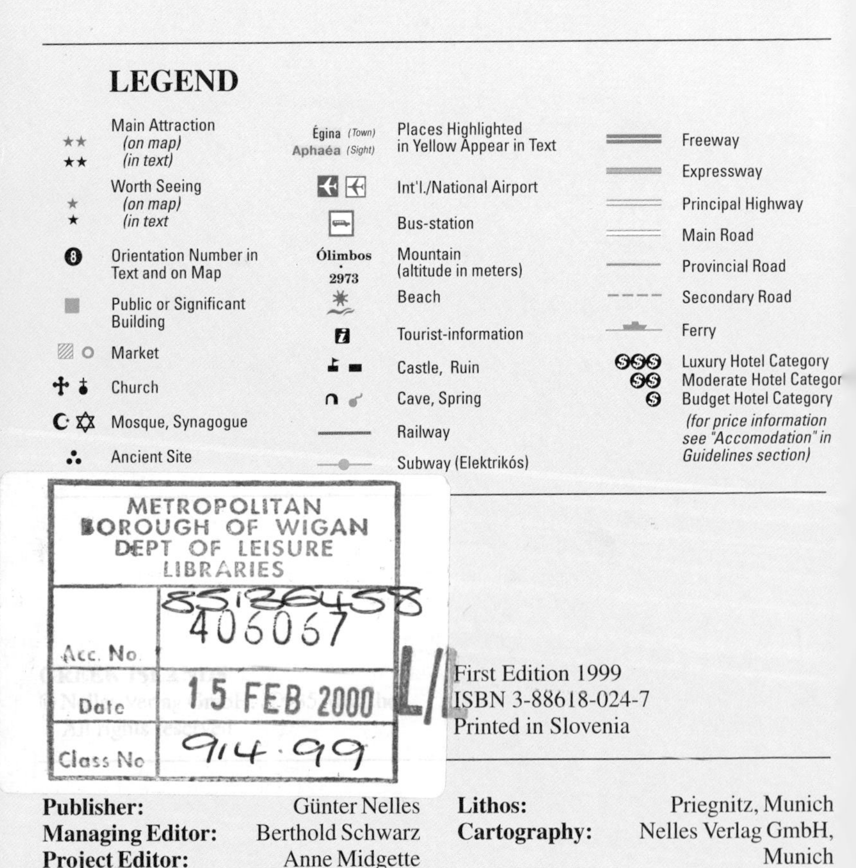

METROPOLITAN BOROUGH OF WIGAN
DEPT OF LEISURE
LIBRARIES
Acc. No. 85136458 406067
Date 15 FEB 2000
Class No 914.99
L/L

First Edition 1999
ISBN 3-88618-024-7
Printed in Slovenia

Publisher: Günter Nelles
Managing Editor: Berthold Schwarz
Project Editor: Anne Midgette
English Edition Editor: Chase Stewart
Lithos: Priegnitz, Munich
Cartography: Nelles Verlag GmbH, Munich
Printed By: Gorenjski Tisk

No part of this book, not even excerpts, may be reproduced without prior permission of Nelles Verlag.

- S01 -

TABLE OF CONTENTS

Imprint / Legend 2
List of Maps 6

HISTORY AND CULTURE

The Greek Islands: An Introduction 13
History and Culture 17
Greek Art and Architecture 32

ATHENS – ANCIENT AND MODERN CAPITAL

The Acropolis 39
The Agorá and Pláka 42
Monastiráki and Omónia Square 45
Sindágma Square and Vassílissis Sofías Boulevard . . . 46
Dafní Monastery / Piraeus 49
INFO: Hotels, Restaurants, Sights 50

THE GREEK ISLANDS

THE ISLANDS OF THE SARONIC GULF 55
Salamína (Salamis) 55
Égina (Aegina) 57
Póros / Ídra (Hydra) 60
Spétses 62
INFO: Hotels, Restaurants, Sights 63

THE CYCLADES 67
Northern: Ándros, Tínos, Míkonos, Dílos Síros 67
Western: Kéa, Kíthnos, Sérifos, Sífnos, Kímolos, Mílos . 80
Central: Páros, Andíparos, Náxos, Erimoníssa, Amorgós 90
Southern: Folégandros, Síkinos, Íos, Thíra, Anáfi 98
INFO: Hotels, Restaurants, Sights 104

THE SPORADES 111
Skiáthos 111
Skópelos 113
Alónnisos 114
Évia (Euboeia) 116
Skíros 119
INFO: Hotels, Restaurants, Sights 120

THE TRACIAN ISLANDS 123
Thásos 123
Samothráki 125
INFO: Hotels, Restaurants, Sights 127

THE NORTHEAST AEGEAN ISLANDS 131
Límnos 131
Lésvos (Lésbos, Mitilíni) 134
Híos 140
Ikaría 145
Sámos 149
INFO: Hotels, Restaurants, Sights 154

THE DODECANESE 159
Pátmos 159
Lipsí 162
Léros 163
Kálimnos 167
Astipálea 169
Kós 170
Nísiros 173
Tílos 176
Rhódos 177
Sími 187
Kárpathos and Kasós 189
Kastellóriso 192
INFO: Hotels, Restaurants, Sights 192

CRETE 199
Iráklio and Knossós 200
Lasíthi 202
Réthimno 203
Haniá 204
INFO: Hotels, Restaurants, Sights 205

THE IONIAN ISLANDS 209
Corfu (Kérkira) 210
Páxi 218
Lefkáda 219
Itháki 222
Kefaloniá 224
Zakínthos 226
Kíthira 228
INFO: Hotels, Restaurants, Sights 230

FEATURES

Literature and Music 232

Flora and Fauna 234

Sailing the Aegean 236

GUIDELINES

Preparing for Your Trip . . . 238
When to Go . . . 238
What to Pack . . . 238
Currency . . . 239
Visas and Customs . . . 239

Traveling to Greece . . . 239
By Plane . . . 239
By Boat . . . 239

Traveling in Greece . . . 240
By Plane . . . 240
By Boat . . . 240
By Flying Dolphin . . . 240
By Bus . . . 241
Car and Motorcycle Rental . . . 241
Taxis . . . 241

Practical Tips from A to Z . . . 242
Accommodation . . . 242
Crime . . . 242
Deportment . . . 242
Eating and Drinking . . . 242
Electricity . . . 244
Emergency Phone Numbers . . . 244
Handicapped Facilities . . . 245
Holidays and Festivals . . . 245
Hours of Business . . . 245
Maps . . . 245
Money . . . 246
Newspapers / Media . . . 246
Sports and Activities . . . 246
Telephones and Post . . . 246
Time . . . 247
Water and Plumbing . . . 247

Addresses . . . 247
Internet . . . 247
Embassies and Consulates in Athens . . . 247
Greek National Tourist Organization (EOT) Offices . . . 247

The Greek Language . . . 248

Author / Photographers . . . 249

Index . . . 250

LIST OF MAPS

Greek Islands 6-7
Athens. 40-41
Piraeus 49
Saronic Gulf 56
Ándros 68
Tínos 71
Míkonos / Dílos. 73
Ancient Dílos 76
Síros 78
Kéa 81
Kíthnos 81
Sérifos 83
Sífnos 85
Kímolos / Mílos 87
Páros / Andíparos. 90
Náxos 93
Erimoníssia 95
Amorgós 96
Folégandros / Síkinos / Íos 99
Thíra / Thirasía / Anáfi 102
Skiáthos / Skópelos / Alónissos . . 115
Évia (Euboeia) 117
Skíros 119
Thásos 124
Samothráki 126
Límnos 132
Lésvos 134
Híos 140
Ikaría 147
Sámos 150
Pátmos / Lipsí 161
Léros 164
Kálimnos 167
Astipálea 170
Kós 173
Nísiros 175
Tílos 177
Rhódos and Rhódos-Town 178
Sími 188
Kárpathos 191
Crete 200-201
Corfu 211
Páxi 218
Lefkáda 221
Kefaloniá / Itháki 225
Zákinthos 227
Kíthira 230

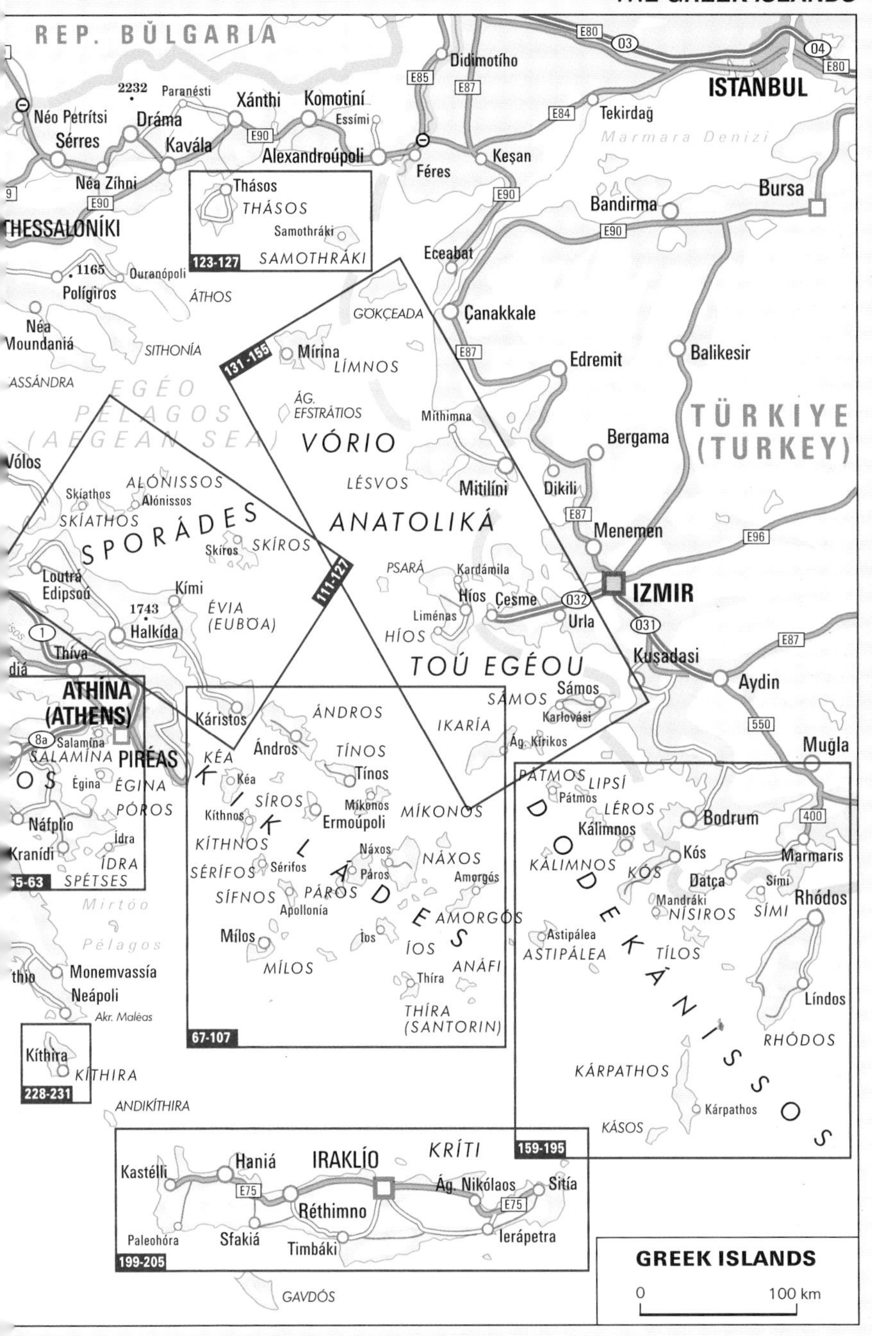
REP. BŬLGARIA
ISTANBUL
Didimotího
Néo Petrítsi
Paranésti
Xánthi
Komotiní
Essími
Dráma
Kavála
Sérres
Alexandroúpoli
Féres
Keşan
Tekirdağ
Marmara Denizi
Néa Zíhni
Thásos
THÁSOS
Samothráki
SAMOTHRÁKI
123-127
THESSALONÍKI
Bandirma
Bursa
Eceabat
Ouranópoli
Políğiros
ÁTHOS
GÖKÇEADA
Çanakkale
Néa Moundaniá
SITHONÍA
Mírina
LÍMNOS
131-155
Edremit
Balikesir
ASSÁNDRA
EGÉO PÉLAGOS (AEGEAN SEA)
ÁG. EFSTRÁTIOS
Míthimna
VÓRIO
TÜRKIYE (TURKEY)
Bergama
Vólos
LÉSVOS
Mitilíni
Dikili
ALÓNISSOS
Skíathos
Alónissos
SKÍATHOS
ANATOLIKÁ
Menemen
SPORÁDES
Skíros
SKÍROS
PSARÁ
Kardámila
Loutrá Edipsoú
Kími
111-127
Híos
Çesme
IZMIR
Urla
1743
ÉVIA (EUBOA)
Liménas
HÍOS
Halkída
Thíva
Kuşadasi
TOÚ EGÉOU
Aydin
ATHÍNA (ATHENS)
Sámos
SÁMOS
Karlovási
Káristos
ÁNDROS
IKARÍA
Salamína
SALAMÍNA
PIRÉAS
KÉA
Ándros
TÍNOS
Ág. Kírikos
Muğla
Kéa
Tínos
PÁTMOS
LIPSÍ
Pátmos
Égina
ÉGINA
SÍROS
Kíthnos
Míkonos
MÍKONOS
LÉROS
PÓROS
Ermoúpoli
Kálimnos
Bodrum
Náfplio
Ídra
KÍTHNOS
KIKLÁDES
Náxos
NÁXOS
KÁLIMNOS
Kós
Marmaris
Kranídi
ÍDRA
SÉRIFOS
Sérifos
Páros
Amorgós
KÓS
Datça
Sími
SPÉTSES
55-63
SÍFNOS
PÁROS
Mandráki
NÍSIROS
SÍMI
Rhódos
Mirtóo Pélagos
Apollonía
AMORGÓS
Astipálea
Mílos
Íos
ASTIPÁLEA
TÍLOS
DODEKÁNISSOS
Monemvassía
ÍOS
ANÁFI
MÍLOS
Thíra
Neápoli
Akr. Maléas
Líndos
THÍRA (SANTORIN)
67-107
RHÓDOS
Kíthira
KÍTHIRA
228-231
KÁRPATHOS
ANDIKÍTHIRA
Kárpathos
KÁSOS
KRÍTI
159-195
Haniá
IRAKLÍO
Kastélli
Ág. Nikólaos
Sitía
Réthimno
Paleohóra
Sfakiá
Timbáki
Ierápetra
199-205
GAVDÓS
GREEK ISLANDS
0
100 km
E80
03
04
E85
E87
E84
E90
E96
032
031
E75
550
400
8a
1
2232
1165

THE GREEK ISLANDS: AN INTRODUCTION

People say, "I'm going to the Greek Islands," as if that statement established a specific locale. In fact, it only clouds the issue. There are more than 1,400 islands in Greece, about one-fifth of the country's land area, although "only" 169 of them are officially inhabited (every book, moreover, will quote you different figures). Are "The Greek Islands" better described as vacation hot spots (Íos, Thíra, Kós) or remote mountain wildernesses (on Lésvos); rural outposts (Donússa) or urbane centers (Corfu); are the white Cycladic buildings of Míkonos Town more "typical" than the ochre neoclassical façades of Sími, the chilly Macedonian winters on Thásos less "in character" than the *meltemi* winds that scour the Cyclades in summer or the balmy climate of Rhódos, where the sun shines 300 days a year? All – and none – of the above. When John Donne wrote of "an island, entire of itself," he might have been talking about the distinct, individual worlds that comprise the Greek Islands.

Mainland Greece is a mountainous country, and the mountains run into the sea to form the Greek Islands, most of which are formed by sedimentary rock deposits. Nísiros, Thíra (Santorin) and Mílos are volcanic, and eruptions and earthquakes have continued into this century. The Ionian Islands were rocked by an earthquake in 1953, and Thíra in 1956.

The islands are divided into six main groups, more for administrative convenience than anything else. Along its western flank Greece abuts onto the Ionian Sea, named for the nymph Io (whom the goddess Hera turned into a cow as punishment for having attracted Zeus), and not to be confused with Ionia in Asia Minor, now Turkey. Of the **Ionian Islands**, Kérkira, or Corfu, is the largest and best-known; it represents many tourists' first introduction to Greece, as it's the first stop on the ferry route from Italy to Pátras. Other important Ionian islands are Kefaloniá and lovely Zákinthos.

Athens is perched on the southeastern coast of the Greek mainland, just above the Peloponnese, on the Saronic Gulf. Nearest to Athens and therefore popular day-trip destinations, the **Saronic Gulf Islands** bear resounding names from Greek history: Salamína, where the Athenian navy beat the Persians in 480 B.C., today a rather plain suburb, or Ídra and Spétses, whose ships formed the core of the Greek navy in the 1821 War of Independence. The latter two aren't really in the Saronic Gulf at all; they're tucked up against the Peloponnesian coast.

An hour north of Athens sprawls **Évia**, known to classicists as Euboeia, so big and so close to the mainland that people forget it's an island at all. Above it is a group of islands called the "Scattered Ones," or **Sporades**: popular Skiáthos and Skópelos, Alónnisos and Skíros.

In the northern reaches of the Aegean, Thásos and Samothráki are individualists with no taste for joining a group. Límnos, however, is administratively allied with the **Northeast Aegean Islands**, large islands which have in common forested interiors, rocky shores, and a definite independence and character: these are Mitilíni (better known to many as Lésvos), Híos, Sámos and Ikaría.

South of these, the **Dodecanese**, or "Twelve Islands," do have a common political and historical identity. There are in fact around 16 of them, from Pátmos in the north to Kásos in the south. Close to Turkey, these islands (also called the Southern Sporades) remained technically Turkish until the Italians arrived in 1914;

Preveious Pages: Holiday atmosphere with a view of the Aegean, Thíra. Easter on Kárpathos – women adorn the Epitaph with flowers. Left: Happy hour for sailors in the harbor of Megísti, Kastellóriso.

the Dodecanese didn't become Greek until 1945. At the center of all of these, the **Cyclades** are the best-known and most-visited of the Greek Islands. Most famous of this group are Náxos and Páros, Thíra (Santorin) and Íos; here, too, are beautiful Sérifos, cool Ándros, Tínos, "the Lourdes of Greece," and Amorgós. All of these "encircle" the sacred island of Dílos, supposedly the reason the "Cyclades" (deriving from the word for "circle") were so named.

Then there's the largest of the islands, **Crete**, so big that it deserves a book by itself. The chapter herein outlines a few highlights; anyone staying longer is referred to the *Nelles Guide Crete*.

Traditionally, islanders lived from shipping, fishing and cultivating what crops they could on the islands' sparse, generally poor soil. The latter has prevented the development of large-scale agriculture; the average Greek farmer has only about one hectare of land. Main island products are olives, grapes and other fruits, wine, herbs and the ubiquitous Greek honey.

Above: Mílos, one of the three islands of volcanic origin. Right: Waiting for the boat to the next island!

The earth has been slightly more forthcoming with mineral resources, exploitation of which began on the islands when Neolithic explorers traveled to Mílos for obsidian in the sixth millennium B.C. Other island minerals include marble (Náxos, Páros, Tínos), gold and silver (Sífnos), iron and copper (Sérifos), and such volcanic by-products as pumice (Nísiros) and bauxite. There's also oil exploration and drilling; the Prinos Oil Field, off Thásos, has been producing since 1981.

The principal source of revenue in the island world has always been from the sea. Today, the waters of the Mediterranean are grievously overfished, forcing many fishing fleets to remain in harbor in the summer months. Fish farms have opened on some islands, providing local employment on the one hand, and lively controversies about pollution and commercial development on the other.

Shipping was long a more reliable source of wealth. Island magnates began developing shipping empires even under the Ottomans: Ándros and Síros, Ídra and Spétses, Híos, Skópelos and Sími all enjoyed varying degrees of prosperity throughout the 19th century. Some of this wealth has continued to the present; Híos and little Inoússes, for example, are known as centers for shipping tycoons. But the opening of the Corinth Canal in 1893 turned Piraeus into Greece's major port, cutting out island harbors such as Síros; and progress, such as the advent of steam and diesel power, meant that boats could travel farther without having to refuel and resupply, depriving the islands of a major traditional function.

As the Greek economy struggled to rebuild after the cruel devastation of World War II, workers went wherever they had

to in order to feed their families, and large-scale emigration, especially to America and Australia, left whole island villages empty. Other island men traveled the world with the merchant marine. Today, however, the big international ships are registered in other countries and hire cheaper, non-EU labor. Many former sailors have returned home to try to profit from the islands' greatest, and steadiest, source of revenue: tourism.

Shoreline development is a relatively recent phenomenon. In past centuries, towns were built inland, where they were safer from pirates, and beaches were seen as poor land because of the impossibility of farming the sandy soil. After tourists began to arrive in the 1960s and people saw a way to bring in the money they needed so desperately, building began unchecked; careful planning was the least of their concerns. The result is a surfeit of ugly concrete blocks, from hotels to souvlaki stands. Worst is when the money runs out halfway through construction and the eyesore is left unfinished. Now, the tourist market has raised waterfront real estate prices to a point that some Greeks can't even afford to buy at all. Since the resident English, German or Scandanavian expats don't pay local taxes, their presence is something of a drain; though they do bring in foreign currency. Foreigners have also reclaimed some of the abandoned old houses. These aren't always empty as a result of emigration: tradition dictates that parents build a new house for their daughter when she marries; the old one is eventually left empty. Dowries have been outlawed since 1983, but the practice continues, nonetheless.

Although foreigners represent a large percentage of holiday-makers, plenty of Greeks take their vacations on the islands, too. Greece is one of the countries with the largest number of stay-at-home vacationers in Europe. As one Athens resident put it: "People come from all over the world to vacation in my country, and there are so many parts of it I haven't seen; why should I go somewhere else?"

HISTORY AND CULTURE

Browse through your average bookstore for volumes on Greek history and you'll discover that for a great many authors, "Greek history" ends with the death of Alexander the Great in 323 B.C. This fact is one of the basic problems with modern Greek identity. Greek history comes in two separate packages: the ancient world, which English and German university professors seem to regard as their own exclusive property, and everything since, a patchwork grab-bag of events and place names that Western Europe and the Americas seem all too ready to disregard.

Certainly Greece's ancient history produced such a glorious wealth of art and thought that those who love it may be excused for feeling possessive. Greece – specifically the Greek Islands – was home to some of the earliest civilizations in Europe. In the early Bronze Age, the islands were the seat of a Cycladic culture (3000-2300 B.C.) which produced remarkable marble figurines that in their simplicity seem direct precursors of 20th-century sculpture. Although little is known of their daily lives, the islanders must also have been skilled seafarers.

Superceding Cycladic culture was the rise on Crete of the civilization known today as "Minoan." Many of Greece's most famous archeological excavations were undertaken in the 19th century by foreigners determined to prove that the Greek myths and epics actually contained a grain of truth. A love of Homer, for instance, inspired Heinrich Schliemann to search for Troy, a quest which his contemporaries viewed as people today might regard a person who, armed with a volume of Lewis Carroll, set out to discover Alice's Wonderland (they were astounded when Schliemann actually found it).

Left: Figure of Athena from the west gable of the Aphaéa Temple, Égina, ca. 500 B.C.

Similarly, Sir Arthur Evans, excavator of Crete, named "Minoan" culture for the legendary King Minos who, in the myths, had Daedalus build his massive palace with a labyrinth to conceal the dreadful Minotaur. To early excavators, the massive palaces of Knossós, Phaistos, and other Cretan sites did seem veritably labyrinthine, although their efforts to restore their masonry and bright frescoes go somewhat against the grain of modern archeology.

Whatever the names of their rulers, the Minoans were expert seafarers who dominated the Aegean and maintained trade links from Egypt to Sicily, something demonstrated by finds of their metalwork and distinctive pottery. Of the Minoan settlements on other Aegean islands – at Rhódos, Kéa and Sámos, to name a few – one of the greatest was at Akrotíri, on the island of Thíra (Santorin); excavations begun in 1967 have uncovered a significant village with magnificent frescoes. Yet this island may have contained the seeds of the Minoan Age's destruction: a major explosion of Thíra's volcano around 1500 B.C. not only blew the top off that island, but sent a tidal wave across the Aegean that probably put a damper, to put it mildly, on life at Knossós. Certainly it was around this time that the Minoan Age began to peter out, and power in the Greek world shifted more and more to the culture named for the fortress at mainland Mycenae.

For travelers to the islands, the most significant thing to know about the Mycenaean Age (about 1500-1100 B.C.) is that it was the period of the Trojan War in Homer's epic poem the *Iliad* (which dates from around the 8th century B.C.; centuries after the events it recounts). Homer's "catalogue of ships" in Book II of the *Iliad* gives then-contemporary characterizations of a few of the islands,

including Rhódos, Sími and Crete. Greek legend tells of a bitter sequence of family murders at the Mycenaean court: King Agamemnon sacrificed his daughter Iphigenaia to the gods on his way to Troy; on his return home, he was killed by his irate wife, Clytaemnestra; their son, Orestes, then avenged his father by killing his mother. The tale forms the basis for Aeschylus' 5th-century B.C. trilogy *Orestaia*. Again, history and legend overlap; archeologists dubbed a golden burial mask found at excavations of Mycenae the "Mask of Agamemnon."

The next great chapter in Greece's history began around the 8th century B.C., when the "Dark Ages" that had swallowed the post-Mycenaean world began to be displaced by the radiance from more enlightened forms of government and a new flowering of culture. This age saw the rise of the city-state, or *polis*, a small autonomous administrative unit comprising a village and the lands immediately around it. Size was less a factor in a *polis*' power than such considerations as naval might, and city-states on many of the islands flourished. Égina, near Athens, was for a time the leading naval power in the Aegean, and the first city to mint coins; while the main power in the eastern Aegean was the Dorian Hexapolis, a six-city union that included Kós, as well as Rhódos' three powerful city-states: Líndos, Ialysós and Kámeiros.

Above: Female idol, Cycladic, ca. 2400 B.C. Right: Red-figured vase painting, "Trojan Warriors," 6th century B.C.

In the early days of the *polis*, many city-states were governed by tyrants. Although supporters of democracy soon gave this term the negative connotation it still has today, some tyrants were actually wise and benevolent rulers. Kleobolos, the tyrant of Líndos (on Rhódos), was a liberal thinker who was later accounted one of the Seven Sages of ancient Greece (ancient Greek writers were inordinately fond of drawing up "greatest-hits" lists: Seven Sages of Greece; Seven Wonders of the Ancient World).

Another memorable 6th-century island tyrant was Polycrates of Sámos, who wielded considerable power in the eastern Aegean and left his island with such architectural monuments as the mighty Temple of Hera. But tyranny was ultimately supplanted by democracy, the rule of the people (*demos*), who convened at regular assemblies to decide on matters of state. In Athens, the classic democracy, there was also a smaller council selected on a basis of proportional representation, members of which oversaw day-to-day administration. "People," in this context, were adult males: no women, children or slaves need apply. These "people" also represented the *hoplites*, or foot-soldiers, who formed the army in time of war.

Overshadowing the Greek world's political development was the rise of Persia. By the end of the 6th century B.C., King Darius' Persian armies had taken over the whole coast of Asia Minor (now Turkey)

and the islands off its shores – the territory known as "Ionia." The Ionian Greeks attempted a revolt against the Persians in 498 B.C., but it was put down in fairly short order, and many Ionians, including the famous philosopher Pythagoras of Sámos and other islanders, fled the region altogether. And Persia began marshaling its forces for a full-scale invasion of Greece.

Persia represented a tremendous existential threat to the informal alliance of small Greek city-states that comprised the Peloponnesian League; the Greeks seemed destined for complete subjugation to the heathens from the East. Many island rulers decided that alliance with the Persians was preferable to defeat at their hands; as if to underscore this, the Persians wasted Náxos utterly on their way toward Athens in 492 B.C. Miraculously, however, the Greek forces, mainly Athenians, were able to defeat the numerically superior Persians on the plain of Marathon. Persia retreated to lick its wounds and regroup for an all-out attack led by the new King, Xerxes, in 480 B.C.; this time, the Persians wiped out a Greek army at the pass of Thermopylae; they then entered the hastily-evacuated city of Athens and destroyed its Acropolis. Yet again, David-like, the Greek navy waited to engage the Goliath of the Persian fleet in the narrow straits off the island of Salamis; and here, the Greeks (led by the Athenians, a rising naval power) were able to carry the day.

Driving off the Persian threat cemented a basic Greek identity that has carried on to the present. The ensuing cultural renaissance was centered in Athens, which emerged in a leading role after the Persian Wars. Rebuilding its ruined Acropolis gave the city an excuse to engage some of the leading architects and artists of the age, notably the great Phidias, to create the Parthenon and other still-unforgettable buildings; the theater on one side of the Acropolis hill hosted annual festivals presenting comedies and tragedies by Aeschylus, Sophocles, Euripides and Aristophanes; while at the hill's foot,

Socrates conducted dialogues with fellow-citizens in the Agora.

Yet the glorious, enlightened cultural development was only one side of Athens under Pericles, the popular general who was Athens' leading elected official until his death in 429. Pericles was a true Renaissance man, a humanist and a thinker; but he was also an imperialist who sought to expand Athenian influence. Immediately after the Persian defeat, a number of Ionian city-states voluntarily pledged their allegiance to Athens: the resulting alliance was called the Delian League, because its treasury was on the sacred island of Delos.

But membership in the league grew less and less voluntary as Athenian power grew. By 454 B.C., Athens had forced a number of islands to join or compelled them to remain (Náxos, Thásos and the Evian *polis* of Kárystos, to name a few), and shifted the treasury to the Acropolis. It wasn't the last time the Greek Islands would be made to feel their political helplessness vis-à-vis the interests of the mainland.

Above: Pericles speaks before artists and philosophers (painting by Philipp von Foltz, 19th century). Right: "Aristotle and his Student Alexander," wood engraving, 19th century.

However, the proud and independent city-states of the Greek world couldn't put up with this kind of subjugation for long, even if Pericles' goals of a unified Greek confederation may ultimately have been in their best interests. The Peloponnesian War, which was sparked by a dispute between Corfu (Kérkira) and Corinth in the year 431 B.C., pitted the two main powers of Athens and Sparta against each other, involving most of the other major players, including Égina, Athens' bitter enemy. Athens ultimately capitulated in 404, and never regained its former importance.

Because Periclean Athens produced some of the greatest art and thought the world has ever known, foreign scholars venerate it as the acme of Greek culture. To Greeks, however, the glory of ancient

Greece is best symbolized by Alexander the Great (365-323 B.C.), a young military genius who very nearly succeeded in his goal of bringing the entire known world under Greek control. Alexander had himself deified during his lifetime, and he's still a god for some modern Greeks, who don't want to speak of him in the past tense. "Refined" Athenians saw the boy-king's homeland of Macedonia as an uncouth frontier region, but it was for a brief time the center of a kingdom that Alexander's conquests extended all the way to the Indus River in present-day Pakistan.

In 1992, when a splinter province of the former Yugoslavia titled itself the Republic of Macedonia, the Greeks reacted with a screech of horror heard around the world. Ostensibly, they feared that the republic would lay claims to the Greek province of the same name; a more deep-seated problem was that an independent non-Greek state named "Macedonia" represented out-and-out heresy to the descendants of Alexander.

Alexander epitomized the Greek version of manifest destiny, the idea that the Greeks were foreordained to subjugate the barbarians around them. He also underlined the influence of the East that remains so pervasive in Greek culture, which is exactly the flavor that Western scholars tend to downplay. Greece is supposed to be the cradle of Western culture; it's hardly in keeping with this image that the man still venerated as the country's greatest-ever ruler embraced the Oriental splendor of his conquered territories. But this Eastern color is an essential component of the bright palate of Greece: gold and incense, mosaics and embroideries are as much elements of the Greek world as of the Persian one.

Alexander's eastward-turning kingdom brought prosperity to the islands along the coast of Asia Minor, especially Rhódos. But as unifying as Alexander's rule was, the emperor's early death threw his huge, unsteady kingdom quickly into disarray. Ultimately, the Romans were able to beat the Macedonians in the Mac-

edonian Wars of the 2nd century B.C., and Rome annexed the Greek world. The Romans' attitude toward Greece was mixed. On the one hand, they greatly respected their province's cultural achievements: Roman emperors used to embark on what amounted to Greek "grand tours," and shipped many of the best treasures back home to their capital (setting a precedent for foreign occupiers to come). On the other hand, they saw the Greeks as a subject people, and treated them accordingly. Under the Romans, the sacred island of Dílos became the Aegean's trading center, supporting a thriving international merchant colony.

By the time Emperor Diocletian ascended the throne in A.D. 284, the Roman Empire was weakened and overextended. Diocletian's attempted solution was to divide the territory into separate administrative units, creating an Eastern Roman Empire and a Western one. Inevitably, this opened up the possibility of strife between the individual rulers, a problem resolved in its turn, in A.D. 324, when Constantine emerged victorious from civil war as the sole ruler of a newly-reunified Roman Empire. Constantine proceeded to take some of the most significant steps in European history: he adopted Christianity, and he moved the empire's capital to Byzantium, rechristened, after him, Constantinople.

The Byzantine Empire flourished for 11 centuries, making it one of the longest-lived political entities in the history of Europe. However, it marks yet another border between Western and Eastern Europe – not only geographically but also in terms of world outlook. Conventional wisdom in the West names the period between the 5th and 14th centuries A.D. the "Dark Ages," when people were confronted with barbarian invasion, plague,

Above: The two-story House of Hermes in Dílos is a marvelous relic from Hellenic times. Right: In Greek Orthodox churches children are completely submerged in water during baptism.

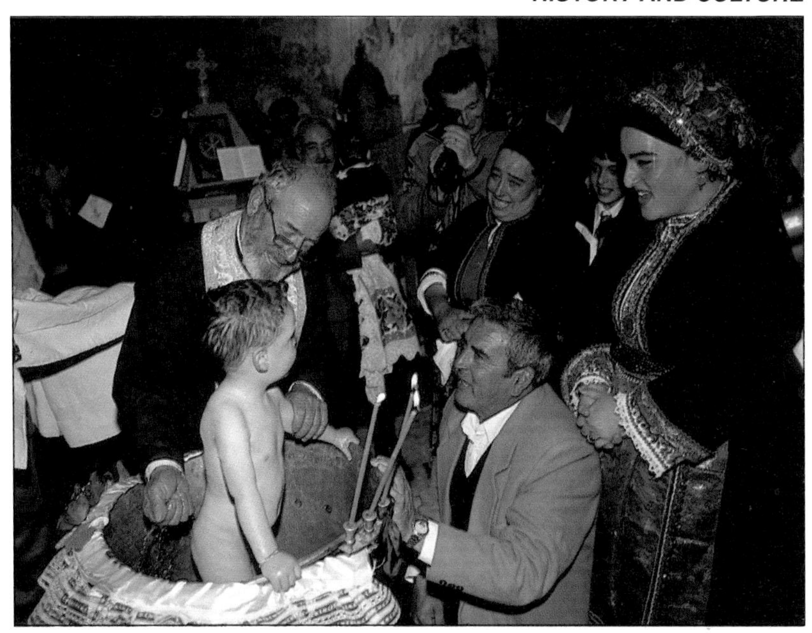

and the hardships of everyday life in a feudal peasant society; this ends with the "Renaissance," a return of learning, culture and light.

To the Greeks, this period was anything but "dark"; rather, it was the heyday of Byzantium, the East's greatest flowering of civilization, thought and culture. In the Greek view of history, there was no 5th-century "decline and fall" of the Roman Empire; for the powerful Byzantine Empire *was* the Roman Empire, and continued to regard itself thus throughout its history. In fact, the adjective *Romeikos*, Roman, is still used to denote "Greekness," its opposite being *Tourkikos*, Turkish; you can find the designation on some street names or beaches on the islands, distinguishing a "Greek" beach from a "Turkish" one.

Furthermore, the Byzantine Empire remains, historically, the only point at which the Greek world was Europe's major political power. Not that the Empire was always on top; its whole history is one of struggle with the countries around it, which entailed great fluctuation of its borders and internal strife, particularly over questions of religion. Yet the fact is that it endured; and it is still a cornerstone of Greek identity. Greeks still refer to Constantinople as *O Polis*, "The City," and remind you that the Turkish word Istanbul derives from the Greek *eis tin polis*, "to the city." Too, the Empire was the leading Christian empire, and it remains the spiritual center of what, to Greeks, is the one true form of Christianity: Orthodoxy. In fact, ecclesiastical law still dictates that the spiritual leader of the Greek Orthodox Church has to come from Constantinople: a law that's very difficult to obey, since there are so few Greeks left in that city.

The difference between Orthodoxy and Roman Catholicism, which began in the 5th century and was cemented when Pope Leo IX condemned the Patriarch of Constantinople in 1054, remained a tremendous obstacle to diplomatic relations between East and West in the ensuing centuries. Adherents of both faiths had,

and still have, trouble remembering that the other side is Christian, as well. This problem peaked around 1095, at the time of the First Crusade. Byzantium was located at the crossroads of East and West. For Western Europeans, it was a bulwark against the "menace" of the Ottoman Empire, expanding since 632 A.D., but it was also a site of heresy and otherness. The raw Westerners, accustomed to a sort of frontier lifestyle, looked askance at Constantinople's sophistication, its architectural masterpieces (such as the great cathedral of Hagia Sophia, built by Emperor Justinian in A.D. 532-537) and "decadent" golden mosaics.

The Crusaders or "Franks," a huge and unruly mob, moved east (through the islands) to start their fight against the "infidel"; many of this ignorant lot failed utterly to differentiate between Christian Greeks and Turkish Moslems, much to the detriment of the hapless population who became their victims. This Crusade proved a failure, but it whetted the West's taste for Eastern blood. And in the end it was Europeans on the Fourth Crusade, rather than the "infidel," who in 1204 sacked Constantinople, marking the beginning of the end for the Byzantine Empire.

Above: The Crusaders conquer Constantinople (1204), fragment of a painting by Tintoretto. Right: Greek freedom fighters pursuing the defeated Turkish army (tapestry, 1828).

The decline of Byzantium brought real problems to the Greek Islands. Small as they were, they stood to benefit from being used as strategic bases by friendly powers, and had little defense against hostile ones. Now, in the absence of a unified political force, they were more vulnerable than ever to invasion. Piracy was rampant – the reason that medieval island towns were built inland, at a safe distance from the sea and preferably on a hilltop, allowing them to see who was approaching. Islanders still keep alive half-remembered myths of pirate caves, smugglers' coves and buried treasure.

Some measure of protection remained. The Venetians, who had firm bases on Corfu, Zákinthos and Kefaloniá in the Ionian Sea, gained control of the Cyclades after the Fourth Crusade, and continued to rule the Duchy of Náxos until 1537, erecting new castles on their islands or shoring up old Byzantine ones. Another naval power, the Genoans, held Híos, Sámos and a few other islands. The Crusaders, meanwhile, driven out of the Holy Land, had fallen back to their stronghold on Rhodes (Rhódos), where the Knights of St. John held sway until 1522. But there was another major power on the horizon: the Ottoman Empire, which in 1453 decisively conquered Constantinople and delivered the Byzantine Empire the *coup de grace*.

Nothing now stood in the way of the Ottoman conquest of the Greek world. In 1522, the Turks drove the weakened Knights out of Rhódos; and after 1537, they moved into the Cyclades, as well. By 1566 they had claimed the Duchy of Náxos from Venice and the Northeast Aegean islands from Genoa; Crete alone remained in Venetian hands until 1669.

Now it was the Ottoman Empire that was the largest in the European world; and "Greece" was no more than a collection of territories within it, and a fond memory. The Greeks were a people bound by a common language and religion, rather than a country, living scattered around the globe. Many Greeks dreamed of reestablishing an actual territorial homeland (*Enosis*) and throwing off the foreign yoke. There are plenty of parallels between the Greek community under the Ottoman Empire and the Jewish community before the establishment of Israel; in fact, some Zionist writings were inspired by the events leading up to the Greek War of Independence.

The Ottomans were rather laissez-faire rulers; they weren't too picky about who was running day-to-day affairs as long as they had the overall power. As a result,

the Orthodox Church remained the focal point of the lives of its Greek subjects, fostering Greek traditions and Greek ideals. The Ottomans even tolerated the establishment of Greek schools, such as the one on Pátmos, which promptly became hotbeds of revolutionary thinking. Young rebels were inspired by the American and French revolutions, especially the latter, since Napoleon briefly took power on the Ionian Islands, declaring them "more important to me than all of Italy." A revolutionary group calling itself the "Society of Friends" (*Etairia Filike*) sought support for its nationalist dreams, and finally launched an "attack" on the Ottomans in 1821 that was wiped out in a matter of hours.

This attack, however, sparked a blaze that rapidly spread over and around the Peloponnese, and the islands were able to play a significant role. For one thing, their shipping tradition was all to the good: the prosperous islands of Ídra, Spétses and Psára had been able to develop one of the largest merchant fleets in the Mediterra-

nean under the Ottomans, and they made sure that the Greek navy, at least, could withstand attack. For another, some of the smaller islands made great hiding places. The population of little Skópelos swelled, at one point, to an unbelievable 70,000.

The first capital of the new country was on an island, Égina. Another island, Chíos (Híos), one of the Sultan's favorites, became a symbol of the revolution when the Sultan made an example of it in 1822; Delacroix's painting of the Ottoman massacre of the island's inhabitants won great popular sympathy for the Greek cause in Europe.

In Western Europe, the Greek revolution was in any case an easy sell. Ancient Greece's language and art were a part of the intellectual property of the educated classes, and they felt a proprietary interest in saving "their" country. Joining the Greek cause seemed like participating in the Trojan War, fighting in a fairy tale come to life. Lord Byron was the most famous of the many Westerners who flocked to Greece to fight for Plato and Aristotle; there to come into contact with the "real" Greeks, rough peasants and chieftains of mountain tribes (*klefts*) who had no idea what they were talking about and who were fighting for their land.

Romantic as it was, Western interest saved the revolution; for after Mehmet Ali, Pasha of Egypt, marched into Greece at the Sultan's behest in 1824, the Greek cause would have foundered if Russia, France and England hadn't stepped in. Ostensibly acting in the international interest, these three powers drew up the Treaty of London establishing a Greek principality, to be ruled by the Sultan. When the Sultan rejected this treaty, the allies' efforts to enforce it led to the Battle of Navarino (1827), where the Sultan suffered a decisive defeat. All of a sudden, the Greek state was a reality after all, albeit wholly under the control of three for-

Above: Athens around 1805 (aquatint by E. Dowell). Right: Elefthérios Venizélos, Greek patriot and several-time Prime Minister.

eign powers. Its first president was the Corfiot Ioánnis Kapodístrias; when he was assassinated in 1831, the powers decided to try monarchy instead, looked around for an available royal dynasty, and settled on that of Bavaria. Thus the 17-year-old Otto, son of King Ludwig I, became Otto I, King of Greece.

So Greece continued, in a way, to be a story of the past told by foreigners, who derived their ideas about the country from writings 24 centuries old. Greece's very language became a charged issue: *katharévusa*, a half-artificial language based on Classical Greek, was implemented as the official language rather than demotic Greek, *demotiki*, the *lingua franca* of Greeks around the world (which was officially reinstated in 1978).

King Otto himself never mastered any version of the language. Instead, he devoted himself to adorning Athens, which had degenerated into something of a mule town under the Ottomans, with splendid neoclassical buildings evoking its ancient past, but looking more like something from his native city of Munich (logically enough, considering that he brought his Munich architects with him). Bavaria's colors, blue and white, even graced the new Greek flag.

The Greeks themselves had mixed emotions about their new nation. It was still effectively governed by foreign powers; its economy was struggling; living standards were fairly poor. Furthermore, large parts of the Greek world lay outside its borders. The Ionian Islands were British until 1862; the Dodecanese and the Northeast Aegean remained Turkish. Even the two Greek cosmopolitan centers, Constantinople and Smyrna (Izmir), were in foreign territory; in fact, some Greeks were packing up and moving from the new Greece back to these more prosperous Greek cities in the Ottoman Empire.

Rising out of this sense of unfulfilled promise was the *Megáli Idéa*, the "Great

Idea" that Greece had a quasi-divine right to follow in Alexander the Great's footsteps and govern the entire Greek-speaking world. Its chief advocate was Elefthérios Venizélos, Greece's Prime Minister after 1909, who brought the nation out of the Balkan Wars of 1911-13 with its borders nearly doubled in size, bringing the Northeast Aegean Islands and Crete, as well as much of northern Greece, into the fold. At the Paris Peace Conference that followed World War I, Venizelos made his territorial claims to his allies Britain and France. Italy, which still occupied the Dodecanese and had its eye on Asia Minor, was not amused; to forestall Italian action, Greece moved in to occupy Smyrna and Anatolia, much to the rejoicing of the area's predominantly Greek population.

Unfortunately, the Greeks' arrival coincided with the rise of the Turkish nationalist movement; its leader, Mustafa Kemal or Atatürk, had already declared his own people, not the Western European powers, the victors in the Ottoman

Empire's fall. Fighting on their home turf, the nascent Turkish army was able to hold its own against the overextended Greeks. Venizelos' unexpected loss in the 1920 elections weakened Greece's ties to the great European powers he had worked so hard to cultivate. When the Turks launched a final push against the Greeks in 1922, the international community sat by and watched the destruction of Smyrna and the massacre of its citizens as the Greeks fled.

The consequences of this debacle have decisively stamped modern Greek consciousness. As they established their borders, Greece and Turkey agreed on huge population exchanges that would finally solidify their communities: the entire Greek world would now be contained within Greek territorial borders. This meant forcibly removing more than a million Greeks from their ancestral lands in Asia Minor: Constantinople was the only city in Turkey where a Greek presence was still tolerated. Formerly well-to-do families found themselves uprooted and homeless; Greek towns and cities, especially the Northeast Aegean Islands and Athens, were swamped with refugees. The displacement worked in both directions: since religion, rather than language, was the decisive criterion for citizenship, Cretan landowners who had converted to Islam found themselves transported to Turkey, while Turkish-speaking Orthodox believers were shipped to Greece.

Above: Ohi Day (October 28, 1940) is still a national holiday. Right: German paratroopers occupy Crete during the Second World War (1941).

In a sense, Greece profited: the refugees brought skills, experience, and in some cases a cosmopolitan flair that the new country had been lacking. Among the refugee families were names that later rose to international prominence, such as Onassis and Kazan. But the melancholy nostalgia for a lost homeland, the sense of an unfulfilled destiny that had long been part of the Greek consciousness, was now indelibly stamped into the country's psyche.

In 1936, King George II appointed General Joannes Metaxas Prime Minister; Metaxas soon talked the King into altering the constitution and abolishing freedom of the press, whereafter he governed as the country's unchallenged, if unloved, dictator. Although he had decidedly Fascist tendencies and did little for the country, Metaxas at least tried to maintain Greece's neutrality. When Mussolini announced he was sending Italian troops over the Albanian border, Metaxas in fact replied, "*Alors, c'est la guerre*," but the story in Greece is that his answer was simply *Ohi*, "no." The date was October 28, 1940, and October 28 is still celebrated as a national holiday, "Ohi Day," with speeches and parades.

In the difficult terrain of the northern mountains the Greeks were able to keep the Italians at bay, but this resistance interfered with Hitler's expansionist plans; he needed Crete as a supply base for Rommel's Africa Corps. Even fighting valiantly and causing the Germans far more losses than they'd anticipated, notably in the Battle of Crete in May 1941, the Greeks couldn't keep the Axis occupiers out. By the end of that year, the country was divided up between Germany, Italy – who had most of the islands – and Bulgaria. The Germans, who controlled Athens and much of the mainland, were the harshest masters. Some 500,000 Greeks starved to death on strict wartime rations, and the Nazis deported the country's considerable Jewish population – 50,000 from Thessaloníki alone – within weeks, most headed straight for the gas chambers of Auschwitz.

But resistance continued, particularly in the mountains, the country's traditional stronghold. EAM formed here, the National Liberation Front, with its army ELAS (National Popular Liberation Army), which saw getting rid of the Germans as only the first step in its program

of reforming the country. Both liberation armies had support from Greece's communist party, the KKE. But other, right-wing resistance groups also sprang up, such as EDES (Greek Democratic League). Even before the end of the war, there was fighting between these various factions, which flared up after the German withdrawal and the arrival of British troops in 1944. Winston Churchill, stoutly committed to the Greek monarchy and therefore against the communists, had informally agreed with Stalin that in the postwar redistribution of power, Britain would be largely responsible for Greece; Stalin therefore enjoined his followers on the Greek left to lay down their arms and go along with what the British wanted. ELAS-EAM held a protest demonstration in Athens; when the police fired on the crowd, it sparked a month-long altercation known as the Battle of Athens, which claimed more than 13,000 lives. The right continued to terrorize the left; the repressive situation was exacerbated when the KKE boycotted the 1946

elections, which meant the election of a right-wing government. The left, forced to flee, regrouped in the mountains, forming guerilla troops and embarking on open civil war. The British had their own postwar privations at home; this situation was more than they could cope with. Enter the United States, embarking on the first leg of its postwar fight against communism that was to involve it in so many ill-starred foreign conflicts. With their considerable financial and strategic support, the right was able to drive out the KKE by 1949. America continued to pour financial and military aid into Greece, thereby shoring up its own strategic position vis-à-vis Russia in the Cold War.

Under Constantine Karamanlis, Greece's Conservative Prime Minister after 1955, the Greek economy began to rebuild and grow. In 1961, however, the coalitionist Center Union party of George Papandreou, a popular politician who had already led a provisional Greek government at the end of World War II, made a significant showing in an election which the right did everything in its power to influence in its favor. By 1964, Papandreou was the elected head of Greece, but he didn't have long to institute his program of reforms. Greece's perennially shaky politics suffered an unexpected blow when, on April 21, 1967, a group of military colonels staged a successful coup d'etat and took over the government.

Above: Constantine Karamanlis becomes Prime Minister in 1974 after the military junta is toppled. Right: Since its entry into the EEC in 1981, Greece has been producing fruits and vegetables for the European market.

The United States has played an inglorious role in modern Greek history; the CIA propped up the Third-World style military junta that now reigned over the country. The colonels' ideology hearkened back to the days of Metaxas: they sought a better, purer Greece free of such modern evils as long hair and mini-skirts (a pose which didn't do much to help Greece's burgeoning tourist trade). Those who didn't agree with them were exiled to remote prison camps, many of them on the Greek Islands; prisoners included Papandreou and his son, Andreas, who, although a Harvard man, gained little appreciation for the Americans during this period of his life. One of the bitterest episodes in the junta's history was the student protest at Athens Polytechnic in November 1973: tanks drove into the crowd, and several students were killed.

It was the volatile situation on Cyprus that proved the junta's downfall. Led by Archbishop Makarios, the Greek Cypriots – a clear majority – had demonstrated for union with Greece since the 1950s; Cyprus' Turkish minority, on the other hand, favored partitioning the island. When the occupying British finally withdrew, the island was declared an independent republic in 1960, with Makarios as its first president. Now, in 1974, the junta planned the assassination of Makarios, aiming to install an authoritar-

ian right-wing official in his place. Their plan backfired: Makarios escaped, and Turkey, spurred to action, invaded the north of the island (also ostensibly with American support) in 1974. The resulting partitioning of the island into Turkish and Greek sectors established an impasse that continues unresolved today, creating a divided island that since 1984 has had two governments, one of which no one but Turkey officially recognizes.

The colonels didn't survive this fiasco, and Karamanlis was summoned back from exile to help lead the country out of turmoil once again. One of his main goals was membership in the EU, achieved in 1981 – the year PASOK, the Panhellenic Socialist Union, came to power. Led by Andreas Papandreou, PASOK won on a platform of anti-US and anti-EU measures, but failed to carry through on them – fortunately for the country, which has leaned on EU loans to carry it through some government crises. In spite of this and a number of scandals, including his affair with a young airline stewardess whom he ultimately married, Papandreou was reelected, with interruptions, until he died in 1996; Karamanlis, his old rival, remained opposition leader until his own death in 1997. PASOK continues to enjoy popular support.

The collapse of the Soviet Union shifted the power structure in the Balkans; from NATO's point of view, Greece ceased to be the kind of "last outpost" it had represented during the Cold War. Extensive military facilities on the islands, particularly those nearest to Turkey, remind of the frostiness of Turkish-Greek relations; but most of the disputes these days are over drilling or fishing rights in Aegean waters. In the 1990s, Greece's real border issues were in the north, with the influx of Albanian immigrants (a presence on the Greek Islands, as well) and the uproar about the name of the Republic of Macedonia. But multiculturalism has always been a part of Greek island life; and the only invasions anyone's really concerned about here are the annual ones of Brits and Germans.

GREEK ART & ARCHITECTURE

The Greek Islands' most distinctive and unique artistic expression is some five millennia old. Expressive and abstract, the figures of women and men grouped under the blanket heading of Cycladic Art have today regained the kind of cult following they probably enjoyed in a more literal sense when they were created. It is unclear exactly what function they served; one can only establish that they date from between 3000 and 2000 B.C., and that they were originally painted. The figures evolve from simple, almost two-dimensional goddess figures into more complex seated figures, often of musicians; but they retain the simple, stylized, geometric forms that evoke, in modern viewers, comparisons with Picasso and Henry Moore.

Above: A beaked pitcher from Minoan times (ca. 1800 B.C.), Festós, Crete. Right: Geometric-style vase. Far Right: Archaic kouros from the island of Sámos.

After 2000 B.C., **Minoan Culture** began to flourish on Crete: sprawling palaces and an absence of fortifications are indications of a truly peaceable kingdom, reflected in exuberant art. Minoan figures in frescoes and ceramics are stylized, but their energy is palpable: wasp-waisted boys tumble atop a bull; a goggle-eyed octopus splays his tentacles across an amphora. Minoan frescoes were executed directly in wet plaster; the best are at Knossós on Crete and Akrotíri on Santorin. The **Mycenaean Culture** that followed (1500-1100 B.C.) is known for its fortified citadels (the ruins at Mycenae are magnificent), visible on some islands in the form of "cyclopean walls."

As little as shelves of dusty vases may appeal to the average museum-goer, Greek pottery is considerably more interesting when you learn to follow its stylistic evolution from one age to another, and when, in addition, you've learned to differentiate between different kinds of container. An amphora is a jug with a narrow neck and two handles; small ones were

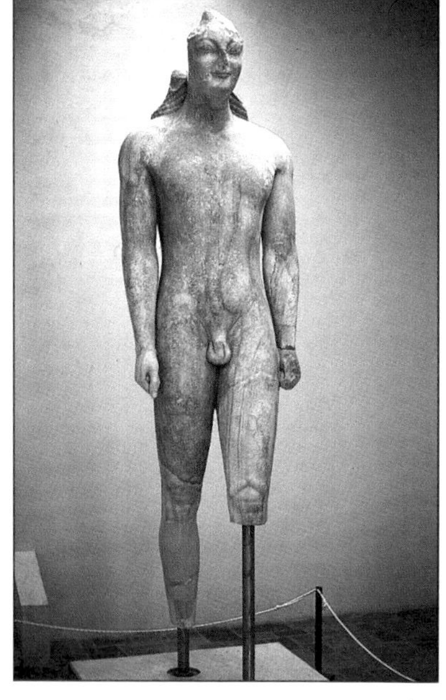

decorated, large ones used for storage and transport (unadorned ones are often found around shipwrecks). Other common forms are the krater, a wide-mouthed vase or bowl, generally also with handles, and the kylix, a broad bowl or plate mounted on a base.

The art historical term for the 9th and 8th centuries B.C. is the **Geometric Period**, so called for the abstract, geometric, non-figural ornamentation of its pottery, some of the only testimony to the age. Gradually, the human figure begins to reappear on amphorae and kraters in scenes that become, with the passing of time, increasingly narrative.

Around the beginning of the 7th century B.C., figurative Greek sculpture began to take the first steps toward its glorious future. Works from this **Archaic Period** (about 700-500 B.C.) demonstrate the active trading culture in the ancient Mediterranean world in that they bear distinct features of Babylon and of Egypt. Archaic sculptures are highly stylized, idealized human figures of either a young man (*kouros*) or young woman (*koure*), their long hair in neat coils on either shoulder, the women in drapery that falls in even folds, the man naked. The figures stand with one foot slightly in front of the other, caught in a static stride, and their faces are fixed in gentle, otherworldly, Mona Lisa smiles. Some of these archaic *kouroi*, which fulfilled a devotional function, were on a mammoth scale: *kouroi* found on Sámos and Náxos are as much as 10 meters high.

480 B.C., when the Greeks drove off the Persian menace, was a watershed in Greek consciousness; and this shift was immediately reflected in Greek art. The stiff figures of the *kouroi* suddenly turned a bit on their rigidly vertical axis, took on a new roundness – became, in effect, infused with life. Greek statues of the dawning **Classical Period** (480-323 B.C.) were still idealized, but they were far more realistic, and far more dynamic. This shift coincided with the magnificent buildings which Athens erected to replace those the Persians had destroyed on

its Acropolis. These temples were adorned with magnificent sculptures and reliefs, developing from the stately, measured pace of the procession depicted on the frieze of the Parthenon (448 B.C.) to the half-liquid flow of the drapery of the victory goddesses adorning the Temple of Athena Nike (410 B.C.).

Greek temples were shrines built around votive statues, generally with an eye to integrating or celebrating the surrounding landscape. The god's cult statue stood in the *naos*, or inner room; sometimes there was a treasure chamber behind this, with its own separate entrance. This was surrounded by a colonnade; from outside, the columns were the temple's most distinctive feature. A triangular pediment at either end, under the roof, afforded more space for sculpture. The temples were probably brightly painted, and the cult statues of the gods, now all long vanished, were the focal point in every sense. Phidias' statue of Zeus at Olympia was one of the Seven Wonders of the World; his huge ivory statue of Athena in the Parthenon represented a good part of the city's financial holdings, and lost a lot of her golden trappings as the city grew increasingly strapped for cash during the Peloponnesian War.

Above: Ionian columns from the north hall of the Erechtheion, Acropolis, Athens. Right: Icons – as much an expression of Byzantine art as of Orthodox religious faith.

Today, many temples remain only as foundations and a few columns. On the mainland, these columns tend to be plainer, of the Doric Order: simple, fluted shafts with plain, unadorned tops, or capitals, holding up the roof. Doric columns are featured in the Parthenon, the Temple of Athena Aphaia on Égina, or the Temple of Apollo on Dílos. Stemming from Ionia, the Ionic Order set its columns on a base and topped them with a double volute, a spiral on either side of the column. The lone remaining column of the Temple of Hera on Sámos is Ionic; better-preserved examples are in Athens' Erechthion. Less common are the ornately carved large capitals that typify the Corinthian Order.

Sensuality and softness gradually stole into sculpture in the "Baroque" **Hellenistic Period** (336-23 B.C.). Beauty takes precedence over magnificence in the works of Praxiteles and other later sculptors who created some of the best-known Greek sculptures: the Winged Victory of Samothrace and the Venus di Milo, both in the Louvre, or the Vatican's Laocoön, all created in the 2nd and 1st centuries B.C. Many of these are visible today only because of the industrious copying activities of the **Romans** (88 B.C.-391 A.D.), whose villas also sported mosaic floors and smaller decorative sculptures.

Non-Orthodox viewers can have a hard time warming to **Byzantine Era** (395-1204) art. It's helpful to note that it is a direct continuation, both thematically and stylistically, of Classical Greece. In the very early phases of the Christian Church

you can actually see one religion adapting elements of another: Orpheus with his lyre becomes King David; the Artemis fertility image from Asia Minor becomes Mary. Too, both Classical Greece and Byzantium idealize the human figure. The stasis of Archaic Greek sculpture, the recurrence of certain types, is incorporated into Byzantine icons, which represent figures for their symbolic rather than realistic merit – giving visible form to an idea which has a firm place in the church's theology.

In the Orthodox Church, icon painting is itself an act of worship: an icon is a window onto the reality of heaven, which is why the representations of a particular saint must not vary from one icon to another. Icons must also be two-dimensional: three-dimensional representation is strictly forbidden. One has to familiarize oneself with the style a bit before one can appreciate the greatest of its products: the magnificent frescoes in Híos' Néa Moní, for example. This church is also a perfect example of Byzantine architecture: a Greek cross, with the dome at the center, which places the viewer in a spatial context very different from that created by the elongated Roman Catholic model.

Much island architecture of the **19th and 20th centuries** reflects the influence of other countries: Corfu's copy of the Rue de Rivoli, Italianate villas on Síros, the neoclassical mansions of Sími, or 1930s Italian Futurist buildings on Léros. There are, however, a few distinctive gestures. Houses in the "mastic villages" on Híos sport unique black-and-white geometric designs painted on their façades. Also black and white are the pebble mosaics in church courtyards, public squares and private gardens, in patterns or figurative compositions called *krokalia*.

And of course, the term "Cycladic architecture" conjures up visions of square, whitewashed walls with blue trim. These buildings are not unlike adobe houses in the American Southwest, and have long since become favored subjects for visiting photographers.

ATHENS
Ancient and Modern Capital

ACROPOLIS / AGORÁ / PLÁKA
MONASTIRÁKI
OMÓNIA SQUARE
SINDÁGMA SQUARE
VASSÍLISSIS SOFÍAS BOULEVARD
PIRAEUS

Crowded and bustling, dirty and gritty, modern yet ancient, Athens is, for many travelers, something of an acquired taste. The transportation hub for all of Greece, it's a logical stopover for anyone flying in from abroad: here, you can recover from jet lag and visit the incomparable Acropolis before journeying on to the island paradise of your dreams. But there's no denying that returning to hot, sweaty Athens in the height of summer after a week or two on an island beach is like being doused abruptly with dirty water.

Still, Athens is a taste worth acquiring. A city which has seen many stages of historic evolution at wide intervals, it displays the layers of its past as clearly as the rings of a tree, open to the eyes of anyone who cares to look. Tiny gems of Byzantine churches stand matter-of-factly at the center of busy squares, parting the stream of car and pedestrian traffic as indifferently as a rock in a river; classical columns rear up from the dark coolness of cypress groves as if oblivious to the gray concrete of the roads and buildings around them. Many parts of the city bear witness to the years of the mid-19th century, when a foreign king and his administration sought to create as rapidly as possible a capital that was worthy of the city's classical past and capable of holding its own with the other capitals of Europe: an ambitious transformation of a town that, in 1834, when the capital of the new country of independent Greece was transferred here from Nauplia, numbered all of 4,000 residents and about 300 houses. Other building booms followed: in 1923, when the city was hit with an influx of Greek refugees from Asia Minor, and in the years following World War II.

This juxtaposition of antiquity and youth is what gives Athens its unique character: on the one hand, it seeks to present the façade of calm serenity indicated by the gorgeous ruins on the Acropolis, still towering over the town; on the other hand, it has a kind of adolescent quality understandable in a city that has only existed, in its present incarnation, for some 150 years.

Previous Pages: Inside Athen's market hall. Left: The Minoan frescoes from Thíra are among the most beautiful items on exhibit in the National Archeological Museum.

THE **ACROPOLIS

Nearly every town in ancient Greece had its own acropolis, a local hill supporting a "high city" of temples and shrines to the gods. But Athens' **Acropolis** ❶ is so outstanding, and has preserved so much of its former glory, that it has become for

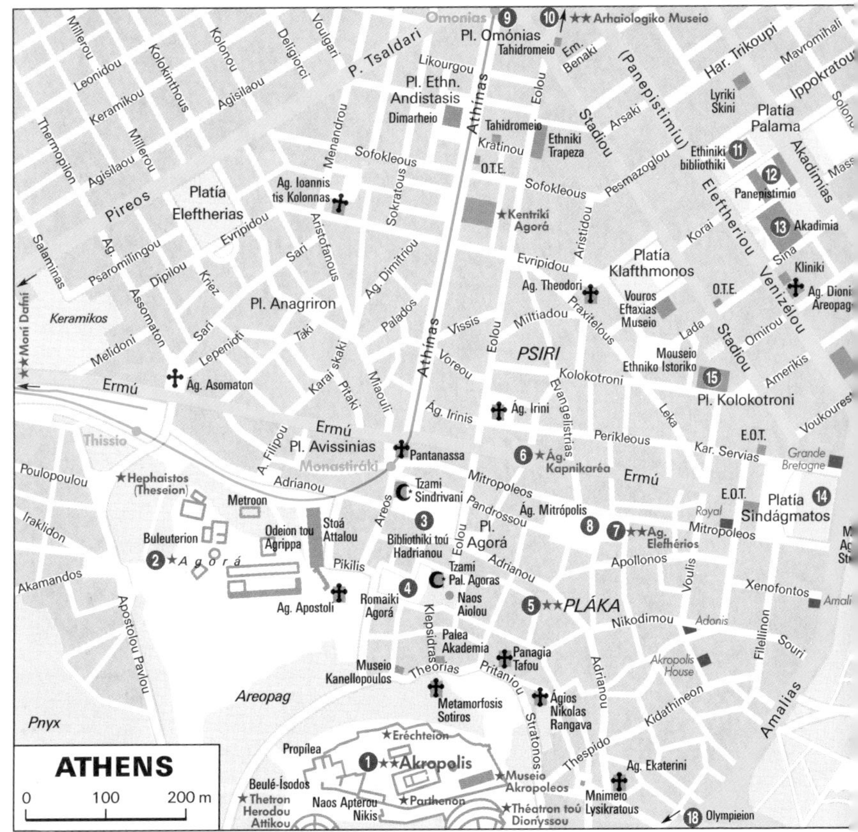

many visitors *the* Acropolis, the only one worthy of the name. In spite of the 17th-century Venetian shell that reduced the Parthenon, until then intact, to a noble ruin – the Turks were using the building to store ammunition at the time – and in spite of the arguably misguided ongoing course of renovations that are to return the buildings to their former splendor, the Acropolis of Athens remains perhaps the best place in Greece in which to appreciate what the classical world was all about.

The Acropolis, of course, didn't always have marble temples: in the 5th century B.C., many of the devotional structures were made of wood. These early structures fell victim to the Persian onslaught. Persia's growing might became a concrete threat in 490 B.C., when King Darius led a huge force against Greece, only to be improbably defeated by the army of the much smaller city-state of Athens in a long battle on the plain of Marathon. Ten years later, Persia's King Xerxes led a punitive expedition against the upstart Athenians; this time, his forces overran the city of Athens and burned the Acropolis, but were ultimately defeated at Salamis (Salamína) by the already ascendant Athenian navy.

Scoring such decisive victories against what had seemed an invincible Eastern host gave the city of Athens a new self-confidence and pride which it expressed both materially, in a navy which soon dominated the whole Aegean, and artisti-

Info pp. 50-51

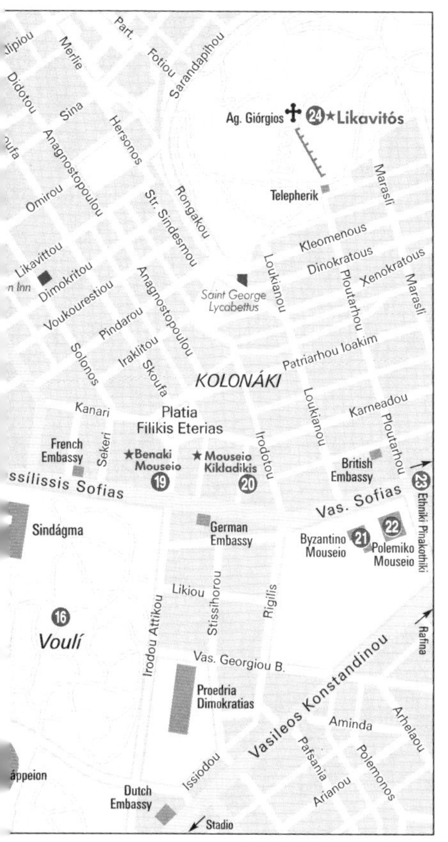

cally, in the temples which the city now erected on its Acropolis in thanks to the gods who had given them victory. Under its elected general, Pericles, Athens reflected its golden age in the buildings and sculptures of some of ancient Greece's greatest artists, notably Phidias.

The Acropolis was a sacred site, used in the context of rituals and religious festivals, especially the Panathenaic Festival, which began in 566 B.C. Festival processions snaked along the Panathenaic Way through the city and **Beulé Gate** (so named for the archeologist who "discovered" it) and up to the massive **Propylaea**, the entrance gateway to the site, an architectural masterpiece which was never completely finished because of the outbreak of the Peloponnesian War. On the left is the airy **Temple of Athena Nike**, built in 420 B.C. to commemorate the city's victory (*nike*) over the Persians (although the present edifice is a reconstruction). Thanks in part to the temple's fine vantage point – on a clear day (before the smog gets too heavy) you can see to Piraeus and the Saronic Gulf – there were sacred structures on this site long before the days of Pericles. Here, legend has it, King Aegeus watched for the return of his son Theseus from Crete, whither he had voyaged to free the city of Athens from its obligation to send 14 youths and maidens each year to feed the dreaded Minotaur. Theseus had arranged with his father to raise a white sail if he were victorious; but he forgot, distracted by his adventure with the princess Ariadne, and Aegeus, seeing a ship returning under blood-red sail, threw himself over the cliff in despair (though Cape Suninon might also have been the location).

A central legend of the Acropolis is that of Athens' patron goddess Athena; the story goes that she and Poseidon vied on this very hill to see who had more to offer Athens' citizens. Poseidon created a spring with a mighty blow of his trident; but Athena presented an olive tree, which was even more useful, providing people with food and oil, shade and wood, and the city therefore took on both her and her name. Athena was a virgin, or *parthenos*, and her main temple, which became known as the ***Parthenon**, remains one of the masterworks of world architecture. Forty-six Doric columns are arranged on a slightly curved base, and the columns themselves are slightly curved and slightly angled, all to create the illusion of perfect straightness. The Parthenon's sculptures were another of its glories. One recurring theme was the triumph of civilized man over the raw forces of nature and barbarism, a reflection of Athens' sense of supremacy after having defeated the Persians and brought the Greek

Info pp. 50-51

seas under its control. This was reflected less in the pediments (now lost), which illustrated Athena's birth and her contest with Poseidon, than in the 92 metopes, depicting scenes from the mythological battles between gods and giants, Greeks and Amazons, and centaurs and Lapiths. The theme carried over into the magnificent Parthenon frieze, a continuous band running around the building showing a Panathenaic procession very like the ones that would have taken place here: some of the finest moments are details of horsemen reining in their steeds or handlers controlling sacrificial oxen. The works were designed and supervised by the master sculptor Phidias, who was also responsible for the centerpiece of the Acropolis, the votive statue of Athena, fashioned of ivory and gold, standing some 10 meters high. Regarded in contemporary society as one of Phidias' masterworks, the statue vanished at some point in the early Byzantine period, and is known to us today only through copies.

Many of the other Parthenon sculptures and reliefs are gone, as well. Much of what wasn't destroyed by that fateful Venetian shell went off to London with Lord Elgin around 1800, and is now displayed in the British Museum. In light of the damaging effects of Athens' trademark *nefos*, or smog, on the fragments that remain, Lord Elgin's move may actually have been in the best interests of conservation, however defensible or indefensible from an ethical standpoint.

The on-site statues are only copies of the originals; in the ***Acropolis Museum**, you can see a few blackened, weathered lumps of rock that used to be proud reliefs of horsemen and coaches (the museum also displays some marvelous archaic sculpture that predates the Acropolis' current buildings: 6th century B.C.). Lord Elgin also removed one of the graceful caryatids from the south porch of the ***Erechthion**, the last of the triumvirate of great Acropolis buildings, constructed from 420 to 406 B.C. on the traditional site of Athena's first olive tree; although part of this disparate building was actually dedicated to the loser of the contest, Poseidon.

Right: View of the Acropolis and the Likavitós from the southwest.

Another important aspect of religious ritual was theater; the plays of Aeschylus, Sophocles, Euripides and Aristophanes were performed as part of festivals to the god Dionysus (the standard format was a trilogy of tragedies followed by a satyr-drama; Aeschylus' *Orestaia* is the only complete trilogy to have survived). The marble elements of today's ***Theater of Dionysus** were built in the 4th century B.C. to replace earlier structures of wood; the theater held 17,000 people, who were so captivated by the spectacle that some pregnant women miscarried out of sheer terror when Aeschylus' Furies made their entrance. More striking today, however, is the Roman Theater or ***Odeion of Herodes Atticus**, a semicircular amphitheater with a masonry backdrop; dating from A.D. 161 and originally roofed over, it now hosts performances of the annual Athens Festival.

Athens was also a seat of government; the city council met on the nearby hill of the **Areopagus**, where, in A.D. 51, Saint Paul first preached to the Athenians. Farther to the west lay the **Pnyx**, where the combined citizenry of Athens assembled after the city's democratic process had been established and a minimum quota of 5,000 people – not counting, of course, women, children or slaves – was required to transact the business of government.

THE *AGORÁ AND **PLÁKA

Since its earliest history, Athens' bustling center has been located at the foot of the Acropolis. The city's ancient market- and meeting-place was the **Agorá** ❷; while the Acropolis' buildings repre-

City Map pp. 40-41, Info pp. 50-51

sented the city's glory, it was in the Agorá that the actual day-to-day business of city life and government was carried out. Located here was the **Buleuterion**, or council chamber (now only a foundation); the **Stoá Basileios**, or Stoa of Zeus, housing the law courts; and the administrative center of the **Tholos**, where the Council of Five Hundred convened starting in around 500 B.C. A *stoá*, incidentally, is a roofed colonnade, although nothing remains of the Poikile Stoá at which Zeno taught here, and which gave the name to "stoic" philosophy; Socrates was also active in the Agorá.

Nor is there much left of the **Gymnasium** which was built on the site of the **Odeion of Agrippa**, which was later used as the University of Athens until that institution was closed in the 6th century A.D. Still in place, however, is the restored **Stoá of Attalos** (built around 150 B.C.), a kind of early shopping mall with stores running the length of its two stories, now an **Agorá Museum** filled with objects found here since excavations began in the 1930s. Running through the middle of the Agorá up to the Acropolis was the paved **Panathenaic Way**. One hub of this was the **Sanctuary of the Ten Eponymous Heroes of Athens**: these were the figures who gave their names to the 10 tribes of Attica; public announcements were rather prosaically posted on their pedestals.

There were other religious monuments here, as well: the **Sanctuary of Twelve Gods**; the **Altar of Ares** and the **Temple of Ares**, and the so-called Theseion, or ***Temple of Hephaistos**, a splendid Doric construction rising in near-perfection above the rubble of the past, the best-preserved classical temple in all of Greece. On the east side of the Agorá stands the red-roofed Byzantine church of **Agioi Apostoli** ("Holy Apostles"), built in the 11th century.

East of the Ancient Agorá is testimony to the days of the Romans. The **Library of Hadrian** ❸ was built for that emperor in A.D. 132 near the site of the **Roman Agorá** ❹, an extension of the ancient

City Map pp. 40-41, Info pp. 50-51

Agorá dating from around the time of the birth of Christ, which has yet to be completely excavated. A Roman landmark is the **Tower of the Winds** (Naos Aiolou), built in 40 B.C. and named for the reliefs of the eight winds that adorn the outer walls of this octagonal structure.

This area represents the border between ancient and modern, however, for the district closest to Athens' number-one tourist attraction has developed into a busy tourist center. Narrow pedestrian streets and stairways lined with neoclassical façades define the neighborhood known as **Pláka** ❺. In the evening, brightly-lit souvenir stands spill vases and statuettes into the streets; eager waiters try to lure passers-by onto the illuminated terraces of their restaurants; bouzouki music throbs from the interiors of eateries and bars. It's crowded, yet everything is rather convivial and wonderful, like a small-town fair: tourism notwithstanding, the Pláka has managed to retain some of the air of a village, especially in the afternoon heat when its streets and steps are populated only with dusty tendrils of wisteria and mangy cats. When Athens became the capital of Greece in 1834, the Pláka was basically all that there was of the city, and its neoclassical façades bear witness to the early attempts of King Otto to dress it up in appropriate style. Before that, this was the heart of the Albanian quarter: the neighborhood's name, which signifies a slab or paving-stone in Greek, is Albanian for "old," as in "old quarter."

Anyone who still has energy for museums after the wealth of ancient sites can stop in at the **Museum of Greek Folk Art**; the **Museum of Greek Folk Music Instruments**; or the **Kanellopulos Museum**, originally a private collection of *objets* from antiquity through to the 19th century, housed in a mansion from the latter period. There's also the **Children's Museum** on Kidathinéon.

Above and Right: Old Athens (Pláka) and the modern city (Café Neon at Omónia Square) – a wonderful contrast.

City Map pp. 40-41, Info p. 50-51

But Pláka's main attractions remain its atmospheric tavernas and its music – all a little too touristy, perhaps, and a little too crowded, but who really cares in the soft air of a summer night illuminated with strings of colored lights in the trees overhead?

MONASTIRÁKI AND OMÓMIA SQUARE

After the last Turks left Athens in 1833, King Otto was able to construct the core of what remains today the heart of modern Athens. Helping him in this endeavor was an architect from home, Leo von Klenze, who tightened up the plans of a Greek-German architectural partnership, Schaubert and Kleanthes, outlining the grand squares (*platía*), boulevards (*leoforos*) and public buildings of the business center of today's city.

As its tourist paths combine ancient and modern, Athens' newer sections blend East and West. The spirit of the East is alive in the **Monastiráki** quarter, the bazaar of the city during Ottoman rule, still crowded with little shops purveying all manner of wares to tourists. Strewn through here are some of Athens' finest Byzantine churches: ***Kapnikaréa** ❻, on Ermú Street, an 11th- to 13th-century church to the Presentation of the Virgin, or the beautiful ****Ágios Elefthérios** (Little Mitrópolis) ❼, a 12th-century church built of fragments of ancient marble, now standing in the shadow of the flashier, but perhaps more shallow, 19th-century edifice of the **Ágios Mitrópolis** ❽, Athens' main cathedral.

The main north-south axis from Monastiráki to central **Omónia Square** ❾ is the **Boulevard Athínas**, the city's main drag, which runs past the ***Central Market** (Kentrikí Agorá) and **City Hall**. "Unity Square" hardly projects the image of harmony that one might expect from the central spot of Athens, although there's a certain internationalism present in the foreign workers who crowd the kafeníon tables of this run-down, dirty district of anonymous office blocks.

From here, the parallel avenues of September 3 and October 28 run north through a district of boutiques (passing Athens' signature department store, **Minion**, which bears more than a touch of East Bloc character in its cheerless chambers) and fast-food stands toward one of Athens' greatest treasures, the **★★National Archeological Museum** ⑩.

Gathered in this neoclassical building, behind its rectangle of dusty lawn, is the cream of archeology from all of Greece. Every visitor is resigned from the outset to the fact that it's impossible to do justice to the riches here in a single day, and yet every visitor is compelled to try. People who are heading for the Greek Islands may want to focus on relics from the islands, such as the frescoes from Minoan-Age Santorin, preserved Pompeii-like in a volcanic explosion around 1500 B.C. But even these will find it impossible to bypass the golden mask of Agamemnon, found at Mycenae, or the magnificent bronze Striding God of Artemesion, whose authority is in no way diminished by the fact that scholars have not been able to agree on whether he is Poseidon in the act of hurling a trident or Zeus throwing a thunderbolt.

Above: Garlic seller in front of the market hall. Right: The impressive Corinthian columns of the Olympieion (Temple of Zeus).

SINDÁGMA SQUARE AND VASSÍLISSIS SOFÍAS BOULEVARD

The hypotenuse of the triangle of modern Athens are the diagonal avenues of Panepistimíu and Akadimías, which lead down to Sindágma Square. On Panepistemíu, also called Eleftheríu Venizélou, are three public buildings constructed to show off the majesty of the new Greek state after independence: the **National Library** ⑪, the largest in the country; the **University** ⑫, with its frescoes of classical themes; and, most blatantly neoclassical of all, the temple-like **Academy of Athens** ⑬. All three buildings were designed by the Hansen brothers, two Danish expatriot architects, between 1839 and 1884.

Sindágma Square ⑭ is another focal point of modern Athens. For visitors, it's even more important than Omónia Square: near here are the main offices of the tourist authority, **EOT**; private buses depart from here for some out-of-town destinations; leading off the south end of the square is Filellínon Street, lined with travel agencies of all descriptions; and the range of eating and dining facilities runs the gamut from McDonald's on one side to the stately and very expensive Hotel Grande Bretagne on the other.

By the end of the year 2000, the city's extensive new subway line may even be completed, so that a subway stop will replace the large construction site which occupied the center of the square through much of the 1990s.

Dominating the square's eastern side is the **Parliament Building** (Sindágma),

City Map pp. 40-41, Info pp. 50-51

built as King Otto and Queen Amalie's palace around 1840. Before this stands the **Tomb of the Unknown Soldier**, where visitors congregate to watch the changing of the guard of skirted *evzones* every hour on the hour in summer. The original seat of Parliament, just north of Sindágma Square on Stadíu Street, now houses the city's **Historical Museum** ⑮, devoted to Greece from the fall of the Byzantine Empire to the present day.

Extending around the current Sindágma building are the sprawling **National Gardens** (Voulí) ⑯, the city's main public park, complete with botanical gardens and a small zoo. Adjacent to the south is the park of the **Záppeion** ⑰, a congress and exhibition hall also built by one of the Hansens in the 19th century.

South of the Záppeion are the 13 remaining stately Corinthian columns of the ***Olympieion** (Temple of Olympian Zeus) ⑱, begun in 515 B.C. and not completed until A.D. 131. Thankful to the Emperor Hadrian for finally completing this lengthy project, the Athenians erected the nearby **Arch of Hadrian** soon thereafter.

At the northeast of Sindágma Square broad **Vassílissis Sofías** begins; a boulevard of embassies, hotels and museums. The ***Benáki Museum** ⑲ houses what was originally a private collection of Byzantine and Islamic art and artifacts. Further down the street are the fruits of another private collector's activities, of particular interest to anyone heading for the islands: the ***Goulandrís Museum of Cycladic Art** ⑳. Originally from the island of Ándros, which they have also generously endowed with museums, the Goulandrís family made their fortune in shipping, something that enabled Nikolaus P. Goulandrís to build up one of the leading collections of Cycladic art in the world. Signature displays here are the white marble figurines, which in their simplicity and elegance of abstracted form presage Picasso by some four millennia.

The **Byzantine Museum** ㉑, on the same street, is essential to anyone's un-

derstanding of how the forms of classical Greek art evolved into the icons and gold mosaics of the Byzantine world, which dazzled Europe for centuries but today seem unfamiliar and impenetrable to many Western eyes. Yet from the stylization of classical funerary stelai, depicting the deceased in a few regular poses, it was but a short step to the stylization that governs the Byzantine icon. Some of the objects show the early church taking over and adapting "pagan" themes – Apollo morphing into Christ – as well as pagan sites: the Acropolis temples were used as sites of Christian worship. Next door, incongruously, is the **War Museum** ㉒, with weapons from the Stone Age to World War II.

Further along, on Vasiléos Konstandínos near where that street runs into Vassílissis Sofías, is the **National Gallery** ㉓. Born, like so many other Athens museums, from private collections, it mainly documents the course of Greek art of the last few centuries, including early works by El Greco (who was born on Crete) and "The Greek Rider" by Delacroix, up to contemporary Greek artists.

Above: The Pantocrator Mosaic in the monastery of Dafní in the western part of the city is worth a detour.

To unwind from museum-going, head for a café in the exclusive residential district of **Kolonáki** behind the Benáki Museum. This is one of Athens' trendiest and most upscale neighborhoods, home to ambassadors and international businessmen, and with a fine array of boutiques for window-shoppers and serious purchasers alike. It nestles under ***Likavitós Hill** ㉔, which, legend has it, was a rock that Athena absent-mindedly dropped on the city on her way to attend to other business. When the Turks departed, the hill's steep slopes were barren, but a reforestation program begun in the 1880s left it blanketed in pines and cypresses. Anyone daunted by the steep footpaths can take the funicular, which departs from the corner of Aristípou and Plutárhou, up to the top, where in addition to stunning views

City Map pp. 40-41, Info pp. 50-51

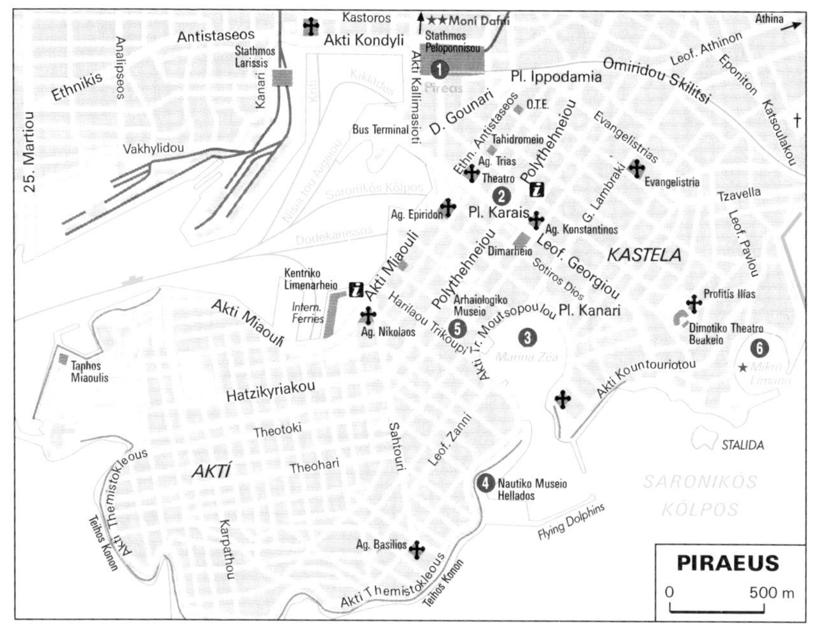

there's a restaurant, the church of Ágios Giórgios, and an open-air theater.

DAFNÍ MONASTERY

For those with a little extra time on their hands while in Athens, a visit to **★★Dafní Monastery**, 10 kilometers west of the city center, is recommended. The monastery's 5th-century church is world renowned for its wonderful Byzantine mosaics from the 11th century.

PIRAEUS (PIREAS)

Anyone traveling to the Greek Islands by ferry in summer knows Piraeus as a hot, crowded, confusing headache of a place, mobbed with cars and resounding with the stentorian horns of departing ferries. But Piraeus also includes exclusive residential districts, yacht harbors, tavernas, beaches and a couple of noteworthy museums; and knowing where these are can transform a stopover in Piraeus from a necessary evil to a pleasant adventure.

Piraeus has been Athens' harbor since the needs of this maritime power outgrew the capacity of Phaleron, the old port, in the 5th century B.C.; the Athenian general Pericles was responsible for the construction of the "Long Walls" that linked the port to the town. Later known as Porto Leone because of the lions that guarded the entrances to each of its three harbors, the town was built after plans by Hippodamos of Mílos, and his original plans were used again for the street layour of the modern city in 1834.

The **metro station** ❶ is a short walk from the main ferry basin, where boats depart for the Saronic Gulf islands, the Cyclades, the Northeast Aegean Islands, the Dodecanese and Crete. In general, the atmosphere around here is one of utter chaos, so that it seems incredible that foreign visitors are ever able to find their way to the boats they want. On Sunday mornings there's diversion, albeit only augmenting the hustle and bustle, in the **flea market**, one of the largest in Attica, held in the streets around the Metro station. Duck into the new large church of **Agías Paraskeví**, across the street from the harbor, for a moment of quiet.

Cutting over on Dimokratias or one of the parallel streets, you come to a still busy, but less touristy part of the city. Locals convene in the numerous coffee shops around the open square in front of the **Municipal Theater** ❷. One can also linger in the yachting-oriented establishments around Piraeus' second harbor, **Marina Zéa** ❸. Not only for pleasure craft, Zéa is the departure point for Flying Dolphins to some destinations. Green squares and lawns frame the banks of pleasure craft; at the southern end of the marina, in a modern building, is the **Maritime Museum** ❹, displaying more than 3,000 years of Greek naval history.

The finest museum in Piraeus, and one of the finest in Athens, is the **Archeological Museum** ❺ on Harilaou Trikoupi, with the ruins of a classical theater in its back yard. Among the sculptures here is a lion that may be a copy of one of the original guardians of the harbor (which the Venetians carted off); other objects were found at the bottom of the harbor, such as fragments of a Parthenon-like frieze that was bound for Italy when the ship it was on sank. Most impressive of all are four stunning bronze sculptures from the 4th century B.C. and earlier, including an archaic Apollo and a figure of Artemis who has retained her original, absolutely naturalistic eyes that seem to gaze back into your own. Three of these bronzes were discovered in a warehouse where they were hidden before the sack of the city in 86 B.C.

On the other side of **Kastela**, the area's most exclusive residential district, Piraeus' third harbor, ***Mikró Límano** ("Small Harbor") ❻, is lined with a row of bars, cafés and fish tavernas. On the other side of Mikro Límano are the beaches of Piraeus, although the sight of ferries and freighters does little to recommend the purity of their water.

ATHENS (☎ 01)

EOT has several offices in Athens. The head office is at 2 Amerikis, tel. 3223111; there are branches at the airport's Terminal East and the National Bank of Greece on Sindágma Square, tel. 3222545.

PLANE: Construction is underway on a modern new airport in Spáta, 23 km east of the city, scheduled to open in March 2001 (for information call 3698300 or go to www.athensairport-2001.gr on the Internet). Until then, flights still arrive at and depart from the old airport at Ellinikó, 10 km south of Athens. There are two terminals: **Terminal West** for Olympic Airways flights, and **Terminal East** for everyone else. If you're flying in on another airline and making an Olympic connection to the islands, you'll have to take the airport bus from one terminal to the other.

BUS: **Express Bus 91** connects Omónia Square (downtown Athens) with Terminal East; **Bus 90** runs to Terminal West. To get from downtown Athens to Piraeus, take **Bus 40**. There's also an Olympic Airways bus from Leofóros Singroú 100 to Terminal West every half-hour. Buses to **Rafína** depart from smaller Terminal C, at Egyptou Square, tel. 8210872. For further information on long-distance buses, see "Guidelines," p. 241.

METRO: The new, expanded Metro is supposed to open in 2001. Until then, the city's sole **metro line** remains a direct, quick and cheap option from downtown Athens (Omónia Square or Monastiráki) to Piraeus (20 minutes). **Public transportation information**: Tel. 185 (daily 7 am to 9 pm).

TAXI: Taxis in Athens are an adventure in themselves. If you're trying to hail one on the street, you have to shout out your destination as it drives by (sometimes with other passengers in the car). If you fit on the driver's itinerary, he'll stop; otherwise, he'll drive on imperviously.

Keep in mind that the meter rates rise once you leave the taxi's operating area. You can tell where the taxi is from by looking at the license plate: A is Athens (town), Z is the airport. Taking an A-plate taxi from Sindágma Square to the airport will run you around 4,500 drachmas; a Z-plate taxi costs about 1,500. So try to hail a cab from the area you want to go to.

You can save some of the headache by calling a radio taxi, such as **Athina 1**, tel. 9217942; **Kosmos** (downtown & Piraeus: tel. 4200042; Glifáda/airport: tel. 9642900); **Protoporia**, tel. 2221623; or **Piraeus 1** (Piraeus and downtown), tel. 41823335.

LEFT LUGGAGE: At the airport, you can leave and pick up bags round the clock across the street from Terminal West (Olympic Airways terminal). Some of

the hostels around the Plaka will let you leave luggage, such as **Festos**, at Filellinon 18, tel. 3232455.

$$$ **The Grande Bretagne**, Sindágma Square, tel. 3230251, fax. 3228034. Athens's leading hotel, may make you yearn for the more lowbrow Greek friendliness. **St. George Lycavitos**, 2 Kleomonos (Kolonaki), tel. 7290711, fax. 7290439; attractive, nice views, pool. **Amalia**, 9 Xenofontos (corner of Amalia), tel. 3237301, fax. 3238792, e-mail: hotamal@netor.gr, website: http://www. greekhotel.com/amalia/. Modern, pleasant hotel across from the National Gardens, down from Sindágma Square.

$$ Apollonos, between Sindágma Square and Pláka, has a number of hotels; try **Omiros** at number 15 (tel. 3235486, fax. 3228059) or **Hermes** at number 19 (tel. 3235514, fax. 3232073), with an in-house travel agency. **Hotel Museum**, 16 Bouboulinas, tel. 3605611, is right behind the Archeology Museum. **Athenian Inn**, 22 Haritos (Kolonaki), tel. 7238097, fax. 7218756, was once patronized by Lawrence Durrell.

$ There are some cheap hotels around the Pláka, but the **Hotel Royal**, Mitropoleos 44, tel. 3238596, has some high-ceilinged rooms with showers and a distant sense of (much-) faded elegance. Pretty **Pension Adonis**, Kodrou 3, tel. 3249397, and **Akropolis House**, Kodrou 6-8, tel. 3223244, are more up-market and higher priced.

EXPENSIVE: **Gerofinikas**, Pindarou 10, Kolonaki, tel. 3636710, among Athens' finest. **Apotsos**, Panepistimiou 10 (Sindágma), tel. 3637046, long-time haunt of upscale Athenians.

MODERATE: **O Thespis**, Thespidos 18 (Pláka), tel. 3238242; pleasant outdoor dining with views of the surrounding countryside; quite good standard food. **Strophi**, Rovertou Galli 25 (Propyleon), tel. 9214130. A rooftop terrace with Acropolis view, decent food; but crowds of tourists lead to harried, peremptory service. **Ithaki**, Agías Filotheis 2 (Mitropoleos Square); a great location under the trees, near the cathedral. **Sokrates' Prison**, Mitsaion 20 (Makriyianni), tel. 9223434, perennially and deservedly popular.

BUDGET: **Peristeria**, Patroou 5, tel. 3234535, simple taverna, standard repertoire, no décor, very popular with Greeks.

Acropolis Museum, tel. 3236665. Open Mon 11 am to 2:30 pm, Tue-Sun 8:30 am to 2:30 pm, until 8 pm in summer. **Ancient Agora**, tel. 3210185. Open 8:30 am to 3 pm, closed Mon. **National Archeology Museum**, Tositsa 1/Patission 44, tel. 8217717. Open Mon 10:30 am to 5 pm, Tue-Sun 8:30 am to 3 pm, in summer until 8 pm. **Museum of Cycladic Art**, Neophitou Douka 4, tel. 7228321, fax. 7239382. Open 10 am to 4 pm, Sat until 3 pm, closed Tue and Sun. **Byzantine Museum**, Vassílissis Sofiás 22, tel. 7231570. Open 8:30 am to 2:45 pm, closed Mon. **National Gallery/Alexander Soutsos Museum**, Vasiléos Konstantínu 50, tel. 7211010. Open 9 am to 3 pm, Sun 10 am to 2 pm, closed Mon. The marvelous **Benáki Museum**, Koumbari 1/Vassílissis Sofiás, tel. 3611617, is unfortunately closed for renovations at least until the year 2000.

The **Athens Festival** takes place in July, with outdoor performances in the amphitheater of Herodes Atticus. Festival Office: 4 Stadiou, tel. 3221459.

The **National Welfare Association** shops feature hand-made crafts, from icons to weaving to needlepoint pillow-cases. Ipatias 6 (corner Apollonos), tel. 3211761, or Vassílissis Sofiás 135, tel. 6460603. The **Benáki Museum** and the **Museum of Cycladic Art** both have large museum shops, with reproductions and a broad selection of books (the shop in the Benáki Museum is open despite the renovation work). **Compendium Bookshop**, Nikis 28 (Sindágma), tel. 3221248, is an English bookstore with magazines, a used book exchange, and lots of books about Greece.

Police: 100. **Ambulance**: 166. **SOS Medecins** (24-hour medical service): 3310310. See "Guidelines," p. 244, for more emergency numbers.

PIRAEUS

See above for information on public transportation. Taxis from downtown Athens will run you about 2,000 drachma. The metro stop is right across from the main harbor.

Some of the Flying Dolphins for the Saronic Islands and Sporades leave from Marina Zéa, on the other side of the Piraeus peninsula (about a 500-drachma taxi ride from the main port).

Express Bus 19 links Piraeus and the Ellenikó Airport (both terminals).

$$ **The Park Hotel**, Kolokotroni 103, tel. 4524611, fax. 4524615, "all mod cons" and an upscale air, on a central square not far from either port.

$ **Noufara Hotel**, Iroon Politechniou 45, tel. 4115541, fax. 4134292. Clean, central, on main north-south artery.

Dipylo, Kodrou 3/Syndagmatos 34, tel. 4172105. Impressive, appealing selection of Greek dishes, prepared and served with both sophistication and comfort. Dinner only.

Archeological Museum, Charilaou Trikoupi 31, tel. 4521598, open 8:30 am to 2:45 pm, closed Mon. **Maritime Museum**, Akti Themistokleous, tel. 4516822, open Tue-Fri 9 am to 2 pm, Sat 9 am to 1 pm, closed Sun & Mon.

THE ISLANDS OF THE SARONIC GULF

SALAMÍNA (SALAMIS)
ÉGINA (AEGINA)
PÓROS
ÍDRA (HYDRA)
SPÉTSES

Close to Athens and in the shadow of the Pėloponnese, the islands in the Saronic Gulf are rather a mixed bunch, ranging from the suburban and semi-polluted sprawl of Salamína, right at Piraeus' back door, to the jet-set ambiance of barren Ídra. One draw for visitors is their proximity to the mainland, which makes them easy of access; another, particularly in the case of the islands of Póros, Ídra and Spétses, is their reputation for being magnets for celebrities and as artistic centers.

For anyone who likes to be where the action is or seeks to combine an island vacation with exploration of the Peloponnese, or who has a day to kill in Athens and would like one last (or first) island experience, the Saronic Gulf islands are the place to go.

SALAMÍNA (SALAMIS)

To classical scholars, the name of **Salamína** ❶ resounds with glory, since it was here that the Athenian navy magnificently defeated the Persians in the year 480 B.C., an event which ushered in the golden age of Periclean Athens. Today, however, Salamína is anything but golden; leaden would probably be a more appropriate adjective for this island nestled up against the dirty coast off the shipping lanes to and from nearby Piraeus. Still, there are some decent beaches, especially along the southern coast; and Salamína has a very "real" flavor as the weekend spot of choice for less well-to-do Greek families.

Salamína, the island's capital, offers a not very nice beach and an **Archeological Museum**. Buses run to the northwest of the island and the convent of **Faneroméni**, one of the island's highlights: built on the site of an ancient temple around 1660, its church contains some stunning 18th-century frescoes, and peacocks wander about the garden.

Avoid the beaches around here, however, in favor of those further south, by **Eándio** (the ancient town of Telemon), or the stretch of coast between **Kakí Vígla** and **Peristéria**. The aforementioned battle was fought in the straits between **Ambelákia** and the mainland, but the port towns here today are rather smelly and polluted, with no trace left of the murex shells from which a purple dye was produced – related to the dye the Phoenicians made and sold from the same creature – until World War II.

Previous Pages: The Temple of Aphaéa in Égina. Left: Whitewashed walls and brilliant blue doors – these colors are the hallmark of the Cyclades.

ATTIKÍ
Mándra
Elefsína
Kólpos Elefsínos
Pérama
ATHÍNA
Piréas
Mégara
Makriplági
1369
1132
Paloúkia
Faneroméni
Salamína
Ambelákia
Loutráki
Kinéta
Órm. Salamínos
Akr. Petrítis
Selínia
Eándio
Kakí Vígla
Ág. Theódori
SALAMÍNA 1
ΣΑΛΑΜΙΝΑ
Peristéria
Akr. Kóhi
Kórinthos
Órm. Kehrión
Saronikós Kólpos
DIAPÓRII
KORINTHÍA
Ág. Nektários
Souvála
Mesagrós
Órmorfi Ekklisía
Aphaéa
Kolóna
Paleohóra
Agía Marína
Égina
Hriseleóntissa
Marathónas
532
2 ÉGINA
ΑΙΓΙΝΑ
Ó. Marathón
Agístri
Skála
Pérdika
AGÍSTRI 4
3 MONÍ
Akr. Pirgos
Limenária
Trapezóna
1137
Néa Epídavros
Paleá Epídavros
Arahnéo
1199
HER. METHANON
740
Ligourió
Méthana
Kólpos Epidávrou
Akr. Ahérdo
ARGOLÍS
Poseideíon
5 PÓROS
ΠΟΡΟΣ
Néorio
Zoodóhou Pigís
Póros
Galatás
Dídimo
1113
Kólpos Ídras
Akr. Zoúrvas
Ermíoni
Ídra
Mandráki
Agía Triáda
Argolikós Kólpos
Kranídi
DOKÓS
Vlihós
Mólos
6 ÍDRA
Profítis Ilías
ΥΔΡΑ
Agía Efpraxía
588
Epikopí
Portohéli
Órm. Kranidíou
Akr. Bísti
Kósta
SPÉTSES 7
ΣΠΕΤΣΕΣ
248
Profítis Ilías
Spétses
Agía Paraskeví
Agía Marína
Bekíri
Agía Anárgiri
SPÉTSOPOULA
MIRTÓO PÉLAGOS
PÁRNON
Paralía
SARONIC GULF
0
10
20 km
Paralía
Monemvasia

*ÉGINA (AEGINA)

A mere 45 minutes by hydrofoil from Athens, **Égina** ❷ is practically within commuting distance, and is accordingly overrun with Athenians on weekends and holidays. But for all the suburban sprawl along the island's north coast and the frequency of hydrofoil and ferry traffic, Égina is a genuine Greek island. Its shady, light-dappled pine woods and ancient ruins are a world away from Athens' hustle and bustle, and pistachio orchards, rather than *nefos*, are the characteristic features of this countryside. Add to this a host of ruins and Byzantine churches, a respectable array of beaches and *psarotaverna*, fish taverns, and, the ultimate accolade of a place's Greekness, the fact that Nikos Kazantzakis lived here while writing *Zorba the Greek*; and Égina can easily make you forget that Athens is a mere day trip away.

At the start of its history, it was Athens that was close to Égina, rather than the other way round: Égina, that is to say, was a stronger, more successful entity than the mainland city. After becoming a part of the seven-city alliance called the Heptapolis in 950 B.C., it grew into a flourishing trade center, and even became the first place in Europe to mint coins in 650 B.C. As Athens gained in power and prestige, the two places found themselves in frequent stand-offs. To keep Égina from siding with Darius and the Persians in 490 B.C., Athens kidnapped a few leading Aeginans as hostages. Égina did come in on the Greek side at the Battle of Salamis, and was even decorated for the leading role of its navy; but the reconciliation with Athens was short-lived.

In 458 B.C., the Athenian navy defeated those self-same triremes; three years later, it forced the islanders to tear down their walls and hand over their fleet; and in the Peloponnesian War, to forestall inimical retaliations, it deported the island's population altogether. The Aeginans found a ready welcome on Sparta. Evidence of Byzantine influence can be found in the island's liberal sprinkling of Byzantine churches. Two 13th-century gems within walking distance of Égina Town are **Ómorfi Ekklesía** or "Beautiful Church," so named on account of its frescoes, and little **Faneroméni**, actually an underground chapel in a cave.

In the War of Independence in 1820, Égina became one of the first places to shake off the yoke of Ottoman rule: one reason why it was selected to be the first capital of free Greece in 1828. It only served in this function for a year before relinquishing pride of place to Nauplion; still, the island's main town bears traces of its proud past in the form of a number of erstwhile government buildings, including the mint where the first coins of free Greece were produced more than a millenium after Égina began its tradition of coinage (located in the **Residence**; today's public library). Égina has continued a couple of its old commercial traditions, as well. The island still produces attractive glazed pottery, for instance; but even the most lustrous ewers and jugs can't compete with the pistachio. Harvested in August, the nuts, with shells or without, are mounded at stalls and stores around the harbor for visitors' perusal and purchase; while the orderly rows of pistachio trees in the orchards are a characteristic feature of the island's interior.

Certainly **Égina Town** has a tidy, civic air that shows it's not "just" another island capital; the dominant architectural style is neoclassical rather than Cycladic, and buildings public and private run to ocher tones and red tile roofs; apart from the white-painted chapel of **Ágios Nikólaos** at one end of the harbor pier, built to celebrate the harbor's completion in 1826. The building was financed by Samuel Gridley Howe, a young American who had come to Greece to help fight for independence and funded the harbor project as a way to create employment in

Info p. 63

the struggling young country; he was the husband of Julia Ward Howe, author of the well-known American song "Battle Hymn of the Republic."

As the ferry from Piraeus rounds the point to head into Égina harbor, you can see a single broken column affixed like an admonishing finger to the headland: all that remains of a classical-era **Temple of Apollo**, this monument has also given the name to the site known as the **Hill of Kolóna**. The temple is actually a relic of one of the later stages of habitation here; the hill was settled in prehistoric times, and excavations of the numerous walls and remnants of structures here are still in progress; though the site is of more interest to archeologists than the average layman. More concise explanations are to be found in Égina's **Archeological Museum** nearby; although many of Égina's archeological treasures have been exported to Athens or even farther afield (take the British Museum's "Aegean treasure" of Minoan gold ornaments, believed to have been brought to Égina from Crete), there are some noteworthy things preserved here, including the mosaic floor of a 7th-century synagogue.

Above: Pistachios – Égina's most important product. Right: The gigantic modern church of the monastery of Ágios Nektários is the destination of pilgrims from throughout Greece.

The 19th-century **Town Hall** on the shore promenade houses two cafés. In the town center the church of **Agía Tríada** and a Venetian tower, **Pírgos Markéllou**, are also both from the 19th century.

While rife with history, Égina has been somewhat prodigal with its archeological treasures; the rest of the Temple of Apollo was used to build the new dock in the infancy of the Greek state. Even more egregious was the case of the ****Temple of Aphaéa**, Égina's most famous archeological site, and the best-preserved ancient temple to be found on any Greek island, if not in the whole of Greece. "Best-preserved" refers to the fact that most of its columns are standing, including the second, upper-story row around the inner sanctum or cella; the original sculptural decoration, however, is gone. This is because peasants in the early 19th century were cutting it up to use as fuel for their lime kilns; Bavarian crowned prince Ludwig (mercifully) bought it up and transported it to Munich, where you can still see it in that city's Glyptothek, partially restored according to 19th-century conceptions of archaic perfection. The temple, however, remains *in situ*, gloriously commanding the top of its windswept hill, looking down over the water on two sides and dominating the town of Agía Marína, whose concrete hotel blocks seem ludicrous in the forced comparison. For walkers, there's a trail down to the water through the trees.

Before it reaches the temple of Aphaéa, the bus from Égina stops at the church and monastery of **Ágios Nektários**. Locals claim that this church is the second-biggest in the Orthodox world after Hagia

Map p. 56, Info p. 63

Sofia, and the largest in Greece; it commemorates the former Archbishop of Libya, who died here in 1920 and was canonized in 1961, making him one of the newest additions to the list of Orthodox saints. The faithful honor him on November 9, the anniversary of his death.

Architecturally more interesting are the many old Byzantine churches – 32 or so, many with remains of frescoes – on the hill of **Paleohóra**, the medieval city of Égina, abandoned some 200 years ago, which lies just behind the monastery. Although the hill is always accessible, the best time to visit is the morning, when the caretaker is on hand to let you into the locked churches (dating from the 13th to the 17th centuries). Walkers can continue on to the 17th-century convent of **Hrisoleóntissa** ("Golden Lion"), originally a fortified monastery, about an hour on foot from Paleohóra.

The island's second town, and arguably its main resort, lies on the eastern coast. **Agía Marína** boasts the dubious blessing of a relatively broad sand beach; the sand is that particularly Greek shade of beige, rather than sparkling white, but that hasn't prevented the town from developing into a crowded tourist center in summer, with the requisite complement of accompanying attractions: fast-food joints, souvenir shops, and bars serving overpriced cocktails with English names. Overshadowing the whole is an unfinished concrete block defacing what must once have been a picturesque hillside. Still, if you like swimming and nightlife – two reasons many people come to Greece – this is the place for you. Smaller beaches dot the north coast; **Souvála** is the largest resort along here, which is also serviced by ferries to and from Piraeus.

The other main road out of Égina town leads along the west coast, a route which, as it moves in and out of the trees, affords dramatic views of the mainland as well as two smaller nearby islands, Agístri and Moní. On the way, you can stop off for a swim at some of the small beaches, or for fish at **Marathónas**; from where a steep path leads up **Mount Óros** (532 meters).

But if it's fish you're after, it's worth waiting until you get to **Pérdika**, a quiet (in the off season) fishing village where you can eat in sight of the local fleet. Pérdika is also known for its animal shelter, a facility which cares for sick or injured animals, wild or domestic. Continuing this theme is the mountain goat refuge on the otherwise uninhabited island of **Moní ❸**.

Wooded **Agístri ❹** has a few hotels, if not much in the way of activities; it's a quiet, unassuming place, with three little villages: **Skála**, the local resort; **Agístri** (Mílos), the main town; and the settlement of **Limenária** in the south.

PÓROS

"The Grand Canal of Greece" is how writers have described the narrow **channel** that separates **Póros Town** from the mainland: some 300 meters across, it's crowded with pleasure craft and small boats ferrying back and forth, and lined, especially on the Póros side, with white houses rising steeply from the water's edge. This volcanic island of **Póros ❺**, actually created when two smaller islands, Kalouria and Spheria, were joined together, offers, like many of the Saronic Islands, more in terms of atmosphere than of sights per se. However, thanks to its attractive approach and closeness to Athens, it's become the leader in package tours of all the islands of the Saronic Gulf. From the crowds, you wouldn't know that Póros was only sparsely populated at the beginning of this century, until it became a haven for Greeks expelled from Asia Minor after 1923. In the 7th century B.C., however, it was populous enough to serve as headquarters of the Kalavrian League, a naval alliance; Póros may also have played this function because the island's patron deity was the sea god Poseidon, who could be expected to protect "his" ships.

Right: Since cars have been banned on Ídra, mules once again transport luggage.

The **Temple of Poseidon** underwent a number of incarnations even before Demosthenes the Orator sought sanctuary here from the Macedonians, who were understandably annoyed at the way he kept trying to stir up Greek sentiment (and armies) against them, in 322 B.C. The Macedonians, being "barbarian" northern savages by the elitist standards of some Athenians of the day, had no respect at all for the sanctuary of the temple and came in to kill Demosthenes, but he beat them to the punch by swallowing poison; Pausanias later reported visiting his tomb in the marble temple.

Today, the most interesting sight at the temple is the view; only a few stones are left. You can walk or drive down to the 18th-century monastery of **Zoodóhou Pigís**; the beach below, called **Kalavreias**, is pebbly, which is about the average for this island. Boats bear visitors from Póros Town to swimming spots on the more secluded north coast.

As on all the Saronic Islands, shipping and the navy have played and continue to play a significant role; there's still a **Naval Training School** here, although the battleship Evangelos Averof, which used to be moored off Póros as a kind of memorial, now floats in Piraeus harbor. A local son whom islanders are not eager to claim is General Papadopoulos, a member of the infamous junta who is still in prison; his family is from Póros, and is engaged in a dispute with the local government about retaining their lands.

*ÍDRA (HYDRA)

"The Greenwich Village of Greece" is an epithet for cosmopolitan **Ídra ❻**. Pioneered, like so many trendy spots, by artists seeking a new arena in which to work and play, it's become a playground for the international jet set. The island itself is gray and barren; but since cars, motorcy-

Map p. 56, Info p. 63

cles and buses are prohibited here, it does have a special charm.

Since the island didn't offer early settlers much in terms of ways to make a living, they took to the seas, building up a redoubtable fleet of ships in the services of merchant shipping and, less overtly, piracy. Its navy won it the nickname "Little England." Although Ídra was not an initial leader in the War of Independence, it came in, when it did, with a will: Ídra's ships made up two-thirds of the entire Greek fleet. Andreas Vokos, a.k.a. Admiral Miaoulis, was one of the legendary leaders in the story of Greek independence. He's commemorated every year on his native island with a big festival called the Miaoulia, culminating with the arrival of a Greek Air Force plane to drop a laurel wreath for the hero, around June 20. A new **Historical Museum** contains memorabilia from the War of Independence.

The picturesque main town, **Ídra**, is scattered with art galleries of greater and lesser degrees of seriousness, vegetarian restaurants and discos. Prosperity has long set the tone in Ídra Town, at least since the 19th century, when sea captains made their fortunes in shipping and built their stone mansions here, now put to various uses: the **Tombázis Mansion**, once a branch of Athens' School of Fine Arts, is now used as accommodation for art students; the **Satouris Mansion** contains the National Merchant Marine Academy; and one of the **Koundouriotis Mansions**, formerly a museum, is currently being renovated by the Greek Ministry of Defense.

The Koundouriotis family, which produced the first President of the Greek Republic, was Albanian, like many of Ídra's early settlers, who fled here from the Turks in the 15th century. Despite popular mistrust of the Albanians today in the face of a new wave of immigration, elements of Albania have penetrated into Greek culture: the *foustanella* or kilt that's a part of the formal attire of Greek soldiers is based on Albanian fighting gear, and is sometimes referred to as the "Albanian kilt."

Traces of the island's oldest history exist around Episkopí, to the west, where the first settlers, Driopian shepherds, lived around the 10th century B.C. Recent forest fires have, however, done little to ease the general dearth of foliage. Another walk of about an hour and a half leads up to **Profítas Ilías** and the convent of **Agía Efpraxía**, where the nuns sell some of their textiles; if you bring food and water, you can head from here down to **Limoniza Bay**. Popular swimming spots along the north coast are **Mólos**, attractive **Vlihós** with its tavernas, and the fishing harbor of **Kamíni** with the so-called "baby beach" popular with families, all west of Ídra town; and **Mandráki**, to the east, a natural harbor once used by shipbuilders, later in wartime, which boasts Ídra's only real beach.

Ídra's religious highlights include the church of **Panagía tis Theotókou**, a striking 18th-century edifice in the main town, and the island's newest church, **Ágios Konstandínos** of Ídra, dedicated to the island's patron saint and built on the site of his residence. The island holds a festival on his name day, November 14. Also worthwhile is the monastery of **Agía Triáda**, a little way out of town.

SPÉTSES

Farthest from Athens of the Saronic Gulf islands, **Spétses** ❼ seems truly more like a piece of the Peloponnese with its pine forests and tranquil air. Spétses, like the other Saronic islands around the Peloponnese, made its money through shipping and shipbuilding; but the defining factor in its identity was its role in helping to launch the fight for independence, becoming the first naval fleet to fly the Greek flag after the outbreak of rebellion on the Peloponnese in 1821.

One heroine is Spétses' "lady admiral" Laskarina Bubulína, who won a number of victories for the Greek side; her bones are preserved in the island's **museum** in Spétses Town, along with one of the original flags bearing the slogan of the war, "Freedom or Death." The museum is housed in the elegant 18th-century mansion of Hadzigannis Mexis, a wealthy supporter of the Greek cause at the time. **Bubulína's Statue** also graces the main square of **Dápia**, which is adorned with the *krokalia* (black-and-white pebble) images at which Spétses excels.

Another noteworthy house in town is the **Hotel Possidonion**, built by a local tycoon, Sotirios Anargiros, who put some of his fortune to the service of his town by creating the first-ever hotel in all of the Greek Islands in the 1920s. Anargiros was also responsible for foresting part of the island with pines, as well as opening a school based on English public schools; it's closed now, but the building is still occasionally in use. Author John Fowles taught here when he was living on Spétses, which is the setting of his novel *The Magus*.

Above the harbor is the lovely church of **Ágios Nikólaos**. East of town is the church of **Panagía Armada**, built to commemorate one of the most important victories Spétses' ships won in the War of Independence, on September 8, 1822. Every year on September 8, this battle against the Turks is recreated, complete with burning ships, which make a dramatic impression at night on the dark water. Further on, **Agía Marína** is the main town beach. Finds made near here established that there has been settlement on Spétses since before 2000 B.C.

Some of the best (and most popular) beaches are to be found on the island's southwest coast, at **Agía Paraskeví** and **Agía Anárgiri**. Near the latter is **Bekíri Cave**, with a few stalactites.

Another lovely corner is around the beach of **Vréllou**, also known as "Paradise." From here, any hiker with time and energy can make the ascent up through the trees to **Profítis Ilías**, the highest point on the island at 248 meters.

Map p. 56

ÉGINA (☎ 0197)

There are several commercial tourist offices in Égina Town, mostly open Apr-Oct.
Colona Tours, tel. 22334, can book rooms and also sells ferry tickets.

FERRY: 90 Minutes from Athens, 45 minutes by Flying Dolphin to Égina Town (there's also less frequent service to Agía Marína): an easy day trip, although on weekends the last boat back to Piraeus is in the early evening – so check times in advance!
Port Authority, tel. 22328.
CAR AND MOTORCYCLE RENTAL: **Trust Rent a Car**, tel. 27010 or 26478.

ÉGINA TOWN: $$ **Hotel Pavlou**, Pavlou Aeginitou 21, tel. 22795. Pleasant blue-and-white building tucked behind palm trees. **Areti**, tel. 23593, near the ferry dock, facing the sunset.
MARATHONAS: $$$ **Moondy Bay Hotel**, tel. 25147, fax 61147; on the beach; the island's nicest bungalow complex.
AGÍA MARÍNA: $$$ **Hotel Apollo**, tel. 32271, large, renovated, with tennis courts. $$ **Hotel Liberty**, tel. 32353, by the beach.

ÉGINA TOWN: Of the restaurants lining the harbor, one standout is **To Spiti tou Psarou** ("The Fishermen's House"), filled with locals even in the low season. If you can't get a table there, nearby **Maridaki** is also acceptable. **Lekkas** (tel. 22527) is another local favorite.
PERDIKA: Miltos is one of the better tavernas.

Archeological Museum, tel. 22248, open Tue-Sun 8:30 am to 5 pm. Ask here if you want to visit the (locked) church of Omorphi Ekklesia.
Temple of Aphaia, tel. 32398, open weekdays 8:15 am to 7 pm, weekends 8:30 am to 3 pm.
The small **Archeological Museum** here can be viewed by arrangement with the guard, at 9 and 11 am, 12 and 1 pm.

The non-profit **Hellenic Wildlife Hospital** in Pérdika is a unique organization that treats wild animals until they are sufficiently recovered to be set free. For more information, call 9596988.

PÓROS (☎ 0298)

There are a number of travel agencies at the harbor. **Tourist Police**, tel. 22462

PÓROS TOWN: $$ **Sirena**, tel. 22741 or 22880, the island's best, with casino. **Latsi**, tel. 22392, small and pleasant.

The restaurants along the waterfront in Póros Town are generally good; try the **Sailor**.

Archeological Museum, tel. 23276.

ÍDRA (☎ 0298)

The **Saitis Tourist Office** by the harbor, tel. 52184, fax. 53469, can help with itineraries, accommodation, and excursions, as can **Ídra Tours**, tel. 53718. **Tourist Police**, tel. 52205.

BOATS: Flying Dolphins (1 hour) and ferries (4 hours) from Piraeus; Flying Dolphins from Piraeus depart from Marina Zéa. Ferries and water taxis also run across from Ermioni on the Peloponnese (20 minutes).

ÍDRA TOWN: $$$ **Bratsera Hotel**, tel. 53971, fax. 53626, restrained elegance in a converted sponge factory, with a chic colonnade around the pool. **Miramare Bungalows**, tel. 52300, fax. 52301, comfortable complex on the island's only sand beach. **Mistral Hotel**, tel. 52509, fax. 53412, an old stone building with modernized rooms, centrally located.
$$ **Ippokampos**, tel. 53453, fax. 53454, in an old villa with a lovely stone courtyard. **Hydra Hotel**, tel. 52102, fax. 53330, in another old villa in the heart of town looking out over the water. **Pension Antonios**, tel. 53227, and **Pension Alkyonides**, tel. 54055, are two other nice old villa accommodations.
$ **Hotel Sofia**, tel. 52313, small, central and somewhat loud.

ÍDRA TOWN: O Kipos ("The Garden"), tel. 52329; outdoor taverna dining. **Xeri Elia**, tel. 52886, expansive inside and out, with leafy green terrace, good fresh fish. **Christina**, tel. 53516, on the beach, reasonable prices.

Historical Museum, tel. 52355, focuses on events of the Greek War of Independence.

The weekend nearest June 21 sees the **Miaoulia**, a big festival (with fireworks) honoring the Greek freedom fighter Admiral Miaoulis. An international **Puppet Theater Festival** is held every July.

SPÉTSES (☎ 0298)

Takis Tourist Office, tel. 72215; listings of accommodations and excursions. **Port Authority**, tel. 72245.

BOATS: From Piraeus there are ferries and Flying Dolphins (from Marina Zéa), and small ferries to and from Kósta in the Peloponnese.

SPÉTSES TOWN: $$$ **Possidonion**, tel. 72206, fax. 72208, Greece's first tourist hotel, going strong since 1914. **Kasteli**, tel. 72311, large, modern hotel/bungalow complex.
$$ **Villa Christina**, tel. 72147, nice pension. **Akroyiali**, tel. 73695, on the beach.

SPÉTSES TOWN: Patralis, on the water, is deservedly popular, but not cheap. **Lazaros**, also very good, is lower priced.

Museum, tel. 72994.

SUPERFERRY II
STRINTZIS LINES

BAR

THE CYCLADES

NORTHERN CYCLADES
WESTERN CYCLADES
CENTRAL CYCLADES
SOUTHERN CYCLADES

Many travelers who refer to "the Greek Islands" generally mean the Cyclades, the heart of Greece's Aegean territories. Yet some of the most popular of these much-visited islands are at first glance among Greece's least inherently prepossessing. Most of the Cyclades are lumps of dry earth sparsely covered with a thin veil of tough vegetation, with tamarisk-lined beaches of brown sand, scoured in summer, on their north shores, by the *meltemi*. Their white villages, with earthen walls rounded as if grown from the land around them, are their most immediately identifiable feature. With a minimum of fertile land and natural resources, islands like Míkonos and Íos have at times ranked as among the poorest areas in Greece.

To imply that there's no beauty in the Cyclades is, of course, nothing short of slanderous: whether your tastes run to the white sands of the beaches of Míkonos or the black ones of volcanic Thíra, the fertile valleys tucked between the dry hills of Ándros or the ancient ruins of Dílos, there's plenty here to admire. But the Cyclades' beauty is more subtle than overwhelming: a poetry of empty windmills and deserted-looking farms amid the terraced fields, of stone walls snaking across hillsides that grow tawny rather than green in the relentless summer sun, which mutes the ocean's blue into a whitish haze.

And in fact, beyond the obvious appeal of active beach scenes or night life, it's in this subtlety that the Cyclades weave their spell. Only here do you find just this quality of limpid air, laden even at night with the smell of sun-warmed thyme, shimmering with the vibrato of cicadas in the olive groves, as soft as the warm water, sparkling in the moonlight, licking against the shore in a gentle darkness spangled with glowing stars hung thick and low as grapes.

The Cyclades offer an indefinable sense of well-being, suspending visitors in a state of womb-like comfort: and it's this, in the end, that keeps drawing people back again and again.

Previous Pages: Arrival in Míkonos. Left: Sunset turns the sea to gold (Thíra; Catholic church in the neighborhood of Firostefani, Firá).

– NORTHERN CYCLADES –

ÁNDROS

Ándros modestly hides its charms. Ships on the main channel along its western coast see only rocky flanks, battered by high waves. And Gávrio, the main

ferry port, is enough to make the heart of any disembarking traveler sink: an obligatory row of eateries and ferry offices lined up along the dusty quay. Not, it would seem, a place to fall in love with at first sight.

So Ándros remains an inside tip. Those who get past that first impression often end up buying vacation homes: license plates from Belgium, New Jersey and Ontario grace cars parked in front of hillside villas. Ándros' proximity to the mainland – "two hours from Athens," any smitten local will assure you – hasn't hurt; many people use it as a summer retreat, making occasional forays into the city to check up on business.

Northernmost and second-largest of the Cyclades, Ándros was once called "Hydroussa," the watery one, because of its many springs. These rise especially along the island's eastern coast, creating verdant valleys bristling with the glossy foliage of fruit trees and the silver sparkle of olive leaves, all pinned into place with the dark sedate fingers of cypresses. Another signal element of the landscape are the distinctive stone walls, or *xerolithies*, draped across the hills like well-wrought chains: within a regular stone wall, slabs of local slate are placed upright and horizontal, like windowpanes.

Right: Fishing nets must be regularly checked for holes and mended.

Arriving ferries dock in **Gávrio ❶**, toward the island's northern end. From here, it's about an hour's walk to Ándros' best-preserved antiquity, the 20-meter-high round tower of **Ágios Pétros** (2nd century B.C.), a type of Hellenistic construction relatively common in the Cyclades. It was probably a defensive residence; the upper floors were reached by ladders, which could be pulled up in time of danger.

Some eight kilometers off the southbound road from Gavrio, the still-operational convent of **Zoodóhou Pigís** boasts one of the island's seven genuine Byzantine churches, and contains a great wooden iconostasis. The convent, the largest on Ándros, also offers a lovely panoramic view of the surrounding region. By contrast, the next town on the coast, **Batsí ❷**, seems to have been erected wholly for the benefit of package tourists: Ándros' tourist center, it has all the requisite amenities, from hotels to jet-skis to a reasonable town beach from which water taxis will bear you to even nicer, remoter ones.

In the early days of Ándros' history, the island's capital was at the spot now known as the "old city," **Paleópoli ❸**. From the road, you can see the ancient harbor mole cupping a segment of turquoise sea; more than 1,000 steps that lead down the hill to the small stony beach. The tiny **museum** in modern Paleópoli's Town Hall exhibits finds from the site, but it's only open once a week; other objects are in the museum in Hóra. More extensive excavations have been made at **Zagorá ❹**, where a complete

Info pp. 104-107

Geometric village (900-700 B.C.) has come to light, but it isn't open to the public. Visitors can, however, avail themselves of the beach at **Halikolimniónas** to the north.

Ándros Town ❺, is a cosmopolitan settlement for a Greek island. It is no longer the island's main port because it's on the wrong side of the island to be within easy reach of Athens; therefore, the town beaches are clean, and are crowded with swimmers and windsurfers.

The town's wealthy shipowners started erecting ornate villas here not long after Greek independence; there are plenty of 19th-century dates inscribed over doorways. The elegant mansions and sophisticated museums are set on a promontory of land sticking out into the water, tipped by the island with the ruined Venetian **castle**, built when the Venetians moved into the Cyclades in the wake of the Fourth Crusade (1207). The delicate arc of a slender stone bridge connects the islet to town; the castle itself was destroyed by German bombs in 1943.

Farther offshore is the **Tourlitis Lighthouse**, a replica of an older edifice. As for museums, as well as the **Naval Museum**, located near the town's main square (and statue of "The Unknown Sailor"), there are two museums that wouldn't be out of place in a cosmopolitan capital. The Goulandrís family, Andriot shipowners who funded Athens's Cycladic Museum, presented their island with the **Museum of Modern Art**, with a permanent collection of works by Greek artists and major rotating exhibitions, and the excellent, informative **Archeological Museum**. A highlight is a 2nd-century B.C. copy of a 4th-century B.C. Hermes by Praxiteles; when it was found in 1833, King Ludwig of Bavaria, father of Greece's King Otto, made a special trip to Ándros to see it.

Churchgoers can visit the **Panagía Paltiana**, built in the 13th century and restored in 1712, the oldest church in town. Also of interest are **Theosképasti** (1555) and the cathedral of **Ágios Geórgios**. The lush valleys around Ándros Town contra-

Info pp. 104-107

vene all stereotypes of Greek island barrenness. The liquid burble of fresh spring water underlies the throb of cicadas; bottled water, as a matter of fact, is one of Ándros' exports. From the beach at **Giália**, north of Ándros, **Steniés** extends back in a carpet of green; you walk inland on verdant shaded paths (the town is closed to cars).

The most famous source of mineral water here is the spring of **Sáriza**, at **Apikía**; one of its outlets is the mouth of a stone lion's head. Here, too, is the venerable monastery of **Ágios Nikólaou**. More lion's-head gargoyles spout in green **Ménites ❻**, rowed along a mossy wall under the trees (the town's name derives from "maenads," the female acolytes of Dionysus).

A few kilometers south of Ménites, at **Messariá**, one of the oldest settlements on the island, the gray-brown stone

Above: On August 15, the faithful make a pilgrimage to the icon of the Holy Virgin in Panagía Evangelístria on Tínos.

Taxiárhis Church dates from the 12th century. Even older is the monastery of the Immaculate Virgin, **Panahrándou**, on the hill of Katafigi above **Fallíka**, founded in the 10th century.

To the west, there's a stalactite cave worthy of a visit, **Forós**, at **Aladinó**. South of this, walkers can follow the old Hóra-Korthos road along the river through the green ravine of **Dipotamata**, near **Vouní**, a valley punctuated with a number of water mills.

Órmos Kórthiou ❼ is Ándros' other main resort, located to the south. A pleasant cove with hotels and restaurants, it was settled during the Turkish occupation. Watching over the bay to the north are the remains of the Venetian **Paleókastro**. In the water below, off **Mélissa Beach**, is a stone known as **To Pídima tis Griás**, "The Old Lady's Leap"; the old lady in question, a passionate enemy of the Venetians, let the Turks into their castle one night and then, horrified at the massacre they carried out, leapt from its heights to her death.

Map p. 68, Info pp. 104-107

★TÍNOS

"The Lourdes of Greece" is Tínos' epithet – at least to the Greeks, who every August 15 flock here to do homage at the icon of Megalohóri, the all-graceful Virgin. The key event in the island's history took place in 1823, when the nun Pelagia saw in a vision that an icon of the Virgin was hidden in the hills. The icon was duly found, and the church of the Evangelistria built to house it. Appearing as it did at a time when Greece was fighting for its freedom, the icon took on a special significance for the nationalist movement, and thus, by extension, for the whole country; even today, everyone in the land tunes in to television broadcasts of the annual processions and festivities.

At first sight, Tínos seems barren and brown. Yet its valleys contain fruit and olives, and garlic and honey are produced in the verdant orchards around spring-watered towns where Cycladic white is tempered by deciduous green. Under the Venetians, wheat was even cultivated here. Some 80 windmills helped with irrigation, many of them operating well into this century (some farmers crept out during the German occupation of World War II to mill flour at night for the people suffering under strict wartime rationing).

Below the fertile soil is stone, another of Tínos' trademarks. Granite boulders litter the slopes around **Vólax**, creating a lunar landscape known as "Little Mexico." But the island is better known for slate and marble. The latter is quarried around **Pírgos**, long an established center for marble sculptors, with its **Fine Arts Academy** and legion private studios. And flaky slices of slate are geometrically placed in the square ornamented dovecotes (*peristeriones*) for which Tínos is also famous; more than 600 of them are scattered around the island, home to pale pigeons kept for food and for the fertilizer provided by their guano. Basket weaving, another traditional occupation, is dying

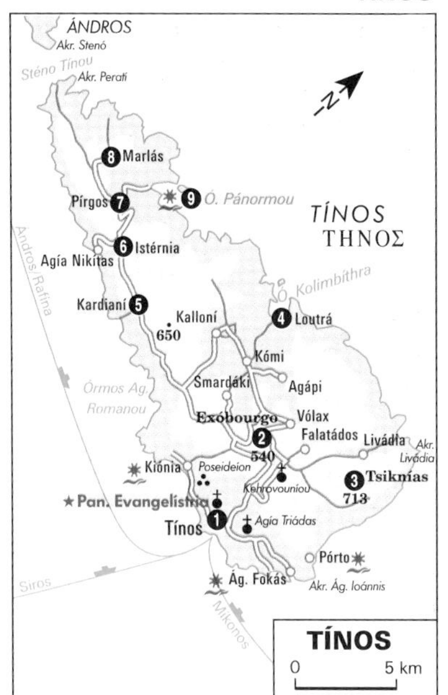

out; but at Vólax you can still see one or two practitioners of the art at work.

Dominating the port of **Tínos Town** ❶ is the massive church of **★Panagía Evangelístria**; many of the people disembarking from the ferries make their way directly up the hill. Some proceed laboriously on their knees, praying as they go; others stop on the way to purchase icons, crosses, or the devotional candles, taller than themselves, that stand like idle lances in booths along the sidewalk. The church is a huge, new, almost gaudy complex; within the main building, the icon, allegedly painted by St. Luke, is almost completely obscured by a crowd of votive offerings given as tokens of thanks. The chapel of Evressis, where the icon was found (the name means "discovery"), is below the church. The "holy water" that is said to have sprung out of the ground when the cornerstone was laid bubbles from a tap now. The complex also includes **museums** of Greek painting, the works of local sculptors, icons and ecclesiastical objects.

Pagan sites are kept outside the complex, such as the island's **Archeological Museum**. Tínos was a site of devotion long before the icon's discovery: a **Temple of Poseidon and Amphitríte** was a sacred spot in antiquity, and pilgrims on their way to Dílos used to stop off here for purification. The museum displays artifacts from the temple; what's left of the building is still visible by the beach at **Kiónia**, three kilometers west of Tínos Town. East of town, there are good but crowded beaches at **Ágios Fokás** and **Pórto**; the latter of which has become a veritable resort. Also out of town, to the north, is the convent of **Kehrovouníou**, built in the 10th century; it was here that St. Pelagia lived and had her visions of the icon.

Rising from the cluster of inland villages is **Exóbourgo** ❷, where stood a Venetian fortress so impregnable that it was never taken by force. Invaders obviously took one look at the steep climb and abandoned their efforts; die-hard modern visitors can ignore their example and park by the little church at the roadside to follow the path to the rocky summit. The winds here are so strong that it's easy to understand why Tínos was said to be the home of Aeolus, god of the winds. There's a "cave of the winds" on the island's highest mountain, **Tsikinías** ❸, near the village of **Falatádos**. One 18th-century traveler described the northwest wind as the "doctor of Tínos," claiming it blew the germs out of people.

Above: There are said to be over 600 of these richly ornamented dovecotes on Tínos.

The road north leads through the lunar-like landscape from **Vólax**, and along the green valley from **Kómi** to pretty **Loutrá** ❹, on the bay of **Kolimbíthra**, where there are nice sand beaches and seafood tavernas.

As you go northwest toward the marble villages, the hills to your right are golden and majestically barren; while those on the left slope are a tangle of lush foliage and water trickling down to the sea. **Kardianí** ❺ is a village so green it's al-

 Map p. 71, Info pp. 104-107

most tropical, the humidity exacerbated by the springs that issue from carved spouts of marble. Marble is the specialty of this end of the island. Further on, at picturesque **Istérnia** ❻, there's a small art museum, as well as the abandoned but beautiful monastery of **Katopolianí**. From here it is worth making a detour to the lovely sand beach of **Ágios Nikítas**.

At **Pírgos** ❼ (see p. 71), in addition to the school and legion marble workshops, the cemetery is noteworthy for its 18th-century gravestones, and you can see the house-turned-museum of the late local sculptor Jannolis Chalepás. **Marlás** ❽ is one place where the marble was actually quarried. **Pánormou Bay** ❾ has a lovely fishing harbor with a little beach.

*MÍKONOS

In and of itself, this overpopular island doesn't seem to warrant all the attention. At best, you can describe its barren slopes as "golden," rather than the more pedestrian "brown." For those who love it, however, "golden" describes the sand of the island's many beaches (what you can see of them between the umbrellas), or the late sun striking the boxy white houses in the winding white warren of Míkonos Town, where the buildings look like toys – dollhouses that could be moved at will.

And Míkonos is indeed like some kind of giant playground. The tanned crowds jamming its capital's narrow streets are visibly ready for fun, smiling at members of the opposite sex, or the same sex (Míkonos is ranked alongside San Francisco, California and Sydney, Australia as one of the three poles of the gay world), and pushing their way into the clubs that at night open their doors and turn all the town into a giant disco. You can sun and shop, drink or dance until dawn, and hundreds of other people will go right along with you. Certainly Míkonos has its assets. Crowded as they are, the town's nar-

row streets are like something from *Alice Through the Looking Glass*, twisting in unexpected directions and suddenly depositing you in a narrow white alley with flowering vines where it seems no tourist has ever set foot. The houses are pleasingly organic in form, with rounded corners and chunky domes; epitomizing their rustic earthiness are the signature windmills above the town.

And the town's tame pelican, Petros, with his pinkish-white plumage and yellow beak, is a true local character, whether he's yawping at a tourist or waddling down the steps of a store from which he has been ignominiously ejected by the broom of a long-suffering proprietor, portly and breathless, like an avian Mr. Pickwick.

Míkonos Town ❶ is where you'll start and where you'll eventually finish. In the port, ferries and cruise ships litter the waters like flotsam. The ferry dock is north of town, and boats to Dílos leave from the pier of **Karaoli Dimitriou** at the south end of the harbor. Between these

two poles are a small town beach; **Mantó Square**, featuring a statue of its eponymous heroine, a wealthy local who gave all her money to the fight for Greek independence; and the promenade of **Akti Kambani**, where crowds sit in sidewalk cafés and watch other crowds go by.

Extending into the water past the Dílos quay is the neighborhood of **Paraportianí**, with the sprawling **church** of the same name at its center, a complex grown together from four smaller buildings from the 16th and 17th centuries. Churches are almost as common on Míkonos as tourists; many families erected private churches for their burial vaults. Across from the Paraportianí church is a small **Ethnographic Museum**.

The other flank of Paraportianí is the stretch called "Little Venice," simply because it features some quaint old houses abutting directly on the water, and is almost as much-photographed as the six coy windmills on the other side of Alefkandra Bay. Between the two is the Catholic **church**, incongruous among the Orthodox surroundings.

Above: Time for an evening stroll around the harbor basin (Míkonos). Right: Panagía Paraportianí, the most-photographed sight in the Cyclades.

The **windmills** are private: if you want to have a look inside one, go up to the ring road around the port, where there's another windmill that is open to the public. The ring road leads on back to the ferry dock, near which is the ***Archeological Museum**. Other museums include the **Maritime Museum** and **Lena's House**, the 19th-century home of a member of the local middle class with its original furnishings.

A majority of visitors come to Míkonos for sea, sand and sun. Life on the island's beaches is one big spectacle: music drones from the doorways of tavernas, jet-skiers and parasailers maneuver their way between swimmers, and beach umbrellas and lounge chairs mark out the territory like flags on a map. To some, Míkonos is synonymous with Paradise –

Paradise Beach ❷, that is, southeast of town, the most popular of the island's many beaches. This is the epicenter of a number of popular beaches stretching along the southern coast. Nearer town, **Ornós** sports some of the island's leading luxury hotels. **Psaroú** is small and sandy; **Platís Gialós**, larger and sandy. **Agía Ánna Paránga** is slightly less photogenic, and certainly less crowded, than bopping **Paránga**.

Super Paradise, tucked at the end of a cove, used to be the "gay beach," but is today democratically equivocal as to who uses its umbrellas. Further out, **Agrarí** sports rare patches of green around its new hotel complex; its wide beach is less crowded than others.

At the center of the island, **Áno Méra** ❸ is Míkonos' "real" town: the population here is actually higher than in Míkonos Town itself (during the off season). It's also spread out, agricultural, and not particularly geared to tourists. It does have the lovely 17th-century monastery of **Panagía Tourlianí** with its graceful tower, containing a **Church Museum** and an **Agricultural Museum**; and a broad, unshaded town square lined with tavernas. The town comes alive for the monastery's three-day festival which begins on August 15. A bit further north stand the remains of the the Venetian fortress of **Paleókastro**.

Kalafáti ❹, most easterly of Míkonos' beaches, is not as hectic as its brethren, though it does offer a full range of water sports. It's in full view of little **Agía Ánna Kalafátis**, where fishermen mend their yellow nets to the beat of the music from Kalafáti on the other shore of the cape. Nearby, **Kaló Livádi** lives up to its name ("Beautiful Harbor") with a pleasant, sandy, not-too-crowded beach.

Míkonos' ancient settlements centered around **Panórmou Bay** ❺ in the north of the island, where there's a beach at **Fteliá**. On this shore are caves such as **Mávri Spilia**, but they're often closed to the public. The northwestern shore, between Míkonos Town and **Fanarí**, is more attractive for sunsets than beaches;

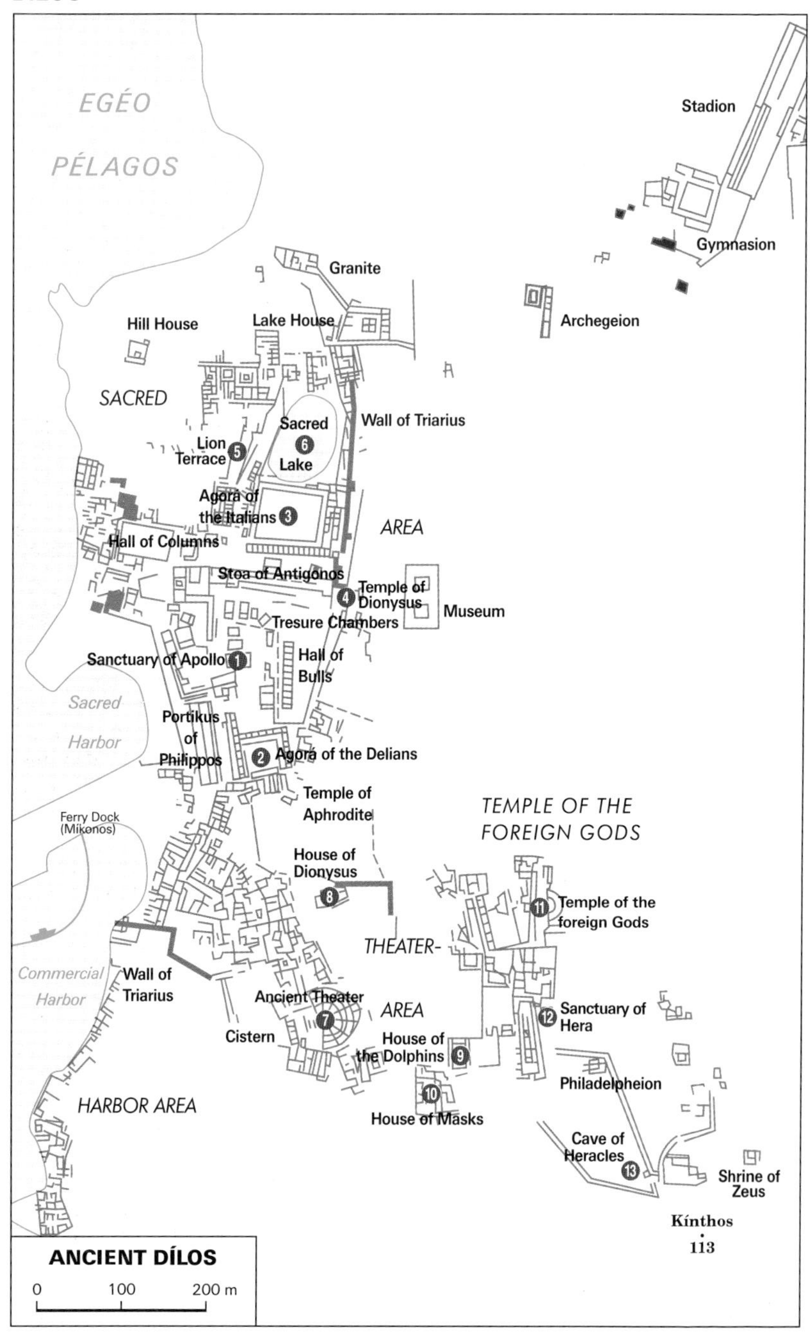
EGÉO
PÉLAGOS
Stadion
Gymnasion
Granite
Archegeion
Hill House
Lake House
SACRED
Wall of Triarius
Sacred
6
Lake
Lion
Terrace 5
Agorá of
the Italians 3
AREA
Hall of Columns
Stoa of Antigonos
4 Temple of
Dionysus
Museum
Tresure Chambers
Sanctuary of Apollo 1
Hall of
Bulls
Sacred
Harbor
Portikus
of
Philippos
2 Agorá of the Delians
Temple of
Aphrodite
TEMPLE OF THE
FOREIGN GODS
Ferry Dock
(Míkonos)
House of
Dionysus
8
11 Temple of the
foreign Gods
THEATER-
Commercial
Harbor
Wall of
Triarius
Ancient Theater
7
AREA
Sanctuary of
Hera 12
Cistern
House of
the Dolphins 9
Philadelpheion
10
House of Masks
HARBOR AREA
Cave of
Heracles
13
Shrine of
Zeus
Kínthos
113
ANCIENT DÍLOS
0
100
200 m

there are many hotels and a full complement of night life, especially in chic **Ágios Stéfanos** ❻.

**DÍLOS (DELOS)

When Zeus impregnated his mistress Leto, Zeus' jealous wife Hera enjoined the earth not to let her give birth to her twins anywhere under the sun. Leto wandered around the Aegean, seeking a place to lay her head; finally, Poseidon helped his brother Zeus by creating the island of Dílos, little more than a rock, with a mighty blow of his trident. It was here that Leto bore Apollo and Artemis, two of the most revered of the Olympian pantheon of gods.

Many people regard the trip to Dílos as an obligatory part of a stay on Míkonos; but if you don't have a real interest in archeology and clambering around old ruins, you probably won't enjoy it. The crossing from Míkonos can be rough; the sun on Dílos hot; and tourists visiting "because it's there" can be heard complaining loudly.

However, anyone willing to invest a little time and imagination can have a wonderful time wandering through the foundations of Roman businessmen's houses, adorned with mosaic floors, or completing the steep ascent of **Mount Kínthos** to stand by the **Shrines of Zeus and Athena**, where victorious athletes were crowned, with spectacular views of the surrounding islands.

By the 9th century B.C., Dílos was home to a cult of Apollo; this was regarded as such a sacred site that even the Persians, on their way to attack Athens in 492 B.C., left it alone. After the Persian Wars, the island became the nominal center of the Delian League, which was basically an Athenian alliance. As Athens grew in power, it made increasingly free with its allies, and finally moved the League's treasury from Dílos to its own acropolis in 546 B.C. A plague subsequently hit the city and the Athenians, seeing this as Apollo's wrath at this misdeed, imposed a process of purification (*katharsis*) on Dílos that prohibited birth or death from taking place on the island; the sick and pregnant were taken over to nearby Rínia.

Above: One of the five extant archaic lion sculptures that can be seen at the Lion Terrace in Dílos.

The Romans made Dílos their main commercial port in the Aegean, at the expense of Rhódos; and the island flourished during the last three centuries before the Christian era, as Romans and Egyptians, Athenians and Syrians settled and traded here. Prosperity came to a sudden end, however, when Mithridates, King of Pontos, conquered the island in 88 B.C.; after that, Dílos sank into relative obscurity, not really to emerge again until archeologists began exploring its ruins in the 19th century.

The focal point of Dílos' buildings was the complex of the **Sanctuary of Apollo**

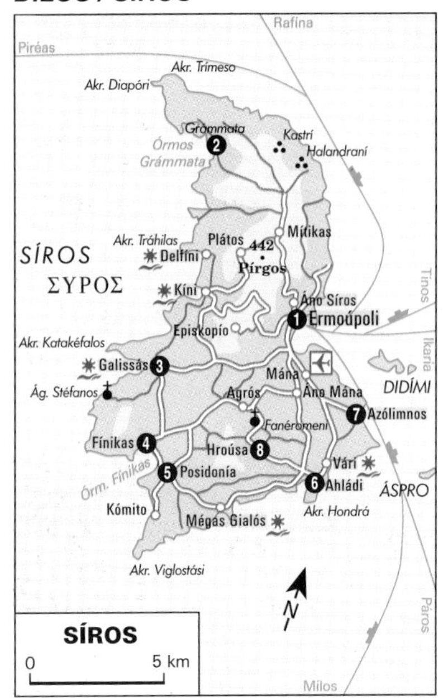

❶, which was originally accessed via a ceremonial road. It was here, by the sacred statue of Apollo, that the treasure of the Delian League was stored; little is left today of the several temples and other edifices that once stood here.

Flanking the sanctuary were the **Agorá of the Delians** ❷ and the **Agorá of the Italians** ❸, a large rectangle surrounded by the scant remains of a colonnade. More striking are the remains of the **Temple of Dionysus** ❹, marked out by corner pillars supporting what remains of some mighty phallic symbols.

Past this to the north (to the left, as you come from the harbor) is one of Dílos' most famous highlights, the **Lion Terrace** ❺, where the five eroded lions that remain of the original nine from the 7th century B.C. (they are supposed to be moved to the **Museum** some time in 1999; it is still not clear whether in situ copies will be displayed here) exude an unparalleled grace and power. Facing the Lion Terrace is the irregular circle of the **Sacred Lake** ❻, which has long since dried up. It is on the shores of this lake that Leto is said to have given birth to the twin gods Artemis and Apollo.

Right: Ermoúpoli (Síros) – administrative center of the Cyclades with urban character.

On the other side of the harbor (to the right as you disembark) is the so-called "Theater District," an area of exclusive villas and commercial buildings around the **Ancient Theater** ❼. By the theater are the well-preserved remains of an old vaulted **cistern**, still gracefully bridged by its arches.

As you move uphill toward Mount Kínthos, you can spot some of the best mosaics on the island in the **House of Dionysus** ❽, the **House of the Dolphins** ❾ or the **House of the Masks** ❿. Further up the hill there is the **Temple of the Foreign Gods** ⓫; the **Sanctuary of Hera** ⓬; and, close to the mountain's top, a **cave** ⓭ where Heracles was worshiped.

SÍROS

The "Aristocrat of the Islands" is a fitting sobriquet for the island of Síros. Slightly aloof, and with a faded elegance of days gone by, Síros tolerates visitors with unerring friendliness, but doesn't rely on them; one senses that life continues at a similar pace here in or out of the tourist season.

Among the Cyclades, Síros is definitely *ancien regime*. For one thing, it was a seat of Cycladic culture (3rd millennium B.C.), also termed the "Síros-Keros Culture" by archeologists. Documenting this period are some wonderful female torsos in the small, dusty **Archeological Museum** of the island's capital, **Ermoúpoli** ❶. For another thing, much later in its history Ermoúpoli became Greece's first capital after independence in 1821. It is still the administrative capital of the Cyclades.

Ermoúpoli is full of relics of its heyday: the neoclassical **Town Hall**, repre-

 Map (Dílos) p. 77, Info pp. 104-107

senting the Bavarian architect Ziller's conception of King Priam's palace at Troy; Greece's first opera house, the **Teatron Apollon**, modeled on Milan's La Scala; and Greece's first high school (*Gymnasion*).

Síros was also Greece's leading port, sending ships around the world; passenger ships departed twice a week for the United States. But with the opening of the Corinth Canal in 1893, Piraeus suddenly became Greece's leading port, and Síros withdrew into island isolation. Still, it hasn't lost the flavor of its former internationalism. Rather than whitewashed Cycladic huts, you find here neoclassical villas, even in the countryside, amid gardens of palms. In the evening, the café tables on the broad square before the town hall are filled, and you can sit out in the soft apricot twilight and nibble on "Síros delight," or *lukumia* – not "Turkish" delight, however similar the confection may appear to the uninitiated.

Dominating one side of the harbor are the hulking **Neorion Shipyards**, now operational again after a few years of having been shut; at the other end of town are the elegant mansions of the **Vaporia Quarter**. Neoclassical **Ágios Nikólaos** fits right in with the town's 19th-century façades; an older note is struck in the church of **Kimisis**, with an icon by the Cretan icon painter Doménikos Theotokópoulos, better known to the world as El Greco.

From the water, Ermoúpoli rises into two church-topped peaks. Nearer the center of town, atop the hill of **Vrondádo**, is the church of **Anastásis**, a Byzantine gem. Farther back, the Catholic cathedral of **Ágios Geórgios** tops the hilltop district of **Áno Síros**, the older part of town. This picturesque quarter has retained its village character. Two medieval city gates and two monasteries, a Jesuit and a Capuchin, survive. This is where the Catholic faith arrived with the Venetians in the 13th century and where it is still embraced today. The vacation crowd generally heads across the island to the beaches of the west coast. From **Kíni**, a little fish-

Info pp. 104-107

ing village, or **Delfíni**, to the north, people take *káikis* (boats) to the more deserted northern reaches, where road access is as difficult as the sunsets are spectacular. The rocks by **Grámmata** ❷ are inscribed to ward off shipwreck. **Kastrí** was the center of prehistoric settlement; excavations have uncovered finds from 3000 B.C.

South of Kíni, **Galissás** ❸ is the epicenter of Síros' tourism, in no small part because of its long sand beach – fertile soil for a range of tourist amenities, including a campground. **Fínikas** ❹ is more genteel, and more attractive, with tavernas along the limpid waters of its generous bay; it was named for the Phoenicians who arrived here long ago. The area around here is rife with old, elegant houses, many of which started life as *nouveau riche* abodes; some of the houses in **Posidonía** ❺ or Delagrátsia, Fínikas' neighbor to the south, replicate medieval castles. The beaches on the point are quiet, overlooking little islets which are uninhabited.

Above: This stone lion from the 6th century B.C. is Kea's trademark.

The southern coast between **Mégas Gialós** and **Vári** is also lined with beaches, but is somewhat less charming, although the sheltered harbor of **Órmos** is attractive, with a little town beach of smooth sand at **Ahládi** ❻. To the east, **Azólimnos** ❼ has a wide beach, the hill behind it faced with houses and hotels. Driving through the interior of this part of the island you can see plenty of sedate old villas, hidden in the dark, dusty shade of their palm fronds, around the village of **Hroúsa** ❽, for example. Not far from here, the church of **Fanéromeni** commands stunning island views.

– WESTERN CYCLADES –

KÉA

Kéa can be reached by ferry from Pireaus in only three hours; from Lávrion on Attica's southern tip the journey takes

Map p. 78, Info pp. 104-107

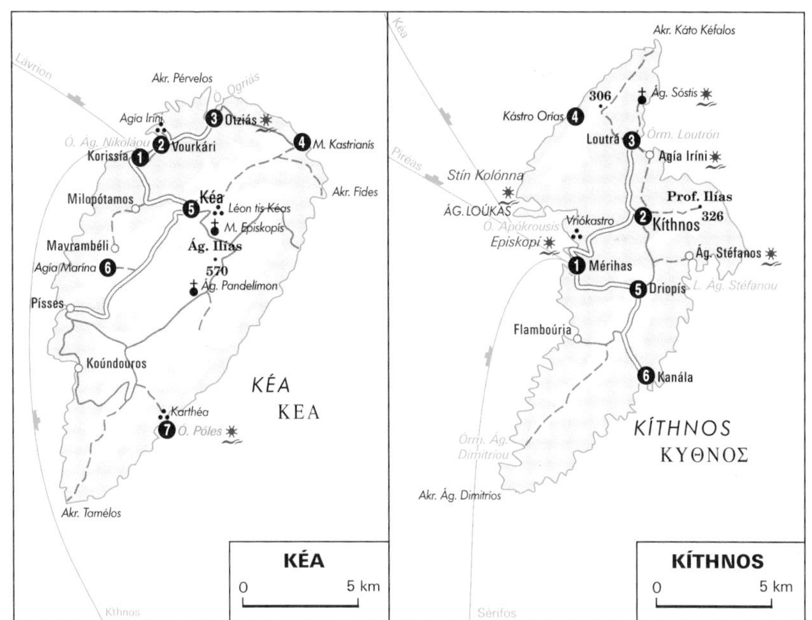

just one hour. Because it's not on the main ferry routes, the island tends to draw lots of Greeks and relatively few tourists. But there's no reason to overlook this pleasant green island; in fact, visitors should hurry to get here before the masses of vacation crowds turn their attentions here, as Kéa is being increasingly developed.

In antiquity, Kéa had four independent city-states – Ioulís, Korissía, Karthéa and Poiiessa (modern Písses) – and all four live on in some form, whether as ruins or modern settlements.

Ferries dock at **Korissía** ❶ (also called Livádi), a protected natural harbor on the western coast where the island's services are concentrated. North of here, the one-time fishing village of **Vourkári** ❷ has been somewhat taken over by vacationers, especially yachtsmen. On the point of **Agía Iríni** are the excavations of an ancient city inhabited from the Bronze Age through the Minoan and Mycenean periods; a temple foundation is staked out with a few column drums. Moving further eastwards, you can stop off for a swim at the bay of **Otziás** ❸ or visit the monastery dedicated to **Panagía Kastrianís** ❹, the island's patroness.

Built safely inland to guard against possible sea attack, **Kéa Town** ❺ (also called Ioulís), the island's capital, is perched on a hill commanding views out over the island. The highest point, known as the **Kástro**, occupies the site of the ancient acropolis, of which only a few stones are left. Another highlight with old stones is the **Archeological Museum**. Yet another is Kéa's hallmark, the **Lion of Kéa** (Léon tis Kéas; 6th century B.C.), about a kilometer north of town. It's not certain what story lies behind this figure, which is six meters long and carved into the living rock, but his expression is benevolent.

South of Kéa, the road passes the old ruined monastery of **Agía Marína** ❻, where there's a striking and relatively well-preserved Hellenistic tower, on its way to the west coast resorts of **Písses** (ancient Poiiessa) and **Koúndouros**. The

Info pp. 104-107

roads are less good over to another fine beach at **Póles** ❼ and the remains of the island's fourth ancient city, **Karthéa**, where the poet Simónides, an island native, had his school in the 5th century B.C.

KÍTHNOS

On Kíthnos, you can experience the Cyclades on your own terms. It's near enough to Athens that it gets its fair share of tourists, but not being one of the most popular Cyclades, and not boasting any major tourist attraction, it has managed to retain much of its own personality and flavor. It does get a lot of Greek visitors, both weekenders and expatriot Athenians who've relocated, as well as yachtsmen. And it offers two lovely villages with plenty of character, two pleasant port towns, some ancient ruins, some pleasant walking, and inordinately friendly villagers who are still curious about non-Greek arrivals.

Above: Climbing up to the main town of Hóra on Sérifos.

Ferries and Flying Dolphins dock at narrow **Mérihas** ❶ harbor. This is the busiest and most tourist-oriented town on the island, which is to say it has some supermarkets and shops, as well as a number of restaurants, hotels, and rooms to let. From here, roads run in two directions: northeast along the coast toward Kíthnos (Hóra), or south and inland toward the island's "second town" of Driopís, also known as Horió (just to confuse the issue).

If you're in a hurry for a beach, though, take the first of these roads to **Episkopí**, or further to **Ágios Nikólaos**, which locals account the best beach on the island: notable here is the islet of **Ágios Loúkas**, connected to the mainland by a firm tongue of beach called **Kolóna** that's fine for swimming on both sides. On the headland between the two are the remains of **Vriókastro**, the ancient capital of Kíthnos, which dates back to the 10th century B.C.

Map p. 81, Info pp. 104-107

Kíthnos (Hóra) ❷ is a beautiful little white Cycladic village, tucked away a good distance inland, and pinned, as it were, between progress and tradition: a row of modern windmills generate energy for the island in the so-called "Windmill Park," while in and around town are venerable churches such as **Agía Triáda**, the island's oldest; **Ágios Savás** and **Sotíros**, containing a 17th-century iconostasis; and the monastery of **Pródromos**, with an even older iconostasis from the 16th century.

From here, it's five kilometers to **Loutrá** ❸, named for the medicinal springs that were historically one of the island's main attractions; in fact, Kíthnos is also known as Thermia. Iron deposits – there was an iron mine on Kíthnos until 1940 – give the waters a reddish hue; they're supposed to be good for rheumatism, arthritis and "female complaints." Good beaches can be found near **Ágios Iríni** and **Ágios Sóstis**.

From Loutrá you can walk up to **Kástro Orías** ❹, the old Byzantine-Venetian fortress that controlled the island from the 10th century A.D. on.

Inland, the poor roads are actually dirt tracks that defy drivers but make great walking. From Kíthnos to Driopís it's a pleasant stroll through the countryside past the little white chapel of **Taxiarhis**, with a possible detour down to the beach at **Ágios Stéfanos**.

The counterpart to Kíthnos' "Windmill Park" are the old deserted windmills above **Driopís** ❺. This town is known for the **Katafáki Cave**, once a refuge in times of danger, but now itself posing a danger because of the risk of collapse, and therefore closed. Visitors can, however, peruse the folk art in **Ágios Minas** church, seek out local ceramics, and then go on to the beach at **Léfkes** or catch a bus to **Kanála** ❻, the island's most picturesque port and a popular resort. The church here contains a beloved icon of the Virgin Mary.

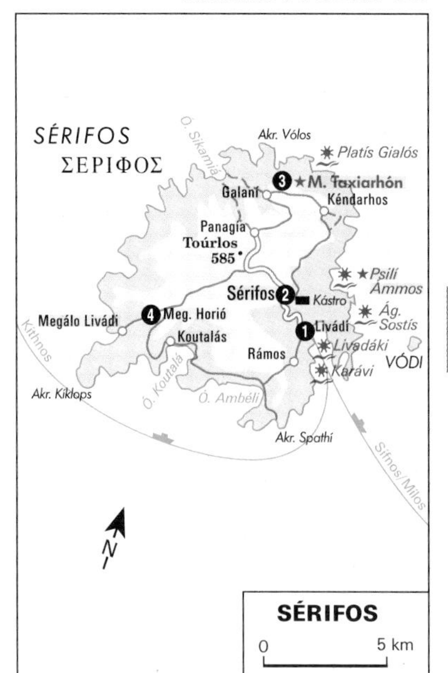

*SÉRIFOS

Although it is becoming increasingly popular with tourists, Sérifos seems particularly dry and barren; its very name means "rocky." This island was a mining center from antiquity until the 1960s, and some of the dust of the mines seems to have lingered in the air over the harbor, Livádi, which accommodates most of the island's visitors and manages to be both bustling and, at the same time, somehow nondescript. Yet this island "does it" for many people, including a number of architects from Athens and elsewhere who have transformed old houses in Sérifos (Hóra) into dream vacation homes featured in the pages of international architecture magazines.

The white port town of **Livádi** ❶ has the basic vacation essentials: a long sand beach shaded by tamarisk trees, and the usual tavernas, shops, hotels and nightlife. Further attractive beaches can be found south of town near **Livadáki** and **Karávi**.

The fit of foot can set out to climb the long trail of concrete and stone steps that leads up from Livadi to **Sérifos** (Hóra) ❷; the latter is also served by bus from the harbor, as well as by the occasional donkey plodding up under the weight of an elderly resident. Sérifos is a sprawling hilltop mass of narrow lanes opening out onto squares large enough to accommodate big churches, such as **Evangelístria Church**, built in 1907, next to the Town Hall on the main square, or leading up to the remains of the haughty Venetian **Kástro**, upon which a small church, **Ágios Konstandínos**, stands today. From here you can see down to the approximate locations of the beaches of ***Psilí Ámmos** and **Ágios Sostís** on the east coast, but these are easier to reach from Livádi, unless you have a guide or a very good map.

By foot, bike or car, you can continue from Sérifos through the village of **Galaní** to the monastery of ***Moní Taxiarhón** ❸; but unless you've made prior arrangements, your chances of getting in are rather slim. The sole monk can sometimes be prevailed upon to show off the treasures in this 15th- to 17th-century building, including illuminated manuscripts and frescoes of the sufferings of the damned in Hell; but if he's out, you'll have to move on to the brown, unspectacular beach of **Platís Gialós** west of Galaní, or to **Sikamiá Bay** to the east.

In the southeast of the insland is **Mégalo Horió** ❹, once site of the island's mines and possibly marking the site of Sérifos' ancient capital. This brings you to a concentration of miniature "resorts": **Mégalo Livádi** and, on the other side of the point, **Koutalás**. This southwestern stretch of coast has two caves, one traditionally held to have been home to the Cyclops Polyphemus.

Above: Unique manner of transporting sheep on Sífnos.

*SÍFNOS

Sífnos is a treasure-chest of an island. Its increasing popularity with visitors is deserved, if regrettable to those who had hoped to keep it to themselves. The harsh Cycladic landscape here is tempered with agricultural terraces; there's a big beach resort, little medieval villages, bays with lovely beaches, harbors difficult of access, and plenty of religious and ancient "sights."

Sífnos was once quite literally a treasure chest: the mines that began operating here in the 3rd millennium B.C. were in the business of finding gold and silver. Because of their yield, Sífnos was one of the wealthiest Greek islands, and its treasury at Delphi among the most splendid at that shrine. The story goes that the islanders contributed a golden egg to Apollo at this treasury every year; one year, they sent a gilded rock instead. Apollo, furious, flooded the mines, evidently removing the island's wealth forever; attempts to revive the mines in the late 19th century were not lucrative. Some say that the island's name derives from the emptiness of the place after Apollo's revenge; but most islanders will tell you that their home is named after the son of the Attic hero of Sounion.

Other traditional sources of livelihood have fared marginally better. Sífnos' other two hallmarks are cooking and ceramics. Many of Sífnos' great chefs left the island for the Continent, but there are still traces of a culinary legacy. Some tavernas serve such local specialties as *revithia*, made of chickpeas and olive oil baked overnight at a very low temperature to create an unctuous puree with a dark, smoky flavor. The cooking vessel is a special *revithia* pot, which you can see in the island's ceramics outlets, although there aren't as many of these left as there used to be. Many houses sport a ceramic chimney ornament called a *koutsonara*.

Although it's the island's main port, **Kamáres** ❶ is a relatively new town, born with the effort to revive the mines; the first jetty wasn't built here until 1907. There's a decent town beach and a con-

centration of hotels and bungalows, all guarded by the church of **Agía Marína** perched on a slope over the water. South of town you can hike up past the old iron works to the cave of **Mávris Spiliás**.

The road inland to Apollonía, the island's capital, goes through some of the olive groves that supposedly produce the Cyclades' best oil. It also passes the convent of **Theodorous tou Mongú** ("The Mute Ones"); these quiet beings were nuns from wealthy Venetian families, who, it's said, used to receive lovers here.

Capital of the island since 1836, **Apollonía** ❷ is one of a pair of villages named after the twin gods Apollo and Artemis. Apollonía's **Ethnographic Museum** recreates the musty jumble of a grandmother's attic, with faded photos of local heros and worn farm tools. Standing on the site of an old temple of Apollo that gave the town its name, the church of **Panagía Ouraniophóra**, the "Sky-Bearer," holds a *Lolopanagirio* or "crazy festival" every February 2.

Info pp. 104-107

As befits a lady, **Artemón** ❸ is slightly more demure. Shops and restaurants testify to the increased presence of visitors, but they haven't obscured the towns' own character. By going up a stone stairway you can visit the church of **Panagía Pouláti**, which looks out on a bay.

Walkers can set out from Apollonia for the island's heights. One trail leads up to **Ágios Andréas**, where there are remains of a walled prehistoric settlement that was, in its day, impregnable. Ancient watchtowers have also been found in this area; some are still visible. From here, you can continue up to the peak of **Profítis Ilías** ❹ (678 meters); atop it is an 8th-century Byzantine **church**, the oldest on the island. Plan on the walk taking a good hour.

It's an easier walk over to ***Kástro** ❺, about three kilometers from Apollonía, site of other early settlement. An Ionian city here from the first millennium B.C. was later superceded by a castle of the Knights of St. John, built after they recaptured the island from the Venetians. Much of today's village still dates from this period; there are bits of ruins scattered around the whitewashed town, almost as varied as those found in the small **Archeological Museum**. **Panagía Eleussa**, "Our Lady of Mercy," used to be the main church on the island; it was most recently restored in 1635. Sitting on a promontory is the little white church of **Elia Martiras**; from here, steps lead down to a cove where swimmers can sun on the rocks or plunge into the perfectly blue water.

South of Apollonía, the first town on the main road is **Exámbela** ❻, long a gathering-place for artists and musicians. Because of the lax nature of its café scene, the Turks dubbed it *Aksham Bela*, "Trouble in the Evening," which was corrupted into the village's present name. Further along is the monastery of **Kíria Vrisiánis** or simply "Vrísis"; the name

Above: Panagía Hrisopigí contains an icon that is said to have protected Sífnos from disaster twice in its history.

Map p. 85, Info pp. 104-107

means "well," and the water here is supposed to be the best on the island. Founded by prosperous 17th-century Sifniot merchant Vassilis Logothetis, the monastery contains a wonderful iconostasis and a **Museum of Ecclesiastical Art**. But the monastery that Sífnos holds most dear is further on, near **Fáros**, a nice little fishing harbor.

***Hrisopigí ❼** sits on a point of land like a white marker holding the sea and sky in place. It was built in 1650 on the spot where fishermen found an icon in the sea, and Our Lady of Hrisopigí ("Golden Springs") has since twice saved the island from disaster, averting the plague in 1675 and locusts in 1928. Inside, the church, which incorporates an ancient column, has a carved iconostasis laden with votive thanks, including a great ship-lamp hanging from the ceiling. The baptismal font sits outdoors, at the very tip of the point, as if the new baby were to be named in the foam of the breaking waves. Swimmers go down to the sands of adjacent **Apokoftó Beach**.

Platís Gialós ❽ is the most modern and most crowded resort on Sífnos, though its ancient remains include a Bronze Age burial ground. Its beach has lovely sand, and claims to be the longest in the Cyclades, but it is overrun in summer. Seekers of solitude can continue on foot to some quieter, less accessible beaches, such as **Fikiáda**. There are also boat taxis available.

Taking a boat taxi was once the only way to get to the sheltered natural harbor of **Vathí ❾**, doomed to be less peaceful since the road was built in 1996. The white monastery of **Taxiárhis**, which offers overnight accommodation to visitors, is in danger of becoming something of a motel; and the old-fashioned pottery that was once only accessible by boat has now established a sales outlet in the little hamlet (preferable, in fact, to negotiating the long, steep, and badly rutted road that leads down to the pottery itself). The

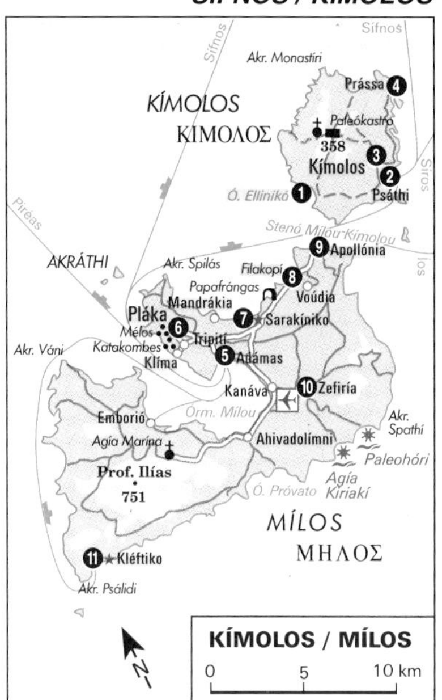

beaches of the west coast of the island are accessible only on foot or from the water. From the one at **Vliháda**, there's a trail up to **Mávro Horió**, called the "Black Village" because it was burned by pirates. There are two other popular beaches at the north of the island: **Vroulídia** and the fishing harbor of **Herónissos ❿**, also known for its traditional pottery, an old church of **Ágios Geórgios**, and the circular foundations of an ancient **tower**.

KÍMOLOS

Lying cheek by jowl with Mílos, Kímolos was actually once a part of the larger island until the land between them was swallowed by the sea. Billed as the hilliest island in the Cyclades, Kímolos is also the chalkiest: in fact, its name means chalk, once one of this dry white island's main exports, and Kímolos is still mined for a chalk-like mineral similar to fuller's earth. Because it is comparatively small and not heavily visited, this is a good island for anyone looking for privacy and

tranquility – one reason, presumably, that Kímolos was long a popular hide-out for pirates.

There's sign of the ancient settlement that once graced the vanished isthmus at **Ellinikó** ❶, on the island's southern shore, where there's an ancient **necropolis** with graves dating as far back as the Mycenean period. The little islet facing this, **Ágios Andréas**, has remains of the ancient – Mycenean – city itself. Of more immediate interest to anyone who's made the walk here from Kímolos (Hóra) in the hot sun is the beautiful beach; swimmers can investigate more ruins of old walls underwater.

Kaikis land at **Psáthi** ❷, from where arrivees can easily walk the two kilmeters up to the town of **Kímolos** (Hóra) ❸, a white Cycladean cubist construction scattered over a hilltop. The crest of the hill is crowned by castle from the late Middle Ages which has given its name to the two quarters lying within its walls: in **Messa Kástro**, the inner castle, the houses are built side by side and so form a defensive wall, with entrance gates at four points; the other section is **Exo Kástro**, the outer castle. Outside of town another castle, **Palaeókastro**, sits on the highest elevation on the island, a Venetian ruin with the island's oldest church, 16th-century **Hristós**.

Above: The Roman Theater in Mílos. Right: Sea horses are common in the Aegean.

Prássa ❹, the island's northernmost settlement, is also the mining center of Kímolos; the local mineral that is mined here has contributed to the curative powers of the radioactive springs, sought out by rheumatics.

**MÍLOS

Mílos is one of the Aegean's volcanic islands. Eruptions in the long-distant past have left a wealth of mineral deposits for which the island has been mined throughout its history. Today, all that remains of the volcano's crater is the island's shape; the harbor at Adámas, one of the largest

Map p. 87, Info pp. 104-107

in the Aegean (large enough to shelter Allied fleets in the Crimean War and World War I), is the old crater. Some geothermal heat still erupts in the form of hot springs. The volcano must have calmed down a very long time ago indeed, for Mílos was home to one of the Aegean's oldest civilizations, dating from 3500 B.C.

Adámas ❺, the main port, is fitted out with most of the tourist amenities, and more are coming all the time. The island boasts a new airport, and there has also been talk of developing the harbor as a yachting marina. If this development continues, Mílos could easily become one of the next truly popular Greek island destinations for Mediterranean-bound tourists. Certainly there are beaches to meet every taste; the waters are even calmer, of course, at the long sand beaches around the Bay of Adámas, such as **Ahivadolímni**.

In town, the church of **Agía Tríada** contains some old Cretan icons; visitors can also sample the island's mineral waters in the public baths near town, which are housed in a cave.

Like any good Cycladic island, however, Mílos has its main town at a safe distance from the water – even if today's invaders are tourists rather than the pirates of old. Called **Pláka** ❻, it has orderly white Cycladic architecture. Its **Archeological Museum** contains some of the ancient finds from Filakopí; more recent artifacts are displayed in an appealing **Ethnographic Museum**, recreating a 19th-century home.

At the edge of a steep slope is the church of **Panagía Korfiatissa**, a 19th-century edifice with some older icons. Guarding the town is the obligatory Venetian **Kástro**, from which there is a spectacular view; on the way up to it you can stop at the ancient and beautiful church of **Thalassítras** ("Of the Sea").

Tripití translates roughtly into "perforated with holes," and this suburb of

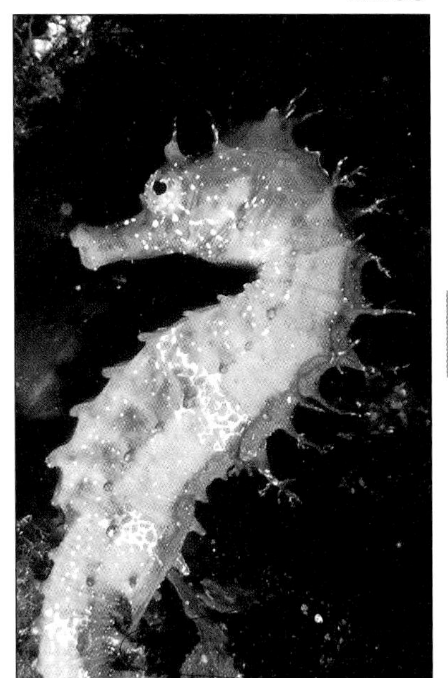

Pláka most probably gets its name from its **catacombs**, which are some of the best-preserved Early Christian relics in Greece (from the 2nd and 3rd centuries). While only a limited section of these are open to the public, it is still enough to provide a sense of this underground passage where the arched niches on the wall were used for burials. From the catacombs, it's an easy stroll to the archeological site of **Mélos**, excavated in the hillside above Klíma.

Particularly clear and impressive here is the **Roman Theater**, with the ocean as a backdrop; this is being overhauled to a degree, and hosts occasional performances. Most laymen know at least one of Mélos' treasures, but that one isn't even on the island; the **Venus de Milo**, dating from around the first century B.C., which a local farmer discovered on his land in 1820, is a highlight of the Louvre Museum in Paris. The only thing that Mélos has to show of it is a plaque marking the site of the farmer's discovery and a copy of the famous statue in the island's

Archeological Museum. There are also bits of a temple to be seen. **Klíma** itself was ancient Mélos' harbor; it is still a fishing port, and its white houses sport parti-color trim.

Also well worth seeing are the fantastic rock formations that twist the island's shores. From the road, you can reach the gorgeous cove of **Mandrákia** on the north shore, or the white moonscape of ***Sarakíniko** ❼, where the bizarre white stone looks like ice floes on the edge of the sea. **Papafrángas** is another popular "cave": an arm of water reaching deep into a corridor of rock, with little grottoes at its end.

Remains of an ancient city, inhabited until the Mycenean period, were excavated in the 19th century near **Filakopí** ❽, at the north of the island; but although there might once have been a magnificent palace and fine homes here, there's not much to see today; there are a few nice small sandy bays, however. Past Filakopí, you come to the village of **Apollónia** ❾, extremely popular with tourists; its harbor and beaches face nearby Kímolos.

In the central part of the island is **Zefiría** (Hóra) ❿, long the island's main town, now a quiet village. There are also popular beaches on the south shore: **Paleohóri** and **Agía Kiriakí** are two pleasant, sandy ones. A scenic highlight here is at ***Kléftiko** ⓫, where a kind of rock castle rises out of a blue bay, perforated with natural sea arches.

Right: In the picturesque harbor of Náousa, Páros.

– CENTRAL CYCLADES –

PÁROS

Large, fertile and gentle, Páros has something of a bovine air about it, in keeping with the pastoral nature of its agricultural interior. But rural tranquility is but a brief illusion for anyone who hits town in the months of July or August. Good beaches, Cycladic charm, and a position on the main ferry route attract tourists like flies; and Páros' gentle sweetness is mitigated by buses packed like sardine cans and cement hotel complexes. Anyone turned off by the "scene" can take refuge inland, where stone villages seem more resistant to the crowds.

Even in antiquity the island was known for its agriculture and its marble. It prospered continuously from the early Cycladic period on; and from the size of its annual contribution to the Delian League in the 5th century B.C., it's evident that it was well-to-do even then. When the Romans came to the island, they were most interested in Páros' white marble. But the island gradually declined in importance; pirate attacks drained it of inhabitants at one point.

The point of entry and departure for most visitors is the town of ****Parikía** ❶, built on the site of ancient Páros. Protecting, at a distance, the busy waterfront

Map (Mílos) p. 87, Info pp. 104-107

is an old Crusader **castle**, which incorporates the ruins of ancient temples. Parikía's most important building, however, is not the castle but the huge church of ***Ekatontapilianí**, one of the most significant Byzantine structures on any Greek island. Supposedly founded by the mother of the Emperor Constantine, St. Helena, when she was driven here by a storm in the 5th century, constructed under Emperor Justinian a century later, and altered several times since, this "Church of a Hundred Doors" allegedly only sports 99; the legend is that the city of Constantinople will revert to Greece when the hundredth door is found.

It's a magnificent building, with huge boxy interior spaces that aren't quite like those of most Roman Catholic churches, to say nothing of the chandeliers and gold leaf that glitter in the candlelight with that truly Byzantine opulence, both lavish and somehow cold. The oldest part of the building is the baptistery by the entrance. Also by the entrance is a rather good **Ecclesiastical Museum**.

Parikía also boasts a new **Archeological Museum**, which displays, among other things, inscriptions by the poet Archilochus, a Parian who lived in the 7th century B.C. and is credited with the invention of iambic pentameter. From Parikía, buses run to ***Náousa** ❷, the island's second harbor. Náousa so perfectly fits the stereotype of a white Cycladic fishing village that you can hardly see the wood for the trees; it's surrounded by a ring of tourist facilities far larger than the heart of the village itself. An old Venetian castle extends out into the harbor where boats sit waiting to carry beach-goers off to **Monastíri**, **Santa Maria**, **Kolimbíthres**, with its strange rock formations, or **Lagéri** (where there's nude swimming if you walk down the beach a ways). In the town, the tavernas are festooned with octopus hanging out to dry after having been tenderized through repeated beatings on a rock.

The other main bus route cuts across the island. Passing through **Maráthio** ❸, where you can still visit the marble quar-

ries that were active from the 3rd millennium B.C. to the 15th century A.D., you come to the charming little village of **Léfkes** ❹, with its winding alleys and views out over the hills. Here, there's a tiny **Ethnographic Museum** and a pottery workshop. An old Byzantine stone footpath leads down from Lefkes to **Pródromos**. A single roof unites two churches here, and travelers have to pass under it to enter the village.

Márpissa ❺, arguably the prettiest of the inland villages, is also the starting point of a rather heavily-trafficked stretch of shore extending down to Driós. Rising up near Márpissa is the hill of Kéfalos, magnificently topped with the ruins of a Venetian castle and the shining white planes of the monastery of **Ágios Andónios**, built in the 16th century. The town's port is **Píso Livádi**, from which ferries depart for some other islands; its beach is **Logarás**.

Above: Fun in the sun on the beach of Kolumbíthres in the north of Páros.

Driós ❻ is a green village, with a slender white beach. From here, you can walk to **Kalpakis Cave**, a stalagmite and stalactite cave that was once used as a prehistoric dwelling. There are other remains of prehistoric settlement on the promontory of **Piragaki**. The beaches along this southeast coast are fine, and windy, which has made them particularly appealing to windsurfers. In fact, **Hrisí Aktí** ❼ ("Golden Beach") offers some of the best windsurfing in Greece, and has hosted Greece's only World Cup windsurfing race since 1993.

Going south from Parikía, toward **Alikí** and the airport, you can see the ruins of the Doric **Asclepion** (4th century B.C.) and the associated **Pythion**, sacred to Apollo who was a kind of ally of Asclepius, god of healing. The inland route continues on to **Petaloúdes** ❽, the valley of the butterflies, although the tiger moths resident here in July and August have become a bit wary or weary of the mobs of visitors, and have dwindled in number.

Map p. 90, Info pp. 104-107

ANDÍPAROS

From **Poúnda**, day-trippers board the small ferry over to **Andíparos**, which is much quieter than its larger neighbor – although crowded in summer – and has some nice beaches. The large cavern of **Spíleo Stalakitón** ❾ on **Ágios Ioánis** hill was discovered in the days of Alexander the Great, and has been visited ever since.

**NÁXOS

Náxos is a green island with long sand beaches, mountain hiking, ancient sites, and numerous Venetian watchtowers (*pírgi*). It's been popular with foreign tourists since the time of Byron, who said it was his favorite island. Because of its size, however, it's still possible to find places where you can get away.

Largest of the Cyclades, Náxos has played a defining role in the archipelago's history as a center of commerce, administration, and as the source of the word "archipelago." In 1207, after the Fourth Crusade, the Venetian Marco Sanudo arrived and established the island as the center of a Duchy of Náxos that was to endure under Venetian control until 1566. The Byzantines had used the word "archipelago" to denote the Aegean Sea, their "main ocean" (*archos* and *pelagos*); the Venetians took it over to denote the group of islands under their control, investing it with its current meaning. The enduring myth of Náxos is the story of Ariadne: after she had helped Theseus find his way through the Labyrinth of Knossós (Crete) to slay the Minotaur, Theseus set sail for home, taking Ariadne with him; but after they had landed on Náxos, he sailed off and left her. Ariadne mourned her fate until the god Dionysus found her and made her his bride. Dionysus was also associated with the island; in one legend it was here that he discovered wine.

Although Náxos' marble is coarser than that of Páros or Tínos, it's been an is-

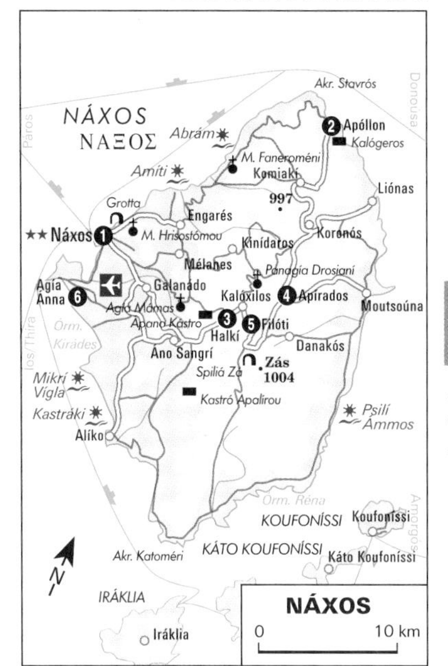

land hallmark since antiquity. There are several old **quarries** near **Apollón**; in one of them is a 10.4-meter ***kouros**, or statue of a boy, left incomplete and still attached to his rocky foundations. Apollón itself, however, has become a rather run-of-the-mill tourist trap. Another similarly incomplete **kouros** lies near **Mélanes**, at the island's center.

****Náxos** (Hóra) ❶ is also the island's port. Náxos' trademark, visible as one enters its harbor, is supposed to be a piece of a Temple of Apollo, which may have been for Dionysus, as well. The **Portára** is a huge square stone gate rising on the little island of ***Paláteia** before the town. Never completed, the temple was further reduced when the Venetians borrowed pieces of it to help build their castle.

Presumably to compensate for the lack of a safer hilltop location, the town's builders made its streets winding and narrow to confuse invaders; they now successfully confuse modern visitors. At least the rise toward the hilltop helps one get one's bearings. Clearly the site of the

Info pp. 104-107

ancient acropolis, the hilltop was later used for the Venetian **Kástro**, within whose walls are displays of ostentation – such as coats-of-arms over the doorways of palazzi – that would have been frowned on in Venice itself. There are also two churches here, one the 13th-century Catholic cathedral, **Ipapandi**, dedicated to the Virgin Mary, restored in the 17th century. The ★**Archeological Museum**, also here, is strongest in the areas of Cycladic and Mycenean art. Churchgoers can also visit the Orthodox cathedral, **Mitrópolis Zoodóhou Pigís**, with its elaborate iconostasis.

Fifteen minutes from town is the 17th-century convent of **Hrisostómou**, perhaps less interesting for its miraculous 1818 icon than for its fabulous views. On the shore north of Hóra, in the area called Grotta for its caves, are remains of ancient (Mycenean or Cycladic) buildings underwater. On the road north to Apollón stands the white monastery of **Faneroméni**, dating from 1603. Nice beaches on the northwest coast are **Amíti** and **Abrám**. **Apollón** ❷ is an important center of tourism that is worth visiting, especially for the kouros outside of town.

Above: The Portára, the immense stone gate of an ancient temple ruin, greets visitors at the harbor of Náxos.

Traveling east from Náxos Town you pass by **Ágios Mámas**, one of the oldest churches on the island (9th century), containing a very old icon. The white neoclassical houses of **Halkí** ❸ create a distinctive, attractive townscape. ★**Panagía Drosianí** can claim to be the island's oldest Byzantine house of worship (6th century A.D.). Some two kilometers from town are the ruins of the fortress of **Ápano Kástro**, which the Venetians, true to form, built atop an ancient site; its foundations are Cyclopean, and there are also remains of Mycenean tombs.

Due east of here is **Apírados** ❹, nicknamed *Marmarinas* ("Made of Marble"). The town has preserved some of its traditional offbeat quirkiness. There's an **Archeological Museum** here, and **Agía**

Map p. 93, Info pp. 104-107

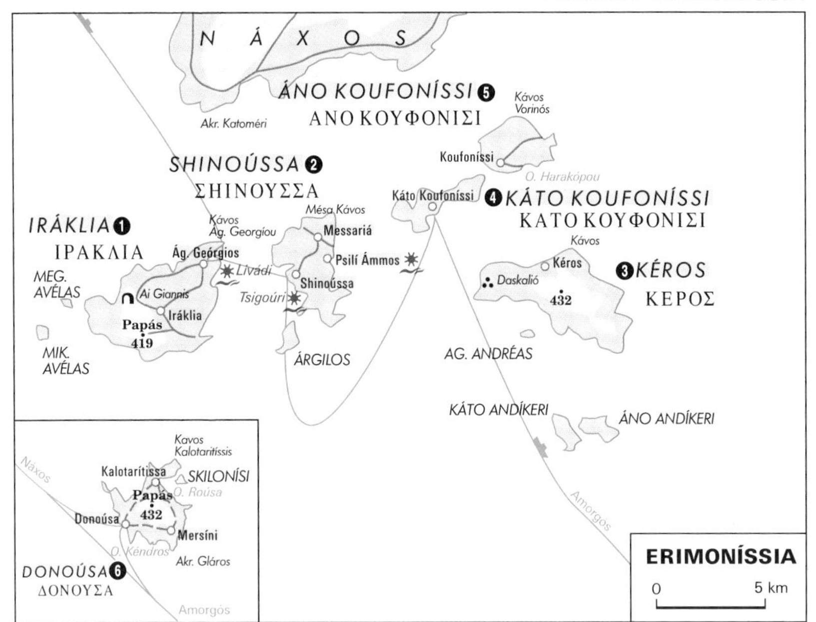

Kriakí contains Byzantine-era frescoes. From here, a long winding road leads to the beach at **Moutsoúna**, from where an even longer road, in poor condition, goes on to another good beach, **Psilí Ámmos**.

Filóti ❺ is the largest village in this area. South of here is the island's highest point, **Mount Zás** or Zeus, known in antiquity as Driós. Hikers can ascend its slopes to the 1,000-meter peak, or follow trails around them to some of the ancient towers at its foot, such as the remarkably well-preserved Hellenistic **Chimaron Tower**, built more than 2,000 years ago.

South of Náxos, serious beach-goers come into their own. **Agía Ánna** ❻, one of the closest to town, gets very crowded; but beaches continue all along the coast, with white and crowded sands. Two of the best are **Mikrí Vígla** and **Kastráki**.

ERIMONÍSSA – THE LESSER EASTERN CYCLADES

Scattered between Náxos and Amorgós are a cluster of small and unspectacular islands (*Erimoníssa* means "back islands") which are perfect for anyone who really, truly wants to get away from it all. **Iráklia** ❶, the largest of them, boasts all of two towns: **Ágios Geórgios**, the settled area around the harbor, and old, sleepy **Iráklia** (Hóra), about an hour's walk uphill. **Livádi** boasts a gorgeous white sand beach. Another attraction is the striking stalactite cave of **Ai Giannis**. Traces of Cycladic civilization have also been uncovered on the island.

Ruins of a later date characterize the Hóra of **Shinoússa** ❷; the town boasts a medieval fortress. There are traces of other fortifications at little **Messariá** on a bay. Nearby **Psilí Ámmos** is the swimming spot of choice, although it's a bit of a trek; more accessible, and thus busier, are the grayish sands of **Tsigoúri**.

Kéros ❸, although largish, is almost completely uninhabited, and is without regular boat service. In the burial sites at **Daskalió** archeologists discovered two 4,500-year-old Cycladic idols (now in the National Museum in Athens).

Map (Náxos) p. 93, Info pp. 104-107

There are actually two Koufoníssi islands, but the smaller of them, **Káto Koufoníssi** ❹, is mainly inhabited by goats. **Áno Koufoníssi** ❺, the main island, is also small, but is the most active of the "Back Islands," with a working fishing fleet and a real hotel. The *meltemi* is strong here, but it doesn't stop people from spending time on the lovely beaches on **Harakópou Bay**.

Seemingly adrift in the sea east of Náxos, **Donoúsa** ❻ is the most geographically isolated of the "Back Islands." The first settlement here was established in the Minoan Age, but since water and food can get scarce even today, it's small wonder that it was eventually deserted. The current population is descended from settlers from Amorgós. Amenities are still modest: there are a number of rooms to let, three tavernas, and a little store in the main town of **Donoúsa**. Even the drinking water has to be imported: the island's only freshwater spring is in the village of **Mersíni**, under a spreading shade tree.

Right: Hozoviótissa Monastery on Amorgós is famous for its spectacular location.

From **Papás**, the island's highest point (383 meters), walkers can make out a sunken ship of World War II vintage offshore by the beach of **Kéndros**. Boats from the harbor take visitors to the cave of **Fokiospiliá**; other visitors unwind on the beaches of Livádi and Kéndros.

⋆AMORGÓS

Easternmost of the Cyclades, long, rocky Amorgós served on and off as a place of exile from Roman times to the period of the military junta. One prisoner of the junta, George Milonas, escaped in his son-in-law's motorboat, later to serve as Greece's Minister of Culture. But Amorgós has also undergone periods of popularity – it supported three flourishing ancient cities – and today, private motorboats tend to race toward the island rather than away from it.

The island's main port is at **Katápola** ❶, a port since the days of the ancient city of **Minóa**, sitting above the modern town, founded in the 4th century B.C. Little remains on the site today, except for views over the harbor and its beaches.

South of Katápola is the village of **Léfkes** ❷; near it, the church of **Ágios Géorgios Valsamítis** is lined with frescoes. The church was built over a spring said to have curative powers, notably for leprosy. The island's southern half is known as **Káto Meria**; from the village of **Vroútsis** you can walk north to the ruins of another of the island's three ancient cities, **Arkesíni** ❸, by Kastrí. Modern Arkesíni is a distinct settlement further south, where there are the ruins of a Hellenistic tower from around 200 B.C. at **Agía Triáda**.

North of Katápola is ⋆**Amorgós** (Hóra) ❹, the island's main village, around a defiant upthrust of rock that bears the 13th-century Venetian **Kástro** and, lower

Map (Erimoníssia) p. 95, Info pp. 104-107

down, forms part of the inner wall of the church of **Keras Leousas**. The **Archeological Museum** is housed in the Gavras family mansion, built in the 16th century. Among the island's souvenirs are shadow-puppets, reflecting the influence of Asia Minor.

Below steep Amorgós are the fine beaches of **Agía Ánna**. But the main track leads to the hallmark of Amorgós, the monastery of ****Hozoviótissa** ❺, starkly white at the base of a cliff, like a pedestal supporting the living rock. It was founded around A.D. 800 to house a miraculous icon of the Madonna, painted by St. Luke, from the Palestinian monastery of Choziva; in 1080, the Byzantine emperor Alexis Comnenos rededicated it. From its beginnings in a cliffside cave, the building has grown, more or less vertically, into dozens of rooms and chapels. It's still an active monastery, albeit with only a couple of monks in residence to guide visitors through the premises, past the treasures and superb views from 320 meters above the sea.

You pass the offshore island of **Nikouriá** ❻, site of an ancient settlement and, later, of a leper colony, on the way north to Amorgós' second harbor, **Egiáli**, site of the third of the island's ancient towns. Modern Egiáli is comprised of three settlements: waterfront **Órmos**, **Potamós**, and pretty **Langáda**. The bay of **Órmos Egiális** ❼ boasts the island's best sand beach. **Tholária** ❽, to the north, is near the ancient city of Egiáli; there are said to be Roman tombs near the village, though they're somewhat difficult to find.

From Langáda, hikers can head up **Mount Kríkelo**, at 822 meters the highest mountain on the island and from which there are some spectacular views. Or they can seek out two old churches: the Byzantine church of **Panagía Epanokori** has large festival grounds which are overrun on August 15; nearer the coast is the monastery of **Ágios Ioánnis Theológos**, coeval with Hozoviótissas, dating in parts from the 5th century A.D. Both churches have remains of old frescoes.

Info pp. 104-107

– SOUTHERN CYCLADES –

*FOLÉGANDROS

Folégandros' name may derive from the Phoenician word for "rocky," an adjective that applies perfectly to this little, cliff-girt island. Its population is relatively small, although it's positively burgeoning in comparison with the Middle Ages, which saw it depopulated three times; the present residents are descended from immigrants from Crete and Venice. In the 1960s and 70s, the ruling military junta tried to augment the population by banishing political exiles here. Now, it draws plenty of summer visitors, some of them taking refuge from the hordes on Íos. **Karavostásis** ❶ is the island's harbor; the nearest decent swimming is on the rough sands of **Lustria Bay**, where Folégandros' campground is located. From the port, a road leads up to

Above: Threshing grain the old-fashioned way with not always willing helpers.

***Folégandros** (Hóra) ❷, a picture-perfect Cycladic village perched atop the cliffs. Its oldest section, the ***Kástro**, was built by the island's Venetian rulers in the 13th century; its houses are built side by side so that their outer walls form a defensive enclosure, with arched gateways leading into the town.

Dominating the village, however, is not its castle but its **Panagía**, the massive white-domed church above the old city walls. The centerpiece of this church is an icon of the Virgin which, it is said, was stolen three times in pirate raids, but each time came floating back to its home island; on the last occasion, it bore with it the lone survivor of the pirate vessel's shipwreck.

Not far away from the church, the stalactites and stalagmites of **Hrisospiliá**, the "Golden Cave," are another main attraction, although visitors will need a guide to go exploring. The cave got its name, according to local legend, when the villagers took refuge here from marauding attackers, taking their golden

Info pp. 104-107

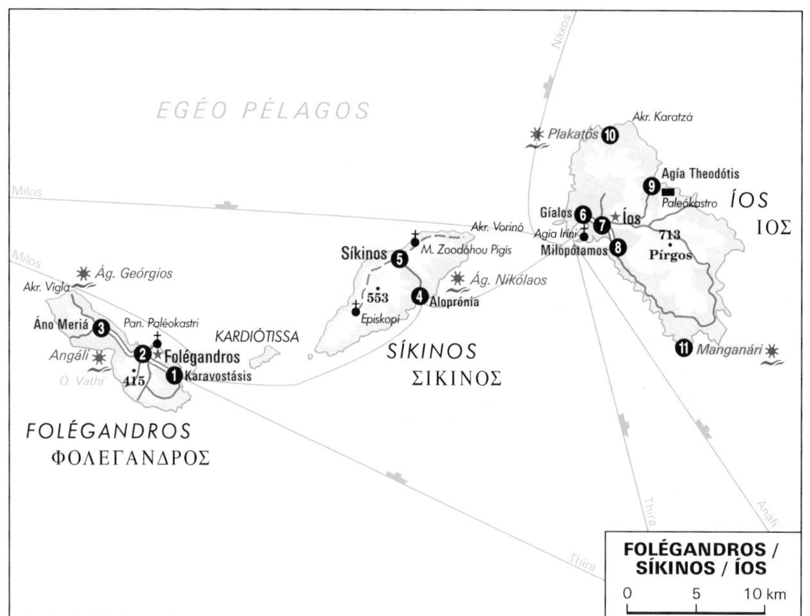

treasure with them; the invaders, discovering their hiding place, plugged up the exits and set the cave on fire, leaving only a pool of molten gold.

Folégandros' second village, **Áno Meriá** ❸, is more like a string of houses extending along the island's road. It does, however, boast an **Ethnographic Museum**, and it hosts a festival on the feast day of Ágios Pandeleímon on July 27.

Just about midway between Folégandros and Áno Meriá, **Angáli** is the island's best beach, as well, inevitably, as its most crowded. Further north, swimmers can skinny-dip at **Ágios Nikólaos**. Kaikis run to both of these and to **Ágios Géorgios**, a large but windy beach at Folégandros' northern tip.

SÍKINOS

Síkinos is a tranquil, leisurely island that has managed to avoid the crowds of Íos. Boats dock at **Alopronía** ❹, and it's uphill all the way to the tripartite capital of the island. **Síkinos** (Hóra) ❺ is comprised of Horió, Kástro and Vuni, and houses most of the local population. It's a lovely village, especially the ***Kástro** part, where stately old houses ring the main square around the church of Our Lady, **Pantánassa**. Some of the buildings are ruined; an elaborately carved stone doorway frames a landscape of hill and sky rather than the interior one might expect.

In town, summer residents are reclaiming some of these old houses; one of them contains an **Ethnographic Museum**. Crowning the whole, the fortress-like monastery of **Zoodóhou Pigís** hearkens back to the dangerous days when an island's main place of worship was also a place of refuge.

To the north, there are ancient ruins at **Episkopí**, originally a Roman shrine before its ultimate conversion into a monastery in the 17th century. Walkers can seek out beaches such as **Ágios Georgiós**, **Ágios Nikólaos**, and **Ágios Pandeleímonas**, or try to locate the island's caves, including **Drakofido**, the "Black Cave."

Info pp. 104-107

ÍOS

Naturally bare and beautiful in the best tradition of the Cyclades, Íos has become one of the most unpleasantly touristed of the islands, as well. A playground for the under-25 set, renowned for outdoor camping, all-night beach parties, and discos that go until dawn, it can be really unpleasant in summer for anyone who's not attracted by this ambiance. But those who come to Greece to swim, meet people and go to parties may have found the perfect spot.

"Little Malta" is yachtsmen's nickname for the harbor at **Gialós** ❻, because it, like Malta's harbor, is sheltered from the wind. From here, stone steps lead up to the island's only real town, ★**Íos** (Hóra) ❼, a solid thicket of tourist amenities within picturesque white Cycladic walls. Two stout white Byzantine churches raise blue domes, and a dozen windmills are another atmospheric hallmark. For visitors who want to meet their cultural obligations, there are the **Archeological Museum** and the **Odysseus Elytis Amphitheater**, which presents events under the summer stars. The most popular beach on the island is the broad stretch of sand at **Milopótamos** ❽, a center for informal camping (it also has two campgrounds) and all-night parties.

Above: Gialós, Íos' wind-protected harbor, is popular with sailors. Right: Hotel complex in Oía (Thíra) – an architectural work of art.

Buses run from Íos to the east coast and the beach at **Agía Theodótis** ❾, where there are tavernas and hotels, as well as the last traditional church festival still held on this crowded island, on September 8. Near here are ruins of a Roman aqueduct, but the most striking monument is the Venetian fortress, or what's left of it, that marks the site of **Paleókastro**, the island's medieval capital. Further south, there's another lovely and popular beach at **Psáthis Bay**, where there are also ruins of an ancient temple.

Beaches on the northern coast include **Plakatós** ❿, near the site known as the

Map p. 99, Info pp. 104-107

grave of the poet Homer, whose mother supposedly came from this island. A festival commemorates the poet every May. At the island's southern extremity is the beach of **Manganári** ⓫, more easily reached by kaiki from Gialos than overland. With a burgeoning holiday community and nude bathing, this was one of the filming locations for "The Big Blue."

**THÍRA (SANTORIN)

In antiquity, Santorin was called Kalliste, "Most Beautiful." Many people would still apply this epithet to this most popular of Greek islands. The only wholly volcanic island in the Cyclades, thrust from the sea and pulled piecemeal back into it in a series of eruptions continuing well into this century, dark Santorin is rimmed with beaches of hot black sand and red cliffs that seem to capture the light of its famous sunsets. Inland, vineyards and orchards flourish in the volcanic soil, producing flavorful fruit, vegetables, and a famous white wine.

Offsetting its rich deep colors are the blue-and-white houses and domed churches, here an especially brilliant contrast to the landscape around them. Another early name for the island was Strongyli, "The Round One," and the islands around the former crater have preserved this circular shape.

Thíra, little **Thirasía** ❶ (sparsely inhabited, with a few tavernas) and **Aspronissi** ❷, the "White Island," mark the edges of the crater; rising blackly at their center are **Paleá Kaiméni** ❸, thrust to the surface in an A.D. 157 eruption, and ***Néa** or "New" ***Kaiméni** ❹, dating from the 18th century. The latter islet is also the location of the present crater; bursts of sulfurous steam rise from its soil, and those visitors who want to can immerse themselves in the malodorous mud of its hot springs.

Parts of Thíra sank after volcanic eruptions in antiquity, which may have given rise to the legend of the lost island of Atlantis. The most recent eruption was in 1956, with a devastating earthquake; Fíra,

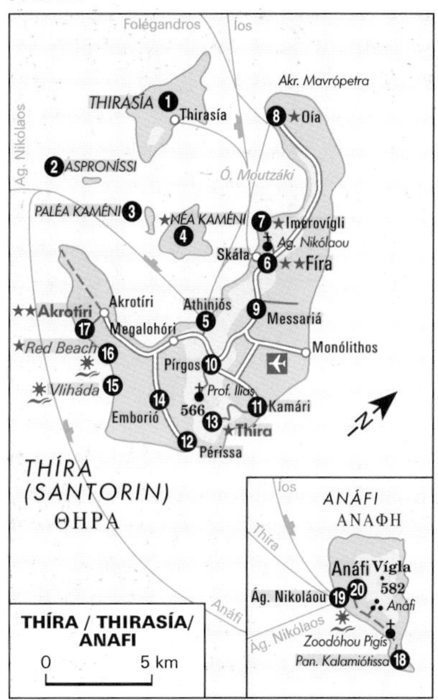

the capital, and Oía, the fishing village at the island's northern tip, were particularly hard hit, and stand today largely as the result of modern reconstruction.

Thíra was named for the legendary king of the island's first Dorian settlers, Thíras, son of a Theban hero. The name Santorin was coined when the Venetians ruled from the medieval capital of Skáros in the 14th century and the little village of Emborió housed a church to St. Irene, or Agía Iríni, their patron saint; "Santa Iríni" was corrupted to "Santorin."

The main ferry port of the island is **Athiniós** ❺, from which a bus runs to the hilltop capital of ★★**Fíra** ❻ or Thíra; but some ships dock at **Skála Fíra**, allowing passengers to make the ascent either traditionally, by donkey, or in more rapid modern style, on the funicular donated by shipping tycoon Evangelos Nomikos. The capital of a tourist-frequented island, Fíra is rife with shops and eateries, bars and discos. The town's **Archeological Museum** displays finds from Fíra's two main archeological sites, the Minoan settlement of Akrotíri and the town of ancient Thíra, which yielded a fine collection of "Thiran" vases from the 7th and 6th centuries B.C. There's also the **Megaron Gyzi Museum**, devoted to local history, in an old mansion.

Right: Exploring a sunken Minoan city – the excavations of Akrotíri.

Not far north of Fíra, ★**Imerovígli** ❼ stands near the site of the medieval capital, **Skáros**, now largely in ruins. The castle that used to dominate the town served mainly as a look-out and defense against approaching pirates. **Ágios Stéfanos** here is the island's oldest church. Imerovígli boasts the still-active convent of **Ágios Nikólaos**, but its most striking attraction are its fine views of the volcano's caldera.

At the opposite, northern end of the island, the village of ★★**Oía** (Ía) ❽ experienced devastation far more recently, when the earthquake of 1956 buried it in a slide of volcanic rock. Partly ruined, partly rebuilt, the town remains a beauty spot for its setting alone, thronged with tourists aiming their cameras at its signature ★**sunsets**. The cave dwellings dug into the soft rock of the cliffs serve today as exclusive holiday homes.

Marking the skyline are the domes of the restored church of **Zoodóhou Pigís** and the blades of the abandoned windmills, called the **Garbini Windmills** after the southwest wind, the *Garbis*, that used to power them. A long flight of steps cut into the cliff leads down to the waterside, where swimmers emerging from the blue water can sunbathe on shelves of the sharp red rock.

At the center of the island are its oldest and most traditional villages. **Messariá** ❾ is at the center of the island's vineyards, which produce a spectrum of distinctive white wines. Pírgos and Emborió suffered the least damage in this century's earthquakes; **Pírgos** ❿, especially, has been able to preserve a medieval flavor, as well as its Venetian **Kástro**. It stands at

Info pp. 104-107

the foot of the island's highest peak, **Profítis Ilías** (566 meters), atop which perches the **monastery** of the same name, built in 1712. This still-active complex includes a **museum** with exhibits about traditional crafts, including replicas of a shoemaker's and a carpenter's workshop, as well as the interior of a Thiran home, complete with weavings and embroideries; note, however, that it keeps irregular hours. Between Pírgos and Kamári is **Méssa Goniá**. **Panagía Episkopí** there sponsors a huge festival in summer.

The most popular black sand beaches on the eastern coast are Kámari and Périssa. **Kamári** ⓫ is very crowded; **Périssa** ⓬ has a campground and is less built-up. Also on the east coast, midway between these two beaches, are the ruins of ***Archaia Thíra** ⓭, ancient Thíra, founded in the 9th century B.C. and excavated in the 19th century A.D. by a team of German archeologists. Highlights here include the **Ancient Theater** and some stunning views from the 300-meter-high cliffs.

By Emborió are the ruins of the ancient settlement of **Elefsina**. **Emborió** ⓮ itself was the site of the Byzantine church of Agía Iríni, whence the island's modern name; the original church has been replaced by a modern building. In the south of the island is **Vliháda Beach** ⓯, which is somewhat less crowded than other area beaches and where striking red cliffs offset the dark sands.

On the southern curve of the island, **White Beach** and ***Red Beach** ⓰ are the two swimming venues nearest to Santorin's leading archeological site, ****Akrotíri** ⓱. Excavations of this Minoan city are ongoing; they've already yielded some of the most stunning testimony extant of Minoan civilization, including the magnificent frescoes in the National Archeology Museum in Athens, which Santorin would very much like to get back some day.

Akrotíri was not discovered until 1967. Professor Spirídon Marinátos, an archeologist working at Minoan sites in Crete, was curious about what could have

Info pp. 104-107

caused the destruction on the island that sparked the decline of Minoan civilization. Determining that it must have been a natural catastrophe, he followed the clue provided by Minoan vases discovered on Santorin, and began excavating there. At first, his work seemed fruitless; not until his team had gotten about five meters down did they break through into rooms filled with storage vases, relics of a flourishing civilization from 1500 B.C. The inhabitants of this "Greek Pompeii" evidently had some advance notice of impending disaster, since no human remains or valuables were found: only frescoes, pots and furniture.

ANÁFI

Remote and wild, at least by Cycladic standards, Anáfi offers an out-of-the-way haven for anyone prepared to rough it a bit. Its pleasant beaches and local color compensate for the relatively sparse tourist amenities. The myth goes that Apollo created the island to shelter Jason and the Argonauts during a storm; Jason built the god a temple in thanks for his support. Traces of the Apollo cult are said to have survived in some of the village rituals; remnants of the temple are overshadowed by the monastery of **Panagía Kalamiótissa** ⓲, which stands nearby, on the peninsula that forms the island's southeastern tip. One reason there's so little left of this temple is that it was stripped for building materials for the monastery of **Zoodóhou Pigís**, not far away. Be aware that nude sunbathing and swimming are strictly forbidden on the beach nearest the monasteries, out of respect for the area's monastic owners.

Ágios Nikólaos ⓳ is the harbor where infrequent ferries dock, not far from the lovely beach of **Klisídi**. From here you can walk up to **Anáfi** (Hóra) ⓴, which is set in the bowl of the island's hills and is guarded by the straggling ruins of a Venetian Kástro.

EOT offices for all the Cyclades: Dodekanessou 10, Síros, tel. (0281) 86275, fax. 82375.

Ferry connections within the Cyclades are good; between island groups they can be a problem (stopovers, transfers). Tourist information and ferry offices can help you further.

ÁNDROS (☎ 0282)

BOAT: Ferry and Sea Jet service to Rafína. No direct service to Piraeus (only via Tínos). Most boats dock at Gávrio, on the west coast, although Flying Dolphins also service Batsí one or two times a day. *CAR AND MOTORCYCLE RENTAL:* **Tasos**, tel. 71040, fax. 71165, at the waterside. **George's Rent a Moto**, behind the post office, tel. 71003.

GÁVRIO: $$ **Ándros Holiday**, tel. 71384, fax. 71097. **Perrakis**, tel. 71456, fax. 71459. $ **Galaxy**, tel. 71228. Seedy but clean, near ferry dock. **STENIES:** $$$ **Pigi Sarisa**, tel. 22187, fax. 22340, right across from the spring. **ÁNDROS TOWN:** $$ **Egli**, tel. 22303, fax. 22159, central, friendly. **Paradise**, tel. 22187, fax. 22340, pool, restaurant. $ **O Neiborsos**, tel. 22052, clean rooms on the town beach. **ÓRMOS KORTHÍOU:** $$ **Korthi**, tel. 61218, fax. 61118. Charmless concrete block, but great waterside location. **BATSÍ:** $$ **Meltemi**, tel. 41016, fax. 41564, and **Erato,** tel. 41943, modern furnished apartments.

GÁVRIO: Camping Ándros, near the harbor.

ÁNDROS TOWN: Ta Delfinia, (Nimborio), tel. 24179. Best of Nimborio's beach tavernas. **ÓRMOS KORTHIOU: To Bintzi**, best of Ormos' tavernas (at the end of the beach). **BATSÍ: Oti Kalo**, tel. 41465, harbor view taverna. **Sirocco**, tel. 41023. **PALEÓPOLI: I Oraia Paleópoli**, tel. 41539, simple taverna.

Museum of Modern Art, June-Sept 10 am to 2 pm, 6 to 8 pm (except Tue, Sun); Oct-May Sat-Mon 10 am to 2 pm. **Archeological Museum**, daily except Mon, 8:30 am to 3 pm.

Sailing School: End of Nimborio Beach. **Water Sports Center:** Batsí, tel. 41247. **Hiking:** Mr. Valmas at Hotel Egli, tel. 22303, fax. 22159. **Water Taxis:** Info from Greek Sun Holidays, Batsí, tel. 41198, fax. 41239 (arranges **excursions** and **trekking tours**.)

TÍNOS (☎ 0283)

BOAT: To Piraeus and Rafína. *CAR/MOTORCYCLE RENTAL:* **G. Vidalis**, Z. Alvanou 16, tel. 23877, fax. 23400; Kionon Ave. 6, tel. 24300. **Dimitris Car/Bike Rental**, Z. Alvanou 8, tel. 23585, fax. 22744.

TÍNOS TOWN: $$ **Aphrodite**, tel. 23556, fax. 22456, near ferry and town beach, with restaurant.

Map p. 103

PÓRTO: $$ **Carlo**, Ai Yiannis, tel. 24159, fax. 24169. Bungalow-style rooms, pool, near beach. **KIÓNIA:** $ **Anna's Rooms**, Kioni, tel. 22877, clean, near beach. **KOLIMBÍTHRA:** $$ **Kolimbíthra Beach**, tel. 51300, fax. 51734, taverna, beach. **PÍRGOS:** $$ **Elena Rooms**, tel. 31694/31840, apartments.

TÍNOS TOWN: O Peristerionas, Fr. Paximadi 9, tel. 23425, good food, central, quiet. **Galera**, Akti G. Drosou, tel. 25551, great harborside fish taverna. **PÓRTO: Taverna Gialos**, tel. 25630, always full, on beach. **PÍRGOS: Tzortzis**, tel. 31477, 31207, good waterside fish taverna. **KARDIANÍ: To Periboli**, tel. 31072.

TÍNOS TOWN: Museums in the Panagía Evangelistra complex include a **Painting Gallery**, **Ecclesiastical Museum**, **Museum of Sculpture**, tel. 22256, 8 am to 8 pm. **Archeological Museum**, tel. 22670, 8:30 am to 3 pm. **PÍRGOS: Museum of Fine Arts** and **House of J. Chalepás**, tel. 31262, 10:30 am to 2 pm, 6 to 7:30 pm. **Fine Arts Academy Exhibitions**, same hours.

MÍKONOS (☎ 0289)

Tourist Police, tel. 22482 (8 am to 9:30 pm); **Hotelier's Union**, tel. 25450; and **Union of Rooms to Rent**, tel. 24860. In town, travel agencies include **Blue Moon**, tel. 24040, fax. 23297, 8 am to midnight.

AIR: The **airport** is 2 km southeast of Míkonos Town; frequent flights to Athens; charter flights in summer. *BOAT:* The main **port** is north of Míkonos Town; connections to Piraeus and Rafína. *CAR AND MOTORCYCLE RENTAL:* **München**, tel. 24772, 27534, one of many near the bus station (southeast side of town).

MÍKONOS TOWN: $$ **Marios**, N. Kalogera 24, tel. 24670, fax. 22704, quiet, central. $ **Margarita**, tel. 22145, on hill north of harbor, sea view. **ÁGIOS STÉFANOS:** $$$ **Princess of Mykonos**, tel. 23806, fax. 23031, favorite of the stars, views of Míkonos Town. **KALAFÁTI:** $$$ **Paradise Aphrodite Beach Hotel**, tel. 71367, fax. 71525. Exorbitant, on nice beach, water sports, pool. $$ **Kalafatis Windsurfing Míkonos**, tel. 71228, nice affordable apartments.

Paradise Beach & Camping, tel. 22852, fax. 24350. **Mykonos Camping Paraga Beach**, tel. 25915, fax. 24578. Both with discos and bus service to town.

MÍKONOS TOWN: Philippi, tel. 22295, fax. 23382. Elegant garden eatery behind the Philippi Hotel (Kalodera). **Sun Set** (Iliovasilema), Scarpa, tel. 27948. Food is merely okay, but the view is a dream. **Alefkundra**, by the Catholic church, tel. 22450. Big, busy, good food. **O Kipos**, in tranquil garden, cheap, quiet. **AGÍA ÁNNA PARÁNGA: Nicolas**, tel. 23566, beachside taverna, also rents rooms (tel. 25762). **ÁNO MERA: Taverna Vangelis**, Plateia Anomeras, tel. 71577, good Greek dishes. **KALAFÁTI: Fish Taverna Markos**, tel. 71497, simple, on the waterfront. **KALÓ LIVÁDI: Kaló Livádi Beach**, tel. 71298, upscale crowd, fish and Indonesian cuisine.

Archeological Museum, tel. 22325, Mon, Wed-Sat 9 am to 3:30 pm, Sun 10 am to 3 pm. **Folk Museum**, Mon-Sat 4 to 8 pm, Sun 5 to 8 pm. **Lena's House**, 7 to 9 pm.

Windsurfing School (Fanatic Board Center, Kalafáti). **Greek Diving Center**: Contact Aphrodite Beach Hotel, tel. 71368, fax. 71525. **Mykonos Diving Center**, Psarou Beach, tel./fax. 24808.

DÍLOS (☎ 0289)

Ancient Sites and **Museum**, Tue-Sun 8:30 am to 3 pm, tel. 22259.

Excursion boats from Míkonos. Check return times carefully (no accommodation or supplies on Dílos).

SÍROS (☎ 0281)

EOT office (for all the Cyclades), Dodekanessou 10, tel. 86725, fax. 82375. **Galissas Tours**, tel. 42801, fax. 42802 (books rooms, rents cars and motorcycles).

AIR: **Síros Airport** is south of Ermoúpoli. Olympic Airways: Tel. 87025, 22634. *BOAT:* Ferries to Piraeus, Rafína, Crete and the Dodecanes. *CAR AND MOTORCYCLE RENTAL:* **Moto Rent Club**, Finikas, tel. 43708.

ERMOÚPOLI: $$$ **Hermes**, Platea Kanari, tel. 23011, fax. 87412, impressive, central, good restaurant. $$ **Villa Nostos**, Spartiaton 2, tel. 84226, 120-year old villa. **Ipatia Guest House**, Babagiotou 3, tel. 83575, another charming villa, pricey. **GALISSÁS:** $$ **Francoise**, tel. 42000, fax. 42024. Near beach, modern but pleasant. $ **Rooms**, Panaiota Sigala, tel. 42643, flowering terraces, near beach. **POSIDONÍA:** $$$ **Kyklamino**, tel. 42518, elegant villa near beach. **MÉGAS GIALÓS:** $$ **Alkyon**, tel. 61761, fax. 61000, sea view, pool, tennis, restaurant. **AZÓLIMNOS:** $$ **Galaxy**, tel. 61586, 61497. On hillside with views of the bay.

ERMOÚPOLI: Taverna Folia, A. Diakou 6, Vrodado, tel. 23715, good food, view. **GALISSÁS: Aisthima**, tel. 42862, worth the climb. **FÍNIKAS: To Doublino**, tel. 42696, grilled squid. **To Kima**, tel. 43526. **Hroussa**, tel. 61813, no frills but good. **AZÓLIMNOS: Batis**, tel. 61545, for a really good meal.

KÉA (☎ 0228)

At the ferry landing, tel. 31256. **Tourist Police**, tel. 21100.

BOAT: Ferries to Piraeus and Lávrion. **Port Authority** in Korissía, tel. 21334. Flying Dolphins to Piraeus (Marina Zéa), tel. 21435 or (01) 428001.

KORISSÍA: $$ **Karthea**, tel. 21204, on harbor. **Tzia Mas**, tel. 21305, central, restaurant. **KOÚNDOUROS:** $$$ **Kea Beach Hotel**, tel. 31230, fax. 31234, luxurious, also bungalows, night club.

PÍSSES: E. Politis, tel. 31332/5.

KORISSÍA: Astéria, taverna beneath trees, on beach. **KÉA: To Stéki**, edge of town, simple, good.

Archeological Museum, Kéa, tel. 22079, Tue-Sun 8:30 am to 3 pm.

KÍTHNOS (☎ 0281)

Small office in **Mérihas**.

BOAT: Ferries to Piraeus and Lávrion.

LOUTRÁ: $$ **Meltemi**, tel. 31271, fax. 31302. Pleasant, family-run, homey. **MÉRIHAS:** $$ **Romantza**, tel. 32237. Also apartments, central.

MÉRIHAS: Ostria, tel. 32263. **To Kantouni**, tel. 32220. **LOUTRÁ: O Koutsikos**, tel. 31185.

SÉRIFOS (☎ 0281)

Coralli Holidays, tel. 51488, fax. 51073, rents cars and bikes, and has info about water taxis.

BOAT: To Piraeus via Kíthnos.

LIVÁDI: $$$ **Asteri**, tel. 51891, fax. 51789. Leading hotel on the island. $$ **Areti**, tel. 51479, fax. 51507, attractive, clean and appealing. $ **Sérifos Beach**, tel. 51209, slightly overpriced but adequate.

Coralli Camping, tel. 51500, fax. 51073, near the ferry dock, friendly staff.

LIVÁDI: O Mokkas, tel. 51242, best place for fresh fish. **Perseus**, 51273, good standard taverna. **Margerita's**, at the end of the beach, is very good.

Folk Art Museum, 6 to 9 pm, Sat, Sun also 10 am to noon. **Archeological Museum**, daily except Mon, 9 am to 2 pm.

SÍFNOS (☎ 0284)

In **Kamáres**, across from the harfbor, tel. 31145 or 31977. There's a branch in **Apollonía's** main square.

BOAT: Ferries to Piraeus via Sérifos and Kíthnos. *CAR RENTAL:* **Thrifty Rent a Car**, Kamares, tel. 33383, fax. 31709.

KAMÁRES: $$$ **Boulis**, tel. 32122, fax. 32381, comfortable, near the beach. **Alkyonis Villas**, tel. 33101, fax. 33102, apartments with views of mountains and the harbor.
ARTEMÓN: $$$ **Petali**, Ano Petali, tel./fax. 33024, restored old building, views of Apollonía. $$ **Artemon**, tel. 31303, fax. 32385, modern, pleasant. **APOLLONÌA**: **Anthousa**, tel. 31431, with courtyard and pastry shop.
PLATÍS GIALÓS: $$$ **Simon Platís Gialós**, beach hotel and bungalows, tel. 71224, fax. 71325, on the waterfront, nice terrace. **Alexandros**, tel. 71300, fax. 71303, pool, restaurant, near beach. $$ **Euphrosine**, tel. 71353, 32140, all rooms with sea-view balcony, on the beach.
VATHÍ: $ **Taxiarhis Monastery**, also rents rooms.

ARTEMÓN: **To Liotrivi** (Manganas), tel. 31246, excellent, local specialties. **PLATÍS GIALÓS**: **Chrissopigi**, tel. 71295, great taverna. **Sophia**, tel. 31890, end of Platís Gialós, upscale, reasonable. **Phoni**, tel. 71308, popular. **VATHÍ**: **I Okeanida**, tel. 31191.

APOLLONÍA: **Folk Museum,** open daily 9 am to 1 pm and 6:30 to 10:30 pm, closed Sat morning.

KÍMOLOS (☎ 0287)

Tourist Police, tel. 51205.

BOAT: Ferries to Piraeus and Mílos.

Most visitors are day trippers from Mílos. If you want to stay overnight, there are plenty of private rooms.

MÍLOS (☎ 0287)

Drougas Travel & Tourist Agency in Adámas also rents cars, tel. 22369, fax. 22388. **Port Authority**, tel. 23360. **Tourist Office**, tel. 21204.

AIR: **Airport** near Zefiría, several flights daily to Athens. **Olympic Airways**, tel. 22380. *BOAT:* Ferries to Piraeus, Rafína and Crete.

ADÁMAS: $$$ **Kapetan Georgantas**, tel. 23251, fax. 23219, apartments. $$ **Hotel Delfini**, tel. 22001, 23195.

Archeological Museum, tel. 21620, open Tue-Sun 8:30 am to 3 pm. **Folk Museum**, tel. 21292. **Catacombs**, tel. 21625, Mon-Tue, Thu-Sat 8:30 am to 2 pm.

PÁROS (☎ 0284)

Parikía, tel. 51220. In **Náousa**, on the central square, tel. 52158, open 11 am to 4 pm, 8 to 11 pm.

AIR: Airport near Alikí; flights to Athens and Crete. *BOAT:* Páros is the hub for Cycladic ferry service; boats to Piraeus, Rafína, Thessaloníki, Crete, Sámos, Ikaría and the Dodecanes.
CAR AND MOTORCYCLE RENTAL: **Spanopoulos**, Naoussa, tel. 51774, fax. 51914.

PARIKÍA: $ **Hotel Arian**, tel. 21490, 22269, lovely courtyard, some rooms with balcony, all with bath.

NÁOUSA: $$$ **Astir of Páros**, tel. 51976, fax. 51985, pool, beach, high-class comfort. $$ **To Spiti Tis Thalassas**, tel. 52198, on seaside cliff.
PARIKÍA: To Tamarisko, tel. 24689, excellent food, touch of class in gorgeous garden. **LÉFKES: Pezoula tis Lihoudias**, tel. 094-371474 (cell phone), tea room with homemade baked goods.
Archeology Museum, tel. 21231, Tue-Sun 8:30 am to 2:30 pm. **Skorpios Folk Museum**, Aliki, tel. 91129, daily 10 am to 2 pm and 5 to 9 pm.
NÁOUSA: Diving Club Santa Maria, tel. 094-385307 (cell phone), fax. 51937, all levels.

NÁXOS (☎ 0285)

Tourist Office, waterfront, Náxos Town, tel. 22993, fax. 25200. **Zas Travel**, tel. 23330, fax. 23419.
AIR: Airport 4 km south of Náxos Town; flights to Athens, charter flights. *BOAT:* Ferries to Piraeus, Rafína, Ikaría, Sámos, Crete, Kós and Rhódos.
NÁXOS TOWN: $$$ **Château Zevgoli**, tel. 22993, fax. 25200, romantic. $$ **Anixis**, tel. 22112, central. **Panorama**, tel. 22330, pretty, small.
NÁXOS TOWN: Lukullus, tel. 24386, one of the best. **Nikos**, tel. 23153, on the waterfront. **APÓLLON: Apollon**, tel. 67005, good standard dishes.
Archeological Museum, open Tue-Sat 8:45 am to 3 pm, Sun & hol. 9:30 am to 2:30 pm.

AMORGÓS (☎ 0285)

Mistis Tours in Katápola, tel. 71409, fax. 71003.
BOAT: Regular ferry service to Piraeus; can be a long trip, as stops are made at other islands along the way.
KATÁPOLA: $$$ **Hotel Aegialis**, tel. 73393, modern. $$ **Pension Lakki**, tel. 73393, fax. 73244, on beach, with garden. $ **Nikos'**, tel. 73310, fax. 73368, taverna and pension.
Archeological Museum, tel. 71289.

FOLÉGANDROS (☎ 0286)

FOLÉGANDROS: Tel./fax. 41285. **ÁNO MERIÁ:** Tel. 41387.
BOAT: Folégandros is on the Piraeus-Thíra (Santorin) ferry route.
Hoteliers' Association, tel. 41205. **KARAVOSTÁSIS:** $$ **Aeolos**, tel. 41205, clean, near the beach. **FOLÉGANDROS:** $$$ **Anemomilos Apartments**, new, all amenities.
KARAVOSTÁSIS: Camping Livadi, on the coast 2 km west of the harbor.
FOLÉGANDROS: Kritikós, nice taverna, good Greek dishes.
Ethnographic Museum, Áno Meriá, tel. 41387, daily 4 to 7 pm.

SÍKINOS (☎ 0286)

Tel./fax. 51238. **Tourist Police**, tel. 51222.
BOAT: Regular ferry service to and from Piraeus.
ALOPRÓNIA: $$ **Porto Sikinos**, tel. 51220, on the beach. $ **Private Rooms** in Síkinos (Hóra).
Small **taverna** at the ferry landing.

ÍOS (☎ 0286)

Port Authority, tel. 91264. **Plakiotis** (travel agency), tel. 91221, fax. 91118.
BOAT: Ferries to Piraeus, Crete and some of the Dodecanes. *CAR AND MOTORCYCLE RENTAL:* **Jacob's**, Gialos, tel. 92097, fax. 91047.
MILOPÓTAMOS: $$$ **Ios Palace**, tel. 91269, fax. 91082, beautiful beach complex. **GIALÓS:** $$ **Corali**, tel. 91272, fax. 91552, on beach. **ÍOS TOWN: Afroditi**, tel./fax. 91546, small, pretty. **Hotel Poseidon**, tel. 91091, fax. 91969, attractive, with pool. $ **Marcos Pension**, tel. 91059, fax. 91060, near a disco.
MILOPÓTAMOS: Far Out Camping, tel. 91468, fax. 92303, upscale campground.
KOUMBÁRA BEACH: Polydoros, tel. 91132, good taverna. **ÍOS TOWN: Pithari**, very good taverna.
Meltemi Water Sports, Milopotámos, tel. 91680.

THÍRA (SANTORIN) (☎ 0286)

EOT, Oía, tel. 71234. **Port Authority**, tel. 22239.
AIR: Airport (tel. 31525) near Monólithos; flights to Athens, charter flights. **Olympic Airways**, tel. 22793. *BOAT:* Ferries to Piraeus, Thessaloníki, Rafína, Crete and the Dodecanes.
FIRÁ: $$$ **Atlantis**, tel. 22232, fax. 22821, volcano views. $$ **Gallini**, tel. 23097, views. $ **Pension Argonaftis**, tel. 22055. **PÉRISSA:** $ **Vassilis Rooms**, tel. 81739, fax. 82070. **OÍA**: **Jack's Village**, tel. 71439, accommodation in all price ranges.
Archeological Museum, tel. 22217, Tue-Sun 8:30 am to 3 pm. **Akrotiri Site**, tel. 81366, same hours.

ANÁFI (☎ 0286)

Town Hall, tel. 61266.
Regular ferry service to and from Piraeus.
Several **pensions** at the harbor; **private rooms** in Anáfi (Hóra) are nicer though.

THE SPORADES

SKIÁTHOS
SKÓPELOS
ALÓNISSOS
ÈVIA (EUBOEIA)
SKÍROS

Sporades means "scattered," and for a long time the term didn't even apply to the islands in the northwestern Aegean, but was used for the Dodecanese. Even after taking over a designation of their own, Skiáthos, Skópelos, Alónnisos and Skíros were for years off the beaten tourist track. Tucked away behind Athens, against the bulwark of Évia (Euboeia), they were difficult to get to, off the main island-hopping routes. By the late 1960s, however, Skiáthos especially was being actively discovered by Greek and German tourists alike. Today, Skiáthos and Skópelos are popular vacation spots.

Slightly further from the mainland, Alónnisos has its own little archipelago of smaller islands; these mark the area of the first ocean reserve in Greece, where monk seals, in particular, can breed in a natural habitat unspoiled by the hand of man. Although linked to these islands by geographical proximity, Évia and Skíros actually belong to another administrative district. Évia is in any case a world unto itself, the second largest island is so close to the mainland that it feels like mainland, where Greek tourists cluster in a few resorts but much of the land is still wild and rural, the province of farmers and hikers out to explore old ruins.

Previous Pages: The beach of Koukounariés in Skiáthos, lined by a shade-giving pine forest. Left: Waiting for the next chance to do a little flirting.

The northern Sporades are considerably greener than the other Greek Islands; their broad pine forests, rocky coasts and wonderful beaches are simply waiting to be exploreded by visitors.

SKIÁTHOS

Skiáthos is known for its great beaches – known, alas, all too well. Nearest to the mainland of all the Sporades, Skiáthos is also by far the most developed. Pensions and hotels line the narrow streets of its main town, and its 62 beaches are crowded, in summer, with tanning bodies and excursion boats moored in the shallows like parked cars, waiting to carry people back to town in the late afternoon.

Even the island's capital commemorates the advent of modernity: not until Skiáthos became part of Greece, in 1830, did the local population desert its traditional home of Kástro, at the island's northern tip, and construct ***Skíathos** (Hóra) ❶ around the harbor. Admittedly, the town's most striking architectural feature was already standing at the time: the fortress on the small **Bourtzi** peninsula was erected by the Ghizzi family of Venice, who took control here around 1207.

Skiáthos was passed back and forth from Byzantine to Venetian to Turkish hands before the Greek War of Independence; today, the ruined fortress houses a restaurant and an open-air theater used for performances in the summer. Swimmers head to the rocky beach here.

Skiáthos prides itself on its local son, the novelist Aléxandros Papadiamántis (1851-1911), one of the first significant authors of modern Greece. Since his work is not widely available in other languages, however, the charms of the small **Papadiamántis House**, today a museum, will be lost on many foreign visitors.

The island's main road leads south and west of town past one beach after another. **Megáli Ámmos** is nearest to town and thus the most crowded, but it starts off a beach "strip" that extends down the coast to the **Kalamáki Peninsula**, a promontory thickly strewn with vacation homes and hotels that command some lovely views. **Kanapítsa** is the main – and most built-up – beach here; look for **Vromólimnos** or **Agrirolimnos** on the other side of the peninsula for more privacy.

While the beaches of **Plataniás** and **Troúlos** are attractive, many travelers head for ***Koukounariés** ❷, the pride of Skiáthos' beaches. A long arc of tree-lined white sand, it extends along a shore near the lake of **Strofilia**; there are footpaths around the lake through the trees to other beaches. The region has been declared a nature reserve and is a refuge for cranes and other birds. From the parking lot it's a short walk to **Banana Beach**, a nudist beach; a longer walk (ca. 20 minutes) brings you to **Mandráki**, on the island's northern coast.

Turning off the main road at Troúllos is a secondary road through lovely countryside to **Asselínos** ❸, where there's another sandy beach facing into the winds. Sightseers can detour by way of the convent of **Kounístra**, so called because it marks the site where a miraculous icon of the Virgin was found in the 17th century;

Above: Skiáthos Town is held firmly in the grip of tourists during the summer months.

 Map p. 115, Info pp. 120-121

she accordingly became the island's patroness. In the northern part of the island is the island's only still-active monastery, **Evangelístria** ❹, which saw the first-ever Greek flag hoisted in 1807, and which contains a museum of icons and other sacred objects. The best way to explore the north, however, is by boat: this allows access to the ruins of ***Kástro** ❺ high above the sea; abandoned in 1829, its 12 churches are currently being restored. Skiáthos' oceanside caves, including **Skotiní** and **Galaziá Spiliá**, can be swum to from the pale pebble beach of ***Lalária** ❻, set off by the delicate gray of the cliffs rising behind. Boats also run out to smaller offshore islands, such as **Tsoungriá** or **Argós**, where a lighthouse shows ships the way.

SKÓPELOS

The calm, tidy contentment Skópelos projects in the off season is a last vestige of the island's prominence as recently as the 19th century. In 1845, when the new Greek state took its first census, Skópelos Town was the third-largest city in Greece, after Nauplia and Athens. Shipping was responsible for its prosperity; the English shipping company Lloyds kept a large office on the harbor. Now, there are plenty of offices that offer their services, but the only international business Skópelos attracts these days is the tourist trade.

***Skópelos Town** ❼ is a pretty, inviting place rich in character, loved equally by artists and tourists. The town is watched over by the ruins of its Venetian **Kástro**, standing high above the water. This fortress, a relic of the Ghizzi family, helped protect the island in the War of Independence; no one wanted to deal with it, and it was left untouched.

A number of churches mark the top of the hill, from which there is a magnificent view; the oldest of these is 9th-century **Ágios Athanásios**, built on the site of an ancient temple. The town is supposed to have a total of 123 churches; one striking one is **Panagía Eleftheria**, which sports a kind of "tile work" of bright ceramic plates on its exterior; while **Hrísto** has a notable iconostasis. The small **Ethnographic Museum**, which displays embroidery and traditional costumes and furniture, is worth visiting.

East of Skópelos there are a couple of monasteries that can be seen in a daylong walking tour. There is a lovely view from **Moní Evangelismoú** (built in 1712). This monastery contains an icon of the Holy Virgin from the 10th century. The oldest monastery on the island, **Metamórfosis** (16th century) is now abandoned. The nuns of the monastery of **Prodómou** (built in 1721) offer their handicrafts for sale. The iconostasis in the church is of interest, and the courtyard is beautifully decorated with flowers.

Stáfilos Bay ❽, in the south of the island, has a large beach to offer. The bay is named for the Cretan prince Staphylos, the son of Ariadne and Theseus – or, according to another legend, of Ariadne and Dionysus – who are traditionally considered to have been the island's first inhabitants. Some of the treasures that were unearthed in the so-called Staphylos Grave near the bay include gold jewelry and battle axes; these objects can be seen in the Archeological Museum in Vólos (Thessaly).

Between Stáfilos and Agnóndas is the cliff where legend says St. Reginos lured a dragon to its death – in one version of the tale, the saint was a local preacher whose sermons were so dull that the dragon sprang to its death of its own accord. Whatever the story, **Drakontoshisma** is worth a look for its scenic charms; as for Reginos, today the patron saint of the island, he was martyred in A.D. 362, and his sarcophagus can be seen in the courtyard of **Ágios Regínou** monastery near Skopelos Town.

Agnóndas ❾ itself serves as the island's port when stormy weather prevents

ships from docking in Skópelos' town harbor; in calm weather, coming out of the trees to espy its clear water, dark with the reflected colors of the pines, you might mistake it for an Alpine lake. **Limonária Beach** boasts soft, white sand. Traveling northwest along the south coast you then come to **Panórmos Bay**, another gorgeous mountain-like arm of smooth deep blue water framed by pines, with a border of pale sand separating the two. At **Miliá** the sand gives way to a broad sweep of pebbles.

Paleó Klíma ⑩, further down the road, was largely deserted after an earthquake shook the island in 1965. It's a good starting point for walks around the northern part of the island. From here, for instance, you can walk to the traditional island village of **Glóssa**, built, like so many old villages, at a safe distance above and away from the sea, and comprised, also like so many old villages, of a rambling assortment of streets through which the uninitiated may have to wander for some time in order to find the town's hidden heart (the locals' distinctive accent makes it that much harder to ask directions). Much of Glóssa dates from the period when the Turks held sway over the island.

Above: Roofs covered with stone shingles – typical of the architecture of Skópelos (Panagía ston Pírgo, Skópelos Town).

From Glóssa, it's about an hour on foot to **Ágios Ioánnis** on the northeast coast, where a church perches on a rock over the restless water. The other option for those seeking water access is the descent to **Loutráki**, Skópelos' second port, where ferries dock by a fairly quiet beach lined with the obligatory taverna tables.

Skópelos prides itself on local produce. The island's almonds are used to make a kind of sweet. White plums are another specialty, found nowhere else in Greece.

ALÓNNISOS

Like Skópelos, Alónnisos was hard hit by the 1965 earthquake; the town of Alónnisos (Hóra) was almost wiped out. Disease had already taken care of many of its traditional grapevines. But the neglected island took on new life when the first-ever ocean reserve in Greece was established around Alónnisos and its archipelago in 1992.

Today, it is more frequented by travelers eager to take one of the carefully restricted tours through the habitat of the monk seal and other marine fauna – including dolphins – and flora; and its orchards and vineyards have made a slow but steady recovery on this now-green island.

There are a number of scattered islands and islets to Alónnisos' east and north. These include the wildlife reserve of **Pipéri** with its monk seal colony, and the wild, once-monastic **Kirá Panagía**, which still belongs to the monastic republic of Mount Athos, and where a sunken Byzantine ship lies off **Ágios Pétros**. Alónnisos' nearest neighbor is **Peristéra**,

Info pp. 120-121

where you can stroll through the olive groves.

Giúra is home to a special breed of mountain goat (Bezoar) and some striking limestone caves, including one of the many caves in the Greek Islands that claim to have been home to the Cyclops. On the distant volcanic island of **Psathoúra** stands a lighthouse, and a sunken city lies just off shore.

Psathoúra doesn't have the only sunken city, and visitors don't need to leave Alónnisos to see such things; the island's 5th-century B.C. capital, **Íkos**, sank into the water, too, and is still visible near Kokkinó Kástro. This area saw even earlier settlement; in 1970, in fact, excavators here discovered traces of some of the oldest human habitation in the entire Aegean, extending back some 100,000 years before Christ.

Alónnisos' main harbor is very much a town of the present, since **Patitíri** ⓫ only became the island's main town after the population was shifted in the wake of the 1965 earthquake. Today, it's a bustling little place with a busy yacht harbor, a **Monk Seal Museum** and even an **Academy of Homeopathy**. The town of **Alónnisos** (Hóra) ⓬, by contrast, is half-empty, although summer vacationers, taverna owners and shopkeepers are steadily reclaiming the old houses. Its walls are supposed to date back to the time of the Byzantines. There is a marvelous panoramic view from the old town. Besides the monk seals, beaches and walking are draws on Alónnisos. From Patitíri, it's not far to **Marpoúnda** and **Vithisma**, the beaches along the southern coast, while Alónnisos' nearest beaches are downhill at **Vrisitsa** and **Giália**. Most of the other popular beaches extend along the east coast, sheltered by nearby Peristéra: tree-lined **Hrisí Miliá** and **Kokkinó Kástro**; **Kalamákia**; and on up to **Ágios Dimítrios**. The latter boasts ancient ruins nearby, including a Byzantine fountain.

The farther north you go, the emptier the island gets. In the town of **Stení Vála** ⓭ you can watch a video in the office of

Info pp. 120-121

the **Greek Society for the Study and Protection of the Monk Seal**. And there are a few beaches around **Gérakas ⓮**. Hikers can tackle the island's greatest height, 472-meter **Mount Kouvoúli**, for views out over the archipelago.

ÉVIA (EUBOEIA)

Each island can claim to be unique, but Évia's claim is based partly on the fact that it hardly seems like an island at all; in fact, some guidebooks to the Greek Islands omit it altogether. Second-largest of all the islands after Crete, it extends its 250-kilometer sprawling length so close to the mainland that its capital, Halkída, actually stretches over both the mainland and island sides of the narrow Evrípou Channel. Évia's tourism is spotty, concentrated in only a few areas, and largely Greek, coming up on weekends from

Above: Monk seals have been saved from extinction thanks to the maritime national park near Alónnisos.

Athens, a mere 80 kilometers away. Much of the island is still fairly wild, and in the small villages farmers raise their herds as they've done for centuries – the island's ancient name, Euboeia, means "well-cowed" – and offer hikers refreshment as they pass on their way to one of the island's many ancient monuments.

Marking the approximate center of the island is **Halkída ❶**, a large modern city with two bridges – the first of which was originally built in 411 B.C. – straddling the ***Evrípou Channel**, which here is only 30 meters wide, but gets attention through the fact that the direction of its currents changes frequently and unpredictably. This has occasioned scientific enquiry and posed difficulties for shipping since antiquity. Aristotle supposedly got so frustrated over his inability to explain the phenomenon that he threw himself into the waters here in 322 B.C.

Continuously inhabited since antiquity, Halkída contains testimony to many ages of civilization. **Agía Paraskeví** is the city's patron saint; her Byzantine basil-

Info pp. 120-121

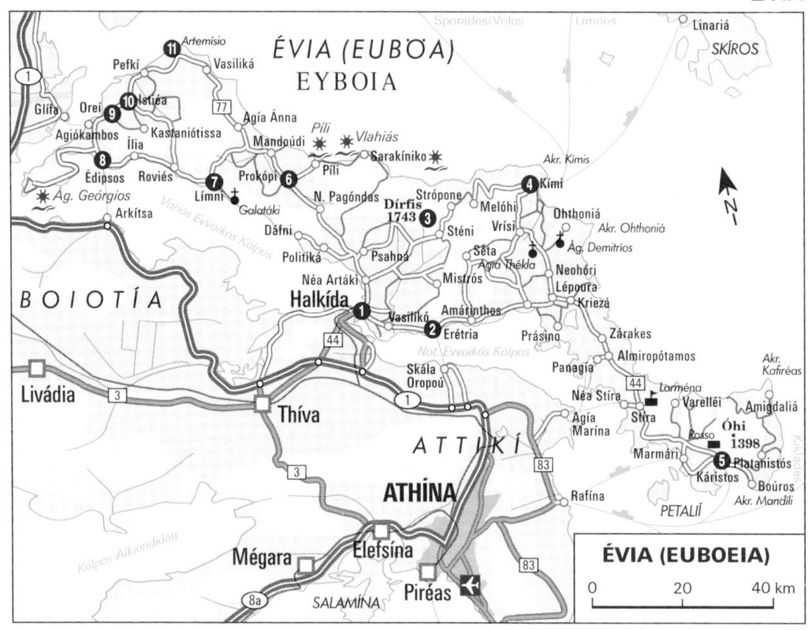

ica, built some time between the 5th and 8th centuries A.D., was converted into a Gothic cathedral under the Crusaders, and is today a collage of contrasting architectural styles. Long years of Turkish rule are reflected in the 16th-century **mosque** (formerly the Venetian Church of San Marco) with its beautiful fountain – the building now houses a collection of Byzantine fragments, as if tacitly to symbolize the triumph of Christianity – and an aqueduct in the **Kástro**, the old Venetian-Turkish quarter. An **Ethnographic Museum** is housed in the only extant portion of the old Venetian fortress. The Turks also built the fortress of **Karababa**, which stands on the mainland section of Halkída. Another ancient neighborhood here was the Jewish quarter, supposed to be one of the oldest in Europe; there's still a **synagogue**, built after an older one burned down in the 19th century, and the **Jewish Cemetery**.

Halkída and **Erétria** ❷, south of the island's capital, were two of ancient Évia's most powerful city-states, and spent much of their time contesting the fertile land of the Lelantine Plain between them. Ultimately, Halkída won out, living on into the present as the modern capital, while Erétria is now merely a striking archeological site. Interesting here are the Theater, the Mosaic House, the West Gate, and the Apollon Temple, which lie in part spread out over the coastal town founded by Ionian refugees in the 19th century. The best finds from are preserved in Halkida's **Archeological Museum**; which is better than the small museum in Erétria.

Mount Dírfis ❸, the island's highest mountain, rises to 1,743 meters at the island's broad middle; this peak and its adjacent mountains divide Évia and slow down the passage of anyone trying to cross the island. A circuitous road leads to the quiet resort of **Kími** ❹ in the east. The village itself sits in green trees and fields 250 meters above the water; it is said that the best figs in the world come from Kími. The town boasts a small **Ethnographic Museum** in an old neo-

classical house. Kími's beach and port is **Paraliá Kímis**, the main ferry port for Skíros with connections, in summer, to the other Sporades as well; there's good swimming off the sands.

Évia's unofficial capital to the south, **Káristos ❺**, has its own ferry connection from Rafína (20 kilometers east of Athens), perhaps an easier means of access than the road from Halkída. Káristos was another of Évia's ancient and powerful city-states, and it's remained one of the island's centers, especially for visiting foreigners. Centuries before, the Venetians created a kind of seaside home for themselves in the form of the **Bourtzi**, a 14th-century fort, partly built with blocks from an ancient temple of Apollo, that borders one end of the long town beach. Above town is the doughty edifice of **Rosso Castle**, first erected in the 11th century by the Byzantines, later appropriated by Venetians, Franks, Turks, and anyone else who happened to be in possession at the time. It was supposed to be so secure that only 30 men were required to defend it. In town, the small **Museum** contains relics of local excavation.

From **Míli**, two kilometers from Káristos, hikers can set out for **Mount Óhi**, the island's second-highest mountain (1,398 meters). The route, which takes some three hours, leads past some old **marble quarries**, where several columns of the distinctive green-and-white stone known as *cipollino*, named for the Italian word for "onion," still lie. Apart from sweeping views, the main attraction here is the **Drakóspito** or "Dragon House," a structure built of huge blocks of unmortared stone, which may have played a role in some form of ritual worship, since libation cups have been discovered around its foundations. There's a similar house located near **Stíra**, some 30 kilometers further north.

The northern part of the island is green and lush. **Prokópi ❻** is a much-visited village, partly because of its landscape –

Above: Sometimes locals in traditional costume can be seen on the island of Skíros.

it's set in a wooded ravine – and partly because of its church of **Ágios Ioánnis o Róssos**, where the relics of St. John the Russian were brought over from Cappadocia in the enforced Greek exodus from Asia Minor in 1924. Another point of interest here is the **Noel-Baker Estate**, at the center of the village. The English family who owned the land since the 19th century, and worked very hard to improve the area and living conditions for its residents, became a target for attack by Greeks resenting the presence of "feudal" landowners on soil not their own, and local protest continued vociferously through the 1980s. The house is now home to a pottery school. From Prokópi, a road leads northeast to the beaches at **Píliou**, **Vlahiás** and **Sarakíniko**.

Many people find the waterside fishing village of **Límni** ❼ to be the most attractive town on Évia; and its beaches boast clear, beautiful water. This is supposed to be where Zeus and Hera either got married or had their honeymoon. Some eight kilometers away is Évia's oldest working convent, **Galatáki**, where the church has lovely old frescoes. Tucked in a harbor near Évia's northern tip, **Édipsos** ❽ is the largest spa town in Greece. It's filled with elderly Greeks taking the waters in the area's many hot springs – between 60 and 80 of them, depending on whom you ask – which are good for curing just about anything. Fans of salt rather than mineral water can swim at **Ília** or pretty little **Roviés**, further south, or venture out along the wooded Lihás Peninsula to the good beaches at, for instance, **Ágios Geórgios** and **Gregolimano**. The island's north coast also offers nice swimming, at **Pefkí**, for one. Southwest of Péfki is **Oreí** ❾, where a marble bull from the 4th century B.C. is displayed on the coastal road.

Inland **Istiéa** ❿, set in the hills, is a center for agriculture – even Homer described it as "many-vined" – but it remains rather poor, despite its attractive

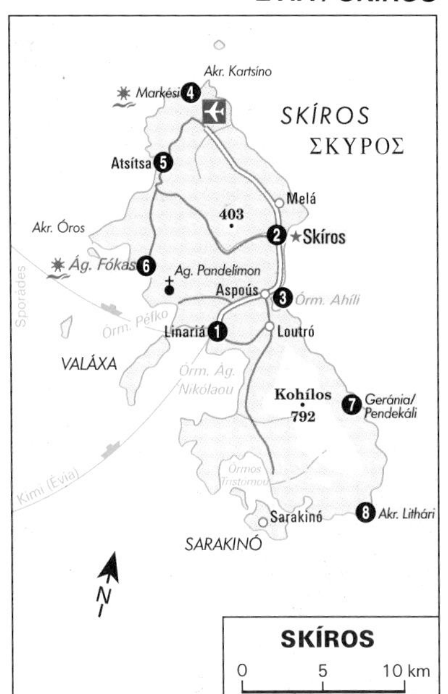

setting. A Venetian **Kástro** graces the town center. Near **Artemísio** ⓫, further east, an ancient shipwreck yielded two of the most famous bronze statues in Athens' National Archeological Museum: the *Striding God* and the *Boy Rider Clinging to his Horse's Back*.

SKÍROS

Isolated from its fellows and thus a bit aloof, Skíros is one of the less-known and thus less-frequented islands. This has allowed it to maintain its own character, traditions, and local dress, still sported by some older residents. Historically, its position has fated the island to serve either as a military base or as a hideout for freebooters. Pirates they were driven out as early as 470 B.C., when Kimon of Athens took the island, but were back in force on and off throughout the Middle Ages. The island was also a place of exile for people who had offended the Byzantine court. In 1821, it became a shelter for freedom fighters in the War of Indepen-

dence. Over the past few decades, the island's residents have untertaken measures to deal with their relative isolation; ferry connections have been established between Skíros and Kími on Évia.

"The Blessed" is an epithet for the island, coined partly because of the natural springs and rainfall that keeps its northern, pine-covered section green. Another natural gift was the particolored marble for which the island was quarried in Roman times. In the island's dryer southern section graze the *pikermies*, miniature ponies native to Skíros.

Linariá ❶, the island's port, is comparatively new; indeed, virtually all of it dates from after 1860. Skíros' main settlement is hilltop ***Skíros** (Hóra) ❷, topped, like any self-respecting island town, with the remains of a **Kástro**. The acme of this is the monastery of **Ágios Geórgios**, which the Byzantine emperors Nikeforas Fokas and John Tsimiskis founded in A.D. 962; the surrounding fortifications are medieval, of Byzantine and Venetian vintage.

The **Archeological Museum** contains finds from Skíros' most ancient settlement, Copper-Age **Palmari**, situated on the northern coast. Also displayed here is a typical Skirian house, its walls lined with plates and its mannequin inhabitants dressed up in local outfits. Another display of Skíros' traditions is presented in the **Faltaits Museum**, which is filled with traditional island ceramics and embroideries.

Below Skíros are the beaches of **Magaziá** and **Mólos**, where the island's nightlife is concentrated. In the extreme north, near **Markési** ❸, there are good beaches. **Atsítsa** ❹, is a charming village. Somewhat south of here, near **Ágios Fókas** ❺, stretches another lovely beach. **Órmos Ahíli** ❻ boasts a yacht harbor. The sea grottoes of **Pendekáli** and **Gerània** ❼ can be easily reached by boat, as can **Cape Litharí** ❽, with its tall lighthouse.

There are hourly buses from Athens to **Ágios Konstandínos** (2.5 hours) and **Volos** (5 hours); from here, boats and Flying Dolphins leave for the Sporades. There is also regular ferry service from Thessaloníki to the Sporades. There are regular boats between Skíathos, Skópelos and Alónnisos. There is also an irregular connection between Skíathos and Kími (Évia). Regular ferry service from Kími to Skíathos.

SKIÁTHOS (☎ 0427)

PLANE: Skiáthos airport (tel. 22200 or 22229) is about 2 km from Skiáthos Town. *BOAT:* See above; there are also connections to the Cyclades and Crete. Round trips from Skiáthos to Alónnisos and Skópelos, tel. 22417.

The **Association of Rooms to Rent**, tel. 22920, fax. 23852, has comprehensive listings. Simple rooms, tel. 21406.

SKIÁTHOS TOWN: $$ **Hotel Alkyon**, tel. 22981, fax. 21643. A generously proportioned modern building on the water, away from the busy section of the harbor, water views. **Hotel Pothos** and **Hotel Bourtzi**, tel. 22694, fax. 23242, central, clean and comfortable, with flowering courtyards. $ **Hotel Kastro**, tel. 22623, vine-draped balconies.

KOUKOUNARIÉS AREA: $$$ **Muses Hotel/ Bungalows**, tel. 49384, fax. 49440. Expansive complex, luxurious layout. **Skiáthos Palace**, tel. 22242. Ugly, but great views. $$ **Golden Beach**, tel. 49395. Decent place with balcony looking over woods. **TROÚLOS**: **Korali Hotel/Apartments**, Troulos, tel. 49212, fax. 49551, by the beach.

KOUKOUNARIÉS: **Camping Kukinariés**, tel. 49250.

SKIÁTHOS TOWN: Limanakia, by the water past the port, has good food geared to Western visitors. **Asprolithos**, tucked away, also has a good reputation. In the port, the *ouzeri* **Aigaion** offers local color, decent food. For a real Greek experience, **O Kiros** has zero décor, lots of cigarette smoke and locals, and cheap food lovingly prepared. **KANAPÍTSA:** Taverna **O Stathis** is the best of the bunch.

SKÓPELOS (☎ 0424)

Harbor Police, tel. 22235. **Port Authority**, tel. 22180. **Madro Travel**, books rooms and excursions, tel. 22145, fax. 22941.

BOAT: See above. *BUS / TAXI:* From the harbor of Skópelos. *CAR AND MOTORCLYCLE RENTAL:* **Moto Center**, tel. 23789.

Map p. 119

Association of Hotel Owners, tel. 23272, 22986. **SKÓPELOS TOWN: $$$ Skópelos Village**, tel. 22517, 23011, fax. 22958. Most upscale place on Skópelos, with comfortable apartments, harbor view, pool. **$$ Kavouris Hotel**, tel. 23238 or 22596, fax. 22596. Modest but modern family-run hotel. **Rooms to Rent**, tel. 22361, sweet little vine-covered building in the heart of the old town. **STAFILOS: $ Rooms to Rent**, 23917, pretty house on the way to the water. **AGNÓNDAS: $$ Pavlina**, tel. 23634, fax. 23272, apartments, located near the beautiful pine-shaded bay. **PANÓRMOS: $ Sandra**, tel. 20361, rooms to rent in a little house in a meadow, surrounded by woods. **LOUTRÁKI: $$ Hotel Avra**, tel 33550, 33526, a modern block, overlooks the island's second harbor.

SKÓPELOS: Two tavernas side by side near the ferry dock, **Klimataria**, tel. 22273, and **Molos**, claim to be the oldest in town; both are deservedly popular. **O Platanos**, tel. 23067, popular summer hangout. **Kipos tou Kalou**, tel. 22349, pleasant outdoor dining, lovely garden. **AGNÓNDAS: Pavlos**, tel. 22409, famous for its seafood. **LOUTRÁKI:** A good if simple waterside restaurant is **I Oraia Ellas**, "Beautiful Greece," tel. 33408.

Ethnographic Museum, tel. 23494.

ALÓNNISOS (☎ 0424)

Alónnisos Travel, tel. 65188. **Tourist Police**, tel. 65205.

BOAT: See above. **Port Authority**, tel. 65595.

Association of Hotel Owners, tel. 65212/3, fax. 65582. **Association of Rooms to Rent**, tel. 65573, fax. 65577. **PATITÍRI: $$$ Alkyon**, tel. 65602, fax. 65195, central, on the sea, balconies. **$$ Paradise**, tel. 65213, fax. 65161, pool. **Galaxy**, tel. 65251, fax. 65110, restaurant. **MARPOÚNDA: $$$ Marpoúnda**, tel. 65212, fax. 65582, bungalow complex with pool and tennis courts, on the beach.

PATITÍRI: To Kamáki, I. Dolópon, tel. 65245, excellent seafood.

ÉVIA (EUBOEIA)

HALKÍDA AND CENTRAL ÉVIA (☎ 0221; Kími 0222)

Eviorama Tours, Halkida, tel. 81420, fax. 88069, offers a range of services for visitors. **Municipality of Kími**, tel. 24000, fax. 22022.

BUS: Évia is connected by two bridges to the mainland at **Halkída**. Buses from Athens' Liossion depot run every 45 minutes from 6:30 am to 9 pm; the trip takes 90 minutes. From **Kími**, on Évia's north shore, 3.5 hours by bus from Athens, you can get boats and Flying Dolphins to **Skíros**. **Bus Station** in Halkída, tel. 22640. Regular buses to Athens (also from Kími). *TRAIN:* **Railway Station** in Halkída, tel. 22386; trains to Athens. *TAXI:* Tel. 22204, 89300 (Halkida), 23666 (Kími).

HALKÍDA: $$$ Lucy Hotel, Voudouri 10, tel. 23831, fax. 22051, looks right over the (bustling) water. **Paliria Hotel**, El. Venizelou 2, tel. 28001, fax. 81959 is modern, with roof garden. **ERÉTRIA: $$$ Malaconta Vogue Club Hotel**, tel. 60544, fax. 62518, pleasant complex with all the amenities. **$$ Delfis**, tel. 62380, nice in this price range. **KÍMI: $$ Korali**, tel. 22212.

HALKIDA: Ethnographic Museum, 13 Venizelou, tel. 76131, fax. 25131. Tue-Sun 8:30 am to 3 pm. **ERÉTRIA: Archeological Site** (and museum), tel. 62206, Tue-Sun 8:30 am to 3 pm. **KÍMI: Archeological Collection**, A. Potamia, tel. 71498, open Sun 10 am to 1 pm.

Káristos (☎ 0224)

BUS: **Bus Station**, tel. 22453. *BOAT:* Connections with Rafína and the Cyclades. **Káristos Port Authority**, tel. 22227. *TAXI:* Tel. 22200.

$$$ Apollon Suite Hotel, Psili Ammos, tel. 22045, fax. 22049, large, new, on the beach, open year-round. **$$ Amalia**, Bouros, tel. 22311.

Archeological Museum, Kriezotou, tel. 22472, Tue-Sun 8:30 am to 3 pm.

ÉDIPSOS (☎ 0226) / LÍMNI (☎ 0227)

Édipsos Port Authority, tel. 23317.

ÉDIPSOS is filled with hotels; there's even a **Club Med** (at Ágios Geórgios, tel. 33281, fax. 33115). **$$ Egli**, 25th Martiou 18, tel. 22217. **$$ Capri**, 25th Martiou 45, tel. 22496, not far from the baths. **LÍMNI: Hotel Limni**, tel. 32445 or 31374

Spa, Hydrotherapy and Physiotherapy Center, tel. 23501, fax. 23500.

SKÍROS (☎ 0222)

Municipality of Skíros, tel. 91716. **Tourist Information**, tel. 92789.

PLANE: **Olympic Airways**, tel. 91607. **Airport** near Markési, tel. 91625. *BOAT:* Ferries to Vólos, Thessaloníki and the Cyclades. **Port Authority**, tel. 91475. **Skíros Shipping Company** (operates boats to Kími), tel. 91789, fax. 91791.

$$ Pension Hara, tel. 91601, fax. 91763, attractive house 2 km away from Mólos, rooms with bath.

Archeological Site and Museum, tel. 91327. Site open daily 8:30 am to 9 pm; museum open Tue-Sun 8:30 am to 3 pm.

229D
CAT

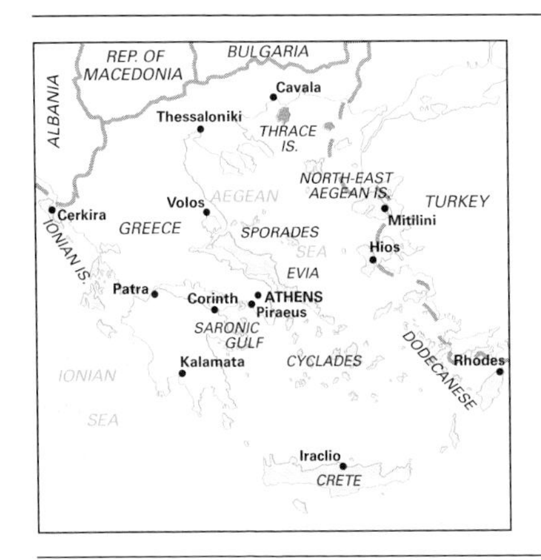

THE THRACIAN ISLANDS

THÁSOS
SAMOTHRÁKI

Both of the islands in the Thracian Sea, Thásos and Samothráki, have far more in common with the northeastern Greek mainland than with the other islands further south in the Aegean. Pine trees, mountains, even cold, snowy winters counterbalance the requisite beaches and blue waters; and the swimming season is far shorter than it is on, say, balmy Rhódos. Well off the Piraeus ferry routes that lead to the main tourist islands, both Thásos and Samothráki are easier to reach from the Macedonian (Kavala) or Thracian (Alexandroupoli) mainland, or by plane from Thessaloníki, than from other islands, including each other, and people who come here to vacation tend to stay put. There's no reason to leave: with plenty to explore, from mountain forests to ancient ruins, and great beaches, each of these islands has more than enough to occupy a visitor for weeks.

*THÁSOS

Its northern climate has the disadvantage of winter snow, reflected in the pitched roofs of its houses; but it also gives it a lushness that made Thásos, in the eyes of Lawrence Durrell, "one of those delights among islands." Freshwater springs and cattle grazing in the meadows are features of the landscape on this perfectly round island, circumnavigated by a coastal road running around its mountainous center.

Left: In the marble quarry by Liménas, Thásos.

In mythology, Thásos was a relative of the Phoenician maiden Europa, who found the island in the course of his search for his sister after Zeus had carried her off. Páros was a close ally of the island, and set up a colony here in the 7th century B.C.; later, the island was hard hit by the Persians who kept passing by on their way to Athens (in 490 and 480 B.C.). Other foreign powers who held sway here included the Russians, who had it for four years in the late 18th century, and, not long after, the Egyptians: Mehmet Ali, 19th viceroy of Egypt, spent part of his childhood here, and loved the island so much that the Sultan turned it over to him in 1813. This meant the island had a lot more autonomy than many other Greek islands, since the viceroy lowered taxes and gave it special privileges; Egyptian rule lasted until 1902.

Thásos ❶, also called Liménas, is built on the site of ancient Thásos, and is chockablock with ruins and relics, some of which are displayed to advantage in the excellent **Archeological Museum**. From the 7th to 5th centuries B.C., the harbor

Map p. 124, Info p. 127

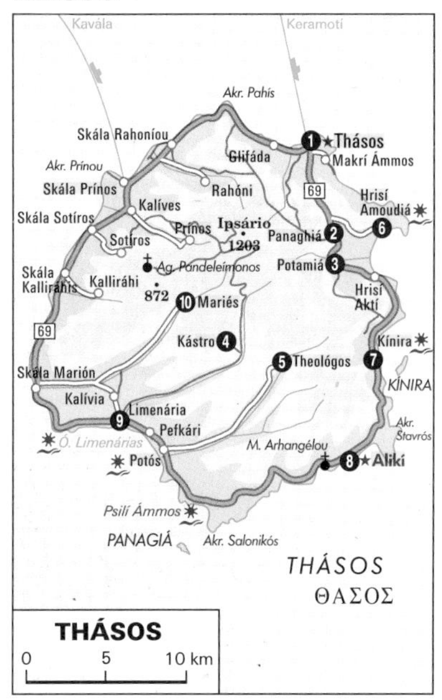

was fortified with walls of the local marble: Thásos was a center for marble export from antiquity until early modern times. One of the older sites is the **Herakleion**, dedicated to the island's patron deity, worshiped here as long ago as Phoenican times. Later, the Romans came, building an **Agorá** which still stands north of the town center. The ancient **Theater of Dionysus** still hosts performances in summer; excavations are still going on nearby. Another highlight are the remains of the ancient **Acropolis**, including a temple to Pythian Apollo later worked into an Italian fortress.

Makrí Ámmos is the town beach, but visitors now have to pay to use it; however, the whole stretch of coast west of it is also strewn with beaches, such as **Glifáda**, accessible by bus. Inland, **Panaghía** ❷ and **Potamiá** ❸ are attractive mountain villages with wooden balconies

Right: At the foot of the mountain villages of Potamiá and Panagía stretches the lovely sand beach of Hrisí Amoudía (Thásos).

and slate roofs reflecting the architecture of mainland Epirus and Macedonia, although the arched doorways which are a distinctive feature of the island's buildings help identify them as uniquely Thassian. The latter's **Museum Vágis** is devoted to the work of a local sculptor, Polýnotos Vágis (1894-1965).

Both villages are nestled in the pine forests on the slopes of **Mount Ipsário**, some 1,204 meters at its highest point and the start of hiking trails up to its summit. Hardy walkers can continue on to **Kástro** ❹, a half-deserted village whose houses are being reclaimed as vacation homes, where there are traces of Byzantine settlement, which can also be reached from Limenária (see below). In **Theológos** ❺, the island's former capital (reached from Potós), the Genoese castle of **Kourokástro** once stood. Near the latter are a number of trails for rock climbers. On the eastern shore, a stretch of beach runs between **Skála Panaghía** and **Skála Potamiá**, with camping at **Hrisí Amoudía** ❻. Further south on this east coast, there's a nudist beach at **Kínira** ❼.

On the southeastern coast, two lovely beaches flank the peninsula of ***Alikí** ❽, which in antiquity was a center for the export of marble from Mount Ipsário, and where marble relics of the past still abound, from an old marble quarry to the ruins of an archaic temple. Nudists frequent the stony beach at **Arhangélou**, below the convent of the same name.

Potós and **Limenária** ❾ are the main towns in the southwest; Limenária, in particular, is popular with tourists, thanks to its beach and its charm. At Easter, the villagers here dance in their traditional folk costumes. Above the village is the "little palace," Palatáki, built as offices by the German mining company Spiedel around 1900. Nearby **Psilí Ámmos** is one of the best sand beaches on the island. In general, Thásos' west coast is less interesting than the rest of the island, though its beaches tend to be emptier. Most of the

 Info p. 127

"Skálas," or waterside villages, along here were founded in the 20th century and are associated with older inland villages, such as picturesque **Mariés** ⓾, whose church has some nice frescoes, **Prínos**, or **Rahóni**, which are among the more untouched on the island. At **Skála Prínos**, ferries dock from Kavala; you can also see an oil platform offshore.

SAMOTHRÁKI

Samothráki, adored by nature lovers and hikers, is best known for the Winged Victory in the Louvre, one of the most famous statues of Classical Greece. As her pose suggests, this *Nike* (Victory) was originally the figurehead of a marble ship; Demetrios Poliorcetes, who also commissioned the Colossus of Rhodes, had her made as part of an offering of thanks to the gods for his victory over Ptolemy II in 305 B.C.

However, those who know Samothráki best for its goddess are taking up an ancient tradition: for Samothráki was a leading religious center of the ancient world. This rocky, rugged island, which doesn't even have a natural harbor, was the base of the cult of the Cabiri, ancient Phrygian or Phoenician gods (the word means "the mighty ones") whose rites predated that of Classical Greece, and persisted, in all their mystery, until the Byzantines forced them to stop in the 4th century A.D. Attesting to the power of this cult is the extensive site of **Paleópoli** ❶, seven kilometers east of the harbor, where ongoing excavations continue to uncover more and more elements of the Sanctuary of the Great Gods; it was here that the Winged Victory was originally found, in 1863.

The ***Sanctuary of the Great Gods** was dedicated to underworld deities; like the Eleusinian Mysteries, little was recorded of the secrets of their cult, although it was less restricted than the Eleusinian Mysteries, and non-initiates were even allowed to view the rites. Initiates or *Saoi* ("rescued ones") included figures from Philip of Macedon to

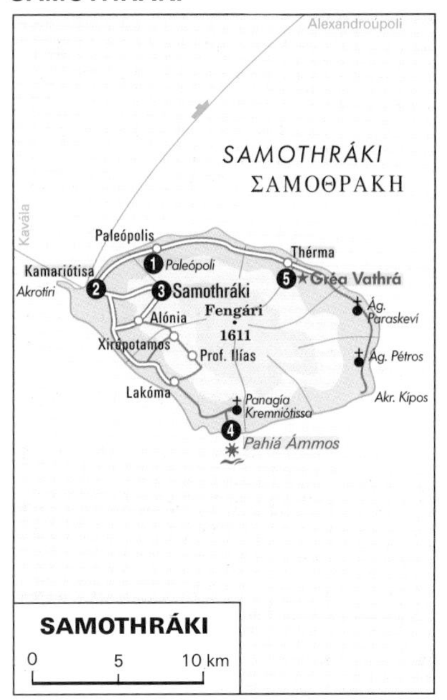

Herodotus; it is still not altogether clear, however, what gods they were worshiping. Certainly they were fertility gods, with a mother goddess figure related to Great Goddesses of Asia Minor; and the Cabiri were later incorporated into Greek and Roman mythology, in a lesser role, as the divine twins Castor and Pollux.

That the fertility gods granted the wishes of mortals is evidenced by the **Arsinoeion**, the ruin of the largest round building in ancient Greece (20 meters in diameter), Queen Arsinoë's gesture of thanks to the gods for the birth of her child (ca. 280 B.C.). More central to the initiation rites were the **Anaktorion** ("House of Lords," 6th century B.C.) and the **Hieron** (3rd century B.C.); five of the latter's Doric columns have been re-erected, framing a view of green pine and blue water through their unsteady drums. The **museum** on site contains other findings from the ongoing excavations, which began in 1948.

Above Right: Only a few of the columns of the Sanctuary of the Great Gods still stand on Samothráki.

Samothráki's port is **Kamariótisa** ❷, with a rocky beach; this is where most of the island's accommodation and tourist facilities can be found. Most of the residents, on the other hand, dwell inland at the idyllic island capital of **Samothráki** (Hóra) ❸, which, with its rustic houses and a bazaar, invites visitors to tarry here. The ruins of a Genoan castle tower above the town. From here, hikers can make the several hours' ascent to **Mount Fengari** ("Mount Moon"), at more than 1,611 meters the highest peak in the Aegean. This snow-capped mountain of white marble was supposedly where Poseidon sat to watch the Trojan War.

From Kamariótisa, you can also travel by boat to the beach of **Pahiá Ammos** ❹ or the **Kremastá Nerá** waterfall, on the south coast. On the north coast is the natural hot spring of **Thérma** ❺, known since antiquity. East of Thérma, near **★Gréa Váthra**, waterfalls and freshwater ponds are inviting places to cool off in.

THÁSOS (☎ 0593)

Thásos Tourist Association, tel. 22289. **Tourist Police**, tel. 23580. **Thásos Harbor Authority**, tel. 22106.

BOAT: Daily ferries to and from Kavála (from Thásos Town and Prínos) and Keramoti (from Thásos Town). Once-daily hydrofoil to Samothráki (from Thásos Town).

THÁSOS TOWN: $$$ **Makriammos Bungalows**, tel. 22101, fax. 22761, situated on a beautiful beach, with all the requisite amenities. **Amfipolis**, tel. 23101, fax. 22110, attractive converted old building, set back somewhat from the water, with its own pool and restaurant.

$$ **Makedon**, tel. 22177, modern block in the trees, with a small pool. **Aithria**, tel. 22310, with pool, on the edge of town. **Pegasus**, tel. 22373 or 22061, functional, basic, but clean rooms, with pool and restaurant. **Timoleon**, tel. 22177, your standard seaside block, but well furnished. **Filoxenia Inn**, tel. 23331, fax. 22231, a modern house with aspirations to villa-hood, with a small pool.

PANAGÍA: $$ **Thásos Inn**, tel. 61612, all rooms with balcony. $ **Theo**, tel. 61284, quiet hotel, friendly owner.

SKÁLA PRÍNOS: $$ **Kazaviti**, tel. 71650, fax. 71812, a pleasant villa with pool and restaurant. $ **America**, tel. 71322, rooms with balconies.

SKÁLA POTAMIÁ: $$ **Ariadni**, tel. 61591, bungalow-style accommodations, with its own restaurant.

SKÁLA RAHÓNI: $$ **Coral**, tel. 81247, balconied house pleasantly surrounded by shade trees, with balconies and a pool.

POTÓS: $$$ **Alexandra Beach**, tel. 51766, green lawns, outdoor terraces, pool. **Coral Beach Hotel**, tel. 52402, fax. 52424, appealing red-roofed complex set on the eponymous swatch of sand beach, outdoor pool. $$ **Hatzigiorgis**, tel. 51212, small but adequate, with restaurant.

PEFKÁRI: $$ **Thásos**, tel. 51596, fax. 51794, with its own beach as well as pool. **Pefkari**, tel. 51341, fax. 51877, pleasant, villa-like building on the beach, with restaurant, at the edge of town. $ **Prasino Velouso**, tel. 52175, fax. 51232, constructed in the blockiest apartment-block style, but carefully tended.

LIMENARIA: $$ **Ralitsas**, tel. 51578, fax. 52878, situated right on the beach. $ **Papantoniou**, tel. 51363, fax. 52070, located above a café, reasonable rooms.

ASTRÍS: $$ **Astrís Sun Hotel**, tel. 51281, fax. 52861, on the busy beach of Astris Bay, not far from Potós.

SKÁLA PRÍNOS: Prinos Campsite, tel. 71171 or 71270, room for 810 people, snack bar and supermarket.
SKÁLA RAHÓNI: Perseus Camping, tel. 81242.
PEFKÁRI: Pefkári Camping, tel. 51595.
HRISÍ AMOUDÍA: Hrisí Amoudía Camping, tel. 61207.
The two latter campgrounds are expecially nice, though somewhat isolated.

THÁSOS TOWN: Iphigi is a popular taverna. The somewhat higher-class **Zorbas** features live music; slightly more expensive. **Platanakia**, on the water, is known for its fish.
SKÁLA PRINOS: Kyriakos Taverna, central, good standard Greek fare.

Archeological Museum, Meg. Alexandrou 18 (Thásos Town), tel. 22180.

EVENTS: A **Festival of Ancient Drama** is held in Thásos' Ancient Theater every summer. Contact the tourist office for information.

SAMOTHRÁKI (☎ 0551)

Tourist Police, Samothráki (Hóra), tel. 41203. **Port Authority**, 21305. **Niki Tours**, tel. 41465, fax. 41304, can help with rooms and transportation.

BOAT: Daily ferry service to and from Alexandrúpolis (approximately 2 hours); also regular service to Kavála and Límnos. Once-daily hydrofoil to Thásos.

KAMARIOTISSA: $$$ **Hotel Aeolos**, tel. 41595, fax. 41810, largest and most pleasant on the island. $$ **Niki Beach**, tel. 41561, is right on the water and open year-round.

PALEÓPOLI: $$ **Hotel Xenia**, tel. 41230, small, by the site of the excavated ruins of the old city.

THÉRMA: $$$ **Hotel Kaviros**, tel. 41577, ideal for those who come to enjoy the hot mineral springs and waterfalls.

KAMARIÓTISA: Orízontas, tel. 41793. Very good taverna at the ferry landing.
THÉRMA: Fengari, fish and meat dishes from the clay oven, rather expensive. **Paradise**, excellent seafood dishes.

Archeological Site and **Museum** (Sanctuary of the Great Gods), tel. 41474, open Tuesday-Sunday, 9 am to 2 pm.

The sulfer-rich mineral waters of the baths at **Thérma** are supposed to be good for arthritis and gynecological complaints. A bath in the thermal waters is also pleasant for those without any medical needs. For information, contact the Town Hall of Thérma, tel. 41218, fax. 41204.

THE NORTHEAST AEGEAN ISLANDS

LÍMNOS
LÉSVOS
HÍOS
IKARÍA
SÁMOS

Large and wooded, nearer to Turkey than to Greece or to each other, the Northeast Aegean Islands are worlds unto themselves, set apart from Greek Island stereotypes. These are not islands to "hop": ferry links between them are regular but infrequent, and each is big enough to occupy at least a week for even the most peripatetic vacationer. Furthermore, interesting boat excursions are offered to the one-time Greek west of Turkey and the world-famous archeological sights found there, such as the ancient cities of Miletus and Ephesus.

Proximity to the Turkish coast helped shape the character of these islands from the 15th to the 20th century. In general, the Northeast Aegean Islands had a less hostile relationship to their Ottoman overlords than many of the other islands in the Aegean; the Sultans especially favored Híos, which supplied them with the mastic that they found so important. These islands didn't even become part of Greece until 1912; not long thereafter, they bore the brunt of the wave of refugees when the Greek population was expelled from Turkish Anatolia in 1923.

Previous Pages: A Byzantine castle looks down on the picturesque village of Míthima (Mólivos), Lésvos. Left: In the 16th-century monastery of Megalí Panagías on Sámos.

Part of the legacy of this historic past is an Oriental flavor that continues to flourish today in the narrow, bazaar-like streets of Mitilíni or Híos Town. Another legacy of the proximity to Turkey is a strikingly high military presence; hikers just might find themselves suddenly confronted by a wire fence marking the periphery of an army installation. It goes without saying that photography in such areas is strictly prohibited.

Being islands, of course, these locales have their share of beaches, and consequently, of the tourist trade: Lésvos and Sámos, in particular, have thriving resorts complete with yacht harbors and active nightlife. Those who want to get away from it all can seek out tiny Psará or the empty and beautiful beaches of green Ikaría for an island holiday with a difference.

LÍMNOS

Assigned to the administrative division of the Northeast Aegean Islands, Límnos has little in common even with its disparate fellows. Scenically, it is pleasant if unspectacular, with low, rolling hills; agriculturally, it traditionally produced cotton and wheat, not common crops elsewhere on the islands, as well as its own distinctively-flavored wine.

Map p. 132, Info pp. 154-155

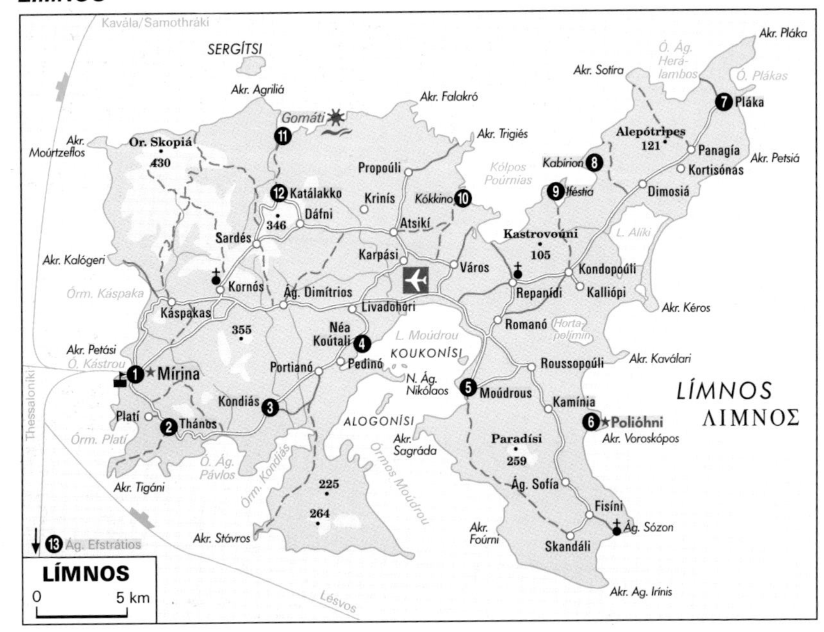

Límnos is known as the island of the blacksmith god Hephaistos, who set up his forge here when his father Zeus cast him out of Olympus. When Hephaistos' wife, Aphrodite, began her affair with Ares, the women of Límnos reported the betrayal to Hephaistos. As punishment, Aphrodite gave them a strong body odor which so turned off their husbands that they went off and got new wives from Thrace. After this, their rejected wives got them drunk and threw them all off **Cape Petrassos**, near the village of **Androni**. Fortunately, according to Homer, the Argonauts passed by soon thereafter on their search for the Golden Fleece and found the island full of unattached women; thus Límnos' population was able to regenerate.

The eruptions of volcanic Mount Moschylos created the sulfurous soil valued for its healing properties since antiquity. So sacred was it that only a small amount could leave the island; in antiquity, a priestess dug it up on a certain day of the year, while in Christian times, a priest performed the task on August 6, the day of the transfiguration. Its source is located near the old Byzantine city of Kotsinas, probably a corruption of the word *kokkinos*, or "red"; the color of the soil.

Right: A good example of the best way to deal with the heat of a summer afternoon.

The ruins of 12th-century **Paleókastro** sprawl across the hilltop by the harbor of ***Mírina** ❶, the island's capital (also known as Hóra or Kástro). The elegant waterfront here consists of sedate 19th-century houses lined along the beach of **Romeikós Gialós**. This "Roman" beach was so called to distinguish it from **Tourkikós Gialós**, the Turkish beach in the former Ottoman quarter down the shore. Along Romeikós Gialós are the **Archeological Museum** and the **Metropolitan Mansion**, which contains an Ecclesiastical Museum.

The beach of **Thános** ❷, a few kilometers southeast of town, is one of the best on the island; and **Kondiás** ❸, further east, is one of Límnos' most traditional

Info pp. 154-155

villages. By contrast, **Néa Koútali** ❹ was first settled in 1926 after the exodus from Asia Minor forced the islanders of Koútali from their homes; its beach is perhaps the best on **Moúdrou Bay**, one of the largest natural harbors in the Mediterranean. It was from this beach that the Anglo-French attack was launched that culminated in the defeat at Gallipoli during World War I (1914-16); the town of **Moúdrous** ❺, across the bay, still has a strong military presence and also tends the Commonwealth War Cemetery.

Located on the island's eastern coast is ***Polióhni** ❻, site of the oldest settlement on Límnos, which dates back to the end of the 4th millennium B.C., and is therefore even older than Troy across the water on the Turkish mainland. Like Troy, the city has several levels of settlement, extending up to as recently as 100 B.C.; also like Troy, it housed a wealth of gold jewelry, excavated in this century, not unlike the gold that Schliemann found at Troy and dubbed "Priam's Treasure." In **Kamínia**, the town nearest the site, an ancient stele is built into the wall of the church of **Ágios Alexándros**; the inscription is written in Greek characters, but in an unrecognizable language.

Pláka ❼, at the island's northeastern tip, is another ancient site. Tradition has it that it was here that Agamemnon ordered the lighting of the first beacon signaling the end of the Trojan War. Offshore, visible on a clear, still day, is a sunken village identified as Homer's **Hrísi**.

Two of the island's other major archeological sites are on the northeastern shore here: the **Kabírion** ❽, where mysteries were celebrated, like the ones at Samothráki to the north, and **Íféstia** ❾, on the other side of the bay, Límnos' most important town from the 8th century to the 11th century A.D., when its harbor silted up and the population center shifted to Kotsinas. Still visible here are remains of the temple to the Great Goddess of Límnos (8th-6th centuries B.C.), as well as the ancient theater.

The fortress of **Kókkino** ❿ was built by the Venetians in the 14th century.

Info pp. 154-155

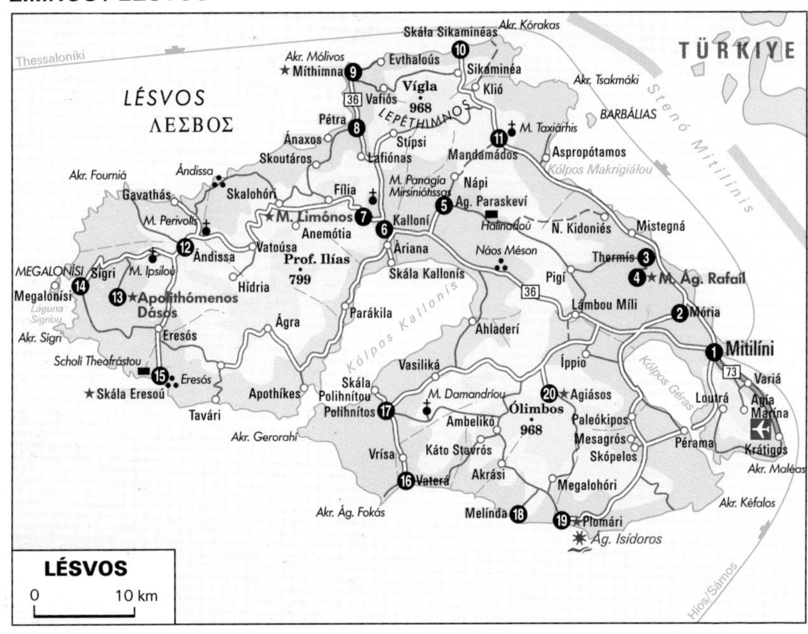

Gomáti ⓫, west of here, is one of the sandiest beaches on the island, facing the uninhabited island of Sergítsi. On a cliff above the beach stands the picturesque village of **Katálakko ⓬**. Fans of smaller islands can also catch a ferry from Mírini to **Ágios Efstrátios ⓭**, a large part of which still belongs to the "Holy Community of Sacred Mount Athos," the autonomous monastic republic on Chalkidike. Settled in the 17th century, it served as a place of exile for political prisoners between 1936 and 1963, poet Jánnis Rítsos and composer Mikis Theodorakis among them. In 1968, it was hit by an earthquake; as a result, today's population resides in ugly concrete houses.

LÉSVOS (LÉSBOS, MITILÍNI)

Lésvos is the third-largest island in Greece after Crete and Évia. The island's common name, Lesbos, is pronounced "Lesvos" in Greek, and has no association whatsoever with gay women. The island is also often called Mitilíni, the name of it's main town. The "Island of the Olives" is a kind of Greece in minature, with extensive olive groves and wooded mountains accessible only along donkey paths, fishing villages and salt flats, medieval castles, a petrified forest, and even its own Mount Olympus – although, since there were more than a dozen Mount Olympuses at last count, this isn't, after all, such a great distinction.

Since earliest antiquity, Lésvos has been a cradle of culture. The first name that comes to most minds is that of the poet Sappho (ca. 615-562 B.C.), although the number of lesbian Lesbians may never have been inordinate: Sappho was notable for her open praise of women and for founding a women's academy in the groves of her native town of Eresós, but she was also married, had a daughter, and ultimately committed suicide out of unrequited love for a man (or so the story goes, at any rate).

Right: The landscape of Lésvos is marked by olive groves.

Before Sappho, before actual history, Orpheus drifted to these shores: at least, his head did, after the poet had been torn limb from limb by frenzied Maenads. The head was still singing, and charmed the beasts with its music until the gods put a stop to it.

The artistic spark has survived to the present century. The novelist Stratís Mirivílis (1892-1969), for example, set his novels in the fishing villages of northern Lésvos. Another local son of Lésvos was Theófilos Hatzimihaílis (1868-1934), a naïve painter who was dubbed "the Greek Rousseau" after a one-man show of his work in the Louvre in 1934. His "discoverer" was another Lesbian, Stratís Eleftheriádis, better known as Tériade, who settled in Paris and made a name for himself as a publisher of limited-edition art folios by Picasso, Chagall, Matisse, Giacometti, and many other leading lights. In **Variá**, just south of Mitilíni, the ***Tériade Museum** has a unique collection of original color lithographs and art books by these and other famous painters.

Lésvos has more olive trees than any other Greek island; more than 10 million of them shimmer silvery-green over its slopes. Lesbian olive oil is supposed to be the best in Greece: some 20 to 30 thousand tons are produced each year. The other signature liquid exported from the island is ouzo, the famous spirit distilled from anis seeds; there are a number of well-known distilleries in and around Plomári.

Mitilíni and Environs

Lésvos' capital, **Mitilíni** ❶, is a tough, scrappy port city with character, framed by a periphery of lovely if fading Italianate villas and by the ruins of the largest medieval **Kástro** in Greece, begun in the 6th century under the Byzantine emperor Justinian. Like the Eternal City, Mitilíni is laid out upon seven hills, though they

are considerably smaller than Rome's; and indeed, the city has continued to regenerate upon the same site since earliest antiquity, something attested to by the hilltop ruins of its **Ancient Theater** (3rd century B.C.), also one of Greece's largest, and famous for its excellent acoustics (summer concerts are also given in the ruins of the castle).

Dominating the waterline today are the domes of **Ágios Therapón**, imposing from a distance but so nestled into the warren of streets that if you're on foot you don't see it until it's right on top of you. It, too, stands on an ancient site – originally, there was a temple here, and then an earlier Christian church – but the building itself is of more recent vintage, dating for the most part from this century. A small **Byzantine Museum** in its forecourt contains icons and other ecclesiastical treasures.

Not far from the ferry landing is the genteel villa that houses part of the city's interesting ***Archeological Museum**. In 1999, the main exhibition was moved to a

new building on Odós 8 Noemvríou Square. On the square's extension, Odós Mikrás Asías, stands the ★**Municipal Art Gallery**, in which more than 80 works of the great painter Theófilos can be seen.

Mitilíni stands on the island's southwestern peninsula; buses run down to the beaches at its tip, as well as to the airport. North of town, at **Mória** ❷, fragments of a Roman aqueduct are tottering testimony to a double-arched conduit that once bore water 26 kilometers. The Romans were well versed in the positive attributes of the local waters; the mineral springs at **Thermís** ❸ saw their heyday during Roman settlement, although they were already in use during the first millennium B.C., and settlement on the site dates back to the Stone Age.

In the Hellenistic period, the area was associated with the goddess Artemis – strong women were evidently something of a Lésvos fixture – whose ruined temple was abandoned after the coming of Christianity. The monastery of ★**Ágios Rafaíl** ❹ to the southwest holds the remains of the wonder-working saints Rafaíl, Nikólaos and Iríni. It is an important place of pilgrimage.

Above: In Mitilíni Town. Right: Women are not allowed into the monastery of Limónos.

Míthimna and the North

The quickest route from Mitilíni to Míthimna (also called Mólivos) leads through the center of the island, where the flat Gulf of Kallonís ends in broad salt marshes where horses graze. The wild horses that once lived on Lésvos have largely been supplanted by the domestic variety, who show their stuff in the annual races at the three-day-long **Festival of the Bull** (on the second Sunday after Orthodox Easter) in **Agía Paraskeví** ❺. Celebrated since 1774, and betraying certain pagan overtones, the festival also involves a procession with a garlanded bull. The ruins of the early Christian basilica of **Halinadoú** (6th century) southeast of Ágia Pareskeví are also worth a look.

Map p. 134, Info pp. 154-155

Another specialty of the **Gulf of Kallonís** is its seafood, especially sardines, which, lightly battered and fried (in olive oil, of course), are one of the island's culinary specialties. They're served in the port town of **Kalloní** ❻, the shallow waters of which attract bird watchers and families with small children to the beach at **Skála Kallonís**.

The 15th-century nunnery of **Mirsiniótissas** is impressive for the flower gardens in its interior courtyard. It is located 2.5 kilometers north of Kalloní. Built in 1527, ***Limónos Monastery** ❼ to the west is an important religious center, but its frescoed church is off-limits to women, although they can get into the small museum.

West of Mólivos is **Pétra** ❽, another holiday town stretched along a strip of beach. A notable landmark here is the church of: **Panagía Glikfoúsa** ("Our Lady of the Sweet Smile"), which sits in the midst of town on an abrupt upthrust of rock (the *petra* – Greek for "rock" – of the town's name). It's reached by 114 steps hewn into the living stone, an ascent the faithful make on their knees during the festival of the Assumption of the Virgin on August 15. Near the foot of this rocky tower is the church of ***Ágios Nikólaos**, less spectacular on the outside, but with 16th-century frescos inside that are lovely, though in sad condition.

On a balcony above Pétra's main square is a sign for the **Women's Agricultural Cooperative**, going strong since 1983. Born of local women's sense of frustration at their lack of muscle in the community, this cooperative has enabled them to bring in extra income by renting out rooms and selling a bit of what they make on the side. Through ups and downs, the cooperative has become successful enough to spawn emulation; there are now 14 such cooperatives throughout the Greek Islands.

If you want a taste of farm life and aren't staying with a member of the Cooperative, it's a pleasant uphill stroll south to the village of **Lafiónas**, where there are great views down over Pétra and

Mólivos, mules are the preferred form of transport, and there are hardly any tourists at all. But the same distance on foot towards the coast will bring you to a string of beaches: quiet **Avláki**; **Ánaxos**, an increasingly booming resort; and, tranquil **Ambélia**.

Capping the northern tip of the island is ★**Míthimna** (Mólivos) ❾, rising up its hilltop to the crown of its medieval castle with picture-postcard perfection. This perfection draws crowds of summer visitors; although Mólivos has the wherewithal to handle them, it's not an ideal destination for anyone looking to get away from it all. Still, everyone should stroll through its narrow shop-lined streets, a verdant and fragrant arcade with a translucent roof of wisteria vines.

There are mementos of Turkish rule in the Arabic inscriptions on some of the stone fountains set into the walls.

Above: Petrified trees – a special attraction on Lésvos. Right: At the beach of Vaterá in windy spring weather.

Mólivos boasts its own small **Art Museum**, with works of local artists, and an **Archeological Museum**. The Byzantine **Kástro** commands a view out over the local beaches and across the channel to nearby Turkey.

A two-hour hike eastward through **Evthtaloús**, with its thermal springs, brings you past the ochre-striped cliffs of pebbly **Golden Beach** to the beautiful little fishing village of **Skála Sikaminéas** ❿, its harbor guarded by a tiny chapel perched atop a rock, charmingly commemorated by Stratís Mirivíllis in his novel *The Mermaid Madonna*. Fishermen carefully mend their nets by the water, while behind them the tables of the tiny village's few restaurants seem to merge into a single giant café under the mulberry tree and vines. Somewhat further south, **Sikaminéa** itself surveys the scene and marks the winding overland road back; unfortunately, there's no bus service between Skála Sikaminéas and Mólivos.

This northeast corner of the island is a good area for hiking, centered as it is around the **Lepéthimnos** range. One trail leads from the village of **Vafiós**, southeast of Míthimna, up to the peak of **Profítas Ílias** (937 meters), from where you can continue on to the main peak, **Vígla** (968 meters), and on down to Evthaloús: however, the route in its entirety is long and strenuous, and should not be attempted in the heat of the day in summer.

Inland from here, although more easily accessible from the south, is the village of **Mandamádos** ⓫ with its stone houses, the largest settlement in this area. Nearby is a monastery dedicated to the island's patron saint, **Taxiárhis Mihaílis** ("Archangel Michael"). Its jewel is a miracle-working dark icon that was supposedly made of the blood-soaked clay from the ground where marauding pirates slew a bevy of earlier monks, and is said to exude the aroma of wildflowers.

Map p. 134, Info pp. 154-155

The West of the Island

The road passes the 17th-century monastery of **Perivólis**, which has some beautiful frescoes, on the way west to **Ándissa** ⓬; today's village, inland, is a few kilometers from the ancient harbor settlement of the same name, which you can reach on foot from **Gavathás** (about one kilometer). Further west, atop the extinct volcano of Ordimnos, sits the monastery of **Ipsiloú**, established in 1101 in the name of St. John the Theologian.

Here, visitors can also see some pieces of petrified wood: part of Lésvos' ***Petrified Forest**. Forested no more, this area is strewn with the fossilized trunks of conifers that grew here some 15 to 20 million years ago. Perfectly preserved by layers of volcanic ash, they demonstrate rings, bark, leaves and seeds. Some of the best specimens are near Sígri in the **Apolithómenos Dásos** ⓭ nature park, and on the offshore islet of **Nissiópi**, and there's even an underwater section of forest. **Sígri** ⓮ itself is a pleasant fishing village with an 18th-century castle built by the Turks and nice bays for swimming.

The highlight of the area is ***Skála Eresoú** ⓯, with a wonderful three-kilometer-long sand beach, simple restaurants and inexpensive rooms. A number of gay women are attracted by the fact that Sappho was born and lived here; in antiquity, the coins of Eresós even bore her portrait.

The South of Lésvos

On Lésvos' southern coast, swimmers can head to **Vaterá** ⓰, at 11 kilometers the longest beach on the island; at one end of the swathe of brownish sand is **Ágios Fokás**, where the ruins of an old temple to Dionysus stand within an old Christian basilica. About eight kilometers north of Vaterá is **Polhinítos** ⓱, with some very hot thermal springs. To the east, the coast is steep and spectacular; in a sturdy car, you can get away from it all in **Melínda** ⓲, with some basic accommodation and a nice beach. From here to Plomári, the

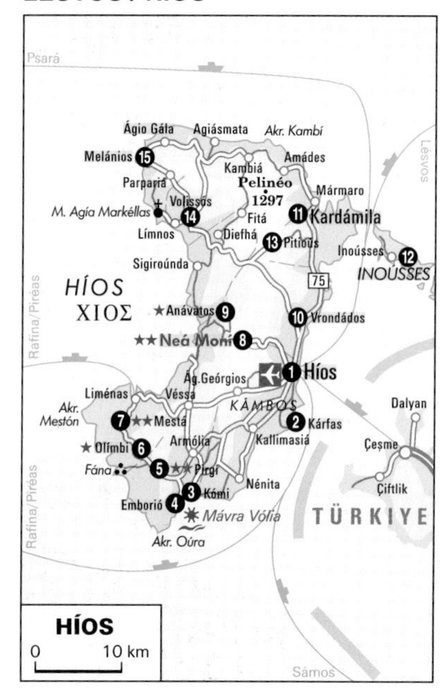

road is high, dusty and very scenic – for those with a head for heights.

***Plomári** ⓳ itself, Lésvos' second-largest town, has retained its original character, and is best known for its ouzo distilleries (**Barbagiánnis** is one of the better-known). It has a pleasant square on the water lined with tourist restaurants, and, a bit out of town, a small ouzo museum. **Ágios Isídoros**, a pebble and sand beach further east, is generally acknowledged as the best beach on the south coast – and is correspondingly crowded. In the inland section of this part of the island rises the 968-meter-high **Mount Ólimbos**. On its slopes is ***Agiásos** ⓴, a much-visited specimen of a "typical" mountain village with a pretty church, to which thousands of pilgrims make their way on August 15. For walkers, there's a trail up Ólimbos (takes about three hours)

Right: The skulls of the murdered monks of the monastery of Néa Moní on Híos are reminders of the massacre of the island's populace in 1822.

and another from here to Plomari past the ruins of ancient **Paleókastro**: it's a good day's hike.

HÍOS (CHÍOS)

Híos is a wonderful island. It has a flavor all its own, and always has. Even in the days of the Delian League, "Chian Life" was proverbially high, and a "Chian laugh" described a person of sunny temperament, even if no one was quite sure what there was to be so happy about (apart from the renowned Chian wine perhaps). The Chians knew, though. They had a great home, with a wide range of landscapes, natural harbors, secluded pebble beaches or longer sand ones, forests and mountains. The Genoans knew, too, when they came in 1346; their Maona company regulated the island's rich trade, while they built residential villas in the plain known as Kambos, south of Híos Town. The Genoans may not have been the kindest masters; still, one traveler described Híos as "heaven on earth." And the Turks, who took over in 1566, knew as well. Híos was the favorite island of the Sultans, accorded special privileges and such a degree of autonomy that the standard of living was higher here than virtually anywhere else in present-day Greece: one reason, no doubt, for the contentment of its residents.

One Chian commodity prized by all of its inhabitants was – and is – the mastic which grows abundantly in the south of the island. Mastic trees, low shrubs related to the pistachio, yield a sticky resin that was used in the Middle Ages as everything from a healing agent to a breath freshener – popular in the Sultans' harems; Híos still produces everything from mastic toothpaste and mastic gum to an ingredient in paint. And mastic (*Pistachia Lentiscus Var Chia*) grows only on Híos, and only in the southern part of the island, where the 21 little towns whose economies centered around its cultivation

Map (Lésvos) p. 134, Info pp. 154-155

and production are still known as the "Mastichochoría," the mastic villages, and have retained their medieval air. Mastic, of course, is no longer as much in demand as it once was. Today, in addition to the above-mentioned items, it is used in the manufacture of "spoon sweets," in this case a viscous white paste, a spoonful of which is submerged in a glass of water. You sip the lightly flavored water as you slowly eat the sweet – probably *very* slowly, unless you develop a taste for this resinous confection.

But Híos' days of happiness were numbered. In 1821, the island initially opted to stay aloof from the War of Independence which the Greek states were waging on Turkey; in 1822, however, a fleet from neighboring Sámos landed and proclaimed the revolution, leaving the Chians with little choice but to take sides. It was a bad move. The rebels were under-equipped and under-prepared, and no help was forthcoming from the central leadership at Athens, already overtaxed. The Sultan, like a lover scorned, demonstrated a hellish fury by making an example of his once-favorite island: in June, 1822, his fleet arrived and basically wiped out Híos, sparing only the mastic area in the south. Men were killed, women and children sold into slavery, buildings and property destroyed. Effective as it may have been, this move was very bad PR on the part of the Turks: the scale of the tragedy drew the attention of continental Europe; Victor Hugo wrote a poem about it (*L'Enfant*); Eugene Delacroix executed a famous painting (*The Massacre of Chíos*; now in the Louvre); and these and other expressions of sympathy inflamed sentiments for the Greek cause. The Sultan tried to cover for the mistake by exiling the general responsible and appealing to those surviving Chians who had left the island to return, but rebuilding was a slow process.

A devastating earthquake in 1881 finished off many of the old buildings that the Turks had left; a lot of reconstruction has gone into preserving many of the monuments extant today.

But Híos eventually struggled back to health. One important branch of the economy has long been shipping; Vrondádos and Mármara in the north, and the offshore island of Inoússes, are known as centers for some of the big shipping families. Yet shipping, too, is fading: more and more boats are registered in Panama, crewed with Panamanian or other cheaper, non-EU labor.

Híos has enough facilities for tourists, yet it's so large, and is still enough of an inside tip, that it doesn't feel overrun, and visitors can still feel they're discovering the island. In some ways, it's a hard nut to crack. As on many islands, most of the original towns were built inland, safe from marauding pirates. The mastic villages, for example, have preserved their original medieval plan, with a tortoise-like carapace of defensive outer wall (formed by the outer walls of the houses on the town's periphery) punctured by a few narrow alleys that twist their way toward the town center. Visitors, like pirates, could easily be fooled into driving right by. But once you've penetrated into the inner sanctum, you find neighbors exchanging news in the alleyways outside their homes, children playing, and men with backgammon boards in the cafés on the town square, before the church with its bell tower.

Híos Town

The island's port and capital, **Híos Town ❶**, isn't impenetrable at all; far from it. A public, bustling warren of streets with chaotic traffic, part of town resembles nothing so much as the Grand Bazaar: boxes of produce and sacks of spices and other goods spill out into the street, and there's even a **mosque** (today housing a **Byzantine Museum**, its courtyard littered with a jumble of stone odds and ends). The island's proximity to Turkey has led not only to Eastern influence but to a certain cosmopolitan flair, as has the large contingent of city-dwellers from Smyrna the island received when the Greeks were forced out of Anatolia in 1923; one result is the county-fair-like ambiance around the harbor, where bright lights and modern blocks of buildings set the tone.

Istanbul has always had a great degree of influence here: long before the Ottoman Empire, the Byzantines built the ***Kástro** (fortress) which, reinforced by the Genoans, dominates the north of town. The little buildings within its walls are being reclaimed by artisans and craftsmen, emphasizing the medieval flavor of its quiet stone streets. The little **museum** in the 15th-century **Justiani Tower**, by the castle's doughty **Porta Maggiore**, houses old icons and other artifacts. There is a wonderful view of the city from the tower.

Híos' Archeological Museum has long been closed following damage in a 1994 earthquake, with no immediate prospects of its reopening; visitors can go instead to the **Korais Library**, where an **Ethnographic Museum** includes various objects from traditional Chiot life.

Southern Híos: Mastichochoría, Néa Moní and Anávantos

The plain south of Híos has more of an Italian than a Greek flavor. The predominant flavor, actually, is one of citron, since the orchards of **Kámbos** are heavy with lemons and mandarin oranges in season; but the look of the medieval mansions, their stones weathered to the color and texture of terra cotta, is very Italian. There aren't many of these left: the earthquake of 1881 was more effective than even the Turks in getting rid of physical aspects of the island's heritage. Those that remain are much photographed, as are the old wooden water wheels.

Right: Xistá façades attest to the former wealth of the Mastix villages (Pirgí).

 Map p. 140, Info pp. 154-155

Nearby **Kárfas** ❷ is one of the island's leading tourist resorts, with a sand beach and shallow waters. Further down, along the southern coast, there's a nice beach at **Kómi** ❸ and an even better one at **Emborió** ❹; between the two, archeologists have unearthed remains of an ancient settlement.

Emborió's beach is known as **Mávra Vólia** for the dark volcanic pebbles that covers it; the best stretch of it is over the point, reached by a pedestrian path. Somewhere to the west of the Kómi-Emborió road is the old **Chion Tower**, now a square ruin very difficult to locate on foot, whose origins are equally misty, even in legend: this was supposedly the home of a princess who defied her father as to his choice of suitor and lived out her days in either voluntary or enforced seclusion.

★★Pirgí ❺ is the largest of the mastic villages, and thus the best place to get a taste of their signature traditions and décor. The trademark of the Mastichochoría is the *xista* or black-and-white designs that cover the houses, made using black sand from Emborió; the designs give the impression that the façades around the main square are tiled. Corresponding to these are the black-and-white pebble mosaics (*krokalia*) in the courtyards of the houses. Another highlight here is 12th-century **★Agía Apóstoli**, modeled on the church of Híos' most famous monastery, Néa Moní, with ornate decorative brickwork and frescoes from the 17th century.

A drive south through the mastic leads to **Fána**, where the fallen stones of a temple surround a little white chapel near a tranquil beach with soft sand, and on to **★Olímbi** ❻, with its fortified tower. Further on, **★★Mestá** ❼ is the best-preserved of all the mastic villages, if not as striking as Pirgí: its oldest church, **Taxiárhis**, has a noteworthy carved iconostasis.

West of Híos Town are two of the island's most famous monuments: Néa Moní and Anávatos. In an idyllic mountain setting some 16 kilometers west of Híos Town, the monastery of **★★Néa**

Moní ❽ is without a doubt one of the greatest and most important Byzantine creations in the world. Founded in 1043 by the Byzantine emperor Constantine IX Monamachos, it is one of the best extant testimonies to Byzantine art of the 11th century, bringing a new expressive element to the regulated stylization of iconographic convention. Decline under the Turks, followed by the 1881 earthquake, did considerable damage to its magnificent mosaics, but most of them have been restored.

A little way east of Néa Moní, it is worth making a detour to the monastery of **Ágios Márkou**, from where there is a fantastic view of the island and the Turkish mainland.

The hilltop village of ***Anávatos** ❾ stands abandoned, a memorial to the struggle for Greek independence and the atrocities of the Turks. In 1822, as the Turks closed in on the villagers and inhabitants of the region who had fled up to this peak for refuge, women threw themselves from the sheer cliff rather than submit to the Turks. Filled only with the whistling wind, the deserted houses seem newly abandoned and indeed filled with the ghosts of the past, something invoked by the busloads of Greeks who come here to pay homage.

The North of Híos

Híos' wealth and industry is primarily concentrated along its northeastern coast: **Vrondádos** ❿, five kilometers north of Híos Town, is popular with local shipowners as a residential spot, while **Kardámila** ⓫, Híos' second town, some 21 kilometers farther north, is the island's shipping center. The richest shipowners in Greece live on **Inoússes** ⓬ across the channel, reached by boat from Mármaro or Híos Town: as many as 60 powerful families have homes here. A curiosity on this wealthy enclave is the convent of **Evangelismoú**, a modern facility built by a wealthy shipping wife after her daughter died of cancer: her body is displayed in a glass coffin.

Right: The mosaics in the monastery of Néa Moní – impressive examples of 11th-century Byzantine art.

Back on Híos there are memorials to another figure who is traditionally held to have been a resident of this area: the poet Homer was supposedly born on Híos, in the mountain village of **Pitioús** ⓭. In Vrondádos, the stone where the poet allegedly taught, known as the **Daskalópetra**, is a popular attraction; it may actually have been part of an ancient temple or altar.

On the other side of the mountainous northern section of the island, badly hit by forest fires in recent decades, is **Volissós** ⓮, with its beautiful beach **Skála Volissoú**. Volissós is a charming, slightly crumbling stone village scattered around a hilltop Byzantine castle, where one of the old buildings is popularly known as Homer's House. More historically demonstrable is the fact that the village was founded by the great Byzantine general Belisarius. Heading from Volissós towards the coast, you arrive at the important pilgrimage church of **Agía Markéllas** after about 10 kilometers. This church is dedicated to Saint Markélla, the island's patroness. From July 22 to July 24 each year, a festival is held in honor of the saint which features, among other things, a large procession.

Similar memories to those of the ghost town of Anávatos are preserved of **Melánios** ⓯, a village and beach at the island's northwestern tip: the village's name means "dark," and the story is that people fled here from the Turks only to find more Turks waiting for them: the carnage was such that the sea became dark with their blood.

It is reckoned that the small mountain village of **Ágio Gála** to the north has been settled for more than 7,000 years. Worth

Map p. 140, Info pp.154-155

seeing here are a stalagtite cavern and a 13th-century church with some beautiful frescoes.

This spot looks out toward **Psará**, a small island which met a similar fate in 1824 when its population was completely wiped out. Today, about 200 people live on the island. Psará is quite a long ride from Híos – some four hours by ferry from Híos Town – and there are only a few connections a week, which makes its pretty little village a great place for those who really want to get away from it all. Hiking is fine here.

Sights around this part of the island include the monastery of **Kimíseos Theotókou** (consecrated to the Virgin Mary) at the northern end of the island, destroyed by the Turks and later rebuilt, and the old castle on the headland behind the little town; **Límnos Beach** is only about 20 minutes' walk away. Psará, like Inoússes, was known for its shipping might. Recently, the EOT has fixed up some of its old traditional houses as accommodation for tourists.

IKARÍA

Of the Northeast Aegean Islands, Ikaría is the least visited by tourists, though this wooded, mountainous island with its lovely beaches is well worth a visit. Ikaría has always tended to go its own way; in 1912, it even proclaimed itself a free state, independent of both Greece and Turkey, and maintained its sovereignty, with its own currency and government, for four months before it was taken back into the Greek fold. Today it is an ideal site for independent visitors; anyone who's willing to go out and explore, and doesn't want sights handed to him on a platter. No quaint crafts shops here; even roads are few and far between, and some places are only accessible by jeep. The rewards for those who do venture here, include a sense of "wilderness" in the forested mountains (the highest is Mount Ahéras, at 1,037 meters), a flavor of the real Greece and, on the north coast, some of the best beaches you could hope to find anywhere.

Ikaría takes its name from Icarus, son of Daedalus. The latter, a mythological forefather of Leonardo da Vinci, was architect of the Minotaur's labyrinth at the Palace of Knossós on Crete; when he realized that his taskmaster, King Minos, was never going to grant him his freedom, he engineered his escape, and that of his son, by building wings of wax and feathers and literally taking flight. In spite of his father's warning not to fly too high, Icarus, intoxicated by his power, tried to rise as high as the sun; Apollo, the jealous sun god, melted the wax that held the wings together and sent Icarus plummeting to earth. He landed in the sea near Ikaría, and the island, variously known through its history as Makris (large) or Ichthioessa (fishy), eventually adopted his name. Today, there's an amateur flying event held here named for Icarus, although why anyone would name a flying contest – let alone Greece's air force academy – after one of the most famous crash-landers of all time is a mystery.

Above: A dream bay for lovers near Thérma on the island of Ikariá.

Ikaría's other claim to fame is its radioactive springs; the sign that welcomes disembarking ferry passengers at Ágios Kírikos to "the island of Icarus" once read "the island of radiation." Ágios Kírikos is flanked by the towns of Thérma and Thérma Lefkádas, each with its own waters with various curative powers; one is said to be especially good for infertile women. The radioactivity is no joke; one spring at Thérma has been closed to people, and its rocks glow red with the heat.

Agíos Kírikos and Environs

Agíos Kírikos ❶, the island's main town, features an idyllic square where locals as well as visitors (for the most part Greeks) sit beneath shady trees at the water's edge playing backgammon and engaging in easy conversation. A few narrow lanes with a couple of bakeries and grocery stores make up the commercial

Info pp. 154-155

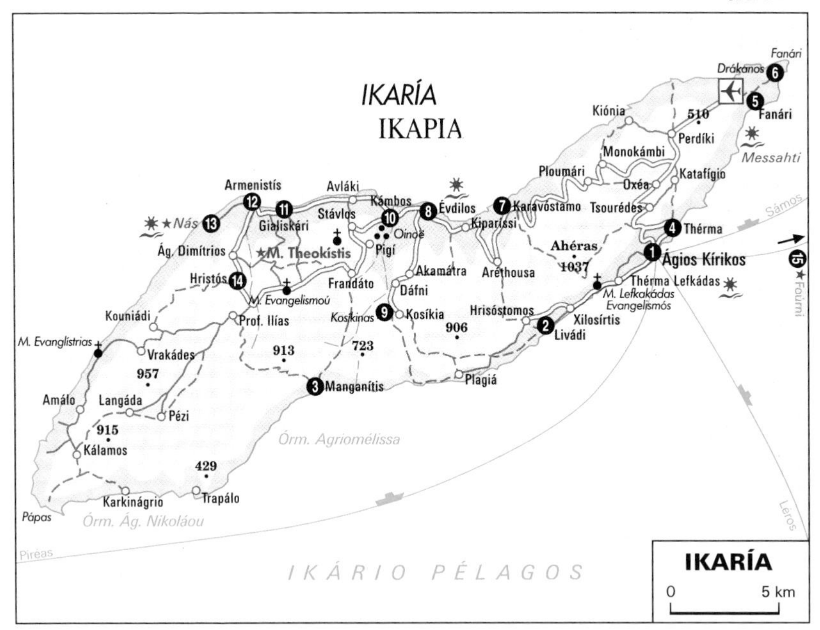

center of this quiet settlement, of which it is said there are more trees than people. The **Icarus Monument** and **Archeological Museum** are the main sights here. In the 1990s, the west of Ikaría was severely damaged by a series of forest fires. A marble plaque on the road through Ágios Kírikos commemorates the 13 islanders who lost their lives fighting those fires.

Ágios Kírikos lies on the south coast, which is quieter and rockier than the more visited north. To the southwest are the charming villages of **Xilosírtis** and **Hrisóstomos**; the beach at nearby **Livádi** ❷ was once a hideout for Aegean pirates. Past **Plagiá**, the road gets bad, but not bad enough to keep young people on Ikaría from congregating at **Manganítis** ❸, where bonfires and all-night parties, far from the restrictive clutches of authority, are a hallmark of summer. East of town is **Thérma** ❹; one of its springs is located in a cave by the harbor. There's a beach here, but a better one farther northeast, at **Fanári** ❺, by the new airport. Crowning the island's northeasternmost tip is the white tower of **Drákanos** ❻, dating from the 4th century B.C., by the ruins of an ancient town supposedly once the home of Dionysus. The tower was part of a castle which Admiral Miaoulis destroyed in "target practice" as his boat passed by during the War of Independence.

The North of Ikaría

It's the north coast of the island, however, that's the real draw for visitors. With the winding mountain roads, distances on Ikaría are no joke; the 57 kilometers between Ágios Kírikos and Armenistís translates into a drive of some two hours. But there's plenty to see along the way, including isolated pockets of brown sand beach, accessible on steep dirt tracks down the crevassed hillsides from the road, and empty even in high season.

Karavóstamo ❼ is one of the island's main settlements, population-wise, but has less to offer visitors than the picturesque fishing harbor of **Évdilos** ❽, the island's second ferry port. The view west-

ward from Évdilos' fine beach is somewhat marred by ongoing work to enlarge the harbor into a proper marina, but to the east there's nothing to obstruct the sight of majestic green-clad hills rising dramatically from the water. A road here leads inland to **Dáfni** and the island's Byzantine castle, **Koskínas** ❾ (near Kosíkia village), with its church of **Ágios Geórgios**, all originally dating from around the 10th century A.D.

Grapevines on terraced hillsides by the road are testimony to a long history of wine on an island where Dionysus supposedly dwelt; the vine type, *pranni petra*, is even sacred to the god. Oinoë, the island's ancient capital, also bore the name of Dionysias. The settlement here existed from antiquity into the Byzantine period (as demonstrated by a ruined Byzantine dwelling); today, the area is called **Kámbos** ❿, and boasts a sand beach, a pension, and a few tavernas, and its museum displays archeological finds. A little ways inland, by **Pigí**, is **★Theokístis Monastery**, painted with frescoes in the style of Mount Athos and featuring a cave chapel, the roof of which is formed by two protruding plates of stone.

Above: A cool bath in the Nás Gorge, Ikariá. Right: Doing some evening shopping in Sámos Town.

On this stretch of coastline, the beaches are simply stunning. **Gialiskári** ⓫ is a little hamlet with a number of rooms to rent; indeed, the roadside here demonstrates the nearest thing Ikaría gets to a blossoming tourist industry, with seaside tavernas and a few hotels. These overlook beaches like **Messahti**, which embodies anyone's dream of a Greek island vacation: pale sand sloping gently into a turquoise sea, with a tiny blue-domed chapel marking one end of the embracing cove, and the houses and trellised restaurants of **Armenistís** ⓬ climbing the hillside at the other. These restaurants are pleasant places to escape from the heat of the day before moving on to **★Nás** ⓭, another lovely if smallish beach guarded by the foundations of an ancient temple to Artemis. It is said that Naiads used to live here; a part of the ancient harbor is the only concrete testimony to past seaside activities.

Inland from Armenistís are the forested mountains of **Rahes**, a wild country of rushing rivers, lakes and waterfalls; hikers can follow the course of a river through a mountain, or step into a waterfall for a refreshing "shower." The main square of the picturesque village of **Hristós** ⓮, surrounded by verdant green woods and orchards, offers a panoramic view of the coast; nearby is the 13th-century convent of **Panagía Mounde**.

Between Ikaría and Sámos are the **Foúrni Islands** ⓯, flanked by Thímena and Ágios Miná. The main island **★Foúrni's** protected harbor was once a pirate cove, but is now better known for its delicious lobsters and other seafood. There are some nice beaches and a little town near **Kámbi** and **Hrisomiléa**.

Map p. 147, Info pp. 154-155

⋆SÁMOS

In antiquity, life on Sámos was held to be so easy and rich that, as the poet Menander wrote, "even the birds gave milk." The beverage of choice, though, was wine; the virtues of Samian wine are legendary. During the 16th century the island was deserted for a time, and today's wine is a new invention rather than the wine of tradition: but it flows no less readily for that and, supplemented by green pine forests, white beaches, antiquities, yacht harbors and active nightlife, has helped to make Sámos one of the most pleasant and most popular islands in the Northeast Aegean, if not in all of Greece.

There's truly something here for everyone, whether your tastes run to the active resort scenes of Kokkári and Pithagório, the ancient ruins of the Heraéon, or mountain walks through old villages or the sparsely populated region around Mount Kerkis, the second-highest peak in the Aegean (1437 meters).

⋆Sámos Town and Environs

The island's main harbor is at **Sámos Town** ❶, whose elegant harbor promenade lends the place an urban character. It is sometimes known as Vathí, although this name is more generally applied to the older, uphill section of town, originally called **Áno Vathí**, which has more of the air of an old village. A café in the thick shade of the palm-lined main square or the museum café in the municipal park offer liquid cool in the heat of the day. The highlight here is the ⋆⋆**Archeological Museum**, with treasures of the island, notably artifacts from the Heraéon on the southern coast, one of the more important religious sites of the ancient world. The centerpiece of this museum is one of the largest archaic kouros figures ever found; more than five meters high (photo p. 33). Excursions from Sámos Town include the chapel of **Agíi Paraskeví**, the 18th-century monastery of **Zoodóhou Pigí**, and the idyllic bay of **Posidónio**, all three with notable views over to Turkey.

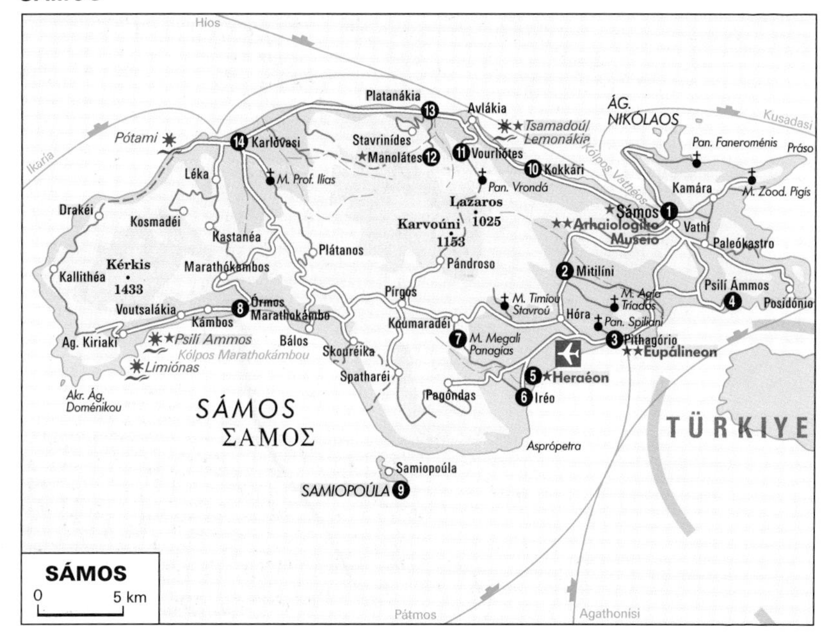

Most visitors head from Sámos Town to the two popular resort areas: Kokkári on the north coast and Pithagório on the south one. An alternate route to Pithagório leads through **Mitilíni** ❷. When, in the 16th century, the Turks went about repopulating what was then a virtually uninhabited island – most of the islanders left when the Genoans did – they brought in Greeks from all over the Greek world, and Mitilíni is one of the names that reflects colonists' memories of their native places, in this case Lésvos. Today, the village prides itself on its modern **Paleontology Museum**, a small but loving assemblage of local fossils, flora and fauna.

★Pithagório and the South Coast

Pithagório ❸ was, in fact, the ancient town of Sámos, renamed for the tourists in honor of Sámos' most famous son, Pythagoras, known to most students today as the author of the Pythagorean Theorem ($a^2 + b^2 = c^2$). There was far more to Pythagoras' philosophy than this: he was a deep thinker on religion, the nature of the soul, and the harmony of the cosmos, and was a signal influence on Plato. Born on Sámos around 580 B.C., he left the island, possibly after a dispute with the tyrant Polycrates, and traveled extensively through the ancient world before, it is believed, returning to his island in his late fifties; although it's hard to pin down his movements with any certainty. Certainly spurious are the many objects on the island that bear his name, including the "Pythagorean cup" made by local potters to illustrate the virtues of moderation: when filled halfway, it retains its contents, but if it's too full, all of the liquid drains out through a hole in the bottom.

Right: The Eupálinos Tunnel, a masterpiece of engineering from the 6th century B.C. (Pithagório, Sámos).

Pythagoras' town echoes little of the seriousness of its namesake: it's an active, fun vacation center with an unspectacular sand beach – the sand-and-pebble beach of Potokaki begins at the edge of town –

 Info pp. 154-155

and a crowded yacht harbor. If there were any justice, the town would be called Polykratio, since Polycrates, ruler here after 550 B.C., was one of the most powerful men in Greece in his day, and was actually responsible for a number of the ancient building projects we see today, including the **Harbor Mole**. The most striking is the ****Tunnel of Eupálinos**, which leads through the hill to connect the aqueduct to Polycrates' capital. It took stunningly exact calculations to measure a tunnel 1,045 meters long through solid rock; excavation proceeded at a pace of about 25 centimeters per day and the project took five and a half years to complete. Today, visitors are allowed to walk a few hundred meters into the narrow passageway to see the ancient source of Pithagório's water; but this is not a descent for the claustrophobic, despite the electric lights. Also atop this hill is the little monastery of **Panagía Spilianí**, with a small church built inside a cave, as well as the **Ancient Theater**, recently restored so as to betray almost no trace at all of its antiquity. Recently begun here is an August music festival celebrating Manos Kalomiris, a 20th-century composer honored as the "father of Greek music" and founder of the Athens Conservatory, and whose family was from the island. About eight kilometers east of Pithagório, near **Psilí Ámmos** ❹, is a sand beach popular with families.

Lovers of antiquities will head down the coast some six kilometers to the ***Heraéon** ❺, the Temple of Hera. Originally, this route was covered along the marble Sacred Way from Pithagório, of which all that remains is a stretch of a few hundred meters. There was a cult site here to Hera as far back as the Bronze Age; the first temples dated from the 8th century B.C.; but the greatest of all is from the time of Polycrates. After an earlier building had been destroyed – altogether there were three successive temples on this site – he erected the third-largest temple ever built in Greece: 25 meters high, and 108 meters long. All that remains today is a single column. A few plaster casts from

the museum help to recreate a bit more of a sense of where the various votive offerings and treasure houses here stood. The town of **Iréo** ❻ has some nice tavernas and pensions along its sand beach.

Inland, the monastery of **Megalí Panagías** ❼ has a beautiful old Byzantine church (16th century) with lovely but damaged frescoes. A few kilometers north of here lies the charming village of **Koumaradéi**, with a herb factory and a carpet-weaving studio. Through hillside **Pírgos** and the pine woods of **Koutsi** you reach beach-tourist country again around **Órmos Marathakámbo** ❽: **Kámbos**, in particular, has quite a number of hotels. As you continue west, the beaches get nicer: a second ***Psilí Ámmos** ("Fine Beach") here is a marvelous stretch of white sand, dotted with umbrellas; and **Limniónas** is even better. From **Votsalákia**, east of Psilí Ámmos, walkers can ascend via the convent of **Agía Evangelístria** to the top of **Mount Kerkis** (1,433 meters), or continue on foot along the coast to the western side of the island. From Pithagório and Órmos Marathakámbo there are boats to the little island of **Samiopoúla** ❾, with a good sand beach and a taverna open in summer.

Above: Copies of archaic statues in the Temple of Hera (Heraéon), Sámos. Right: In the evening, quiet comes to the beach of Kokkári.

The North Coast

Ever popular with visitors is the onetime fishing village of **Kokkári** ❿, with narrow pebble beaches and red-roofed houses clustered on points of land extending out into the water. This is one of the main tourist spots on the island; the beaches of ***Lemonákia** and ***Tsamadoú**, a bit further west, are mobbed during the tourist season. From Kokkári, hikers can embark on the classic tour of Sámos' mountain villages, the heart of the island's wine country. A slightly longer route leads through the 16th-century fortified monastery of **Panagía Vrondá**, "Our Lady of the Thunder," named for the

Map p. 150, Info pp. 154-155

storms which come every year in early September (the climb from here up the 1,035-meter **Mount Lazaros** takes about two hours). **Vourliótes** ⓫ is worth seeing: the first of the hill towns; a green, lush place in the pines, with fresh-water springs and nice tavernas. You can cross the deep wooded ravine called "Nightengale Valley" and head to ***Manolátes** ⓬, surrounded by vineyards; a taverna here, Lukas, serves wine from the barrel. Continue through the lower nightengale valley down to **Platanákia** ⓭, named for the plane trees which provide shade here (total walking time without Lazaros about seven hours). A good stop along the way is the taverna in **Pnáka**, halfway along the mountain road from Kámbos to Vourliótes, which has a great view.

Karlóvasi ⓮ is the island's second port town, divided into New, Middle and Old Towns as you move west. The port itself, for all its hotels and eateries, is a rather cheerless place; while **Néo Karlóvasi**, "New Town," offers everything from deserted tanning warehouses from the town's industrial heyday before the war, to several large, newish churches, such as Panagía Mirtidiotissa. **Paléo Karlóvasi**, "Old Town," however, up above, is a pleasant village-like place where you can eat *loukomades* (pastries) in a little plateia or stroll up to the white church of **Agía Tríada** perched atop the hill. And it's well worth continuing from Karlóvasi, by bus, car or on foot, the two kilometers west to **Pótami**, a lovely sand beach guarded by a white modern chapel that rises like a sail over the coast.

A new unpaved road goes on to even better beaches: **Mégalo Seitaní** and **Míkro Seitaní**. This west coast boasts some of Sámos' loveliest scenery and finest beaches, and there are trails both along the coast and uphill inland; such as to the vineyard village of **Kosmádei** (taverna with view): just make sure you plan ahead as to accommodation and food, if you intend to venture very far afield. **Drakéi** has only modest facilities, so you'll have to continue as far as **Kallithéa** for supplies.

LÍMNOS (☎ 0254)

Tel. 22315, fax. 24100. **Tourist Police**, tel. 22200.
PLANE: Airport 9 km northeast of Mírina, tel. 31202. Flights to Athens, Thessaloníki, Lésvos; charter flights in summer. *BOAT:* Ferries to Kavála, Thessaloníki, Pireaus, Rafína, Lésvos, Sámos, Híos and some of the Dodecanese Islands.
MÍRINA: $$$ **Akti Mirina**, tel. 22681, luxurious, all amenities, right on the beach. $$ **Afrodite Apartments**, tel. 23141, studio apartments, near the harbor. **Katsaraki**, tel. 24508, 51700, central, cozy. **THÁNOS:** $$ **Villa Thanos Beach**, tel. 23496, 25028, on the beach, nice rooms.
MÍRINA: O Glaros, at the harbor. Fish taverna with a nice terrace.
Archeological Museum, Mírina, Tue-Sun 8:30 am to 3 pm.

LÉSVOS

MITILÍNI AND ENVIRONS (☎ 0251)

EOT Aristarhou 6, tel. 42511, fax. 42512.
PLANE: Airport 8 km south of Mitilíni; flights to and from Athens, Thessaloníki, Límnos, Rhódos, Sámos, Híos. Also charter flights. **Olympic Airways**, tel. 28659. *BOAT:* Service to Piraeus, Thessaloníki, Límnos, Híos, Sámos, Ikaría, Pátmos and Aivalic, Turkey. **Mitilíni Harbor Office**, tel. 28659. *CAR RENTAL:* **Payless**, Koudouriotou 49. **Just Rent-a-Car** (cheaper), Koudouriotou 47, tel. 43080. *BUS:* Long-distance bus station is on Venizelou at the municipal park (tel. 28873), local buses depart from the harbor (tel. 28725).
MITILÍNI: $$$ **Hotel Loriet** (or Laureate), Varia, main road, 3 km south of Mitilíni. Rooms in a 150-year old mansion, modern bungalows, pool. $$ **Sappho**, tel. 28415, near the ferry dock.
MITILÍNI: Good fish tavernas on the harbor promenade, such as **Dimitrakis** at the south end.
MITILÍNI: Archeological Museum, Argyri Efaliotli, tel. 22087, open 8:30 am to 2:30 pm, closed Mon. **Museum of Byzantine Art**, Agiou Therapontou (behind the cathedral), tel 28916, 10 am to 1 pm, closed Sun. **Kástro** (castle) and **Theater**, 8:30 am to 3 pm, closed Mon. **VARIÁ: Tériade Museum**, tel. 23372, 9 am to 2 pm, 5 to 8 pm, closed Mon. **Théophilos Museum**, 9 am to 1pm, 4:30 to 8 pm, closed Mon.

MÍTHIMNA AND THE NORTH (☎ 0253)

At entrance to town, tel. 71347.
MÍTHIMA: $$$ **Hotel Delfinia**, 1 km from town, tel. 71502, fax. 71524. Modern complex with pool and tennis courts, restaurant, beach. **Olive Press**, tel. 71205, fax. 71647. Converted olive mill on the beach. $$ **Adonis**, tel. 71866, fax. 71636, clean, comfortable. $ **Giorgos Arapis**, tel. 71072, rents motorbikes and inexpensive rooms, showers, balconies, kitchenettes. **EVTHALOÚS:** $$ **Golden Beach**, tel. 71879, fax. 72044. In an old Byzantine monastery on the beach. **PÉTRA: The Women's Cooperative of Pétra**, tel. 41238, fax. 41309, rooms and apartments in various price ranges.
MÍTHIMA: O Krinos, Agorá, tel. 71135. Open only for dinner, best in town. **Melinda**, Agorá, good international cuisine, expensive. **EVTHALOÚS: Anatoli**, tel. 71181. **PÉTRA:** At the Women's Cooperative (tel. 41238), delicious food on a terrace above the square.

PLOMARI AND THE SOUTH (☎ 0252)

ÁGIOS ISÍDOROS: $$ **Sea Sun,** studios and apartments, 1 km east of town, tel. 31755, fax. 32234. Green grounds with flowers, reasonable rates. **MELÍNDA:** $ **Maria's Rooms and Taverna**, tel. 93239. Isolated taverna with secluded beach.
ÁGIOS ISÍDOROS: Taverna Finikas, tel. 33123. Where the Greeks go. **PLOMÁRI: Platanos**, on the Platía beneath plane trees, good Greek food.

HÍOS (☎ 0271)

Híos Town

EOT, Kanari 18, 82100 Híos, tel. 44389, fax. 44343 (open until 2:30 pm, longer in summer).
PLANE: Airport 3 km south of Híos Town; flights to Athens and charter flights. *BOAT:* Ferries to Piraeus, Kavála, Rafína, Çesne (Turkey), Pátmos, Léros, Kálimnos, Kós and Rhódos. Ferries and hydrofoils to Sámos, Lésvos, Ikaría, Foúrni and Psará. *CAR RENTAL:* **Vassilakis Bros**, Venizelou 15, tel./fax. 25659; Kárfas, tel. 32284, reliable, personal service.
$$$ **Golden Sand**, Kárfas (6 km south of Híos Town), tel. 32080, fax. 31700. Resort complex by the broad beach of Kárfas, pool, outdoor dining, bar. $$ **Kyma**, Prokimea (by the port) tel. 44500, fax. 44600, in an old villa, simple rooms, central. **Chandris**, Prokimea, tel. 4440111, concrete block, with pool. $ **Rooms Alex**, Livanou 29, tel. 26054. People come back year after year, modest rooms, warm hospitality.
HÍOS TOWN: Agrifoglio, Stavrou Livanou 2, tel. 25845, good Italian food, expensive. **Theodosiou**, right by the ferry dock, wonderful food. If you prefer amenities like décor or menus, try **Apoplous**, diagonally opposite. **Two Brothers**, corner of Livanou and Venizelou, has good food and a garden.
Justinian Museum, temporary displays. **Koraís Library/Argenti Ethnographic Museum**, Korai 2, tel.

44246, open Mon-Fri 8 am to 2 pm, Fri also 5 to 7:30 pm, Sat 8 am to noon.

Rural Híos

PIRGÍ: Women's Cooperative, tel. 72496. **Rita's**, tel. 72479; both rent rooms. **MESTÁ:** Four EOT guest houses (contact Paradosiakos Ikismos, EOT Box 25, Híos 81100, tel. 76319). **VOLISSÓS: Stella Tsakina**, apartments, tel. 21413, fax. 21521.

KÁMBOS: Marvokordatiko, tel. 32900, taverna with rooms for rent. **EMBORIÓ: Volcano**, tel. 71136. Great food and décor. **MESTÁ: O Morias**, on the main square, lots of atmoshphere. **VOLISSÓS: Limnia Taverna**, tel. (0274) 21315, on the shore.

Néa Moní (Byzantine monastery), 17 km west of Híos Town, open daily 8 am to 1 pm, 4 to 8 pm.

PSARÁ (☎ 0272)

The EOT has turned the Parliament Building here into an 18-bed guesthouse, tel. 61293, 61181.

IKARÍA (☎ 0275)

PLANE: Airport near Fanári. Daily flights to Athens and Sámos. *BOAT:* Ferries to Piraeus, Sámos, Foúrni, and to some of the Cyclades and Dodecanes. *BUS:* One or two runs a day from Ágios to Armenistís and back (two hours one way).

ÁGIOS KÍRIKOS

$$ **Hotel Kastro**, tel. 23480, fax. 23700. Ágios' one "real" hotel, clean rooms, helpful staff.

Dedalos, tel. 22473, on the square, delicious food. **Klimataria** is also good.

NORTH COAST

ARMENISTÍS: Marabou Travel, tel. 71460, fax. 71325, organizes hikes, car rental and hotel rooms.

GIALASKÁRI: $$$ **Messakti Village**, tel. 71331, the island's best hotel, across from a gorgeous beach. **ARMENISTÍS: Dolihi Apartments**, tel. 41450, fax. 41451, with sea views and kitchenettes. **Hotel Daidalos**, tel./fax. 41410, classical comfort.

There's a **campground** east of Armenistís: it has no phone and no name, but is right on the beach.

SÁMOS (☎ 0273)

PLANE: Airport 2 km southest of Pithagório. Daily flights to Athens and Thessaloníki, charter flights. **Olympic Airways**, tel. 61219. *BOAT:* Sámos has three harbors: Karlóvasi (Piraeus, Ikaría, Híos, Foúrni, Lésvos and some of the Cyclades); Pithagório (Dodecanes, Híos, Foúrni, Ikaría, Lésvos); and Sámos Town (Vathí). Connections from Sámos Town for Kusadasi (Turkey), Piraeus, Thessaloníki, Ikaría, Foúrni, Híos, the Cyclades and Dodecanes. Day trips to Turkey (Kusadasi) also possible. *CAR RENTAL:* **Speedy Rent a Car**, Pithagório (tel. 61502, fax. 61042), good rates.

SÁMOS TOWN (VATHÍ)

EOT, Martinou 25, tel. 28530, Mon-Fri 9 am-3 pm.

$$ **Eolis**, Themistokli Sofouli, tel. 28904, fax. 28063. Rooftop pool. $ **Pythagoras**, Kalistratou, tel. 28601, fax. 28893. Clean, cheap rooms with bath.

Gregori, Mikalis 5, tel 22718. **Ta Kotopoula**, vine-shaded terrace (corner Mikalis/Vlamaris, tel. 28415).

Archeological Museum, Tue-Sun 8:30 am-3 pm.

PITHAGÓRIO

$$$ **Doryssa Bay Village**, 1 km west of Pithagório, tel. 61360, fax. 61463. Lavish complex includes facsimile Greek village. $$ **Stratos**, Konstandínu Kanari, tel. 61157, fax. 61881. Central, reasonably quiet. **Labito 1 and 2**, Dimitrou Rafalia, tel. 61086, fax. 61085, two quiet hotels in the old town.

Vegera, tel. 61436. High-class, at the harbor. **Family House Restaurant**, Konstandínu Karnari, tel. 62260. On side street, good food for the money. **IRÉO: Ireon Restaurant/Taverna**, tel. 95361, great fish.

Eupálinos Tunnel, north of Pithagório, Tue-Sun 9 am to 2 pm. **Heraéon Temple**, Tue-Sun 8:30 am to 3 pm. **Megáli Panagía Monastery**, 9:30 am to 1 pm, 2:30 to 4:30 pm, closed Sun. **Paleontological Museum**, Mitilíni, Mon-Fri 9 am to 2 pm, 5 to 7 pm, Sat 9 am to 2 pm, Sun 10:30 am to 4:30 pm.

SOUTH COAST

ÓRMOS MARATHÓKAMBO: $ **M. Vourliotou**, tel. 37427, fax. 37073, rooms above a taverna on the harbor. **KÁMBOS:** $$ **Alexandra**, tel. 37131, fax. 34895, attractive waterfront hotel. **LIMNIÓNAS:** $$$ **Limionas Bay**, hotel/apartments, tel./fax. 37057. Idyllic setting, near great beach, pool.

ÓRMOS MARATHÓKAMBO: Klimataria, tel. 372 63. **LIMNIÓNAS: Limionas**, tel. 37096, beach taverna.

NORTH COAST

KOKKÁRI: $ **Frangos**, tel. 92257, clean rooms, on the beach. **KARLÓVASI:** $$ **Hotel Erato**, tel. 34600, fax. 35180. These maisonettes are good value and are right across from the beach.

KOKKÁRI: Farmer's Restaurant, main street, good but expensive. **KARLÓVASI: Ouzeri Kima**, Odós Kanári, good seafood.

THE DODECANESE

PÁTMOS / LIPSÍ
LÉROS / KÁLYMNOS
ASTYPÁLEA / KÓS
NÍSIROS / TÍLOS
RHÓDOS (RHODES) / SÍMI
KÁRPATHOS / KASÓS
KASTELLÓRISO

The southeastern chain of Aegean islands, running along the coast of Turkey, are inexactly named: the "Twelve Islands" (*dodeka nisi*) are actually 15 major islands and about 50 smaller, sparsely-populated or uninhabited islets. While it's always difficult to lump groups of islands together, the Dodecanese have been forged into a kind of unity through their recent history. Leaders in the Greek War of Independence, they found themselves given to Turkey in the London Protocol of 1830; later, having managed to attain prosperity and even a degree of autonomy under the Turkish yoke, they were appropriated by Italy after the Italian-Turkish War of 1911. Italy continued in possession until 1943, leaving a distinctive architectural legacy in an odd veneer of neoclassicism with a futuristic-fascistic twist: a particularly striking example is the port of Lakkí on Léros, which looks like a 1930s film set.

History notwithstanding, the Dodecanese are firmly Greek. If anything, their checkered and colorful past has strengthened their individual identities: these are islands with their own distinctive personalities. Tourists tend to congregate on Pátmos, Kós and Rhódos; leaving some of the best islands, such as Kálimnos, Nísiros and Sími, to day-trippers who invade by day and clear the field for the discriminating few at night. Whether you favor popular tourist spots like Líndos on Rhódos or prefer the solitude of tiny Lipsí, the Dodecanese are prime spots for a Greek Island holiday with a memorable difference.

Previous Pages: Like loggias in an opera house, the classicistic houses of Sími line the harbor. Left: Heating the oven for Easter baking (Ólimbos, Kárpathos).

**PÁTMOS

"Island of the Apocalypse" is a rather calamitous-sounding epithet for such a tranquil and, yes, holy place as Pátmos. The "Apocalypse" in question is, of course, one of word not deed: it was in a cave here that St. John had his revelation around A.D. 95.

But Pátmos' popularity has been growing among less fervent believers, as well. From its main population centers – the harbor of Skála and the monastery-crowned hilltop of Pátmos (Hóra) – it is hard to imagine that peace and quiet can be found in the north and south; where Pátmos extends its hilly arms fingered with rocky cliffs and beaches and sprinkled with empty beaches, rustic tavernas, quaint villages. And the island's a comfortable size for the self-propelled: 15

Map p. 161, Info pp. 192-195

kilometers from end to end, it can well be explored on foot or by mountain bike.

In the ancient world, Pátmos had little significance save as the spot where Orestes took refuge from the Furies, protected by Artemis, whose island it was. An inscribed plaque from her temple is in the treasury of the monastery; another inscribed piece of her temple is built into the chapel of the Virgin as a doorstep.

In fact, there was at least one Bronze Age settlement on Pátmos, something demonstrated by excavations on **Kastélli**, the hill up behind **Skála ❶**. Skála didn't even exist as a settlement until the 20th century; before that, everyone lived up in Pátmos (Hóra), where the fortified monastery offered protection from pirate attacks. Skála is modern Pátmos' population center, and it's here you find most of the hotels, restaurants, and other amenities. Dominating the main square is the Italian government building found on virtually every Dodecanese island, now housing the post office, the customs office, and the tourist information office. The narrow streets behind are lined with shops, ranging from icon-sellers to a number of good bakeries with Pátmos cheese pie and *poungi*, a pastry filled with walnuts, almonds and honey.

Above: The Monastery of St. John – mighty fortress and labyrinth of chapels in one (Pátmos).

From Skála, it's about 4.5 kilometers to Pátmos (Hóra) by car; but hikers can still follow the old road, constructed of natural rock in 1794, which shortens the way a bit, since it omits the jackknife turns of the wider street. Not well marked on the Skála end – follow the main street up from the main square, bearing with its various turns, and you'll see the stone road leading off to the right after about 10 minutes – it's a pleasant, if steep, route through the trees.

At the halfway point is the place where it all began, the **Cave of Saint John**. The "cave" is now a chapel at the heart of the convent of ***Apokálipsis ❷**; you have to go down some very steep steps to gain en-

Info pp. 192-195

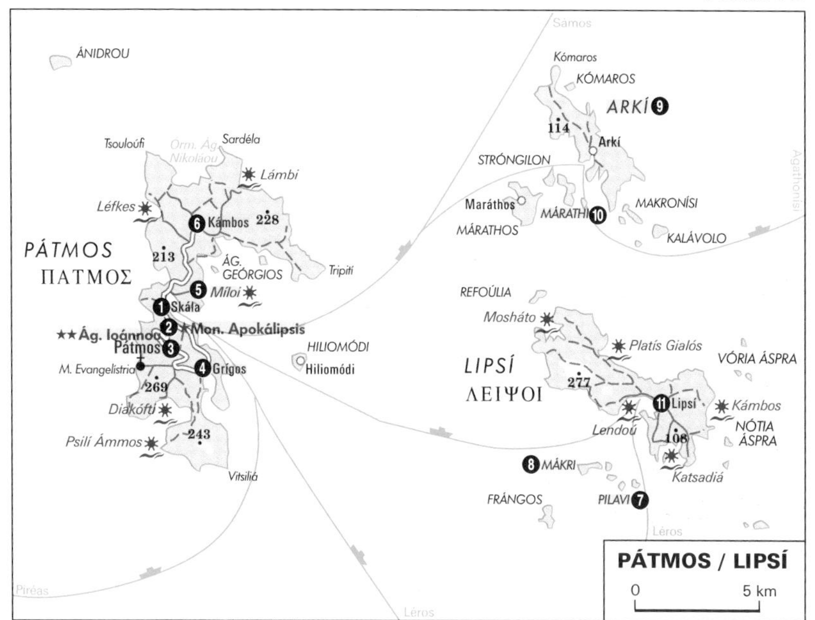

trance, but the inside part still consists of the original living rock. John, exiled to Pátmos by the Emperor Domitian, had his revelation while sleeping; he dictated it to his disciple, Próchoros, who appears in the standard icon treatments of the subject. Highlights include the stone where John supposedly laid his head and the stand where Próchoros wrote.

Patmias School was founded in buildings around the cave in 1713. This was the first official school for the teaching of Greek letters and ideas: it produced some of Greece's greatest thinkers, and incubated the ideas that hatched into the struggle for Greek independence in 1821. Although the Italians shut it down when they occupied the Dodecanese, the school was reopened in modern quarters slightly up the hill in 1947, in a new incarnation as a theological seminary.

Pátmos (Hóra) ❸ is dominated by the ★★**Monastery of St. John** (Ágios Ioánnuo Theológou), which stands like a fortress atop the hill, looking down over the whole island. Although the place remained sacred and popular with pilgrims throughout the next centuries, it wasn't until 1088, when St. Christodulos built the monastery, that Pátmos became established as one of the leading centers of Christianity. The monastery has been growing ever since, resulting in a stylistic conglomerate adorned with layer upon layer of ancient frescoes in various stages of restoration. Today, it's still an active monastery and center of Christian tourism: in season, Pátmos is besieged with excursion ships and weekenders who come for a day or two to do homage.

Inside, it opens out like a rabbit warren over several levels around the arched, pebble-paved main courtyard, surrounded by loggias. Since in Orthodox tradition mass cannot be said more than once a day at the same altar, the monastery contains 10 chapels. The highlight is the **Chapel of the Virgin**, off the main courtyard, which has some of the monastery's oldest frescoes; a side-chapel here is dedicated to St. Christodoulos, with his bones in a silver casket, his shoes, and his walking stick. The **Katholikón**, the main church, contains a much-revered icon of St. John from the 12th century. The **Refectory** also has some wonderful frescoes. In the **Treasury**, valuable objects amassed over the years are displayed, including a whole range of Cretan icons, attesting to Pátmos' once-flourishing trade with that island; a gorgeous 11th-century mosaic icon of St. Nicholas that's one of the oldest objects in the monastery; and an icon of Christ in chains that has been attributed to the young El Greco.

There are dozens of other churches in town, although many of them are locked and it isn't always easy to track down the key. **Zoodóchou Pigís** was the island's first convent; founded in 1607 it has some particularly fine frescoes. The church of **Ágios Dimitrios** is also noteworthy. On a secular note, a museum in the 17th-century **Mansion of the Simantiri Family** allows visitors to examine the interior of a local house. Outside of town is the **Convent of the Annunciation**, or Evangelístria, founded in 1937 on the site of a former anchorite's seat, and today one of the most active convents in Greece.

For beach-goers, a more compelling church complex might be **Panagía Koumana** on the hilltop between Skála and the popular beach of **Míloï** ❹: in addition to two lovely churches, one old, one new, it offers a jungle atmosphere, with lush dense greenery filled with the raucous cries of exotic birds, and sports a blue neon cross that shines down over Skála at night.

Kámbos ❺ is the main village in the north of the island, with tavernas and an active beach. In general, this section of the island runs to wild rocky landscapes, exuding a sense of desertion and majesty. Hikers here will be rewarded with views from the high headlands over the water, where three little islands float offshore, as well as quieter beaches such as **Vágia** and **Livádi Geránou**, east of Kámbos, or **Léfkes**, on the west coast. On the north coast is the beach of **Lámbi**, known for its colorful pebbles.

Right: Fishing lines being baited in the harbor of Lipsí.

A more resort-like feel is in the air at the pleasant vacation harbor of **Grígos** ❻, south of Pátmos, where there's sailing and windsurfing. At one end of Grígos Bay, a spit of sand extends out to the imposing **Kalikátsu Rock**, which has steps hewn into it and a cave at its base that may once have sheltered hermits, but nowadays draws mainly backpackers. The southern part of the island is tethered by a narrow tongue of land to the body of Pátmos; along this tongue is sandy **Diakófti Beach**, held to be the best beach on the island.

Southwest of Diakófti, on the south side of Stavrós Bay, is sandy **Psilí Ámmos**; this is the unofficial nudist beach on Pátmos. It is best reached by boat from Skála.

LIPSÍ

Lipsí is a great place to "get away from it all." The 16-square-kilometer island, with its olive groves and fig trees, lovely beaches and pretty blue-and-white chapels and churches, is absolutely charming in its simplicity. The main harbor has tourist amenities, but the island has no other real villages. You can get everywhere on foot, although there's motorbike rental and a minibus. Excursion boats in the harbor take you to beaches you can't reach on foot, including those on the islets of **Pilavi** ❼ and **Mákri** ❽, the latter known for the natural arches in its cliff sides.

Forty people live on the little island of **Arkí** ❾; there are three tavernas here that rent rooms. Nearby **Márathi** ❿ has only two tavernas with rooms to let, and a gorgeous little beach which, during tourist season, is the destination of numerous day-trippers from Pátmos and Lípsi.

Map p. 161, Info pp. 192-195

Not reliant solely on fishing and tourism, Lipsí's economy also draws on, for example, a carpet factory where young women work to amass money for their dowries, and the local wine; there's a wine festival every August.

In **Lipsí Town** ⓫, however, sightseers have to content themselves with the small **Ethnographic Museum** and the **Church of St. John the Theologian**, funded by Lipsian emigrants to the United States, on the main square. Nearby is the **Monument to Emmanolis Xanthos**. He was a Lipsian who fought for Greek freedom in 1821.

In the off season, this town church also houses Lipsí's miraculous icon, which in summer is kept in 17th-century **Panagía tu Haru**, about 20 minutes from town. This icon incorporates dried lily bulbs which blossom every year in August, an event which is commemorated by a church festival.

This Panagía is on the road to the island's main beach "strip," extending from **Hohlakoúra** to **Xirókambos** on the eastern side, and from **Katsadiá** to **Papantria** on the west. Heading west and north from Lipsí's harbor, you'll pass the beaches of **Lendoú** and **Kámbos**. In less than an hour you will arrive at **Platís Gialós**, encircling a shallow blue bay where white geese lazily swim as if it were a millpond. From this point you can continue along the footpath through the trees to **Mosháto**, another popular "swimming hole."

LÉROS

Léros is something of a standout among the Dodecanese – in good senses and bad. For years, the name was synonymous to Greeks with the "funny farm," thanks to the large mental institution located here. Then, its strategic location and numerous natural harbors made it a logical base for the navies of occupying powers. In the years leading up to World War II, the Italians transformed and expanded the port of Lakkí, a development which had its tragic culmination in the

Battle of Léros in 1943. German bombardments raged around the 14th-century castle above Plátanos, where the Allies had planted their anti-aircraft guns; and so it was that a 20th-century war did more damage than any conflict against which the castle had originally been built for protection.

However, Léros today bears little trace of either insanity or aggression, and more and more people are discovering an island that has been much overlooked.

Lakkí ❶ is where the big ferries dock, and if you're arriving by boat it will give you as clear a sign of Léros' "difference" as you could wish. Lakkí was the Italian harbor, and the Italians decided to turn it into the city of their future: after they arrived in 1923, they razed the existing houses and erected buildings which some see as a manifesto of futurist architecture and others as poor taste. These dilapidated white edifices with their curving walls – including a clock tower, customs house and elementary school, as well as the decrepit former **Hotel Roma** – are like film sets for a fascist director's movie version of the future.

Part of Léros' ongoing transformation involves plans to redo some of the buildings, reproduce the original terrazzo sidewalks, and generally spruce it up. The place still has a military air, moreover, emphasized by the theatrical **Monument to the Fallen** by the water, and the occasional battleship at the quay.

Hard by Lakkí, in the direction of **Lépida**, are the mental institutions that have helped give the island its reputation. After a television crew came in a few years ago and did an exposé on the institutions' dubious conditions, doctors came in from other parts of the EU to help the staff clean things up – with good results. As part of the "new openness," the grounds – with a summer home of Mussolini's – are now open to visitors. It's to the right of the road going south toward **Xirókambos** ❷, one of the island's prettiest little fishing villages, on a bay, as well as the site of some of its oldest ruins. Over the town is **Paleókastro**, an old fortress, as well as the ruins of an old **Acropolis**, probably dating from the Myceanean period; both castle and town saw their heyday around the 4th century B.C. A more recent highlight is the cave church of **Panagía Kavourádena**, southeast of town and halfway downs the side of the steep rocks by the water. This "Chapel of the Madonna of the Crabs" is supposedly so named because a fisherman out looking for crabs found an icon here; an icon inside the church shows the Panagía framed within a crab's body.

The literal as well as the figurative center of the island is **Plátanos** ❸, perched on a ridge at the center of the island under the hill crowned by the Byzantine Kástro. Plátanos lives up to its name with the plane trees that shade its main square. There is also a fountain on the main

Right: Ágios Isídoros, a small chapel on an island in Gournás Bay (Léros).

Info pp. 192-195

square fed by the spring of the ancient Asklepion, or temple of healing. Léros is one of the few islands to have kept its traditional *lehthi*, a kind of café where men gather to play games and trade stories in the evenings.

A long, long flight of steps leads up through the narrow streets, past the old cathedral of **Agía Paraskeví**, to the ★**Kástro**, which has stunning, windswept views out over the island and its "four bays" (including the yachting harbor of the charming village of **Pandéli** on **Vromólithos Bay**, just to the south). A little chapel near the top, where three windmills also stand, has an old bomb casing mortared into its wall like a kind of grisly bell.

The Kástro itself represents many layers of antiquity: the site of a settlement from around the 7th century B.C., it later supported both the Byzantine fortress and a 9th-century **Panagía** ("Church of the Mother of God"), so that the castle is sometimes known as Panagía castle. One of the oldest on the island, this church was badly damaged in the World War II bombardment, but has been beautifully restored. Its magnificent gilt iconostasis dates from around 1745; it contains four 14th-century icons. The church's namesake icon, however, is off to one side. According to tradition it came over from Constantinople by itself in a boat; installed in the town cathedral, it refused to stay there, coming up to the (Turkish-held) castle of its own accord every night until the Turks, spooked, turned the castle back over to the Christians. Thanks to the renovation, the complex now boasts an **Ecclesiastical Museum** and a **Museum of Local History**, including the Bishop's library. Even if these are closed, the views are worth the walk up.

Somewhat hipper and more lively than Platanos is its harbor of **Agía Marína**, where Flying Dolphins also dock. For shutterbugs, there are the arches of the old waterside fortress of **Brouzi** and an old **windmill** posing photogenically on a spit of causeway. For museum buffs, there's a brand-new **Archeological Mu-**

seum, small, but with an attractive, modern presentation of local finds, from prehistoric artifacts to fragments of Byzantine churches.

Further north along the same bay is **Álinda** ❹, the island's main tourist center. Since this is Léros, there are incongruous elements even along the beach strip: the **Belléni Villa**, for instance, the lavish mansion of a wealthy local businessman, which houses an **Ethnographic and Historical Museum** of local objects (including a windmill) and art. Then there's the **Commonwealth War Cemetery**, a tidy, green "corner of England" honoring the Allied soldiers who died in the fighting here.

On a similar theme is the Byzantine **Church of the Forty Martyrs**; you can make out traces of ancient mosaics in the courtyard, although the original structure was stuccoed over in the 19th century. If you continue on foot to the end of the bay, you come to the church of **Panagía**. A rocky path leads over the headland to the beach at **Krífos**, but it's easier to get there by boat.

Above: Kálimnos – the island of the sponge divers.

Across the island, narrow here, is **Gournás Bay** ❺. Near Drimón is **Panagía tis Gourlomatas**, a 14th-century church with some striking frescoes. Gournás' trademark, however, is **Ágios Isídoros**, a little chapel built out on the water, connected to land by a narrow causeway, a sight made famous on countless local postcards.

At present, the northern part of the island is still wild, with a strong military presence; locals say that **Mount Klidí** (320 meters) is hollowed out with subterranean tunnels as a kind of crisis command headquarters. Not so many years ago the junta exiled political prisoners to this area; some of them allegedly contributed to the wall paintings in the little church of **Agía Kioura**. This church lies on a headland between two unspoiled bays, **Parthéni** ❻ and **Blefoúti** ❼. The former is named for a **Temple of Artemis**

Map p. 164, Info pp. 192-195

Parthenos (*parthenos* means "virgin"), the ruins of which are difficult to find, but can still be seen; the latter is a crescent of golden-brown sand around a bay of which the mouth is "corked" by the little island of **Strongíli**, keeping its waters warmer than elsewhere. But the new airport is going in along the Parthéni road, so this area is probably going to be the next to be developed for tourism.

KÁLIMNOS

Sailing in to the main harbor, Kálimnos (Pothiá), you can tell from the ferry deck that this island is special. Not from the landscape, though there's a stark majesty to the steep, gray-pink hills. But it's the town itself, filling its valley with boxy houses whose bright colors are reflected in the fishing boats bobbing in the harbor, that reaches out to enfold the visitor, blending the picturesque and active in an appealing, open, friendly manner.

***Kálimnos Town** ❶ is one of the largest towns in the Dodecanese, and even after the tourist season ends its streets and cafés still bustle with mopeds, pedestrians, coffee-drinkers. Certainly there are tourists, particularly along the gray-brown beach between Kandoúni and Masoúri on the west coast of the island, and it's an open question how the island will develop in the future. For the time being, at any rate, shoppers in town are less likely to find "I Love Kálimnos" T-shirts than fishermen selling *phouskies*, a local mollusk encased in a leathery but flexible "shell" (the name means "balloon") or sea sponges.

For Kálimnos' other sobriquet is "Island of the Sponge Fishermen." Historically, the island's main economy has revolved around sponge divers. Originally, they dove naked, clutching a stone to help them reach the depths where they gathered the black, inky sponges in bags around their necks and brought them to the surface. Once caught, the sponges

were dried and cleaned of their meat; the skeleton is what most people know and use as "sponge." The sponge fleet left in the spring and returned around October, journeying as far as Cyprus and Africa. Besides the weather, hazards to divers included the bends, the crippling result of nitrogen bubbles forming in the blood after a too-rapid ascent to the surface. Those who made it back unscathed were amply rewarded; a sponge diver made up to 10 times more than the local doctor. Sponge diving was pretty much done in by a disease that struck the local sponge population in 1987.

Sponges have slowly made a comeback, but the industry isn't what it once was. Still, Kálimnos has plenty of "sponge factories" where sponges – both the soft Greek ones with the large holes and the firmer and smaller-holed American varieties – are processed, trimmed, and sometimes bleached in a bath of vitriol, which gives the sponge the paler color some people prefer, but also shortens its useful life.

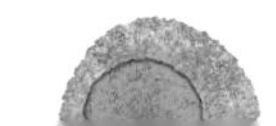

Info pp. 192-195

A collection of material relating to sponge-diving – photographs, diving suits, and sponge tools including a fearsome many-pronged trident – is displayed in the ***Sponge Museum**, housed in one of the many buildings bequeathed to Kálimnos by the Vouvalis family. Local "sponge millionaires" whose empire extended across both sides of the Atlantic, the Vouvalises also donated a number of other public buildings, including the local hospital. An earlier Vouvalis mansion now serves as the so-called **Archeological Museum**; apart from a few marbles and a small collection of Neolithic artifacts found near Vathís, however, this museum is really about the Vouvalis family's life in the 19th century, with furnishings, china and portraits.

Kálimnos runs up a long valley to blend into **Horió ❷**, the island's original town, which has quite a different personality. It's not hard to remember that these steep and narrow streets were built for donkeys, especially if you're daring or foolish enough to try to negotiate them in a car. Three windmills loom over the road. Above them, forming an impressive backdrop when seen from the harbor, are the rangy walls of ***Péra Kástro**, the old Byzantine fortress; it contains nine chapels and the ruins of a medieval village deserted since the 18th century.

Northwest of Horió, the 5th-century basilica of **Hristós tís Jerousalím** was built on the site of a temple of Apollo, and incorporates carved stones from ancient ruins in the remains of its apse, a light, gracefully-curved stone shell. A short walk away through the old graveyard behind the basilica there is the equally old and impressive **Church of the Twelve Apostles** (Ágios Apóstoli). Protective coverings guard the ancient mosaic floors; make sure to replace them after you're done looking.

Right: A beekeeper in the Vathís Valley assesses this year's honey (Kálimnos).

The west coast is the beach strip, sheltered by two offshore islands. **Kandóuni Beach**, where the locals come (it maintained separate men's and women's sections until the 1950s) is the first in a string of beaches. **Platís Gialós** faces the little island of **Agía Kiriakí**, but it's larger **Télendos ❸** that dominates the scene. Télendos used to be part of Kálimnos until it split off in an earthquake in the 5th century B.C., and a few foundation walls of a town that used to stand here are still visible on the beaches and in the water.

Providing a striking silhouette from the Kálimnos side, the island offers a slightly quieter alternative to the beach activity at **Mirtiés**, **Masoúri** or **Arméos**; boats cross to it regularly, and there are rooms to rent and a couple of tavernas. There's a particularly good view of Télendos from **Iéro Horió**, on the slopes behind **Masoúri ❹**, where an ancient village is being excavated. North of the beaches, the island is quieter. Hikers can head into the hills behind **Arginónda ❺** (which has a beautiful beach) and make their way across the slopes of Ilias across the island to the second port at Vathís; but make sure you have a good map or a local guide before you head off.

Emborió ❻ marks the end of the road; its name indicates that this quiet fishing village was once a busy port city, the island's original harbor. Hikers who strike out from here can explore the local caves, such as the one near **Skaliá**, or find their own secluded beaches further along the north coast.

There's layer upon layer of history to be found in the valley of ***Vathís ❼**, the verdant vale of Kálimnos. When you crest over the coastal road from Kálimnos Town, you look down on the island's "fjord," a narrow tongue of sharp blue water reaching deep into the land between the steep dry hills. The water here is extra cold, for it's fed with the runoff from natural springs that irrigate the swath of deep green extending inland:

Map p. 167, Info pp. 192-195

orange and lemon groves dominate here, penned in by whitewashed stone walls. In Vathís village, the springs run through the streets in little canals which feed a huge natural "fish tank"; the food fish swimming unmolested here have attained enormous sizes.

History in Vathís begins in the walls of the fjord, where extensive finds of Neolithic settlement were made in the **Daskalió Cave**; bits are displayed in Kálimnos Town. The cave is supposed to have housed "secret schools" during both Turkish and Fascist rule, since both governments prohibited instruction in Greek. Nearer town, you can see the remains of the old Byzantine village that once stood here. Farther up the valley, amidst the orchards, there are ongoing excavations of two Byzantine **churches** (4th/5th centuries A.D.) near picturesque **Plátanos** ❽; both sites are open to the public, though you may need a local to help you find them. One is located in the ruins of a Hellenistic castle beneath a 12th-century frescoed **Church of St. Michael**.

★ASTIPÁLEA

Halfway between the Dodecanese and the Cyclades, Astipálea has characteristics of both: something illustrated in the main town, where a Venetian castle is enthroned atop a mound of blue-and-white Cycladic houses. Furthermore, it's almost like two separate islands, connected in the middle by a spit of land some 100 meters wide, and the islanders call its eastern and western sections *Méga Nísi* ("Big Island") and *Éxo Nísi* ("Outer Island") respectively.

Astipálea (Hóra) ❶ sits on the inner coast of the latter, its white cubist townscape rising up from its harbor, **Péra Gialós**, and anchored by a row of white windmills aligned with its **Kástro**. The castle belonged to Venice's Quirini family, who ruled here for 300 years and left their coat-of-arms over the door. Within its walls are two white churches: a **Panagía** and **Ágios Geórgios**.

The town has two other churches: the **Megali Panagía** complex, its courtyard

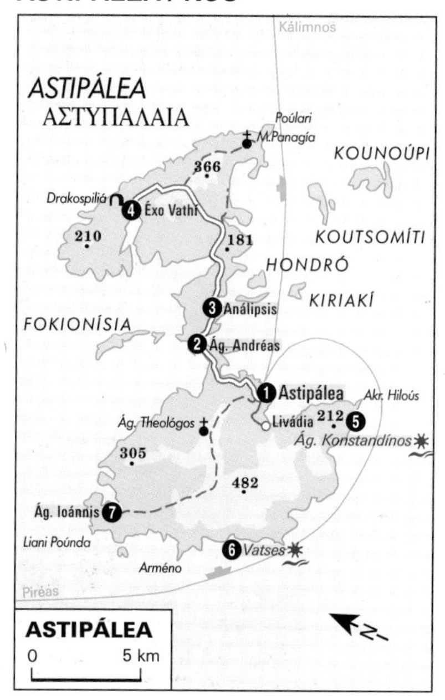

done in black-and-white pebble mosaics, and, especially impressive, **Panagía Portaítissa**, built by the blind St. Anthimos between 1762 and 1771, held to be one of the most beautiful in the Dodecanese. A magnificent gilded iconostasis surrounds an icon which the saint brought with him, a copy of one in the monastery at Ivrion. "Feast of the Gods" is an epithet of Astipálea, coined for its flowers and fruit trees. For visitors, part of the feast is the good walking and the beaches that stud the shores.

Livádia Beach, nearer town, tends to be more crowded. From Livádia, walkers can head to the hills and the monastery of **Flevariotissa**, or seek out the attractive harbor and beach of **Ágios Andréas** ❷. There's good swimming at **Stenó**, the name for the thin tongue of land connecting Astipálea's two "islands." Further east is **Análipsis** ❸, which the Italians called *Maltezana*, possibly because of the Maltese pirates who used to hang out here. Earlier still, Romans built baths with **floor mosaics** (which are still extant) depicting the signs of the zodiac.

The area around here and **Schinóntas** is getting rapidly built up, not least because of its proximity to the new airport. More attractive still is **Éxo Vathí** ❹, a beautiful deep bay off the Gulf of Vai with a little fishing harbor. From here, it's not very far to the stalactite cave of **Drakospiliá**. A bad dirt road leads through the mountains to the monastery of **Panagía**, past the Italian fortification of **Kastellano**.

On Éxo Nísi, there are lovely beaches on the eastern shore around **Ágios Konstandínos** ❺; **Tzanaki** is the place for nudists. At **Vatses** ❻, on the southern coast, are more caves and gorgeous beaches; while the west coast is guarded by the ruins of the **Kástro** of **Ágios Ioánnis** ❼.

Right: Windmills point the way to the Venetian Kástro (Hóra, Astipálea).

KÓS

Kós, within sight of the Turkish coast, has long sandy beaches and mountain villages, ancient ruins and Venetian castles conveniently located and easy of access, an international airport and, thanks to its relative flatness, great cycling opportunities: everything your average tourist to Greece could want. Therefore, the entire island shows signs of the presence of tourism. Villages that once doubtless oozed with genuine charm now market that commodity in various forms in the "Tourist Shops" between the tavernas offering international fare on menus in various languages in the hopes of being able to please everybody. The beaches are beautiful, all right, but hard to see, in season, under the umbrellas. Because Kós is a large island, you can still find lovely scenery and smaller towns, but the atmosphere is surprisingly uniform, and geared to the package visitor. Not that there aren't some very impressive sights.

Info pp. 192-195

Kós was the birthplace of Hippocrates (460-375 B.C.), whose oath still represents a doctor's official entry into the practice of medicine. The island became the site of a major shrine to Asclepius, god of healing, after his death, and its ruins are still imposing. So are those of the ancient city in present-day Kós Town. Classicists may have a field day here – but it's better to come during the off season.

**Kós Town

Kós Town ❶ is a busy and crowded port where ancient and modern are jumbled together in a great deal of heat and bustle. The major building on the waterfront is the old **Castle of the Knights of St. John**, where visitors can roam the remains of parapets and survey the yachts from a cannoneer's vantage point.

Immediately behind the castle is the sprawling piece of plant life dubbed **Hippocrates' Plane Tree**, propped up with metal supports; if it were a pet, it would be put down. There's no way it can date back to Hippocrates' day, but it may be able to claim five or six centuries. It stands at one end of the **Agorá**, a mishmash of buildings and old mosaic floors from different eras, with bits of column drums built into its walls, and a little Byzantine chapel of much more recent vintage. Also here is an informal center for the feeding and care of stray cats.

A delightful introduction to Kós' antiquities is the **museum** off the main square, **Platía Eleftherías** ("Freedom Square"), where there's a pleasant roofed **market** and an old Turkish **mosque**. One enters a room with a Roman mosaic floor in a recreated Roman villa; on the back wall is a stunningly fine mosaic of fish, shimmering with minute tiles.

The "Old Town" is an accumulation of pedestrian streets lined with tourist shops. Roman ruins are scattered around this: a Hellenistic **Temple of Dionysus**, the **Roman Odeon** and a marble **Amphitheater**. On the other side of the harbor, the town degenerates into a mass of bars

and night spots, although Kós Town's beach is broad and sandy – and extremely crowded.

Environs of Kós Town

South of Kós Town, there are beach developments at **Psalídi** (where some of the island's priciest resort hotels are) and **Ágios Fokás**. Continue around the headland, where a military installation displays a huge Greek flag as if to provoke neighboring Turkey, to the natural hot springs of **Embrós Thermá** ❷, where the sand is black. The clifftop drive, with its panoramic views of Turkey, is itself quite spectacular, especially when taken at sunset.

A major "sight" near Kós Town is, of course, the ***Asklipíon** ❸. Try to see it during or after a rain shower, when every plant in the area exudes the fullest measure of its odor and the heavily perfumed cool air seems clearly healing. This was a popular spa for wealthy Romans, with springs, baths and therapy rooms. It also took in the temple complex of the god of healing, Asclepius. The staff of Asclepius, with a serpent entwined around it, was said to aid in the search for healing herbs; it is still the symbol of the medical profession.

Above: The Asklipíon, a health spa from Roman times (Kós).

The Asklipíon is built on three levels, looking out over the creased mountains of the Turkish coast; rising from the Roman baths (3rd century A.D.) to the Doric Temple of Asclepius, with a few of its original 104 columns still standing. This is one of those sites whose original magic still lingers, however many busloads of tourists try to interrupt its spell.

On Kós, the mountain villages have become sanctioned tourist sights: sunset in **Zía** ❹ is as much a part of the official Kós experience as the Asklipíon. Zía is a charming village, and does have great views of the sunset, if you can see them between the cameras; so does nearby **Asfendioú**. Further south, the town of

Info pp. 192-195

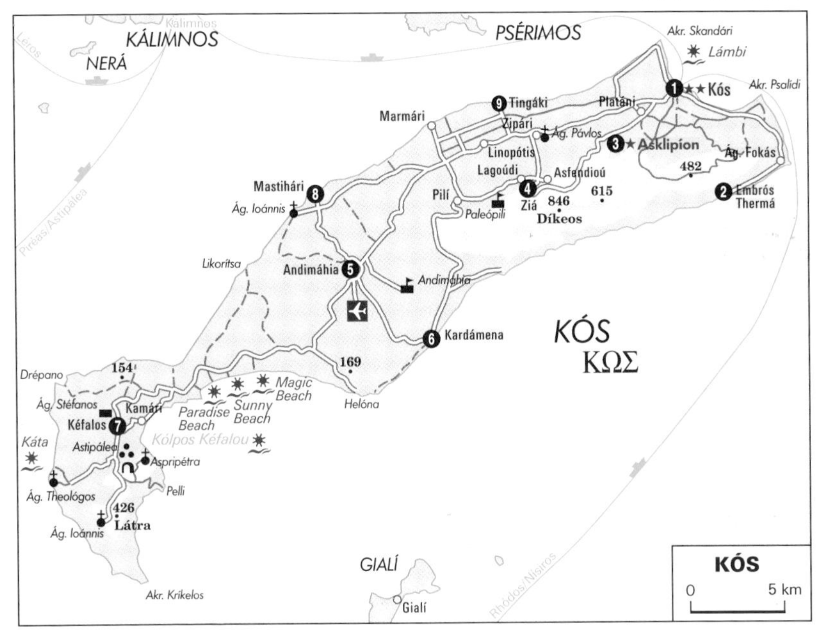

Andimáhia ❺ has managed to remain less touristed – simply because it isn't all that interesting, although it does offer a kind of **museum** with a windmill and a traditional local house. A high point here, literally, is the 14th-century **Kástro** south of Andimáhia, whose tumbled, sprawling ruins are open to visitors and command wonderful views down over the coast and **Kardámena** ❻. In the off season, the latter town betrays traces of what must once have been its considerable charm; in season, it's one big package tour.

From here on, the south coast is virtually one long beach, called by various names: **Paradise Beach**, **Sunny Beach**, **Magic Beach**. Although crowded, these beaches are beautiful; pale sand under high headlands. They gradually peak into the more built-up tourist strip around **Kéfalos Bay**, with its picturesque islet: a Club Med has taken over one end. Hilltop **Kéfalos** ❼ itself sits above it all, and because it's a real Greek village, and away from the water, it's managed to preserve much of its original flavor in the face of the development below. There are also some beach towns along the north coast which nowadays are given over almost exclusively to the tourism industry. **Mastihári** ❽, near Andimáhia, has views of Kálimnos across the water; **Marmári** and **Tigáki** ❾ are the two other places where you can find food, hotels and nice beaches. The latter is near a salt flat, **Alikés**, fairly deserted because of the high grass and humidity, and great for bird watchers.

*NÍSIROS

Many visitors to Nísiros equate the island solely with its volcano. Day-trippers from Kós disembark onto waiting buses and are spirited away into the interior, where they climb down into the crater, take snapshots, and are bussed back to the port for lunch before getting back onto their boats. They don't know what they're missing, for the island has much more to offer. They may have time to look briefly around Mandráki, the island's main port,

but not to fully soak in the charms of its narrow, pretty streets and squares. Nor do they get to swim on volcanic beaches through natural hot springs, or enjoy sunset from the island's 2,000-year-old ruined castle. All these things are missed by day-trippers; though they await visitors to this lush, fertile island who have a little more time on their hands.

The legend of Nísiros' founding is that Poseidon ripped off a chunk of Kós and flung it at the Titan Polyvotis, pinning him to the sea floor under what is now Nísiros; the volcano is Polyvotis expressing his frustration with his enforced captivity. Nísiros is one of only three dormant volcanoes in the Greek Islands, along with Mílos and Santorin; but it's also had other claims to fame. The Phoenicians called it Porphyros, since they found here large quantities of the murex shells which they used for the purple dye; Nísiros was allegedly the first place to produce porphyry. One version of the etymology of the island's name is that it links *nissi*, the Greek word for "island," and *ross*, Phoenician for "red."

Above: Pretty, though sometimes crowded, beaches are found in the southwest of Kós.

Charming ***Mandráki** ❶, extending along the water, is the capital of this community of some 1,200. Well kept-up, it has adorned its squares with little fountains or black-and-white *krokalia* mosaics. Walking along the water, you come to one plaza after another, but you'll entirely miss the main square, **Ilkiomeni**, tucked away inland, where locals come out at night to sit at café tables.

Guarding all this, elevated on a small cliff at one end of town, is the 14th-century castle which the Venetians built when they took over the island, mainly as protection against pirates. Around 1600, a monastery was created inside this castle, called **Panagía to Spilianí** after the little 15th-century church built into the cliff (*spilia* means "cave") at its heart. A steep flight of stone steps leads up the rock, giving onto panoramic views, a little stone chapel, and the **Municipal Mu-**

Info pp. 192-195

seum (which is to be moved to new, grander premises, funded by a wealthy Nisiran, at some future date). In the church a carved wooden iconostasis holds the miraculous Panagía icon. August 15, the Virgin's feast day, is marked with a great local celebration.

A footpath leads around the Spilianí point to the town beach, cradled within high cliffs. The water here is touted as the best on the island, even if the beach isn't the most comfortable in the world, comprised of chunks of the dark rock called **Hohláki**, which is also the beach's name.

None of Nísiros' many monasteries and convents are still operational. A steep six-kilometer road leads uphill from Mandráki to the little convent of **Evangelístra**, with a simple church. About halfway there, at a fork in the road, you can turn off to another "Kástro"; this is not the Venetian fortress, but an older edifice, ***Paleókastro** ❷, which represents the ancient Acropolis of Nísiros. It was first mentioned in the 4th century B.C. Hewn of black basalt, the stones are cut so perfectly that they hold without mortar. One reason it's lasted so well is that basalt is one of the hardest stones in existence; how ancient technicians managed to cut it remains a mystery. From atop the wall, unique in Greece, you can look out over the islets offshore, including **Gialí**, with its pale hill of slag from ongoing, and extremely lucrative, pumice mining. There are some very good beaches on the island, and regular boats from Mándraki.

Apart from the narrow concrete-slab route up to Evangelístra and the Paleókastro, there's basically one road on Nísiros, looping from Mandráki halfway around the island to Avláki on the south shore. As you head out of town, the first settlement is **Loutrá** ❸, a little harbor town. The swimming is excellent at **White Beach** here.

At **Páli** ❹, the island's second harbor, there are also heated waters; anyone swimming off the beach can find "hot

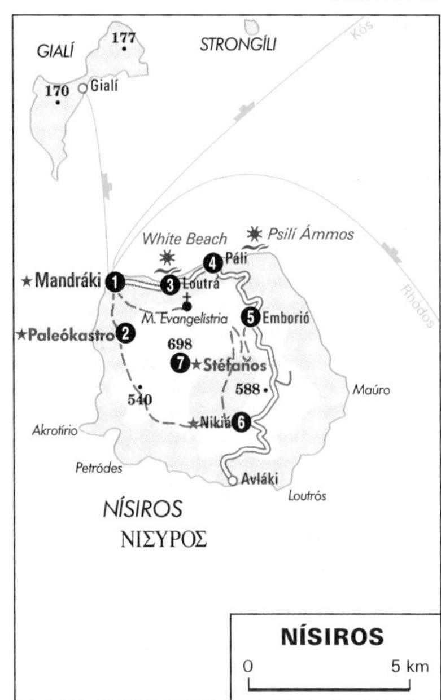

spots" along the coast; and construction is underway on a mammoth spa. The brown beach here is covered with dark volcanic sand and scattered with bits of pumice stone. Anyone looking for more secluded swimming can continue down the shore past all traces of human habitation, park at the very end of the paved road, and continue on foot to get to the island's best beach, **Psilí Ámmos**.

Nísiros has two other villages, both perched on the periphery of the volcanic crater. Emigration has left its mark on Nísiros; a large part of its population has gone off to Canada or the United States, sending home money to finance the construction of local churches, such as that in **Emborió** ❺, which seems almost like a ghost town. At the top of town are the ruins of a medieval **castle**, amid which stands the church of **Taxiárhis**, a little Byzantine gem with very old, somewhat crude frescoes.

***Nikiá** ❻ is another lovely village, a bit more lively than Emborió, painted blue and white and even boasting a

taverna. The elaborate church of **Theotókou**, or the Virgin Mary, was funded by émigrés in the States. There are great views: down to the water on one side, although you'll need a sturdy vehicle to drive down to the beach at **Avláki**; and down into the volcano on the other. You get your first whiff of sulfur here, and a footpath from town leads into the crater.

From whichever side you approach it, the volcano is an impressive sight from any perspective. Within the crater, the island's wooded slopes yield to a flat landscape dominated by heather and orange rock. The singular "crater" is a rather misleading term; for there are actually five craters here, each with its own name and temperament. The largest of these, ***Stéfanos**, is also the most impressive; but you can wander up a footpath through the sharp rocks to find yourself in a miniature Grand Canyon with one of the smaller craters emitting bursts of steam and foul, sulfurous odors at your feet.

Above: The caldera of Nísiros with the Stéfanos crater.

Volcanic activity here is carefully monitored; there hasn't been an eruption since 1933, and busloads of tourists regularly cross Stéfanos each day. Still, caution is in order; if your foot should go through the crust of earth, you might find yourself in scalding boiling mud, such as is evident in the sinkholes that sometimes open up and which, especially after a rain shower, can be seen oozing through the surface of the crater.

TÍLOS

One of the less visited islands of the Dodecanese, Tílos basically remains an inside tip: it is quiet, cheap and pleasant, complete with a full complement of beaches, hiking trails and charming displays of traditional island life. It also boasts some of the earliest traces of habitation, albeit not necessarily human. When the island broke off from the mainland some 10,000 years ago, there seem

Info pp. 192-195

to have been mastodons lving on it; over time, these animals adapted to the size of their new habitat by growing smaller, reaching heights of only 1.3 meters. Their bones have been found in the **Grotto of Harkadió** (Spiliá Harkadió), together with various Stone Age artifacts.

In the 14th century the Knights of St. John arrived on Tílos and set about building no fewer than seven castles on the island, the ruins of which can still be seen.

The harbor of **Livádia** ❶ has a long beach and a modern and lively air, especially when Greek vacationers take over in summer. Following the island road north from Livádia, you pass by **Mikró Horió**, a village whose last residents left in the 1950s (many of them moved to Livádia, taking their tiled roofs with them). The inland capital, **Megálo Horió** ❷, is dominated by the ruins of a Venetian castle. The town was built upon the site of the ancient city of Télos; over 3,000-year-old remains of the city wall can be seen between the houses. From Megálo Horió a road leads to the long beach of **Erístos**.

On the northwest coast of the island lie the beaches of **Ágios Andónios** and **Pláka**. The rock formations of the former are more gruesome than they seem at first: they are made up of the petrified human bones of the victims of a volcanic eruption that occurred around 600 B.C. The walled monastery of **Ágios Pandaleímon** ❸, from the 18th century, sits in idyllic green surroundings and offers stunning views down over the water.

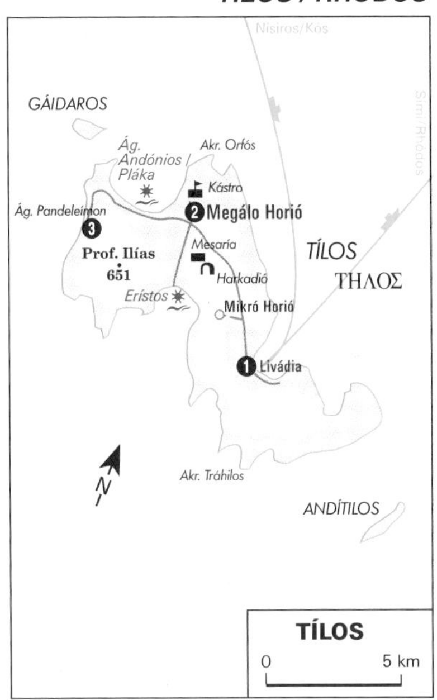

**RHÓDOS (RHODES)

The "Rose Island" (the Greek word *rhodon* means "rose") is the fourth largest in Greece and seems a world unto itself. Larger than all the other islands of the Dodecanes together, Rhódos has many faces. Its capital, Rhódos Town (pop. 41,000), is one of the more urbane cities in all the Greek Islands, with a modern business district as well as an Old Town skyline spiked with the crenellated walls of medieval castles, and some visitors find enough to keep them busy right here. Others park on the beaches closest to town, where the busy resorts stay active nearly year-round on what's supposed to be one of the sunniest islands in Greece: Rhódos, it's claimed, gets 300 days of sun a year. But those who stray farther afield can find other worlds to conquer. Rhódos has preserved a wild beauty in its less-traveled regions, with dark pine woods, emptily beautiful mountainscapes and cliffs toppling into the sea. And fields of ruins mark the sites of cities that were once among the most powerful in the Aegean.

Líndos, Ialissós and Kámiros were the island's three main centers a thousand years before Christ. Named after grandsons of the sun god Helios, this sunny island's patron saint, these cities belonged to a powerful political and economic alliance known as the Hexapolis. In 408

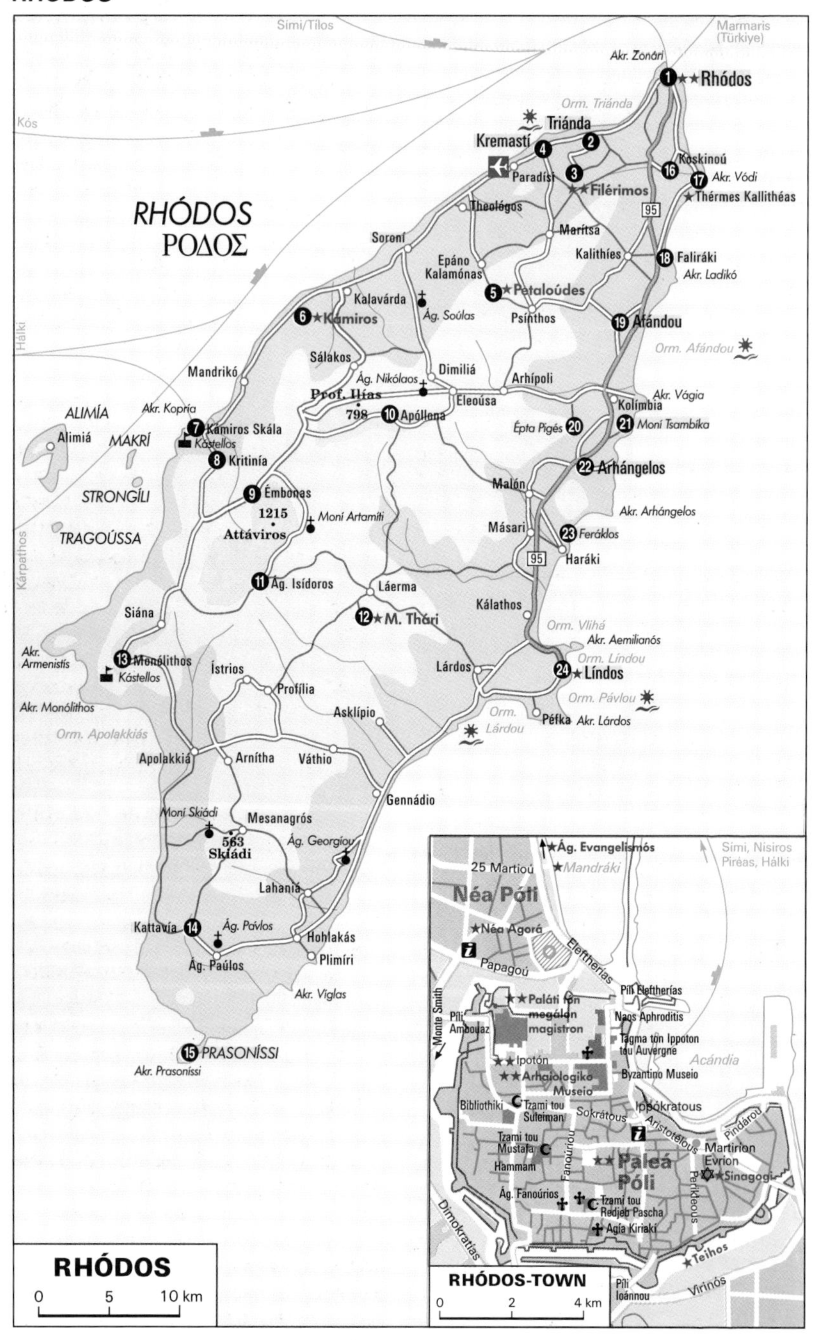

RHÓDOS
ΡΟΔΟΣ
Rhódos
Triánda
Kremastí
Paradísi
Filérimos
Kóskinoú
Akr. Vódi
Thérmes Kallithéas
Theológos
Soroní
Marítsa
Kalithíes
Faliráki
Akr. Ladikó
Epáno Kalamónas
Petaloúdes
Kalavárda
Kámiros
Ág. Soúlas
Psínthos
Afándou
Orm. Afándou
Sálakos
Mandrikó
Dimiliá
Ág. Nikólaos
Prof. Ilías
798
Apóllona
Eleoúsa
Arhípoli
Kolímbia
Akr. Vágia
Moní Tsambíka
Épta Pigés
Arhángelos
Akr. Arhángelos
ALIMÍA
Alimiá
Akr. Kopría
MAKRÍ
Kámiros Skála
Kástellos
Kritinía
STRONGÍLI
TRAGOÚSSA
Émbonas
1215
Attáviros
Moní Artamíti
Malón
Másari
Feráklos
Haráki
Ág. Isídoros
Láerma
M. Thári
Kálathos
Siána
Orm. Vlihá
Akr. Aemilianós
Akr. Armenistís
Monólithos
Kástellos
Ístrios
Profília
Lárdos
Líndos
Orm. Líndou
Orm. Pávlou
Akr. Monólithos
Asklípio
Orm. Lárdou
Péfka
Akr. Lárdos
Orm. Apolakkiás
Apolakkiá
Arnítha
Váthio
Gennádio
Moní Skiádi
Mesanagrós
563
Skiádi
Ág. Georgíou
Lahaniá
Kattavía
Ág. Pávlos
Hohlakás
Ág. Paúlos
Plimíri
Akr. Viglas
PRASONÍSSI
Akr. Prasoníssi
Kós
Sími/Tílos
Marmaris (Türkiye)
Akr. Zonári
Orm. Triánda
Hálki
Kárpathos
RHÓDOS
0 5 10 km
RHÓDOS-TOWN
0 2 4 km
Ág. Evangelismós
Mandráki
Sími, Nisiros
Piréas, Hálki
25 Martiou
Néa Póli
Néa Agorá
Papagoú
Eleftherías
Monte Smith
Píli Eleftherías
Paláti ton megálon magistron
Píli Amboaz
Naos Aphroditis
Tagma ton Ippoton tou Auvergne
Ipotón
Acándia
Arhaiologiko Museio
Byzantino Museio
Bibliothiki
Tzami tou Suleiman
Sokrátous
Ippókratous
Aristotélous
Pindárou
Tzami tou Mustafa
Hammam
Fanouríou
Paleá Póli
Martirion Evrion
Sinagogi
Periklèous
Ág. Fanoúrios
Tzami tou Redjeb Pascha
Agía Kiriakí
Dimokratías
Teihos
Píli Ioánnou
Virinós

B.C., however, they went into voluntary decline after joining forces to found a fourth city as a new capital of the island. Rapidly developing into the island's population center, Rhódos Town became a center for art and learning as well as administration and commerce, the latter partly thanks to its large natural harbor, Mandráki, today still in use as a marina for pleasure boats.

Rhódos is only 18 kilometers from the coast of Turkey, which made the island an attractive base for would-be conquerors intent on moving east. Alexander the Great, for example, favored Rhódos, which during his rule became the leading power in the Mediterranean. But Rhódos always retained a measure of autonomy, and after Alexander's death turned down an offer of alliance with one of his generals. The general's son, Demetrius, summarily appeared to take the island by force. There followed a prolonged and bitter siege during which Demetrius availed himself of a variety of state-of-the-art martial machinery; but the islanders ultimately withstood the attack. When Demetrius finally pulled out, the Rhodians melted down the remains of his machinery and used it to erect the famous **Colossus of Rhodes**, a statue of the island's patron sun god Helios some 35 meters high, which was accounted one of the Seven Wonders of the Ancient World. The fame of the Colossus, completed in 290 B.C., long outlasted the statue itself; it was toppled by an earthquake in 225 B.C. Its remains lay around the harbor for centuries before a Turkish merchant carted them off.

****Rhódos Town**

Remains of the ancient **Acropolis** dominate the skyline on the hill of **Monte Smith** in the western part of **Rhódos Town ❶**; the **Temple of Pythian Apollo** here, reconstructed by the Italians, commands great views of the sunset, and there are remains of an ancient **stadium** and a reconstructed **theater** (where plays are staged in summer) just below the hilltop. But Rhódos Town's most striking architecture is a legacy of some other adventurers who used the island as a base as they looked east: the Crusaders. In the 13th century, when Jerusalem "fell" to the "infidel" Muslims, the Knights of St. John retreated from the Holy Land to a new stronghold, Rhódos. Although the local population initially resisted – many were loyal to the Byzantine Empire, which, after all, was also Christian, although this was too fine a distinction for many Western Europeans – the Knights' presence was advantageous for them, as well: it represented a strong defense against Ottoman attack. For the next two centuries the Knights held sway on the island, constructing the edifices that still characterize the Old Town: the **inns** or administrative buildings for each of the eight "tongues" in the order (England, France, Provence, Germany, Auvernge, Aragon, Castille and Italy); the fortified city walls, which visitors can still promenade around; and the doughty Palace of the Grand Masters.

In 1523, the Turks finally managed to drive out the weakened Knights; Ottoman rule lasted until the Italians were awarded the Dodecanese in 1912. The Turks left their own architectural legacy. In the Old Town, there's the Mosque of Suleiman, which Suleiman the Magnificent built to commemorate his taking of Rhódos; the Moslem Library with its illuminated manuscripts; and the 18th-century Turkish Bath (Hamam) of Mustafa Pasha, which is still in use (though closed for restorations at present).

In this century, the Italians added their own elements to the architectonic mix. One of the most striking edifices that greets a visitor arriving in Rhódos by boat is the **Governor's Palace** on the waterfront, built to resemble a Venetian palazzo. The Italians also reproduced the

vanished Church of St. John, using the knights' original plans, in the church of ***Evangelismós**. And they cleaned up, renovated and restored other ancient and medieval relics all over the island, which is one reason that Rhódos' Old Town has a polished, tidy air incommensurate with its advanced age.

Flanking the entrance to ***Mandráki Harbor** are two columns bearing statues of a stag and a doe, symbols of Rhódos, allegedly marking the site where the Colossus stood (although it's almost certain that the Colossus didn't actually straddle the harbor, as some ancient commentators would have it). Along the harbor mole are three windmills, a reminder that one is, after all, in Greece; but they're overshadowed by the stout city walls of the Old Town, behind. The hexagonal market hall, ***Néa Agorá**, was constructed under the Italians. Here you will find shops and bars as well as the fish market. Day or night, this is a popular center of activity.

Above: The Crusaders fortified Rhódos Town with a mighty protective wall. Right: Activity takes place at night, too – along Odos Sokratóu.

Facing the town from Mandráki, the new arrival has two choices. Going straight or right leads into the cosmopolitan heart of the **New Town**, where Lambráki and Makaríou seem almost like streets from continental Europe. If you walk north along waterfront Eleftherías Street you can visit the **Mosque of Murad Reis** and the adjacent **Turkish Cemetery**. As you approach the northern tip of the island, the cityscape evolves into a complex of high-rise hotels, tourist restaurants and nightclubs, penned in by the town's broad beaches, where ranks of umbrellas shield browning bodies from the strong winds. At Rhódos' northern tip stands the **Aquarium**; this is yet another legacy of the Italians, built in 1924, and is made up of 40 tanks containing a marvelous variety of marine life.

If, instead, you opt to go left from Mandráki, you pass through the **Elef-**

 Map / City Map p. 178, Info pp. 192-195

therías – or "Freedom" – **Gate** into the ****Old Town**. The streets here are narrow, mainly cobbled, and only partly open to cars. Visitors linger over coffee in the squares or cruise along **Sokrátous Street**, the former Turkish bazaar, with its riot of shops and stands in the heart of the Old Town.

Once through the Eleftherías Gate, the first thing you see is what's left of a 3rd-century B.C. **Temple of Aphrodite**, one of Old Town's few ancient monuments. Further on, the **Inn of the Tongue of Auvergne** is of considerably later vintage: it was constructed in the 14th century. The 11th-century **Panagía tou Kastrou** was once Rhódos' cathedral; reconstructed and renovated, it is now the **Byzantine Museum** and displays frescoes and icons. A delightful little **Museum of Decorative Arts** is crammed with local textiles and woodcarvings.

The showpiece of Rhódos' museums is the ****Archeological Museum** in the Knights' Hospital. The statue of Aphrodite here, a beautiful, nearly complete sculpture from the 1st century B.C., was discovered by a fisherman in the harbor basin in 1928.

****Ipotón**, the Street of the Knights, where most of the medieval inns are located, is like a movie set: an alleyway of cobblestones and late-Gothic palace façades, unadorned with any sign of the modern age. At its end is the ****Palace of the Grand Masters**, which Mussolini had reconstructed to serve as his own summer palace during the Italian occupation, adorning it with Roman mosaics brought in from Kós and other trappings more fit for a Roman emperor.

Downstairs, there are rotating exhibits relating to the history of Rhódos. Many of the buildings at this end of Sokratou are undergoing restoration, such as the pinkish **Mosque of Suleiman the Magnificent**; but if you turn off Sokrátous into the alleyways of the former Turkish quarter you can find the **Turkish Bath** (closed for restoration) or, on Fanoúriou, the 14th-century Byzantine church of **St. Fanurios**, lined with aged frescoes.

Sokrátous leads down to **Ippókrates Square**, where the **Kastellanía Building** was probably used for trade by the Knights (it now houses exhibitions).

From here, Aristotelus leads to **Platiá Martíron Evríon** ("Square of the Hebrew Martyrs"), with its seahorse fountain, the center of the old Jewish Quarter. Thriving in the 19th century, the quarter was wiped out by the Nazis; the martyrs commemorated here are those who died in Auschwitz. One ⋆**synagogue** has survived on Perikleous Street, but it isn't always open. Pindárou Street leads on to the square where the ruins of the church of **Our Lady of Victory**, open to the sky, but with its apse fairly intact, commemorate the Knights' victory over the Turks in 1480.

Visitors here should under no circumstances miss a chance to take a walk along the top of the old ⋆**city wall** (Teihos; only possible on Tuesdays and Saturdays). You climb onto the wall at the Amboise Gate; the wall can be walked as far as the Ioánnou Gate. The fortress was never conquered; the last Grand Master had to surrender to the Turkish Sultan and his 200,000-strong army in 1523 because the 300 Knights and 6,000 soldiers ran out of gunpowder. Hedging the city walls is a ring of green parkland; outside the castle, there are festivals and *son et lumière* shows throughout the summer. More tranquil, although more distant (three kilometers from the center), is **Rodini Park**, not far from the Acropolis. It was here that Rhódos' School of Rhetoric was established in 330 B.C., and Rhodians have used the area ever since. Today, there is a **zoo** here, and every year in August this is the site of a popular wine festival.

Above: Odos Omirou offers relief from the sun (Rhódos Town).

The West Coast and Southern Rhódos

South of Rhódos Town, on the island's western coast, **Triánda** ❷ is the fulcrum

Map p. 178, Info pp. 192-195

of one of Rhódos' main tourist strips, where the beach is thick with hotels and snack bars. Here, too, is the turnoff for ancient Ialissós, the least important of Rhódos' original three cities; it's signposted **★★Filérimos ❸**, the name of the monastery later built on the site. Believed to be the site of a Phoenician settlement, the hilltop has since supported a Doric temple of Athena and Zeus (3rd century B.C.) and a Byzantine church; the latter was restored by the Italians, who also constructed the adjacent monastery. A tree-shaded avenue leads up to a huge post-war cross that commands wonderful views.

Kremastí ❹ is known for its miraculous icon of the Virgin, venerated in a big festival every year August 15. Farther along the coast, just past **Paradísi**, is the turnoff to the valley of the butterflies, **★Petaloúdes ❺**. Between June and September this peaceful valley, with its burbling river and old mill, is home to thousands of brown Quadrina butterflies or tiger moths (*Callimorpha quadripuntaria*), clouds of which arise in startled flight when visitors disobey the posted injunctions to leave them in peace and clap their hands or otherwise create a disturbance. Frightening the butterflies is believed to shorten their life cycle; indeed, a dramatic decrease in their population has already been observed.

Back to the sea, the coast road leads on past the village of **Theológos** to **Soroní**. From here, you can turn inland to the wooded glade where stands the church of **Ágios Soúlas** (St. Saul); the July festival that's held here is prominently featured in Durrell's book.

The second of Rhódos' Dorian cities was **★Kámiros ❻**, destroyed by an earthquake in the 2nd century B.C. and not unearthed until British-led excavations began in 1859, as a result of which a number of Kámiros' treasures are now in the British Museum. A later, Italian-led series of excavations between 1914 and 1929 exposed most of the large site of the Hellenistic city with its ruins of temples and houses. Around its **agorá** there are remants of a **Temple of Pythian Apollo** and a temple to local deities and heroes; there are also **bath houses** and the remains of a classical **fountain**.

Kámiros Skála ❼, the nearest beach, is a little curve of harbor guarded by the ruins of the **Kástro** (Kamiros Kastello), an impressive ruin of a building built by the Knights in the 16th century. Ferries run from here to the island of **Hálki**, with its charming harbor town of **Embrió**.

In the town of **Kritinia ❽**, on the winding road south, there is a **Museum of Local History**.

The roads inland lead into mountain country, where wooded slopes plunge into the blue shadows of valleys, dusted with the gold of late afternoon light, punctuated with the white clusters of villages. **Émbonas ❾** is the largest village in the region and center of local viticulture; **Emery**, one of the island's two leading vintners (the other is the cooperative CAIR), has a tasting room in its winery. The grapes themselves grow on the slopes of Rhódos' highest elevation, **Mount Attáviros** (1,215 meters); in antiquity, there was a temple to Zeus atop this mountain where a bull supposedly uttered sacred oracles. Hikers can trek up two to three hours from Émbonas to check out what's left of it and take in the spectacular views.

If you want a somewhat tamer alpine theme, head north for seven kilometers from Émbonas to **Profítis Ilías** (798 meters), where the Italians built two chalets. The road down to **Eleoúsa** passes by the Byzantine church of **Ágios Nikólaos**, which is adorned with some lovely frescoes. In **Apóllona ❿** there is a small **Ethnographic Museum**.

People who prefer less cultivated scenery should bear south and east from Émbonas. **Ágios Isídoros ⓫** is another wine village without the press of tourist

traffic that Émbonas can get in season. Anyone with a four-wheel-drive vehicle can cut across to the Byzantine church at ⋆**Thári Monastery** ⓬, near **Láerma**, which dates from the 10th century. But even the coast road here is wilder and more deserted. **Monólithos** ⓭ is named for a castle built by Grand Master D'Aubusson, a ruin that crowns a magnificent headland on the island. From the 15th-century frescoed churches of **Ágios Geórgios** and **Ágios Pandeleímon** you can watch the sun set over the neighboring islands.

From here on south, you may have the beaches to yourself; and the folk traditions that live on in small towns like **Apolakkía** or **Mesangrós** are not immediately evident in the dusty, unremarkable streets. **Skiádi Monastery**, a tranquil haven, shelters a miraculous icon of the Virgin. **Kattavía** ⓮ offers a couple of hotels and tavernas at the southernmost end of the paved road. Signposted to **Prasoníssi** ⓯ ("Green Island"), a rutted dirt track leads seven kilometers to white sand beaches. The "Green Island" is moored to Rhódos' southern tail by a tongue of white sand; its beaches and waters draw windsurfers and illicit campers. But even this isolated area is threatened: there's a hotel under construction.

Above: The 1,215-meter-high Attáviros is the hightest mountain on Rhódos.

The East Coast

Sheltered from the prevailing winds, on the lee side of the island, with a number of Blue Flag beaches, Rhódos' eastern coast is even more of a draw than the western. Just south of Rhódos Town, **Réni Koskinoú** is the beach settlement of inland **Koskinoú** ⓰, famed for its *krokalia* pebble mosaics.

The next stop is ⋆**Kallithéas** ⓱. The healing waters of the thermal spa here were famous even in antiquity, and an ornate resort facility was built in the 1920s, but the waters dried up in the 1960s; the building is deserted today, and the beach

Map p. 178, Info pp. 192-195

is now a popular spot for snorkelers and divers.

Faliráki ⓲ is one of the island's hottest, and most hopping, resorts, with a shopping mall and a bungee jump, a reptile house and a water slide; the resort strip has run over into the development of Faliráki Bay North. The name of **Afándou** ⓳, to the south, means "unseen village"; it was built to be concealed from the eyes of passing pirates. Slightly less crowded than Faliráki, it draws golfers with an 18-hole course. Nearby **Ladikó Bay** is also known as **Anthony Quinn Beach**; the Mexican-born actor began his long association with Greece along this coast, where he came to film *The Guns of Navarrone* in 1961. **Kolímbia**, an up-and-coming resort, is known for the tree-lined avenue that leads down to the good beaches around **Vágia**.

Turning inland from here, the road to **Eptá Pigés** ⓴, or the "Seven Springs," leads into another world, where clear waters bubble up into a forest pool and peacocks stroll on the grass. There are no ancient legends associated with the site – the water from the springs once irrigated the orange groves of Kolímba – but there is an infamous 170-meter-long tunnel from the springs to the lake. Wading through the ankle-deep water in the darkness is a rite of passage of sorts for many visitors.

Back on the coast, **Tsambíka** is popular with travelers for its sand beaches and with childless women for the miracle-working icon of the Holy Virgin in **Tsambíka Monastery** ㉑, which allegedly bestows fertility upon those who climb up barefoot on the feast day of September 8 to ask for help. Any resulting offspring have to be named for the monastery, and the number of Tsambíkos and Tsambíkas on the island attests to the Virgin's efficacy.

Surprisingly on this visitor-laden coast, sprawling **Arhángelos** ㉒, the island's largest village, surrounded by orange groves, has preserved an unspoiled flavor and a distinctive local dialect. Local products include pottery, textiles, and a special leather boot that farmers wear in the fields as protection against snakes.

Guarding **Vlihá Bay** is **Feráklos** ㉓, a ruined castle which the Knights allegedly took over from pirates; it was the last place on the island to fall to Suleiman.

People who have fallen under the spell of ***Líndos** ㉔ are extravagant in their praises of this white Cycladic-style village on the lower slopes of the acropolis that bears the ruins of what was once Rhódos' leading city. Unfortunately, over the years the town's delicate beauties have been somewhat eroded by waves of mass tourism. One of the first Greek jet-set destinations in the 1960s, Líndos now gets upward of half a million visitors a year. The white buildings lining its sun-dappled streets are bars and souvenir shops; and vendors so line the ascent up to the acropolis that it can be difficult to make out the view through the array of blouses and tablecloths for sale. Embroidery and pottery are two traditional Lindian crafts; examples of both can be seen in the **Papá-Konstantínou House** (now the Líndos Museum) and the **Kashines House**, two of the so-called "Captains' Houses" which rich Lindian sea captains built in the 16th and 17th centuries.

Cars and buses park as near as possible to the tree-shaded main square, where the old fountain bears Ottoman inscriptions and fills with water from the original pipes. Not far from here, but well within the maze of pleasantly winding streets, is the Byzantine church of ***Panagía**, redone by Grand Master D'Aubusson in the late 15th century on the site of a 10th-century church. Its frescoes were executed in 1779 by Gregory of Sími; one of them depicts St. Christopher with the head of a donkey.

Climbing up the 20-meter-high hill to the ***acropolis**, one can see the natural

sheltered **harbor**, the only one on the island except Mandráki, which helped the city to gain its position of importance. Ancient Líndos was much larger than today's town, a shipping power which established colonies around the Mediterranean. In the 6th century B.C. it was ruled by the tyrant Kleoboulos, one of the so-called "Seven Sages" of antiquity, who supposedly advocated "moderation in all things" and allowed women into his circle of learning (a cylindrical building alleged to be his tomb is visible to the north). Kleoboulos' reign saw the erection of some of the acropolis' main buildings, including the Temple of Athena, although this edifice later burned and was rebuilt.

One ancient religious cult here reputedly venerated Heracles by shouting abuse during ritual sacrifices; in antiquity, the phrase "like Lindians at the sacrifice" described people with particularly foul mouths.

Above: Traveling by donkey to the Acropolis of Líndos. Right: Remains of the Stoa of Líndos (ca. 200 B.C., Acropolis of Líndos).

The ascent to the acropolis is dramatic. One of its most famous features is visible on the rock wall before the last stairs up to the summit: the **Relief of a Trireme**, carved in the living rock in the 2nd century B.C., which once served as the pedestal for a statue of Poseidon by the local sculptor Pythokrates, creator of the Winged Victory of Samothráki. The Knights fortified this height in the 15th century; it was they who created the stairs used by modern visitors and left the remains of fortifications and the old church of **Ágios Ioánnis** you see at the top. Here, however, attention focuses on yet another set of stairs, broad and majestic, that seem to lead into the sky, restrained only by the rowed columns of the **Propylaea**. At the top, the **Temple of Athena** stands as the culmination of the journey, but it sits slightly to one side, as if making room for worshipers to take in the majestic view of the harbor and sea before paying homage to the goddess. From the heights

Map p. 178, Info pp. 192-195

you can also see the cave where bulls were sacrificed to the goddess, and a Hellenistic tomb cut into the rock wall behind town.

A swim in **Pávlou Bay** is a good way to relax; this is a natural pool almost completely surrounded by rocks. The beach of **Pallás** is small and pretty. Also pretty are the beaches of **Péfka**, three kilometers to the south, and **Lárdos**, seven kilometers west of Líndos.

*SÍMI

Lying close to the shores of Turkey, its main port turned diffidently away from Rhódos, Sími sprawls languidly in the metal-blue water of the Aegean, its tawny flanks as insouciant and seemingly inaccessible as those of a sleeping animal. But when approached, it turns another face to new arrivals with its spectacular harbor. Sími's hallmark is its yellow neoclassical houses, trimmed glowing blue or red, topped with triangular pediments, lining the steep hills around the harbor like opera boxes. This distinctive architecture gives the harbor a touch of the Riviera, Menton rather than Míkonos; but its elegance is set off by the rugged landscape around it.

Sími may seem remote, but it's always had a somewhat urbane flair, and always stood a bit apart. When Rhódos was settled by the Carians, Sími was settled by the Pelasgians; there are still remains of Pelasgian walls on the former acropolis in Horió. There's a mention in Homer's *Iliad* of the island's handsome King Nereus, who led three ships to do battle at Troy; even in this period, evidently, the island was associated with shipbuilding. Sími's ships maintained their reputation for speed into modern history: after the Turks took over, Sími provided the ships for the Ottoman postal service.

Sponge fishing and shipbuilding were long the island's two economic poles. In 1910, the population was 22,500 – 10

times what it is today – and its shipyards produced 500 boats a year. 1869 saw the introduction here of the first diving suit.

The classic sea approach to Sími leads to its most accessible point, the harbor of ***Gialós** ❶. Pliny mentioned the place as one of the safest harbors of the known world. It's also the site on the island that bears the clearest stamp of modern times, always hearkening back to the past. Take the **clock tower**, built in 1890, modeled on London's Big Ben, or the trireme carved into the rock in emulation of the ancient one in Líndos, on Rhódos. The extreme end of the harbor has been filled in to create a cement town square on which sit the Town Hall and the modest **Nautical Museum**. A bit inland, the church of **Ágios Ioánnis**, with fragments of an earlier temple mortared into its walls, has striking *krokalia* patterns in its courtyard.

From Gialós, many day-trippers in search of immediate beach gratification head off around the point dominated by the clock tower, along **Harani Bay** with

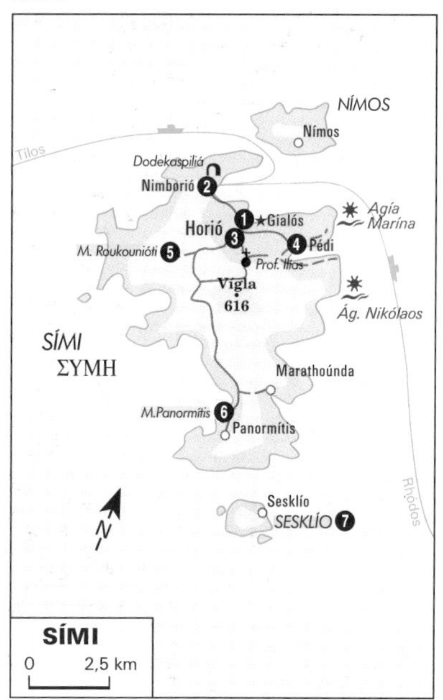

its boatyards, and past the headland of **Ágios Geórgios** to the little shingle beach at **Nós**, packed, in summer, with wall-to-wall bodies. More hardy swimmers continue on the cement track to **Nimborió** ❷, where the beach is longer. This was once the island's main commercial harbor; today, commerce is represented by a fish farm.

Inland, a little **chapel** has Roman mosaics in its courtyard; a little further uphill, a cave leads to ancient, man-made structures whose purpose is debated. There are tales that this was a school of icon painters; another theory is that the old foundations visible at the other end may be remnants of the lost palace of Nereus.

Other visitors in Gialós head to one of Sími's most famous features, **Kalí Stráta**, or the "Good Street." This so-called "street" is a flight of some 400 stone steps, polished and uneven with age, leading up from Gialós to **Horió** ❸, Sími's main village, which lies draped like a saddle atop a ridge crested with old windmills resembling the spines on the back of a stegosaurus. Especially in the heat of day, these steps are a somewhat daunting prospect, requiring good physical condition and a pair of good shoes; but climbing up, rather than making the detour by bus or taxi, brings you from the bustle of the harbor directly into another of Sími's hidden hearts.

Right: Traditional weaving patterns require patience and skill (Kárpathos).

Atop the hill, the stairs suddenly become the main artery of Horió, lined with simple shops and cafés, where people sit on the doorsteps and talk and watch the world go by. Getting lost in side streets, which is very easy to do, is the best way to see Horió, although the town offers a few "sights" as well.

One obligatory stop is the hundred-year-old **Pharmacy**, which has kept its original equipment. Signs lead you on to the **Municipal Museum**, with its small collection dedicated to local history, and to the nearby **Hatzigapitós House** (17th century), also open to the public. The core of Horió's history is the hilltop overlooking Gialós harbor: once the city's acropolis, it still bears traces of Pelasgian walls. Later, it became the site of a castle, first Byzantine, later Crusader. The whole thing, along with a number of surrounding houses, was blown up when the British took the island from the Germans in September 1944; the Germans had been using it to store munitions. There's a church, **Megáli Panagía**, at the top, with a 16th-century icon.

From Horió, it's about a 20-minute walk down to the island's second, quieter harbor of **Pédi** ❹, with fishing boats, a stretch of tawny, tamarisk-lined beach, and a few tavernas. While you can swim here, there are better beaches concealed in the long arms of land on either side of the fjord-like harbor. To the right, as you face the water, a path leads to **Ágios Nikólaos** (wear sturdy shoes, especially

Info pp. 192-195

for the last rocky bit); to the left, a slightly longer path to **Agía Marína**.

A hike of about one hour from Gialós leads you to the monastery of **Rou-koniótis** ❺. There's been a church on the site since the 5th century; the Knights of St. John built atop this in the 14th century, and much of the present edifice dates from the 18th; inside, it's covered with a patchwork of brilliant frescoes.

The first sight many travelers see of Sími is the monastery of **Panormítis** ❻, a long, elegant building standing between rocky arms of land that reach out to embrace a bay of still blue water. The tower atop the large, rather institutional-looking complex was a gift from the seamen of Ídra and Spétses. In the church, there is a miracle-working icon of the Archangel Michael, the island's patron saint, which is the destination of many a pilgrim. Each year, on November 8, the whole island descends on the monastery to celebrate the saint's feast day. The iconostasis attests to the renowned skill of Sími's woodcarvers.

There's also a local museum in the village of Panormítis, where the collection of objects recreates the aura of a farmer's attic.

In the waters off Panormítis are the **Sesklío Islands** ❼. This was site of the last naval battle of Peloponnesian War, which the Athenians lost.

*KÁRPATHOS AND KASÓS

The second-largest of the Dodecanese islands stands apart from the crowd: Kárpathos, with smaller Kasós off its southern tip, forms a link between Rhódos and Crete. A world apart, especially, is the mountainous northern section of the island, which rises to 1,215-meter **Kalí Límni** approximately at the island's center.

Long virtually inaccessible, the villages of this area have been able to preserve their age-old traditions and customs without much interference from the outside world; Ólimbos is particularly famous in this regard, with a dialect that

Info pp. 192-195

bears many traces of Dorian, a form of ancient Greek.

In the south of the island, the land is flatter and greener, and there are more beaches for the vacationers that are starting to come in ever-increasing numbers thanks to the island's airport. Note, however, that access to both Kárpathos and Kasós can be difficult; ferries are not as frequent as they are to the other Dodecanese islands, the way is comparatively long, and there's a risk that visitors will be involuntarily compelled to extend their stays if the sea is high or a storm moves in (especially in the pre- or post-season). In compensation, though, this means that the islands aren't as overrun as some of their more reachable cousins, Kárpathos' burgeoning tourist industry notwithstanding.

Pigádia, or **Kárpathos Town** ❶, is the island's capital. This is a modern place

Above: At the edge of the harbor of Kastellóriso (see p. 192), a mosque is a reminder of the nearness of the Turkish coast.

not far from the site where a few ruins of the ancient city, including Mycenean tombs, are still visible. It is said that Kárpathos gets more money from locals who have emigrated to America than any other Greek island – which is no mean claim, when so many Greek families are financed from abroad – and this is reflected in the newness of its buildings, now increasingly intermingled with hotels and other tourist facilities.

Kárpathos' bay is **Vróndis**, featuring a stretch of decent beach. Ancient Kárpathos was sacred to Poseidon, the god of the sea, who was replaced by St. Nicholas as the protector of sailors after the advent of Christianity; there's a little church dedicated to the latter, **Ágios Nikólaos**, near a spring bearing the name of the former, Poseidonas. **Ágios Kiriakí**, further south, is another Christian shrine on an ancient site, this one sacred to Demeter. The next beach area to the south is **Amópi**.

Inland are older towns: 400-meter-high **Menetés** ❷, southwest of Pigádia, was founded in the Middle Ages, and increas-

Info pp. 192-195

ingly built-up **Arkása** ❸ stands near ancient **Arkesia**, its acropolis dating from the Mycenean era. Early Christian churches are ruins of a later era: the few standing columns and bits of marble wall of **Agía Sophía**, looking down over the sea, illustrate better than any diagram how echoes of ancient art and architecture carried over into the Byzantine tradition. North of both these places, **Óthos** ❹, the highest village on the island (507 meters), has a little **Ethnographical Museum**; similarly, traditional crafts and lifestyles can be seen inside the everyday houses of nearby **Voláda**, where there's an old Venetian castle. Another popular stop, with a beach, on the west coast is **Léfkos** ❺. **Mesohóri** ❻ also contains its share of traditional houses, one of them open to the public.

"Kárpathos is as pure in contour as a primitive sculpture," wrote Lawrence Durrell, whereby he was implicitly referring to the mountainous gray north. Tourists generally access this part of the island through the port of **Diafáni** ❼, which, too, is suddenly sprouting a crop of new hotels and a larger ferry dock. A 15-minute walk north from here will take you to the truly marvelous beach of **Vanánda**. From here, buses run up to ***Ólimbos** ❽. Like many medieval villages in the Greek Islands, Ólimbos was built high inland as defense against pirates; this is a fortified settlement from as long ago as the 10th century. Now that it's an established tourist site, however, its old traditions – from the traditional clothing the women wear to the local music – may disperse more rapidly than they have; but for the time being, the village remains one of the best places in Greece to get a flavor of real tradition and a sense of the islands' medieval past.

From **Avlóna** ❾, to the north, walkers can access the ruins of another ancient city. More ruins are visible on the small island of **Saría** ❿, off the northern coast; this island was colonized by Nísiros, although some of the ruins here date from the Byzantine era, and are the remains of pirates' houses.

Kásos

Kaikis leave from the harbor of **Finíki** in the south for **Kásos** ⓫, while regular ferries run out of Kárpathos Town. Kásos is a small but ancient island, first settled by the Phoenicians. It came to considerable prosperity thanks to its shipping fleet during the 18th century. Its fleet allowed it to play a significant role in the Greek War of Independence, which was punished by the Sultan and his Egyptian allies: they wiped the place out in 1824, an event commemorated in an annual June ceremony in the island's main harbor, **Frí**. Long since resettled, Kásos has few villages, few beaches and few tourists.

Landing in Frí can be somewaht difficult in rough seas; Kásos also has a modest airport, but if the weather is bad this is of little help. **Emborió** is the island's second port; its other towns lie inland, such as **Agía Marína**, near which there's a limestone cave showing traces of ancient cult worship. It's a pleasant walk from Agía Marína down to **Hélatros**, one of the best of the island's beaches, although **Amoúda** is closer to habitation.

*KASTELLÓRISO

The easternmost outpost of the Greek Islands, and the smallest inhabited island of the Dodecanes, Kastellóriso has to assert itself to remind people that it's there. While it is only three kilometers from the Turkish mainland, it is a full 120 kilometers from Rhódos. Its other name, Megísti ("The Largest"), is self-aggrandizement, a reminder that it's the biggest of a mini-group of tiny islands around it. Kastellóriso sits so far from the rest of the Dodecanese and so close to Turkey that the population gets government subsidies just to live here; Greeks fear that it could easily revert to the Turks if deserted. No one has to pay tourists to come, however; a new airport has helped fuel the flow of visitors attracted by the island's clear waters and seafood. There are no beaches, but there's good swimming off the rocks.

Until World War II, Kastellóriso was home to over 14,000 people; today the number is a mere 220. The white neoclassical-style houses of ***Kastellóriso Town** still stand, and are well maintained by their emigrant owners, many of whom spend their summer holidays here. This only adds to the charm of the beachless island. Also attractive are the tavernas at the harbor, whose tables, chairs and small grills stand directly beside fishing boats and yachts. A small **museum** illustrates island history; nearby, a **Lycaonic grave** was carved into the coastal rock in the 4th century B.C.

A four-hour island hike takes in abandoned monasteries and the Venetian fortress of **Paleókastro**. A boat ride to the ***Seal Grotto**, one of the loveliest in the Mediterranean, is a popular activity here.

DODECANES

PLANE: There are large airports on Kárpathos, Kós and Rhódos (domestic flights and charter flights from March to October); smaller airports on Astipálea, Kásos, Léros and Kastellóriso (domestic flights only). Travelers to Pátmos fly to Sámos and continue from there by ferry.
BOAT: Connections between the islands of the Dodecanes with ferries and Flying Dolphins are extremely good, especially in summer. From the larger harbors there are also ferries to Crete and Piraeus. Trips to Turkey (Marmaris and Bodrum) are possible from Rhódos and Kós.

PÁTMOS (☎ 0247)

Tourist Police, tel. 31303. Private agencies such as **Astoria**, tel. 31205, fax. 31975, or **Apollon**, tel. 31724, fax. 31819, can help with tours, accommodations and information. **Tourism Office**, tel. 31666, at the ferry landing in Skála.
CAR AND MOTORCYLCE RENTAL: **Ioannis Apostolidis**, Skála, tel. 31541.
SKÁLA: $$$ **Porto Scoutari,** tel. 33124, fax. 33175. Modern yet classical hotel/apartment complex overlooking the water and islands. $$ **Skála Hotel**, tel. 31343, fax. 31747. 100 meters from the ferry port, yet set back from the water in its own lovely garden with pool and flowers cascading over the balconies. **Blue Bay Hotel**, tel. 31165. Water frontage and views, at the edge of town. **PÁTMOS (HÓRA):** The tourist office has a list of rooms to rent, one to try is **Ioannis Apostolidis**, tel. 31738.
MÍLOÏ: Flowers Stephanos, tel. 31821.
SKÁLA: To Pirofani, tel. 31539, excellent fish restaurant on the waterfront. Also near the water is **Grigoris**, tel. 31515. Across from the telephone office is the very good **Loukas**, tel. 32515. **PÁTMOS (HÓRA):** On the main square, with a flowering rooftop balcony, is **Vagelis**, tel. 31485. **KÁMBOS: Taverna Panagos**, tel. 31076, across from the church.
Monastery of St. John, tel. 31398, hours (subject to change) 8 am to 1 pm daily as well as 4 to 6 pm on Sun, Tue and Thu. **Monastery of the Apocalypse**, tel. 31234, same hours.

LIPSÍ (☎ 0247)

Information Office on the main square. There are also several travel agencies, among them **Paradisis Travel**, tel. 41120, fax. 41110, which can arrange for rooms, excursions, etc.

MOTORCYCLE RENTAL: **George**, tel. 41340

LIPSÍ: $$ **Hotel Aphrodite**, tel. 41000, clean new building just over the hill from town on its own little cove (Lendoú Beach). **Kalypso**, by the water.

LIPSÍ: Kalypso, tel. 41242, taverna and café (rooms, too). **KATSADIÁ: Dilalia**, taverna with campground. **PLATÍS GIALÓS:** Small taverna on the beach.

LÉROS (☎ 0247)

Leros Travel, Plátanos, tel. 24111, fax. 24110, helps find accommodation and organizes excursions.

CAR, MOTORCYCLE AND BICYCLE RENTAL: **John Koumoulis**, Lakkí, tel. 22330, and Álinda, tel. 24646.

LAKKÍ: $$ **Miramare**, tel. 20043, near the ferry landing. **PLÁTANOS:** $$ **Pension Platanos**, tel. 22608, over the café in the main square. **ÁLINDA:** $$ **Hotel Marilen**, tel. 24660, 24100, fax. 22531. Comfortable, spacious apartments with kitchenettes grouped around a large pool, sea views, a short stroll from Álinda Beach.

PANDÉLI: Taverna Psaropoula, tel. 25200. Excellent fresh fish, right on the beach. **AGÍA MARÍNA: Agía Marína**, tel. 24833. A cut above the norm, in quality and ambiance.

Kástro with **Panagía** and **Ecclesiastical Museum**, Wed, Sat and Sun 9 am to noon, 4 to 8 pm; daily during peak season. **Ethnographic Museum**, in Belléni Villa, Álinda, daily 9 am to noon, 4 to 7 pm.

KÁLIMNOS (☎ 0243)

Information Office on the coast road in Kálimnos Town, near Hotel Olympic. **Kálimnos Tours**, tel. 28329, fax. 29656.

KÁLIMNOS TOWN: $$ **Hotel Olympic**, tel. 28801, fax. 29314. Friendly and family-owned, centrally located on the coast road (25 Martiou). **Hotel Katerina**, tel. 22532, the modest villa façade a few minutes up from the port conceals a sparkling blue-and-white courtyard with a pool as centerpiece. $ **Villa Themelina**, tel. 22682, fax. 23970. Simple rooms in attractive old villa up the hill next to the "archeology" museum. **Archontiko**, tel. 24051, fax. 24149, another attractive villa near the ferry dock. **KANDÓUNI:** $$$ **Kalydna Island Hotel**, tel. 47880, fax. 47190. Attractive hotel-bungalow complex on the beach, with pool and restaurant. $$ **Kantouni Beach Hotel**, tel. 47980, fax. 47549. High standards, friendly staff. **VATHÍS:** $ **Hotel Galini**, tel. 31241, on the water, good restaurant.

KÁLIMNOS TOWN: Xefteres, tel. 28642. Traditional cooking (you can still go into the kitchen and examine the contents of the cooking pots). **Barbas Petros**, also known as **Martha's**, tel. 29678, is on the harbor near the fish market and serves excellent fish dishes. **Kambourakis**, tel. 29879, another waterside taverna; try the octopus *keftedes.* **KANDÓUNI: Domus**, tel. 47959. One of the best on the island; fine dining overlooking the beach. **MASOÚRI: The Sun Set**, tel. 47683. Tasty Greek specialties, named for the evening view over Télendos.

Archeological Museum, tel. 23113, open 9:30 am to 2 pm. There are **sponge factories** throughout town, which are generally more or less equipped with tourist presentations, such as **Atsas Sakellarios**, tel./fax. 50530.

Kalymna Yachting offers boat charters with or without crew, and organized tours. PO Box 47, 85200 Kálimnos, tel. 24083, 24084, fax. 29125.

ASTIPÁLEA (☎ 0243)

Gournas Tours, tel. 61334, fax. 61466.

ASTIPÁLEA: $$ **Viva Mare**, tel. 61571, 61292. Pretty and pleasant. $ **Astinea**, tel. 61040, centrally located. **Australia**, tel. 61275, with restaurant and nice terrace.

MARMÁRI BEACH: Camping Astipalea, tel. 61338.

ASTIPÁLEA: Good and popular tavernas include **I Monaxia** and **To Akroiali**.

KÓS (☎ 0242)

EOT, Akti Miaouli 2 (at the harbor), tel. 29200, fax. 29201, Mon-Sat 7:30 am to 3 pm.

CAR RENTAL: **Safari Rent-a-Car**, Kós Town, on the corner of Harmilou and Karaiskaki, tel. 21023, 27918, fax. 21096.

$$$ **Kipriotis Village**, Psalídi, south of town, tel. 27640, fax. 23590. Luxury complex with all the amenities; pools, bungalows, beach, bar, you name it. $$ **Afentoulis**, Evripilou 1, tel. 25321, located on a pleasant side street. $ **Hotel Yiorgos**, Harmilou 9, tel. 23297, fax. 27710. Welcoming and very friendly proprietors add a homey touch to this clean, central hotel. For **private rooms**, try **Irini Vasilopoulou**, Kolokotroni 11, tel. 28298; she also rents out cheap apartments in Psalídi.

Olympiada, Kleopatras 2, reasonably priced and very Greek. In the labyrinth of tourist tavernas on the city beach, **Roditissa** is worth recommending; it is right on the shore. On the other side of town, on the Psalídi road, **Akrogiali** (uses very fresh ingredients) and **Nestoras** are especially good. **Symposium**, on

Artemissias, has very good food. **Kastro** costs more, but is worth it.

Kós Museum (Archeological Museum), Eleftherias Square, tel. 28326, open daily except Mon 8 am to 3 pm. **Castle of the Knights** (by the harbor), open daily except Mon 8 am to 3 pm. **Asklípion** (4 km from town; bus service) open daily except Mon 8 am to 3 pm.

AROUND THE ISLAND

KARDÁMENA: $$$ **Hotel Kris-Mari**, tel. 91642, fax. 91034. At the edge of town, a bit away from the water, modern and friendly, rooms with view of the sea and pool. **KÉFALOS:** $$ **Hermes Hotel**, tel. 71102, fax. 71794. Halfway up to Kéfalos Town, with beautiful views of the bay from terrace restaurant, pool, tennis.

ZÍA: Try **Smaragdi**, up the paved footpath just above the little church of Panagía, or **Olympia** (tel. 29821).

KARDÁMENA: The best restaurant in town is **Giannis**, on the main street, with a range of local specialties.

KÉFALOS: In Kéfalos, the tavernas **Kastro** (tel. 71528) and **Lambada** (tel. 71591) have at least partial views of the panorama below. Of the restaurants lining the beach, **Captain John** (tel. 71152) attracts the most Greeks.

MASTIHÁRI: Dionyssos, tel. 51243 or 51785. Perhaps the best of the waterfront tourist eateries here; they also offer a few specialties besides the ubiquitous moussaka, gyros and souvlaki.

Just about every beach town has its own Water Sports Center; Kardamena's **Arian Diving Center** is something special, though: it operates from a wooden schooner (contact them through the **Porto Bello Hotel**, tel. 91217, fax. 91168).

NÍSIROS (☎ 0242)

For volcano tours, moped rental, accommodation, etc., Dimitris at **Nisyrian Travel** in Mandráki, tel. 31411, fax. 31610, or Páli, tel. 31611, is wonderfully helpful.

MANDRÁKI: $$ **Haritos Hotel**, tel. 31322. Friendly, comfortable pension in a quiet location at the edge of town. $ **Romantzo**, tel./fax. 31340, inexpensive rooms, good restaurant.

MANDRÁKI: Panorama Taverna, tel. 31185, off the central square. This is the best in town. **Taverna Nísyros**, tel. 31460. Simple and good. **PÁLI: Hellinis**, tel. 31453. **NIKIÁ: Taverna Ta Nikeia**, tel. 31285. The only taverna in the village.

Bus tours to the volcano leave every morning from the pier in Mandráki.

TÍLOS (☎ 0241)

Stefanakis Travel, tel. 43310, and **Tilos Travel**, tel. 53259, can help with accommodation and transportation. **Tourist Police**, tel. 44222.

LIVÁDIA: $$ **Irini**, tel. 53293. Near the beach. **Castellos Beach**, tel. 44267, modern hotel, sea view. $ **Stefanakis Appartements**, tel. 44310.

Irina, near the church. Lively taverna, good seafood.

Big **Church Festival** in Ágios Pandeleímon monastery, late July.

RHÓDOS (☎ 0241)

RHÓDOS TOWN

The **EOT** office is extremely helpful: Makariou 5 (corner Papagou), tel. 23655, fax. 26955. They have lots of info on all the Dodecanese, in a number of different languages. **City Information**, Platía Rímini, tel. 35945.

CAR RENTAL: The **Hertz** office here, Griva 16, tel. 21819 (airport: tel. 92902), is remarkably friendly and helpful.

$$$ **Rodos Park**, Riga Fereou 12, tel. 24612, fax. 24613, first-class hotel in the heart of town (in New Town, but a short walk from Old Town), with pool, restaurants. **Grand Hotel Rhodos**, Akti Miamouli 1, tel. 26284, 73333, fax. 35589, luxury hotel on the beach with swimming pools, tennis courts, fitness center, sauna and more.

$$ **Cava d'Oro Hotel**, Kistiniou 15, tel. 36980, 25537. Warm, friendly, personal, in restored old house in Old Town. **Hotel Savoy**, tel. 20721, fax. 21720, very small rooms spruced up with air conditioning and TV, near port.

$ **Hotel Spartalis**, tel. 24371, cheap but decent modern rooms with bath in New Town, steps from the port. **Hotel Sydney**, Apellou 41, tel. 25965, fax. 36980. Good-value central accommodation (Old Town) with personal touch.

In Old Town, the seafood restaurant **Dinoras**, Platía Mousíou, tel. 25824, serves some of the best food you'll find in Greece. If you want to feel safe trying things like sea urchins or *fouskies*, this is the place; don't miss the fish *keftedes*. Rhódos' other leading restaurant is **Palaia Istoria**, tel 32421, which presents a fine array of *mezedes*. At the edge of Old Town, **Chatzikelis**, Solomou Alchadef, tel. 27215, is a cozy and popular place for *mezedes* with tables in the green. **To Rodon**, corner Sokratous/Platonos, tel. 39812, is simple and good. You can eat cheap in the New Town at **Olympia**, 25th Martiou 12, tel. 21620, a "pizzeria"

with good Greek dishes, or the nearby cafeteria **Danaides,** Spartali Arcade, tel. 21547.

Byzantine Museum, **Ethnographic Museum**, **Archeological Museum**, Tue-Sun 8:30 am to 3 pm, tel. 75674 for info. **Palace of the Grand Masters**, Mon 12:30 to 3 pm, Tue-Sun 8:30 am to 3 pm, tel. 23359. **Aquarium**, daily 9 am to 9 pm, off-season until 3:30 pm.

AROUND THE ISLAND

AFÁNDOU: $$ **Afándou Beach**, tel. (0241) 51586, fax. 52003, nice beach hotel. **KOLÍMBIA:** $$ **Allegro**, tel. (0241) 56286, modern hotel on the beach. **LÍNDOS:** The hotels in Líndos are almost exclusively filled with package tourists, making it difficult for individual travelers to find accommodation in town. You can try, though, at $$$ **Lindos Mare**, tel. (0244) 31130, fax. 31131, above the bay, with a pool, or $$ **Anastasia**, tel. (0244) 31547, in the historic center.

KOLÍMBIA: Nissaki, situated on the bay, excellent fish. **LÍNDOS: Mavrikos**, near the main square, tel. (0244) 31232, good food.

The archeological sites of **Ialissós**, **Kámiros** and **Líndos** are open as a rule Tue-Sun 8:30 am to 3 pm; tel. (0241) 21954 for info.

AFÁNDOU: Golf course (18 holes), tel. (0241) 51451. **ÉMBONAS:** Wine tasting at the **Emery Winery**, Mon-Fri 9 am to 3 pm, tel. (0246) 41206.

SÍMI (☎ 0241)

There's a touch-screen information stand by the harbor. **Kalodoukas Holidays**, tel. 72661, at the other side of the port, has loads of info, arranges walks and excursions in a wonderful old wooden boat.

Both **Kalodoukas Holidays** (see above) and **Sími Tours**, tel. 71307, fax. 72292, can arrange for accommodation. For private apartments or villas, contact **Jean Manship**, tel. 71819.

GIALÓS: $$ **Hotel Opera House**, tel. 72034, fax. 72035. Pleasant, livable, spacious apartments with kitchenettes and bath, as well as a hotel, in a quiet location back from the water. Open year-round. **Hotel Albatros**, tel. 71829, in the heart of Gialós, pleasant neoclassical building.

HORIÓ: $$ **Hotel Fiona**, tel. 72088, has airy, spacious, blue-and-white rooms with breathtaking picture-postcard views over the harbor. If you're looking for a small house for a week or two, the cozy, beautifully renovated **Villa Kassandra**, tel. 72157, fax. 72616, offers the same movie views.

GIALÓS: A cut above from the normal tavernas is **O Milopetra**, tel. 72333, a quite elegant and pricey European-standard establishment in a renovated old stone building.

HORIÓ: Dallaras, tel. 72030. Homey, welcoming taverna with reliably good Greek specialties. Also has rooms to rent. **Taverna Giorgios**, next door, also offers good taverna cuisine. For late-night drinks, the **Jean and Tonic Bar** (tel. 71819) is the place to go.

PÉDIO: Ta Valanidia, tel. 72693 (on the road from Gialós to Pédio), very good cooking, Greek with an English touch. Also rents rooms.

Nautical Museum, Gialós, Tue-Sun 10 am to 2 pm. **Museum**, Horió, Tue-Sun 10:30 am to 3:30 pm.

BOAT RENTAL: **Yiannis**, tel. 71931.

KÁRPATHOS (☎ 0245)

Kárpathos Travel, Dimokratias 11, tel. 22148. **Tourist Police**, tel. 22218.

KÁRPATHOS TOWN: $$$ **Possirama Bay**, tel. 22511. Apartments near the beach. $$ **Romantica**, tel. 22461, large pension near the beach. **Sunrise**, tel. 22467, fax. 22089, Internet: http// agn.hol.gr/hotels/sunrise/sunrise.htm, nice, near the beach.

MENETÉS: $$ **Irini**, tel. 22143, friendly staff.

KÁRPATHOS TOWN: I Kali Kardia, excellent fish taverna. **ÓLIMBOS: O Mílos**, tel. 51297, tasty *pita* dishes.

There is an annual **Easter Festival** in Ólimbos, with music, dancing and a wedding market. **St. John's Festival** in the Vorgoúnda cave church (near Avlóna), August 28-29.

KÁSOS (☎ 0245)

Town Hall, tel. 41277. **Tourist Police**, tel. 41222.

FRÍ: $$ **Anagenessis**, tel. 42323. **Anessis**, tel. 41202. In addition to these hotels there are a few tavernas on the harbor that rent rooms.

In the seaside **tavernas** you can generally get very good and very fresh seafood.

A **Memorial Celebration** of the Turkish-Egyptian invasion of 1824 takes place on June 7.

KASTELLÓRISO (☎ 0241)

Town Hall, tel. 49269. **Tourist Police**, tel. 49330.

KASTELLÓRISO TOWN: $$ **Megisti**, tel. 29072, large, modern, the only "proper" hotel on the island. $ **Barbara**, tel. 29295, older pension, also rents apartments

KASTELLÓRISO TOWN: O Meraklis, Ouzeri, very good *mezedes*.

CRETE

IRÁKLIO AND KNOSSÓS
LASÍTHI
RÉTHIMNO
HANIÁ

The 260-kilometer-long "big island" or Megalonissos, dubbed "the small continent" by the Greeks, is veritably a world unto itself. Largest of all the Greek Islands, lying in the middle of the Mediterranean, Crete luxuriates in a wealth of beaches and spectacular mountain scenery, with no fewer than four mountain ranges helping to keep the tide of visitors somewhat at bay from its inner reaches. The island has had its own culture and civilization ever since the Minoans ruled the Aegean from Knossós between around 2500 and 1000 B.C.; in the Middle Ages, Cretan icon painting set the tone throughout the Aegean and Ionian seas (it still dominates in island iconostases); today, the mountain villages are among the few places in Greece to have preserved their own folk traditions, including indigenous songs (*mantinades* and *rizitikas*) and dances, accompanied on the stringed *lyra*.

This long island is also one of the most popular with visitors, who have virtually occupied whole areas of the northern coast in the concrete bunkers of modern quasi-luxury hotels along the sands. It takes some doing, in Crete, to get off the beaten track; and anyone who wants to do so is referred to the *Nelles Guide Crete*, which provides a comprehensive introduction; this chapter is only meant to give you a brief collection of highlights to help orient those island-hoppers who want to stop off here for a couple of days in the course of their vacation.

Previous Pages: A colorful kafenion on the island of Crete. Left: Hiking tour through the Samariá Gorge – the highlight of any trip to Crete.

Because of its size and location, Crete has been hotly contested throughout its history, at least after the age of the Minoans had passed. A mighty sea power with bases throughout the Greek Islands, the Minoans led the island to what arguably remains its heyday as a center for progress and culture, prosperity and learning. In the ensuing centuries, when the centers of power had shifted to Athens, the island sat on the sidelines of history and concealed pirates.

The Romans, and later the Byzantines, used its potential, but had trouble keeping Crete out of the hands of the Arabs; because of its mountainous geography, the island was very hard to defend. After spells of Venetian rule, the Turks finally got the upper hand; they controlled Crete into the 20th century. Greece's first great statesman, Elefthérios Venizélos, himself hailed from Haniá. After abortive attempts in 1897 and 1909, the island managed definitively to join the Greek state in

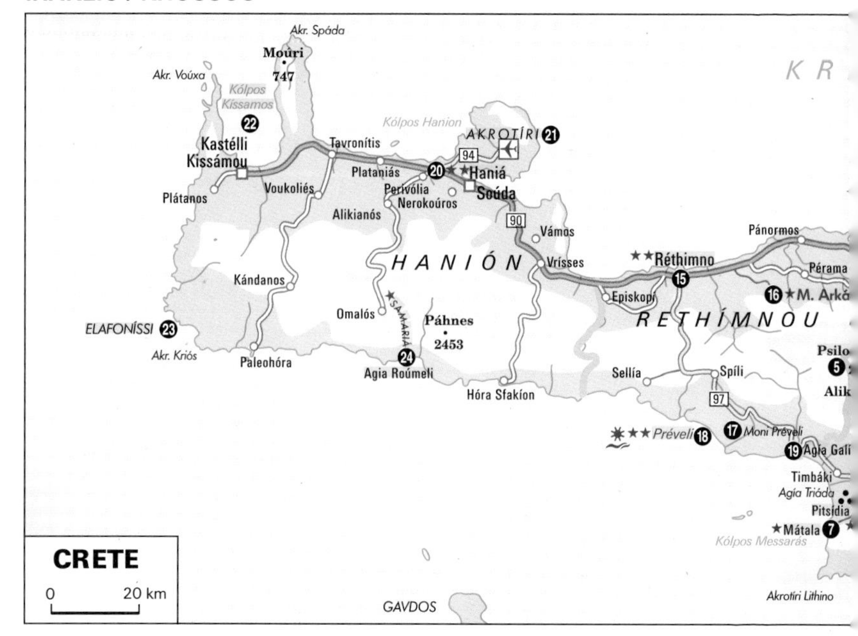

1913, in the wake of the Balkan War. In May 1941, the Germans undertook a successful air invasion of the island, though Cretan resistance continued until the liberation of the island four years later.

IRÁKLIO AND **KNOSSÓS

Crete is divided into four districts or *nomoi*, which section it in bands: these are, from west to east, Haniá, Réthimno, Iráklio and Lasíthi. Most visitors begin at ***Iráklio** ❶, Crete's capital since 1971 and the fourth-largest city in Greece, drawn here not by its beauty – it's a snarling modern tangle of a place – but compelled to pass through because it has the main ferry port, the main airport, and the main archeological museum, with finds from the island's main archeological site, some five kilometers away, Knossós.

Iráklio's huge and important ****Archeological Museum**, preserving many of the fragments too fragile to be displayed on site, is near the Venetian **walls** that ring the city. Guarding the Old Harbor is a small restored Venetian fortress, known by its Turkish name, **Koules**, and the vaulted arched tunnels which are all that remain of the Venetian **arsenal**. At the heart of town is the square called **Platía Venizélou**, also known as *Ta Liontaria* after the lions that adorn the 17th-century **Morosini Fountain** at its center, a city landmark.

Here is the 13th-century church of **Ágios Márkos**, built by the Venetians for their patron saint; a few streets away stands the Byzantine church of **Ágios Títos**, commemorating the patron saint of Crete who Christianized the island in the first century A.D.

Discovered in 1878, the ****Palace of Knossós** ❷ was gradually purchased by Englishman Sir Arthur Evans around the turn of the century; and excavations began in 1900. The buildings are loosely grouped into pre-palatial, neo-palatial and post-palatial periods. After an earthquake in 1700 B.C. wrought considerable destruction on the site, the **New Palace** was constructed, the most splendid edi-

 Info p. 205

fice yet in the area, with some 1,300 rooms; it's this palace, partially reconstructed by Evans, that dominates the site today. This building's size and scope explains the genesis of the legend of Knossós' labyrinth.

According to the story, Queen Pasiphaë bore the Minotaur, a creature half-man, half-bull, after an adulterous episode with a bull. King Minos concealed the beast in a labyrinth in his palace constructed by Daedalus, the master architect; in order to feed it, he exacted annual tribute from his vassal state of Athens in the form of seven young men and seven young women. To free his people from this burden, the prince Theseus went to Crete with one of these sacrificial shipments. Once there, Minos' daughter Ariadne saw him, fell in love with him, and helped him make his way through the labyrinth to slay the Minotaur. Bulls were certainly central to the Minoan religion, judging from votive statues and frescoes on the site.

More prosaically, there is evidence that there was running water supplying the tub and toilet in the **Queen's Bathroom**, off the **Queen's Megaron**, which was adorned with frescoes of dolphins. Other highlights of the palace include the **Throne Room**, containing one of the oldest thrones in the world.

East of Iráklio, the **Gulf of Mália** has some of the island's most popular and peopled beaches. **Liménas Hersónisos** ❸ appeals especially to windsurfers; at **Mália** ❹, there are not only hotels and plenty of nightlife to distract visitors, but also the remains of a Minoan palace (1900 B.C.) located four kilometers east of town.

To the south, the road leads up into the mountains by **Psiloritis** ❺, Crete's highest peak (2,456 meters), otherwise known as Mount Ída. Here, according to legend, the infant Zeus was raised in a cave, hidden from his father, Cronus, who had devoured all of his other offspring in fear that one might overthrow him (Zeus grew up and did).

Further south is the site of **★Festós** ❻, another Minoan palace that echoes some

of the history of Knossós: destroyed in a 1700 B.C. earthquake, it was rebuilt more splendidly, only to be wiped out by the unnamed catastrophe that swept the island around 1450 B.C. **Agía Tríada** is another, slightly later, ancient site. Not far from here is yet another ancient site, that of a palace complex from about the 14th century B.C.

From here, it's not very far to the beaches of the southern coast, which are generally less crowded than those in the north, although far from empty. There's a very good beach down the dirt road about a kilometer past **Pitsídia**; it is located not far from a site that Evans believed to be the Minoan harbor and customs port of Kommós.

Further on is the village of ⋆**Mátala** ❼, now a populous beach resort; chicken wire places the caves that honeycomb its cliffs off-limits to backpackers seeking free overnight accommodation. It was here, according to Greek mythology, that Zeus, disguised as a bull, first landed after his abduction of the maiden Europa from her home in Asia Minor: one further instance of the importance of bulls in this island's legends.

Above: The Minoan palace of Knossós, imaginatively reconstructed by Arthur Evans. Right: Central Cretian landscape in spring.

LASÍTHI

Crete's easternmost district, Lasíthi, is perhaps the island's most varied and is still relatively undeveloped for tourism; wheat thrives on the cool and fertile 815-meter-high ⋆**Lasíthi Plain**, with its charming windmills, at the foot of **Mount Díkti** (2,418 meters), where legend says Zeus was born.

⋆**Ágios Nikólaos** ❽ is the district capital, and the coastal strip around this city, edging the Gulf of Mirabéllo, is thick with hordes of tourists in the summer. The town is built around fresh-water **Lake Voulisméni**, the "bottomless pool" where Athena, the goddess of wisdom, used to bathe; now connected up to the

Map pp. 200-201, Info p. 205

ocean by a channel, it hosts a range of events during the summer months.

From this town, it's 12 kilometers southwest to **Kritsá** ❾, where the 13th-century church of **Panagía i Kerá** stands like some kind of bizarre futurist ensemble. Behind the white triangles of its façade are some magnificent 14th- and 15th-century Byzantine frescoes.

Southeast, back on the gulf, is excavated **Gourniá** ❿, a complete Bronze Age settlement rife with relics of daily life and commerce from the days of the Minoans. From here, a road runs down to the town of **Ierápetra** ⓫, an ancient port that long lay forgotten but has now been transformed into an agricultural and tourist center. Long touted as "Europe's southernmost city," it gets very hot here in summer, drawing visitors to the long beaches around the town itself or else over to the island of **Hrisí**, where there is a cedar forest to offer shady relief from the sun on the golden beaches that gave the island its name. The northern coast between **Pahiá Ámmos** and Sitía, lined with orchards, fields and majestic ocean views, has been dubbed the "Cretan Riviera" on account of its beauty.

Sitía ⓬ is a small, friendly and very Greek town famous for its sultanas, or raisins. **Vái** ⓭, all the way east, has a white sand beach with an idyllic palm grove. Further on, on Crete's eastern shore, is ***Káto Zákros** ⓮. In addition to being a lovely village, it contains some major Minoan finds: the remains of a large palace and a commercial center that was evidently a hub of ancient Crete.

**RÉTHIMNO

Réthimno is the most mountainous of Crete's *nomoi*, embracing the high peak of **Psiloritis** (Mount Ída) and the heights around it. The district's capital, **Réthimnio** ⓯, built on a natural harbor, is less developed than Iráklio or Haniá. It bears clear marks of its Venetian and Turkish history, with the striking **Tis Nerantzés Mosque** and the Venetian **harbor** and **fortress**. Across from the entrance to the

latter, the town's **Archeological Museum** is housed in what was once the Turkish prison.

Twenty-two kilometers southeast, in the foothills of Psiloritis, the ***Arkádi Monastery** ⓰ is the most important on Crete. In addition to the architectural value of its Renaissance-Baroque **Church of Saints Helena and Constantine** (built in 1587), it is a shrine to the martyrdom of hundreds of Cretan rebels who let themselves be blown up in the monastery's gunpowder room rather than fall into the hands of the pursuing Turks in 1866.

Préveli Monastery ⓱, on the south coast, was another refuge in the 1866 invasion; in retaliation, the Turks burned it to the ground (it has since been rebuilt). It's a good half-hour walk down to palm-lined ****Préveli Beach** ⓲, from which hundreds of British soldiers were evacuated after the Nazi invasion of Crete in

Above: Rakish-looking older man from the village of Anógia in the Réthimo District.

1941. Boat taxis make the trip here from **Agía Galíni** ⓳, a former fishing village that is now Réthimnio's main south coast resort. Due north of here is the beautiful and fertile **Amári Valley**, tucked into the foothills.

HANIÁ

The natural boundary of the **Léfka Ori**, or "White Mountains," effectively cuts off the western district of Haniá from the rest of the island, especially in the winter months when the mountain roads are blocked with snow. As a result, Haniá's tourist development has proceeded more carefully – and more attractively – than some of the blight-like building farther east.

****Haniá** ⓴, the capital of the whole island between 1860 and 1913 and still Crete's second city, is an elegant place punctuated with the minarets of mosques and the pointed arches of Venetian façades, with its cruciform **covered market** and **lighthouse**, or Faros, at the end of the harbor mole.

Northeast of here is the **Akrotíri Peninsula** ㉑, increasingly developed with luxury villas, which boasts Haniá's airport, **Venizélos' Tomb**, and a number of noteworthy old churches. To the west, a sprawl of beach development extends along the **Gulf of Haniá**; the **Gulf of Kíssamos** ㉒, by contrast, is framed by two tall points of land that are hardly inhabited at all. The west coast is the place to look for deserted beaches; a highlight is **Elafoníssi** ㉓, a small island off the southwest coast near the monastery of **Hrissoskalítissa**. One of Haniá's scenic highlights is the wild ***Samariá Gorge**, leading through the White Mountains to the southern coast. An 18-kilometer trek, not always easy going, takes you between the spectacular cliffs, past old churches and a deserted village, to **Agía Roúmeli** ㉔, where hikers either stay overnight or catch a boat back to Haniá Town.

Map pp. 200-201

IRÁKLIO (☎ 081)

EOT office at Xanthoudidou 1 (opposite the museum), tel. 228225, 225636, fax. 226020.

PLANE: Iráklio's airport is about five kilometers east of the city. There are regular flights to and from Athens, Rhódos, Thessaloníki, and, in summer, Míkonos , Páros and Santorin, as well as charter flights from Europe. **Olympic Airways**, tel. 229191, at airport, tel. 245644. *BOAT:* Ferries run daily from Piraeus (12 hours), there are links to the Cyclades and Dodecanese, as well as to Haifa, Israel. **Port Authority**, tel. 226073 or 244934. *BUS:* Long-distance buses operate throughout the island, tel. 245019 (eastbound/ Lasíthi), 221765 (westbound/Haniá), or 283925 (within the city).

$$$ **Galaxy**, Leoforos Dimokratias 67, tel. 238812, fax. 211211, with AC and pool. **Agapi Beach**, Ammoudari, tel. 250502, fax. 250731, resort-like feel. $$ **Atrion**, K. Paleologlou 9, tel. 229225, quiet, elegant. **Ilaria**, Epimenidou, tel. 227103, central, rooftop garden. **Pension Dedalos**, Dedalou 15, tel. 224391, near the Archeological Museum. $ **Olympic**, Plateia Kornarou, tel. 288861, simple, clean, nice view. **Hotel Hellas**, Kandanoleontos 11, tel. 225121.

Kyriakos, near the Galaxy Hotel, is a sophisticated taverna. **Ippokambos**, on Mitsotakis, is a good *ouzeri*. **Ta Psaria** on 25 Avgousto is good for fish.

Archeological Museum, Xanthoudidou 1 (off Platía Eleftherias), tel. 226092, Tue-Sun 8 am to 5 pm, Mon 12:30 to 5 pm. **Historical Museum**, Eleftheriou Venizélou, tel. 283219, Mon-Sat 9 am to 1 pm, 3 to 5:30 pm. **Knossós Archeological Site**, tel. 231940, daily 8 am to 5 pm (6 pm in summer).

Greek Mountaineering Association (EOS), 53 Leoforos Dikeosinis, tel. 227609. Information about possibilities for hiking tours.

LASÍTHI (☎ 0841)

ÁGIOS NIKÓLAOS: Information Office at the marina, tel. 82384, fax. 82386, or tel. 22357.

ÁGIOS NIKÓLAOS: $$$ **Minos Beach**, Ammoudi, tel. 22345, fax. 22548, hotel and bungalows. **St. Nicolas Bay**, tel. 25041, luxury beachfront complex with plenty of pools. $$ **Ariadni Hotel**, tel. 22741, fax. 22005, comfortable beach complex. **Panorama Hotel**, Sarolidi 2, tel. 28890, fax. 27268, in the city, with beach views. **IERÁPETRA: Hotel Owners' Association**, tel. (0842) 22306, fax. 61551. $$$ **Ferma Beach**, tel. (0842) 61341, on the beach, pools, tennis. $$ **Blue Sky**, tel. (0842) 28264. $ **Four Seasons**, tel. (0842) 24390, lovely villa with garden.

ÁGIOS NIKÓLAOS: Gournia Moon, between Ágios Nikólaos and Sitía, tel. (0842) 93243.

Ierápetra Archeological Collection, Adrianou Kostoula, tel. (0842) 287221, open Tue-Sun 8:30 am to 3 pm. **Káto Zákros Archeological Site**, tel. 22462, same hours.

RÉTHIMNO (☎ 0831)

EOT, S. Venizelou, tel. 29148, fax. 56350.

$$$ **Rithymna Beach**, tel. 29491, fax. 71002, 7 km east of town, on a lovely beach. **Veneto**, Epimenidou 4, tel. 56634, fax. 56635, luxury apartments in a Venetian palazzo. $$ **Kríti Beach**, east of the town center, near the beach, tel. 27401, with terrace and restaurant. **Mithos**, Platía Dimitriou, tel. 53917, small quiet hotel. $ **Castello**, Platía Dimitriou, tel. 50281, clean, pretty garden.

Avli, near the Rimoudi fountain. Cretan cuisine, inspired creations. **Helona** and **Palazzo** on the harbor have good fish dishes.

Archeological Museum, tel. 54668, Tue-Sun 8:30 am to 5 pm.

HANIÁ (☎ 0821)

EOT office in the Pantheon building, 40 Kriari, tel. 92943, fax. 92624.

PLANE: The airport is 12.5 km east of town; daily flights to Athens, charter flights. **Olympic Airways**, tel. 58005. The airline operates buses to Rethimno. *BOAT:* Daily ferries from Soúda harbor to Haniá from Piraeus (12 hours). **Port Authority**, tel. 89240. *BUS:* Bus station on Kidonias Street, near Platía 1866; regular buses to all parts of the island. *CAR RENTAL:* **Kontadakis**, Konstantinou 31, tel. 25583.

$$$ **Kontessa**, Theofanou 15, tel. 23966 or 98566, old-fashioned, friendly. **Amfora**, Theotokopoulou, tel. 93224. $$ **Xenia**, Theotokopoulou, tel. 91238, modern. **El Greco**, Theotokopoulou 49, tel. 90432, attractive, rooftop garden. $ **Orio**, Zambeliou 77, nice rooms, terrace. **Vranas**, opposite the cathedral, tel. 58618, modern, very clean.

Karnagio, at the old Venetian harbor, good food, somewhat expensive. **Taverna Apovrado**, on Isodon, tel. 58151, local specialties.

Archeological Museum, Halidon 24, tel. 90334, Mon 12:30 to 6 pm, Tue-Fri 8 am to 6 pm, Sat-Sun 8:30 am to 3 pm. **Naval Museum**, at the harbor, Tue-Sun 10 am to 2 pm, Sat also 7 to 9 pm.

The local branch of the **Greek Mountaineering Association** (EOS), Akti Tombazi 6, tel. 24647, operates two refuges in the White Mountains (Léfka Ori).

THE IONIAN ISLANDS

CORFU (KÉRKIRA)
PAXÍ
LEFKÁDA (LEFKÁS)
KEFALONIÁ
ITHÁKI (ITHACA)
ZÁKINTHOS (ZANTE)
KÍTHIRA

Separated from the Aegean islands by the Greek mainland, the islands in the Ionian Sea have a character all their own. They don't seem quite Greek, and indeed, you might say that they're not: for they show a mixture of a number of different influences; whereby the Venetian influence was stronger than the Byzantine. And most of the Ionian Islands were spared the Ottoman yoke. Their fate has been distinct from that of many other parts of the nation – as if the fault line running through them, which has caused severe earthquakes over the centuries, formed a kind of literal barrier between them and the rest of the country.

The Heptánisa or "Seven Islands" of Corfu (Kérkira), Paxí, Lefkáda, Itháki, Kefaloniá, Zákinthos and Kíthira lie in Greece's "other" sea, the Ionian. Unlike Ionia in Asia Minor, which was named for the general Ion, this sea is named for Io, the half-legendary daughter of King Inachus, whom, according to Greek mythology, the jealous Hera transformed into a cow upon discovering that Zeus had seduced her, and drove out of her native land pursued by a gadfly. Herodotus more prosaically, and perhaps more plausibly, had it that Io was kidnapped by Phoenicians. Her sea, in any case, extends south of the sole of Italy's boot to the Cretan Sea, where southerly Kíthira informally marks the boundary between it and the Aegean. Thanks to their western position, these islands have formed a bridge between Greece and Continental Europe since earliest times, for Athenian triremes and Byzantine traders, and into modern times; for this band still binds Greece to the rest of Europe. Ultimately, this proved to be beneficial in that it kept them out of Turkish hands for most of their history; living in relatively good conditions under largely stable administrations, in periods when the rest of Greece was in upheaval, such as during the struggle for independence.

Previous Pages: The beach of Pórto Katsíke in the south of Lefkáda. Left: The Ahillío (Achilleon), residence of Empress Elisabeth of Austria on Corfu.

The overlords here were Venetian, French, English and, briefly, Turkish, together with the Russians. It was in fact the Turks and Russians who created the semi-independent "Septinsular Republic," giving the islands their very first taste of autonomy. Small wonder, then, that many of the leaders in the struggle for Greek independence came from here or based themselves here; though even after Greek independence Britain retained its jurisdiction over these islands, not ceding them to Greece until 1864.

Info pp. 230-231

This distinctive history is reflected in a distinctive architecture, as much Continental as typically Greek, and a cosmopolitan air. Tourism in other parts of Greece is a relatively recent phenomenon, but while foreigners' villas on Míkonos have only sprung up in the last few decades, the Empress Elizabeth was building her summer house on Corfu, the Ahillío (Achilleon), in the 19th century.

Not that Corfu has been spared the ravages of more recent tourism. The last 20 years have left their mark here, too: beaches that were deserted "inside tips" as recently as the early 1980s are now crowded with package holiday-makers working on their tans for the evening disco scene. The fact that Corfu is the first stop in Greece for tourists coming over by ferry from Europe hasn't helped.

Still, once you penetrate the veneer of tourism, or venture a bit off the beaten track, the islands show the beauties that made them beloved in the first place. Their climate is as distinctive as everything else about them: they get some of the heaviest precipitation in Greece, and are more verdant as a result. There are stunning beaches and impressive rock formations, such as the white cliffs of Lefkáda. And spring blankets the meadows of Zákinthos, the "flower of the Levant," with a profusion of wildflowers.

Above: Olive harvest on Corfu.

**CORFU (KÉRKIRA)

Corfu, or Kérkira, is one of the best-known and best-loved of all the Greek Islands. With its lush climate, beautiful beaches, and lovely old Franco-Venetian capital, it offers something for every taste. Thanks to its location and history, it boasts a kind of cosmopolitanism that sometimes looks down on the rest of Greece. In earlier days, Athenian newspapers used to keep correspondents on Corfu; since this was the first port of call for ships form the Continent, the European newspapers arrived here some 30 hours before they got to Athens.

Info pp. 230-231

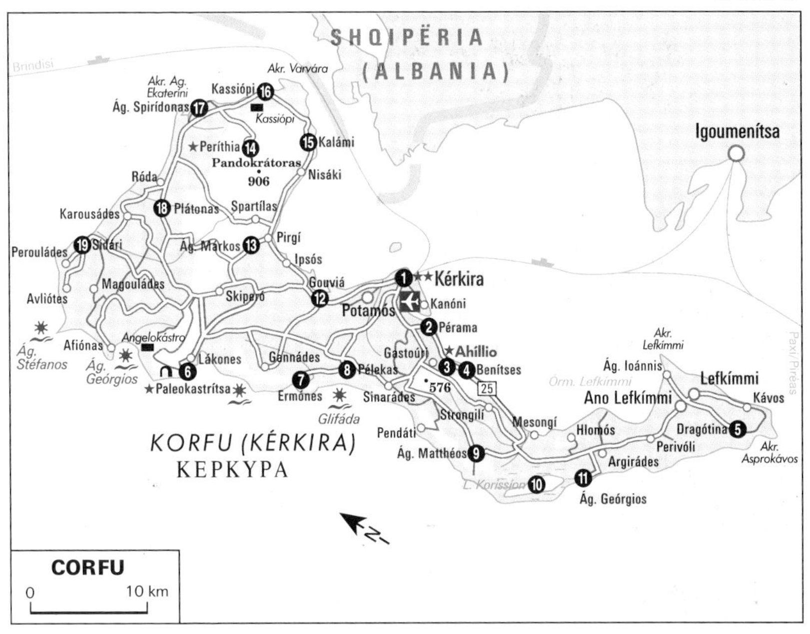

Because of its long, hooked shape, the island is known in legend as the sickle which Cronus (Saturn) used to cut off the testicles of his father, Uranus; the petrified testicles of Uranus are supposedly visible in the two hills or *koryphai* on the promontory occupied by the town's old fortress, which may have given the island of Corfu its ancient name (Corcyra, its other namesake, was a mistress of Poseidon). Corfu appears in Homer's *Odyssey* as the island of the Phaeacians; in Thucydides, more factually, it bows as the first cause of the Peloponnesian War, when the Corinthian colony here rebelled in 435 B.C. and declared itself an Athenian ally after Corinth had come out on the side of Sparta.

Corfu captured the European literary imagination, as well, ever since Shakespeare supposedly used it as a model for the setting for *Tempest*. The young poet and painter Edward Lear lived here and produced a number of stunning watercolors; more recent vignettes are preserved in naturalist and humorist Gerald Durrell's magnificently funny books about island life (*My Family and Other Animals*), which rival the more serious descriptions of his brother, Lawrence Durrell, and his friend Henry Miller (*The Colossus of Maroussi*).

Whether because or in spite of such associations, the English have long had a particular affinity for the place, as evidenced by their readiness to take over its affairs after the Treaty of Vienna divided up post-Napoleonic Europe in 1815. The island still bears a British stamp: it has, for one thing, a long tradition of cricket.

But each of the island's rulers left a lasting mark upon the landscape. In nearly four centuries of (interrupted) dominance, the Venetians left fortifications such as the fortresses of Corfu Town (although the British blew up all the island's fortresses when they pulled out in 1864). The Venetians also left a legacy of olives, thanks to the fact that they paid local peasants a bonus for every 100 trees planted, and allowed them to pay their taxes in olive oil, still a significant Corfu

export. The French, who got the island when Napoleon conquered Venice in 1797, built a copy of the Rue de Rivoli along the capital's Esplanade. Then there's the British Cemetery in Corfu Town, which blooms, in season, with rare wildflowers.

Corfu has its own strongly Greek traditions, as well. A leader among local saints is the island's patron, St. Spirídon, a bishop of Cyprus in the 4th century whose remains were smuggled here in a sack when the Turks took Constantinople in the 15th century. Although a relatively late arrival, "Spiro" remains a powerful presence. The display of his relics allegedly saved the town on four occasions between 1500 and 1716; hence he is borne through the streets in processions four times a year (including his feast day, August 11, and the first Sunday in November), as well as being sought out by the faithful year-round for help and miraculous healing.

Above: Drinking coffee beneth the arcades of Listón – pleasant and expensive. Right: Gorgon Medusa – world-famous monster in the Archeological Museum of Kérkira.

**Corfu Town (Kérkira)

Nowhere is the variety of Corfu's influences more in evidence than the island's capital, where Italian, French, English and Greek coexist in a happy muddle of narrow streets, their façades covered in quietly flaking plaster, that open out onto broad town squares and patches of green park. Corfu Town is also the largest city in the Ionian Islands, with some 30,000 inhabitants.

Corfu Town ❶ stands on a promontory, gazing across at the uncompromising mountains of mainland Albania, a mere three kilometers away. Ferries dock at the new port by the **New Fortress** (Néo Froúrio), a Venetian construction built as "recently" as 1577, with Venice's signature lions over its weathered gates, now open to the public. A companion to this on the other side of the historic center is the **Old Fortress** (Paleó Froúrio), erected around 1550 on a spit of land thrust into the sea and cut off from town by a moat, the *contra fosse*, which the Venetians dug over a period of 100 years.

With its striking, photogenic location, the Old Fortress is a Corfu trademark, but rather than exploring its tunnels, 17th-century cannon and the temple-style British addition of the **Church of St. George** (Ágios Geórgios), Corfu aficionados tend to linger opposite in the sidewalk cafés in the arcades of the **Listón**, Napoleon's "Rue de Rivoli," drinking ginger beer (an English legacy) and watching young cricket players on the green ***Esplanade** (Spianáda).

The latter is the town's imposing main square; at its north end is the **Palace of St. Michael and St. George**, built as a residence for the British High Commissioner, later a summer residence for the king of Greece, and now the **Museum of Asiatic**

Map p. 211, Info pp. 230-231

Art. The **Rotunda** at the park's center is a memorial to the first High Commissioner after the British took power in 1815, Sir Thomas Maitland. A statue here commemorates a famous son of Corfu, Ioánnis Kapodístrias, the first president of independent Greece.

In the Old Town, Corfu's faithful flock to the church of **Ágios Spirídon**, where the relics of the saint lie enthroned surrounded by offerings of thanks for his services, including, from the Venetians, a large silver lamp. Also noteworthy is the **Town Hall**, which the Venetians built as a loggia for merchants in the late 17th century, and which served as the city theater for two centuries before being converted to its present function in 1901.

The 16th-century **Mitrópolis Cathedral** in the Old Town, which contains the relics of the canonized 9th-century Byzantine Empress Theodora, is worth seeing. On the waterfront north of the Old Town, a 15th-century church has been converted into Corfu's ***Byzantine Museum**.

Near the New Fortress is the site of the old Jewish quarter; Venice ingloriously expelled the Jews from its lands in 1571, but the Jews of Corfu were somehow overlooked, and their colony continued to grow until the Germans began deportations to Auschwitz in World War II. A **synagogue** still survives. Of the town's many other churches, the monastery of **Platitéra** is especially worth a look for its beautiful late Byzantine icons, a gift of Catherine the Great (it's located on I. Andreadi, behind Avrami Hill)

But the museum to visit in Corfu, above all, is the ***Archeological Museum** to the south, on Garítsa Bay. Preeminent among its wealth of treasures is the 17-meter-long Gorgon Pediment, an archaic work from around 585 B.C. It once graced the still-visible **Temple of Artemis** at **Paleópolis**, the original "old city" of Corfu, slightly further south.

Another ancient monument near the bay is the **Tomb of Menekrates** (7th century B.C.), a low round building commemorating a consul who was lost at sea.

Of more recent vintage in this area, but no less impressive, is the 12th-century **Ágios Iássonas ke Sosípatros**, the island's only actual Byzantine-era church, with impressive frescoes. Then there's the ornate neoclassical villa of **Monrepos**, built in 1824 for the High Commissioner and his Greek wife; a century later, this elegant stone edifice amid green gardens was the birthplace of England's current Prince Consort, Philip.

Corfu's East Coast

The route south from Corfu Town leads along the **Kanóni** peninsula, named for the French cannon stationed at its tip. From here, causeways lead across Halikiopoúlou Lagoon to the exclusive residential area of **Pérama** ❷, as well as to two small and much-photographed islets, one with the monastery of **Vlahérna**, the other known as "Mouse Island," **Pondikoníssi**, with its own small chapel. Legend identifies this island as the ship in which the Phaeacians brought Odysseus back to Ithaca; as the ship was returning home Poseidon, enraged that the hero had been conveyed against his will, turned it to stone with a blow of his hand. The nearby airport rather dims the romance.

The only mystery or legend associated with the somewhat ostentatious ***Ahillío** (Achilleon) ❸, near **Gastoúri**, is that surrounding its builder, Empress Elizabeth of Austria, who as "Sissi" is still beloved in the German-speaking world. Obsessed with the hero Achilles, and perhaps a bit overwrought after the death of her only son, Sissi filled this villa, built in 1890, with kitschy paintings and statues; the place's next owner, Kaiser Wilhelm II, replaced her "Dying Achilles" with a "Victorious Achilles." The villa continues to fulfill all the requirements of modern foreign visitors, accommodating tourists by day and gamblers – it is now a casino – by night. Inland, you can leave your car at

Above: Popular subject for photographers – monastery island of Vlahérna. Right: Monks in the monastery of Panagía Theotókos.

Map p. 211, Info pp. 230-231

the village of **Ágii Déka** and climb an hour or so to the 576-meter peak of the "Ten Saints," which commands wonderful views of the island, or hike to the nearby monastery of **Pandokrátoras**, set in a green valley.

Not far away, the one-time fishing village of **Benítses** ❹, where there are remains of a Roman villa, has been sacrificed on the altar of package tourism, and the whole stretch of coast from here to **Messongí** is "discovered" in the worst tradition of mass tourism. Further south, the crowds thin out. **Lefkímmi**, the island's second town, has little to offer visitors, and **Kávos** is another crowded tourist center; seek out, instead, the relatively empty beaches around **Dragótina** ❺, at Corfu's southernmost tip.

The West Coast

Homeric tradition has it that when Odysseus washed up on the island of the Phaeacians, he encountered Nausikaa on the beach of ***Paleokastrítsa** ❻. Today, so many tourists have followed his lead to this fabulously beautiful spot – "drugged with its own extraordinary perfection, a conspiracy of light, air, blue sea and cypresses," wrote Lawrence Durrell – that the place is virtually unvisitable in high season. Only a few minutes away from the town center by foot stands the 17th-century monastery of **Panagía Theotókos** at the tip of a peninsula. The lovely frescoes in the monastery church and the flower-bedecked courtyard are worth having a look at; the Monastery Museum contains icons and other sacred objects.

The village of **Lákones** is the starting point of a number of walks. It's about two hours on foot to the ruined Byzantine castle of **Angelokástro**, dominating a headland; built in the 13th century, this fortress served in part to protect locals from the pirate raids that were a constant threat and hardship during the Venetian period (it's a shorter, easier walk from the village of **Kríni**).

Odyssean "scholarship" is notably uncertain: some hold that Odysseus' landing beach was Ermónes, at the other end of the agricultural **Rópa Valley**, a flat plain awash in olive trees, grapevines and fig orchards, as well as the greensward of the Corfu Golf Club, supposed to be among the world's 100 best.

Ermónes ❼ itself is fairly built up, but still offers nice beaches, with blue waters washing on pale sand cuddled within the arms of tree-lined slopes. Even better are the beaches of **Mirtiótissa** further south – once largely deserted save for a few adventurers, it is now crowded with hardy beach-goers prepared to make the trek down the steep track to get there – and sandy **Glifáda**, with its sharp cliffs.

Pélekas ❽ was a favorite with Kaiser Wilhelm II, who built an outlook here from which to observe the sunset; the place is still known today as the "**Kaiser's Throne**."

Farther south, the crowds thin out a bit. **Ágios Górdis**, with its lovely beach, has managed to stay reasonably attractive, and the beaches at and around **Paramónas** can be really quiet. The nearest village to the latter is **Ágios Mattheós** ❾, a quiet place with a plethora of churches, including the eponymous one on the nearest hilltop, which makes a pleasant walk. Another hiking destination might be the octagonal castle at **Gardíki**, built by the same man responsible for Angelokástro by Paleokastrítsa, Michael Angelos II, the despot of Epirus, in the 13th century.

More a lagoon than a lake, the shallow waters of **Korissíon** ❿ extend inland behind a row of dunes with the beaches of Alonáki and Halikaóunas. A paradise for migrating birds, with more than 125 species, the lake draws both hunters and mosquitos; ideal for nature-lovers, it is tranquil rather than spectacular. The same could be said for the broad, windswept beaches of **Ágios Geórgios** ⓫, an increasingly crowded waterside town further south. For the most part, however, this area is off the main drag, and visitors can still find friendly, unspoiled villages in **Kritiká**, **Bastátika**, and **Neohóri**, albeit without much in the way of specific "sights."

Right: Popular place for a swim – the beach of Róda.

Northern Corfu

Wild and wooded, the broad "handle" of Corfu's "sickle" offers a varied landscape. Running across the island here is its highest range of mountains, rising to the highest elevation on Corfu, Pandokrátoras (906 meters); juxtaposed with the mountain woods is Corfu's longest stretch of beach, which extends along the north coast approximately between Almirós and Róda, and has predictably drawn large amounts of tourists.

The coastline north of Corfu is one long stretch of tourist amenities. Foreigners have valued these shores for years; there are remains of Venetian settlement all along here, and the marina at **Gouviá** ⓬ is set in a bay the Venetians once used as a natural harbor (they left a 1716 **arsenal** overlooking the water). Built in the Italian style, but by a Greek, is the Florentine **Castello Mimbelli** (now a hotel) in its green grounds; a 19th-century construction, it was originally a residence of the Greek King George I.

Water sports of various descriptions set the tone at the long beaches along the coast here. Bars, discos and snack bars lined along the road have earned the waterside between **Ipsós** and **Nisáki** the epithet of "Golden Mile." To avoid it, turn inland at **Pirgí** and follow the road some three kilometers to the settlement of **Ágios Márkos** ⓭ with its two churches, one with noteworthy 11th-century frescoes. Another option is the ascent of **Pandokrátoras**.

If the winding and not-particularly-good road is too much for your car, you can go up by foot from **Spartílas**; it's a shorter walk (about one hour) from the at-

Map p. 211, Info pp. 230-231

tractive but half-abandoned village of *Períthia ⓮, to the north. From the 14th-century monastery at the top, there are sweeping views of the Ionian Islands and the Albanian coastline.

Back on the coast, the views from the road past **Nisáki** take in nearby Albania, less than one kilometer away at this point. **Kalámi** ⓯ was where Lawrence Durrell stayed while he was writing *Prospero's Cell* and *The White House*; the house where the Durrell brothers lived is now a taverna and inn, and visitors can stay overnight there.

Kulúra, just north of here, boasts a few 17th-century Venetian villas; nearby is the start of a steep path down to pebbly **Kamináki** beach.

The main town of the northeast is **Kassiópi** ⓰, which was a major settlement even in Hellenistic times, and thrived under the Romans, who built its city walls; Emperor Nero even stayed here and visited its shrine of Zeus, perhaps on the site of the current 16th-century church. The ruined Byzantine castle, a relic of the Angevins, was the first place in Greece hit by the Norman invasions; later, the Venetians left the town largely to its own devices with regard to defense, which meant it was hit hard by marauders, including Turks. Today, the tradition of foreign invasion is upheld by busloads of tourists; to escape them, seek out, in lieu of the beaches around town, the quieter sands of **Avláki**, somewhat to the south, which you can reach on foot.

The quiet waters of the lagoon of **Andiniotissa**, near **Ágios Spirídonas** ⓱, are a hamlet for birds and marine life. From **Almirós** westward to **Róda**, however, you're in tourist country with a vengeance: a long, sunny, sandy beach, littered with umbrellas and bodies in various stages of undress.

A different side of life is preserved in the country around **Plátonas** ⓲, some 4.5 kilometers inland from Róda: this is the heart of Corfu's kumquat country. Imported here in the 1930s from Asia, the kumquat has so successfully taken root

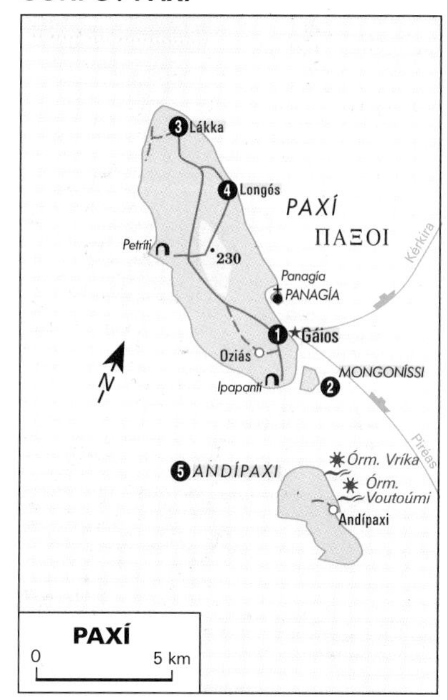

that two local specialties are kumquat liqueur and kumquat preserves.

In the northwest, the waves have wrenched striking formations from the sandstone rocks: at **Sidári** ⓳, another tourist spot where findings of Neolithic pottery attest to ancient settlement, two outcroppings in the bay are supposed to be two lovers, and anyone who swims between them will have love forever. People who feel less gregarious amid the crowds can board a kaiki here to the three little islands of **Othóni**, **Erikoússa** and **Mathráki**, which are very much for lovers of solitude, without many facilities, but with excellent swimming, trails to explore, and friendly inhabitants.

Othóni is the largest and most distant Ionian island, and boasts a grotto that claims to be Calypso's cave; Erikoússa, the most popular, with the best beach. If you opt to stay on the mainland, you have a better chance of enjoying the stone formations in some semblance of privacy in the attractive little cove at **Peruládes** south of Sidári. **Ágios Stéfanos**, still further south, which gets the benefit of east winds, is popular with windsurfers. **Ágios Geórgios** itself boasts perhaps the most attractive beach of the northwest coast, although it, too, is feeling the encroachment of tourism thanks to its proximity to Paleokastrítsa.

Right: The island capital of Lefkáda has been shaken by numerous earthquakes – the last in 1953.

PAXÍ

A miniature wooded jewel, Paxí, the smallest of the Ionian Islands, offers an essence of the Greek Island experience appropriate for anyone who doesn't need the conventional trappings of tourism to feel at home. Only 10 kilometers long and four kilometers across at its widest point, the little island is easily explored on foot, although Aristotle Onassis, a big Paxí fan, subsidized the road which leads between the main port of Gáios and the second port of Lákka, providing a surface for the minibus that represents Paxí's public transportation. En route, passengers can take in the sight of the olive trees that produce the raw material for what's supposedly some of the best olive oil in Greece; some shops in Gáios still sell it from the barrel. Whether or not they were drawn to Paxí by the savor of this oil, Antony and Cleopatra supposedly banqueted here on their last night together before the disastrous battle of nearby Actium in 31 B.C. Modern visitors tend rather to come for the sheltered beaches and striking grottoes that perforate the island's wilder west coast.

Guarding the mouth of the natural harbor of ***Gáios** ❶ are two islands: the one nearer shore is topped with the 15th-century Venetian fortress of **Kástro Ágios Nikólaos** and an old **windmill** that is a Paxí trademark. The more distant island, with a lighthouse and pilgrimage church is that of the monastery of

Info pp. 230-231

Panagía; pilgrims flock here on the Virgin's day, August 15, and in the evening return to shore and dance through the night in the streets of Gáios. **Ozias**, south of Gáios, has natural mineral springs. From the port, you can also board a kaiki to the islet of **Mongoníssi** ❷, off Paxí's southern tip, which is known both for its beaches and for its good restaurant, or **Kaltsoníssi**, even more petite.

At the northern tip of the island is Paxí's second harbor, **Lákka** ❸, also on a natural bay, where boats from Corfu tie up before the brightly-painted houses and little Byzantine church, and there's a relic of the Venetians in the stone mansion of **Grammatikou**. From here, motorboats run out along the west coast for visitors interested in exploring Paxí's caves, especially **Ipapánti**, the largest, which Homer described as having rooms of gold (although these are not in evidence today). What Ipapánti and the other west coast grottoes, such as **Kastanítha** or **Petríti** (whose entrance is guarded by a towering rock), did house, however, was a population of monk seals. Swimming is easier off the more sheltered east coast, where there are rocky beaches near the island's third, little port, **Longós** ❹.

Another excursion is the half-hour boat trip from Gáios to Paxí's "little sister," **Andípaxi** ❺, all of four square kilometers. Andípaxi offers vineyards where Paxí has olive groves, and beaches of soft sand, such as **Vríka** and **Voutóumi**, where Paxí runs more toward pebbles. Hunters come over here to bag migratory quail, in season; but there's little provision for them or other visitors, apart from a campsite at Voutóumi.

LEFKÁDA (LEFKÁS)

It's a matter of some debate whether Lefkáda was originally an island at all. Certainly the Corinthian colonists who settled here around 640 B.C. dug some kind of channel at the point where the island comes closest to the mainland, but whether they were cutting through a land bridge or merely dredging the sand bars

Info pp. 230-231

and silt from a shallow but existing channel has not been definitively determined. It hardly matters: the Romans were the first to bridge the narrow channel, and modern Lefkáda is accessible to car traffic by way of a bridge and causeway. Thus anchored to the land, Lefkáda lacks some of the mystique, not to mention the scenic highlights, of islands farther offshore. On the other hand, this fact has kept it less trafficked, and more private: a boon to those looking for a more "Greek" and less touristed island experience.

Known for its lace-making and embroidery, Lefkáda has something of a literary past, as well. One local son was author Lafcadio Hearn (1850-1904), who went to America to become a journalist before making his name as an expert about Japan; few readers of his English works know that his unusual first name derives from the island where he was born. Another was Greek poet Angelos Sikelianos (1884-1951), twice nominated for the Nobel Prize, who mixed with avant-garde art circles, and who attempted to found a Delphic University and Delphic Festival reviving old Greek traditions of the arts and humanities. Taking up the torch of his festival idea, at least in spirit, is the island's annual Festival of Literature and Art in August.

Above: Waves wash the beach of Káthisma on the island of Lefkáda.

Guarding the access to the island is the old Venetian fortress of **Santa Maura**, laid out in 1300 by Giovanni Orsini, who received the island as part of the dowry in his marriage to a daughter of Byzantine's powerful Comnenos dynasty. The fort acquired its name at a later date: in 1453, when Empress Helena was fleeing Byzantium after the Turks had sacked it, she took shelter on Lefkáda from a storm. The day happened to be the name day of St. Maura; Helena accordingly built a church to her within the fortress, in thanks for her rescue. For a time, the whole island was known as Santa Maura, although the Turks turned the church into a mosque when they took Lefkáda in

Info pp. 230-231

1479. Lefkada was the only Ionian island that was Ottoman for any length of time (from 1467 to 1684)

Lefkáda Town ❶ has been badly hit by earthquakes, with the result that the island's capital sports a high percentage of unusual buildings with upper stories of wood or metal. Some of the old stone churches weathered the quakes. Two of the leading painters of the Ionian School, Panagiotis Doxarás and his son, Nikólaos, left works in **Ágios Dimítrios** and **Ágios Menás**, with its stunning gilt iconostasis; there are other Ionian School works in the **Icon Museum**. The rather unique **Phonographic Museum** here is worth stopping in at, as is the small **Ethnographic Museum**.

Then there's the **Archeological Museum**, housing, among other things, some of the tombs excavated by the German archeologist Wilhelm Dörpfeld. A disciple of Heinrich Schliemann, who "discovered" Troy, Dörpfeld was firmly convinced that it was Lefkáda, and not the island known today as Itháki, that was the "Ithaca" of Odysseus, and spent years excavating on the island in a vain attempt to prove it. Dörpfeld's excavations uncovered remains of the ancient city of **Leukas**, just a few kilometers south of Lefkáda Town. Although rather unspectacular, the site includes an acropolis, traces of city walls, and the remnants of a theater. Better views are to be had, though, from the 17th-century convent of **Faneroméni**, west of town, which was restored in the 19th century.

Nídri ❷ was Dörpfeld's candidate for Odysseus' home town; today, it's Lefkáda's most active tourist center. One reason is its proximity to some offshore islands, the largest of which, **Skorpiós** ❸, is famous as the private island of Aristotle Onassis (he and his children are buried there; his tomb is visible from the water). More accessible to visitors is larger **Meganíssi** ❹, also serviced by boats from Nídri; here, there are several

tavernas, sand beaches, and caves, including **Spiliá tu Daimona** ("Cave of the God") and **Papanikolai Grotto**, one of the largest in Greece.

From Nídri, you can also head inland on foot: in less than an hour, following the **Dimosari Gorge**, you'll come to a waterfall which, although generally tame in summer, still provides opportunity for a swim. Nídri is also close to the narrow mouth of the long, tranquil inlet of **Vlihó Bay**, a wooded, serene locale. Dörpfeld himself lived right across from Nídri, at the other side of this harbor mouth, by the little church of **Agía Kiriakí**, near which he is buried. Farther south is **Póros** ❺, the nearest town to the sheltered pebble beach of **Mikrós Gialós**. Along the deeply cleft southern coast are the protected natural anchorage at **Sívota**, the sheltered sands of the beach at **Agiofili**, and the fishing village of **Vasilikí** ❻, its bay a famous draw for windsurfers.

From here, however, there's no direct route to the island's southernmost tip; so if you're heading out of Lefkáda Town,

it's best to travel along the western shore. Inland, the town of **Kariá** ❼ is a center for the island's traditional crafts of lace-making and embroidery, and holds a major festival of St. Spirídon on his name day, August 11. The shore road leads past **Ágios Nikítas** ❽, a pretty little village at the center of a burgeoning tourist industry on one of the island's most beautiful sand beaches. For another gorgeous beach under the limestone cliffs, continue on to ***Pórto Katsíki** ❾, toward the end of the paved road; the beach is accessed by a flight of stone steps.

Walkers can leave their cars at **Ágios Nikólaos** and continue on foot the seven kilometers to Lefkáda's most famous site, the sheer "white cliffs" of **Cape Leukádas** ❿ (also called Cape Doukáto and Sapphos Cape) that gave the island its name (*leukas* means "white"). Once topped by a temple of Apollo Levkatas, now by a lighthouse, the cliffs drop 72 meters straight into the sea. The ancients believed that this was the end of the western world, and a door leading directly into the underworld; this may have been the beginning of the tradition from leaping from atop them, called *katapontismós*, that developed into some kind of ritual activity. The priests of Apollo's temple did it, often tying feathers or even birds to their bodies; so did those hoping to cure certain ailments; while for criminals, the leap was a test of innocence or guilt (depending on whether or not the leaper survived). The most famous leaper from these heights remains the poet Sappho, who, for all of her present-day renown as a lover of women, leapt in despair to put an end to her life out of unrequited love for a man, Phaon.

Above: Friendly cleric. Right: Evening atmosphere in Vathí (Itháki).

ITHÁKI (ITHICA)

As you set out for Ithaca
hope the journey may be long,
full of adventure, full of discovery.
May there be many a summer morning
when with what pleasure, what joy,
you enter harbors you're seeing
for the first time.
Keep Ithaca always in your mind.
Arriving there
is what you're destined for.
But don't hurry the journey at all,
Ithaca gave you the marvelous journey.
Without her you wouldn't have set out.

(From "Ithaca" by Konstantinós P. Kaváfis, translated by Edmund Keeley and Philip Sherrard.)

Since Heinrich Schliemann uncovered Troy, scholars have been compelled to accept that Homer's epic poems, thereto regarded as pure fiction, contained a grain of historic truth. Still, it is a matter of conjecture whether or not the island today called Ithaca actually was Odysseus' home. By now, however, the island is dotted with sites traditionally associated

Map (Lefkáda) p. 221, Info pp. 230-231

with the Odyssey; and perhaps the main thing is that, as Kaváfis' poem indicates, it is important to all lovers of Greece that there be, somewhere, an actual island bearing the name Ithaca.

Founded by the Romans, developed under the Venetians, the island's capital, **Itháki** ❶ (also known as Vathí), lies at the end of sheltered **Mólos Bay**, a deep natural harbor with the remains of two old fortresses guarding its entrance. An **Archeological Museum** here contains a number of vases and other objects from local excavations.

Ithaca's compact size enables hikers and Homerists to explore on foot. Three kilometers west of Vathí – a fairly steep walk – is **Marble Cave**, the "cave of the nymphs," where Athena and Odysseus hid for safekeeping the presents the Phaeacians had given him. A walk of six kilometers to the south leads to the **Fountain of Arethoúsa**, where, according to legend, the swineherd Eumaios watered his pigs; it was at **Ellinikó** that the disguised Odysseus first met up with Eumaios, who was to become an ally in his attempt to regain his rightful throne. The bay of **Ágios Andréou** is said to be where Odysseus' son Telemachos landed shortly before reencountering his father; but those who have forgotten or never read the *Odyssey* may be more concerned with a swim, either here or at **Pera Pigádi** on the return leg of this several-hour walk.

Other options for hikers are the ascent to what's left of the 17th-century **Taxiárhis Monastery** or the climb up the slopes of Ithaca's highest mountain, **Aëtós**, or "Eagle Mountain," named for the birds that nest here (380 meters). Schliemann mistook ruins found on the latter for evidence of Odysseus' settlement; in fact, they date only from 700 B.C., although they're still generally known as the **Castle of Odysseus**. There are also remains here of an archaic temple. At **Píso Aëtós** ❷ there's an attractive little beach.

It's about 18 kilometers from Vathí to **Stavrós** ❸, Itháki's second town; best driven on the main road. The secondary road is in rather bad shape, but it leads past **Katharó Monastery**, which offers wonderful views from its bell tower, and the charming village of **Anogí**, where there's a 12th-century Byzantine church with frescoes.

Stavrós lies on the **Bay of Pólis**, from where, according to ancient legend, Ithaca's fleet set sail for Troy. Some archeologists believe that the **Loizos Cave**, rather than the Marble Cave to the south, was the actual "cave of the nymphs" mentioned in the *Odyssey*; certainly this cave was a site of cult worship to Hera, Artemis, Athena, and possibly also Odysseus, something demonstrated by archeological finds, including 12 tripods from the Geometric period. Unfortunately, the cave is not open to visitors at the present time.

Pelikáta Hill, north of Stavrós, is another of the island's notable archeological sites: a Venetian fort was built here over the ruins of a settlement dating back as far as 2200 B.C., which is therefore another candidate for Odysseus' home town. The nearby Stavrós **Archeological Museum** contains finds from both these sites.

The valleys of the north are the most fertile section of Itháki. In the northeast, the fishing village of **Fríkes** ❹ is on a bay with pleasant beaches, and is a port and yacht harbor; even less discovered is quiet **Kióni** ❺, a marvelous, traditional village.

*KEFALONIÁ

Mountainous Kefaloniá is the largest of the Ionian Islands, its slopes heavily covered with pine forests. The island has a certain roughness to it, with hard winters as a rule, and rugged slopes dominating the landscape, including the highest peak in the Ionian Islands, **Mount Énos** (1,628 meters). On the sides of this mountain grow the evergreen tree typical of the island, Kefaloniá Pine (*Abies celaphonica*).

The population of the entire island is only about the same as that of Corfu Town; around 30,000. Its distances also make it harder to get around than other, smaller islands. But it is well worth while taking time to discover Kefaloniá: it offers white beaches, blue grottos, green trails, and an air of adventure to anyone curious enough to seek it out.

Sámi ❻, the island's port, offers a few ruins of Roman settlement; but it's more interesting for its proximity to two striking caves. The ***Grotto of Melissáni** ❼, northwest of town, is on the water; in fact, it's a deep lake, with a partially open top through which sunlight streams to create a shifting kaleidoscope of color in the depths. **Drongaráti**, to the southwest of Sámi, has striking stalactites. Because of the incredible acoustics here, concerts are often held in the unique atmosphere of the cave during the summer. Hikers can make a day of it and explore them both on foot from Sámi. **Agía Evfimía**, farther north, is a nicer place than Sámi, with a better beach.

One of the very best beaches on the island is at the neck of Kefaloniá's northern peninsula: **Mírto** ❽ is a crescent of light sand held by rugged mountain flanks against the sapphire water.

Further north, ***Ássos** ❾ is a very attractive town with colorful houses, lots of flowers and trees, and a Venetian castle that stands watch over a natural harbor, originally built to protect it from pirate attacks.

At the northernmost tip of the island, within spitting distance of Itháki, is ***Fiskárdo** ❿, the only village on the island that was spared in the 1953 earthquake. As a result, it has a number of lovely old Venetian houses, some of which have been done over as small hotels, and is popular with yachtsmen and the more well-to-do type of visitors.

Anyone arriving by air flies in near the island's bustling capital, **Argostóli** ⓫, which suffered badly in the 1953 earth-

Info pp. 230-231

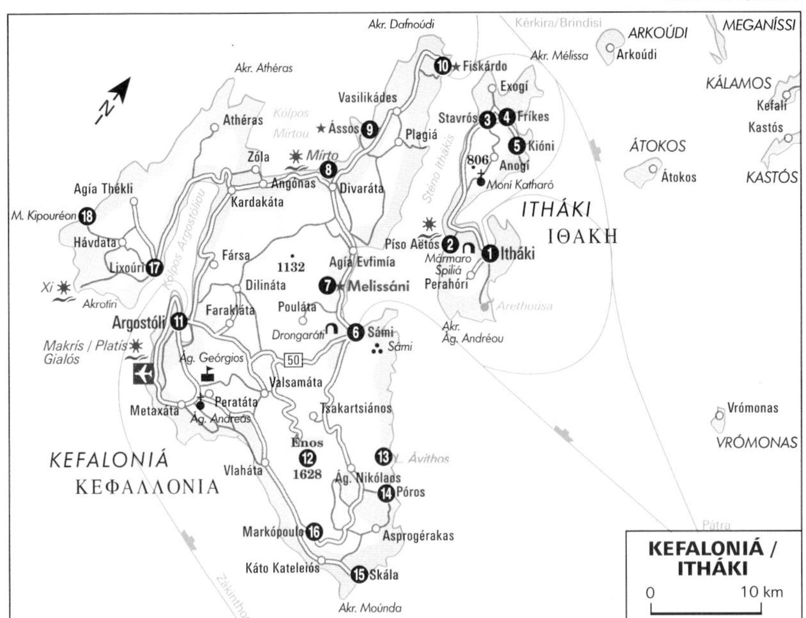

quake. Situated on a promontory thrust into the incut Bay of Argostóli, it's joined to the body of the island by an **arched bridge** the British built in 1813; an **obelisk** by the bridge sports an inscription with the date.

Sights here include the **Archeological Museum**, with a small wealth of Kefalonian finds, and the **Korgialénios Library**, which houses a collection of folk art and local history in addition to old documents from as far back as the Venetian period.

A couple of kilometers south of town are the ruins of **Kráni**, which was the main town here in the 7th or 6th century B.C.; the most striking aspect of the ancient city is its long stretch of cyclopean walls, built of massive blocks of stone. Beachgoers can sun themselves or splash about in the waves on broad **Makrís Gialós** or more rugged **Platís Gialós**, south of town.

Another peculiarity near Argostóli are the **Katavóthres**, two so-called "swallow-holes" into which sea water pours, and then vanishes. Not until the 1960s was it determined that the water ran from here underground to surface at Melisáni, on the other side of the island.

Dominating the southeastern part of the island is Kefaloniá's highest point; **Mount Énos** ⓬, snowcapped in winter, and accessible by car up to an altitude of 1,300 meters, from which it's not hard to walk the last 328 meters up to the mountain's summit, whicht commands stunning views of the island.

Lake Ávithos ⓭ lies not far from the original village of **Ágios Nikólaos**. The lake seems to be bottomless, indeed, it may well be: all attempts to measure its depths have so far failed.

Attractive beaches circle the island's southeastern shore. **Póros** ⓮ and **Skála** ⓯ are the two main tourist resorts in this corner of Kefaloniá; Skála boasts some notable mosaic floors from a 2nd- or 3rd-century Roman villa.

Markópoulou ⓰ is best known not as a bathing resort, but rather much more as a "village of snakes": every year in early

August, before the feast of the Virgin, little snakes with crosses on their heads begin to appear in its streets, all making their way toward the village church. Scientists have explained this away as simple migratory patterns; the faithful, of course, have a more supernatural explanation and wait for the annual occurrence with baited breath.

From Argostóli, ferries run across the bay to **Lixoúri** ⓱, the island's second-largest, but not all that interesting, city on the Palikí peninsula. At the tip of the peninsula stands the **Kounópetra**, a menhir that used to move back and forth for reasons no one could determine; like a clockmaker working in reverse, however, the 1953 earthquake put a stop to its motion. There are some nice beaches along the west coast here: **Ágios Geórgios** and **Xi**, to name but two. Rebuilt after the earthquake, the monastery of **Kipoúria** ⓲ is a great place to watch the sun set.

Above: The sheer cliffs of the west coast of Kefaloniá.

ZÁKINTHOS (ZANTE)

Fior di Levante, the Venetians called this island particularly dear to their hearts. And whether the "Flower of the Levant" was named for the mountain hyacinth or for the sea daffodils which exude a strong perfume on the beaches of the southern peninsula, or for the profusion of wildflowers used in the manufacture of local perfume, there is no question that Zákinthos' outstanding beauty makes it a veritable flower among islands. The Venetians' love of the place is reflected in the strong Italian influence that is still evident here. Like most of the Ionian Islands, Zákinthos has been hard hit by earthquakes over the years, but restored monuments such as the church of Ágios Dionísios, the island's patron saint, in Zákinthos Town would be as much at home in Venice as here.

Links between the two places were also historically evident in a certain amount of cultural exchange. One local son, Ugo Foscolo, is generally thought of as a leading 18th-century Italian poet, since he spent most of his active life in Italy; another, Dionísios Solomós, went off to Italy to study. He wrote on Zákinthos the words that were to become the text of the Greek national anthem. Further evidence of Zákinthos' active arts scene: Greece's first music school opened here in 1815.

In painting, too, Italian influence played a role. When the Turks conquered Crete in 1669, a number of icon painters of the Cretan School took refuge in this area, where a fusion of a certain Italian sensibility with the stylized forms of Byzantine convention resulted in a distinctive style still known as the Ionian School. The **Museum of Byzantine Art** in ***Zákinthos Town ❶** offers a fine overview. Another (restored) church, **Kiría tou Angélon**, contains icons by one of the Ionian School's leading lights, Panagiotis Doxarsás.

Putting a final Venetian seal on the landscape is the **Kástro** above the town; while the town's living pulse is located on the **Strata Marina** along the harbor, where people stroll under the eyes of other people sitting in the outdoor cafés and sweet shops, between **Ágios Dionísios**, with its pretty campanile, and the Renaissance **Ágios Nikólaos tou Molou**.

Zákinthos' main tourist center is **Laganás ❷** in the south of the island, which has become an unbearable agglomeration of the usual range of fast-food joints and stands purveying cheap beach equipment, and night spots. Unfortunately, this development happens to have taken place smack in the middle of what was for years the main breeding-ground of the loggerhead turtle. In the natural course of things, a mother turtle will return to the beach where she was hatched, lay some 100 eggs in a hole in the sand, and return to the sea, leaving the eggs to incubate in the warm sand and hatch some 60 days later. This whole process takes place between June and September, the height of tourist season; and

the few baby turtles that have managed to emerge unscathed by the ends of beach umbrellas or the heels of running children have often been misled by the bright lights around them into crawling the wrong way, and dying of exhaustion and dehydration long before they reached the water. As a result, the turtle population has dropped drastically; and the females have shifted to other, smaller beaches at **Sekánia** and **Dáfni**. The whole issue has become extremely controversial, pitting environmentalists against people intoxicated by the economic possibilities represented by the influx of tourists, but some progress has been made in favor of the turtles: motor boats and jet skis are no longer allowed in Laganás Bay.

The road to **Kerí ❸**, a little village at the southwestern point of the island, passes the natural ***tar pits** mentioned by both Pliny and Herodotos, who visited the island in antiquity, although little is left of the reserves of pitch once used to caulk the seams of myriad boats. Kerí's lighthouse is a great place for sunsets; be-

Info pp. 230-231

low, from Kerí's beach, boats bring visitors out to survey the white cliffs and striking formations that can be seen along the southwest coast.

One popular formation on Zákinthos is at the island's northern tip: the so-called ★**Blue Grotto** (Kianó Spiliá) ❹, where white limestone cliff formations help reflect the sun into the depths in spectacular colors. By contrast, **Xingiá Cave** ❺, on the east coast, has a natural sulfur spring that colors the water white. But perhaps the most famous sight on Zákinthos is on the northwest coast, near the 15th-century monastery of **Anafonítria**: ★**Shipwreck Beach** ❻, a little corner of white sand, walled off by stunning white cliffs and accessible only by water, in the middle of which reclines the hulk of a ship. Its history is less glorious than its appearance: in fact, the boat belonged to cigarette smugglers who ran ashore toward the end of the 1980s.

Above: With their fortress of Kíthira, the Venetians managed to control the trade route to Crete and Rhodes for many centuries. Right: Mighty mooring ropes secure ships in the port of Kíthira.

KÍTHIRA

Southernmost of the Ionian Islands, to which it is linked historically rather than geographically, Kíthira, with its steep coast, has its strongest ties to the goddess Aphrodite. It's here that she was borne ashore on her famous sea shell, born of the foam created when Zeus castrated his father Cronus and threw his genitalia into the sea (ancient Greek myths were nothing if not explicit).

Kíthira (Hóra) ❶, the island's main town on the southern shore, is a pretty blue-and-white place, Cycladic in aspect, dominated by the remains of a Venetian **castle** from 1503. The Venetians called the island Cerigo, as well as the Eye of Kriti; it had strategic value for its position at the entrance to the Aegean, on trade routes to Rhódos, Crete, and even Athens (a position it maintained until the opening

Map (Zákinthos) p. 227, Info pp. 230-231

of the Corinth Canal). A few of the houses and chapels still date from Venetian times, as do the castle's two churches, a **Panagía** and a **Pandokrátoras** with 16th-century frescoes. A little **Archeological Museum** preserves a few island finds. The town port, **Kapsáli**, is frequented mainly by vacationers from Athens. A little lighthouse stands here between two pebble beaches; in summer, thanks to a few hotels and tavernas, this becomes the "tourist center" of the island. Opposite is an offshore islet known as **Avgó**, "The Egg," traditionally held to be the place where Aphrodite was born.

North of Kíthira Town is **Livádi** ❷, where the British left an arched bridge as testimony to their presence on the island (1809-64). From here, a dirt road leads over to the beautiful monastery of **Moní Mirtidió** ❸, which stands uninhabited but still gorgeous with its striking bell tower, surrounded by gardens of flowers. It was named for a gilt relief of the Virgin and Child that still draws plenty of pilgrims, especially on August 15.

Milopótamos ❹ is another attractive village, traversed by clear-running streams. North of here is the abandoned town of **Káto Hóra**, a Venetian settlement still encircled by 16th-century city walls; the gate is surmounted by the Lion of St. Mark. Some of the old houses are now being reclaimed and restored. On the coast here, the beach at **Limniónas** ❺ offers light sand and good swimming. A bit further north is the cave church of **Agía Sofía**, with stalagmites, stalactites and subterranean lakes; fragments of old frescoes and mosaics attest to its earlier use as a church.

Paléopolis ❻ is on the souteast coast of the island. The Phoenicians came here for the murex shells they used to make the purple dye they traded in throughout the Mediterranean, and christened the island Porphyroussa, "Island of Shells." Remains of the settlement dating from this period are located by a lovely beach at Paleópolis. The Cretans who colonized the place were the first people in Greece to worship Aphrodite, but her temple here

was later destroyed by early Christians; all that remains are a few foundation walls of the old acropolis. A bit east of here there's a good beach by the fishing port of **Avlémonas**, guarded by the remains of a Venetian fortress.

Continuing north, you pass **Paleohóra** ❼, the island's ghost town. In 1537, Frederick Barbarossa invaded the island, slaughtering many of its inhabitants and allegedly carrying off 7,000 people. Mothers supposedly threw their children off the hilltop here to fall hundreds of meters to their deaths rather than risk enslavement at the hands of Barbarossa. The deserted town is still believed to be haunted by many islanders.

The largest village in this part of the island is **Potamós** ❽, which was Kíthira's capital under the Venetians. The harbor nearest to it, **Agía Pelagía** ❾, is the dock for ferries coming from the Peloponnese. While there is a beach here, Kapsáli, the harbor of Kíthira Town, is a more attractive destination for yachting tourists and backpackers alike.

BOAT: The ferry connections between the Ionian Islands are rather sparse and subject to change: inquire locally for information. *BUS:* There are buses to Athens from Corfu, Léfkada, Kefaloniá and Zákinthos. The ferry crossing is included in the ticket price

CORFU (KÉRKIRA) (☎ 0661)

CORFU TOWN: EOT, Zavitsianou 15, tel. 37520, fax. 30298. **Corfu Tourism Promotion Board**, Samara 13, 49100 Corfu, tel. 39606, fax. 32525.

PLANE: Corfu's airport (tel. 30180), south of Corfu Town, has regular service to Athens and Thessaloníki, as well as charter flights. **Olympic Air**, tel. 38694. *BOAT:* Ferries to Italy (Venice, Ancona, Bari, Brindisi, Otranto), Igoumenítsa, Pátras; several times weekly to Sarandë (Albania) – book several days in advance because of visa formalities! *BUS:* From Corfu Town there are connections to other towns on the island; several buses daily to Athens. *CAR RENTAL:* **CORFU TOWN: Island Cars**, Paleopoleos 151, tel. 32114; in Paleokastritsa, tel. (0663) 41566. **Payless**, Ethnikis Antistaseos 8, tel. 36882, fax. 25851.

For information about reasonable accommodation: **Corfu Owners of Tourist Villas / Apartments**, tel. 26133, fax. 23403. **CORFU TOWN:** $$$ **Cavalieri Hotel**, Capodistriou 4, tel. 39041, fax. 39283, distinguished old palazzo in the heart of town. **Atlantis Hotel**, Xenofondos Stratigou 48 (New Port), tel. 35560, fax. 46480, modern, comfortable. $$ **Hermes**, in the market quarter, tel. 39321, and **Bretagne**, tel. 30724, are both open year-round. $ **Cyprus**, Agíou Patérou 13, tel. 30032, simple, friendly hotel in the center, shared baths. **KANONI:** $$$ **Corfu Hilton**, tel. 36540, *grande luxe*. **PALEOKASTRÍTSA:** $$ **Zefiros Hotel**, tel. (0663) 41088, one of the few moderately priced hotels in this area.

PALEOKASTRÍTSA: The campground here is gorgeous, 2 km from town, tel. (0663) 41105, .

CORFU TOWN: Xenichtes, Potamou, Mandouki 12, tel. 24911, long established, genteel, pricey. **Rex**, Capodistriou 66, tel. 39649, central, not expensive, inspired Greek dishes. **KASSIÓPI: Tria Adelphia**, tel. (0663) 81211, solid taverna. **PALEOKASTRÍTSA: Chez George**, on the beach, tel. (0663) 41233, very good seafood.

Archeological Museum, tel. 30680, open Tue-Sun 8:30 am to 3 pm. **Museum of Asiatic Art**, Palea Anaktora, tel. 38124, 30443. **Achilleion**, tel. 56210, open daily 9 am to 4:30 pm.

Corfu Golf Club, tel. 94220. **Cricket Club**, tel. 41205. **Association of Amateur Fishermen**, tel. 34407. **Alpine Association**, tel. 39481.

PAXÍ (☎ 0662)

Tourist Police, tel. 31222

BOAT: Regular ferry service to Corfu (3 hours), as well as Párga and Igoumenítsa. **Port Authority**, tel. 32254.

Private rooms in all towns. **GÁIOS:** $$$ **Paxos Club**, tel. 32450, fax. 32097, nice rooms, pool. **LÁKKA:** $ **Lefkothea**, tel. 31408, small, inexpensive.

GÁIOS: Aléxandros, fish taverna at the harbor. **LÁKKA: Nautilus**, at the harber, Greek taverna beneath olive trees.

LEFKÁDA (☎ 0645)

LEFKÁDA TOWN: Municipal Tourist Office, tel. 23000 or 24962. **St. Maura Travel**, Dörpfeld 18, tel. 25319, fax. 25119, with a branch in Nídri (tel. 92141), can arrange rooms, tours, transportation.

PLANE: The airport is on the mainland in Préveza, tel. (0682) 22355; several flights a day to Athens, charter flights. *BUS:* There are buses to Athens (4 times a day) and Thessaloníki (twice a week). **Bus Terminal**, tel. 22364.

$$ **Pension Marina**, tel. 92145, fax. 92818, decent, clean, on the beach. **NÍDRI: Hotel Gorgona**, tel. 92268, 92558, modern villa in the north of town.

PÓROS: Póros Beach, tel. 95452, nice setting in an olive grove at the beach.

Taverna Symposio, on the central square, is very popular. **Vitsounas**, on Dörpfeld Street, is a typical taverna.

Archeological Museum, Faneromenis 21, tel. 23678, open Tue-Sun 9 am to 1 pm.

ITHÁKI (☎ 0674)

Polyctor Tours, tel. 33120.

BOAT: From Itháki (Váthi) there are ferries to Pátras; from Piso Aëtós to Ástakos. **Port Authority**, tel. 32909. *BUS:* Buses from Itháki to Kióni. **Bus Station**, tel 32445.

ITHÁKI: $$ **Mentor**, tel. 32433, largest on the island. **Odysseus**, tel. 32381, attractive small hotel.

ITHÁKI: Thiaki, beside the Town Hall, good Greek food. **KIÓNI: Limáni**, at the harbor, good fish.

Archeological Museum, tel. 32200, open Tue-Sun 8:30 am to 3 pm.

KEFALONIÁ (☎ 0671)

EOT, tel. 22248, fax 24466.

PLANE: Airport 10 km south of Argostóli, tel. 45511. Flights to Athen, charter flights. *BOAT:* From Sámi there are ferries to Pátras, Igoumenítsa, Ástakos and Brindisi (Italy).

FISKÁRDO: $$ **Fiscardona**, at the harbor, tel. (0674) 51484, lovely restored townhouse. **ARGOSTÓLI:** $$$ **Blue Paradise**, Vass. Georgiou 10, tel. 24910-13, fax. 24311, luxury hotel, large rooms, kitchenette. $$ **Armonia**, tel. 22566, attractive simple hotel.
LIXOÚRI: $$ **Summery**, tel. 91771, large hotel, open year-round.

FISKÁRDO: Nikolas, on the shore promenade. **ARGOSTÓLI: Captain's Table**, in town center, cozy, good food. **PÓROS: Romantsa**, at the harbor, good fish dishes.

Archeological Museum, Argostóli, tel. 28300, Tue-Sun 8:30 am to 3 pm. **Grottoes** in Drongaratí, tel. 22439 and Melissáni, tel. 22215.

ZÁKINTHOS (☎ 0695)

PLANE: There are two flights a day from Athens to Zákinthos airport, 6 km south of Zákinthos Town (bus service). **Olympic Airways**, tel. 28611. *BOAT:* Ferries to and from Killíni (Peloponnese); also to Pátras and Brindisi, Italy. **Port Authority**, tel. 28117.

For detailed listings of accommodations, contact the **Hotel Owners Association** at 51590 or 51089. **ZÁKINTHOS TOWN:** $$$ **Stráda Marína**, Lombárdou 14, tel. 22761, beautiful hotel on the shore. $$ **Hotel Park**, tel. 23790, fax. 26121, modern, comfortable large hotel with pool, near beautiful Tsiliví Beach north of Zákinthos Town. $ **Diéthnes**, Lazárou 102, tel. 22286, lovely, simple hotel.

ZÁKINTHOS TOWN: Arebika, on the shore road, typical taverna, good food and wine. **Panorama**, at the Kástro, good food, fantastic view.

KÍTHIRA (☎ 0735)

Skandela Tours, tel. 33522, fax. 33135.

PLANE: Airport (tel. 33292) 20 km north of Kíthira Town; one or two flights a day to Athens. *BOAT:* Ferries from Agía Pelagía to Neápolis, Gíthio (Peloponnese), Crete (Kastélli) und Piraeus. **Port Authority**, tel. 33280.

KÍTHIRA TOWN: $$ **Margarita**, in the center, tel. 31711, lovely hotel in a villa. **KAPSÁLI:** $ **Aphrodite**, tel. 31328, near the beach. **ÁGIA PELAGÍA:** $$ **Filoxenia**, tel. 33610. $ **Kitheria**, tel. 33321, both hotels located near the ferry landing.

KÍTHIRA TOWN: Zorbas, Spirídona Stái 34, very good dishes from the grill.

Traditional **pottery studio** in Livádi, tel. 31124.

LITERATURE AND MUSIC

"Sing to me, muse, of the man of many wiles, Odysseus." So begins Homer's *Odyssey*, the classic literary work about sailing the Aegean, as well as one of the oldest works of Western literature. Not only does Odysseus roam throughout the whole Aegean and its islands on his journey home to Ithaca (which may or may not be identical with the Ionian island that today bears the name), but Homer himself was probably a wandering bard, possibly from Asia Minor, and was very likely quite familiar with the islands. Híos claims to be his birthplace, and preserves a "teaching stone" on which, it is claimed, Homer sat with his students; on Íos, another stone marks his supposed grave. The islands have continued to play an important role in Greece's literature and music ever since.

Part and parcel of the paradigm of the wandering bard – a singer or writer – is the idea of expatriation. Today's model may be the Anglophone with his typewriter – Henry Miller (*The Colossus of Maroussi*), Lawrence Durrell (*Reflections on a Marine Venus*; *Prospero's Cell*), or Patricia Storace, whose *Dinner with Persephone* is one of the finest travel books to appear in some time – but the "expatriates" of earlier days came from considerably nearer by.

Take St. John the Divine, whom Emperor Domitian exiled to the island of Pátmos; there, he had his vision of the Revelations of the Apocalypse, which, as dictated to his scribe Próchoros, have become part of the New Testament of the Bible. The icon image showing the dictation, which is sold all over Pátmos today, is perhaps the first image of an expatriot island writer at work.

The word "expatriot," of course, had little meaning in Greece when the country was a part of the Ottoman Empire. In the 18th and 19th centuries, Greek artists yearning for a homeland were looking to the future, rather than the past: literature was a way of helping to establish a new national identity. Greece's "national" poet, Dionísios Solomós, was born on Zakínthos in 1798 and died on Corfu in 1857. Having received his education in the Italian language, he had to teach himself Greek before he could write such works as "Hymn to Liberty," which is today the country's national anthem (with music by Corfiot composer Nikolaos Mantzaros).

As they formed a literature, writers also helped form a language. Solomós was an innovator in that he used demotic Greek when the accepted "literary" form of the language, *katharévusa*, was a more elegant if rather artificial idiom. The dispute between supporters of *katharévusa* and those who wanted the country's official language to be the everyday demotic was so heated that it led to riots in Athens in 1901.

Most books remained in *katharévusa*, though. As a child, Penelope Delta, née Benakis, who was born on the island of Híos, was reluctant to read books in this difficult, artificial language; as an adult, she set out to create an enjoyable children's literature in *demotiki*. The books she wrote have become enduring staples of Greek children's libraries. Delta, too, was an expatriot in search of her own identity; she was raised largely in Alexandria, Egypt.

Some of the most articulate voices of modern Greek literature have island connections, as well. On Skiáthos, local son Aléxandros Papadiamántis (1851-1911) is still revered as the father of the modern short story. On Lefkáda, Angelios Sikelianos is remembered primarily for his Delphic ideal. Mitilíni trumpets its connection to the 1979 winner of the Nobel Prize for literature, Odysseus Elytis, whose family came from here, although

Right: Nikólaos Filipakis plays the Lyra (Ólimbos, Kárpathos).

the poet himself was actually born in Crete.

Writers who have written evocatively about the islands include Stratís Mirivílis, who brings Mitilíni (Lésvos) to life in his novel *The Mermaid Madonna*, and Evgenia Fakinou, whose *Astradeni* evokes Sími from the perspective of a young girl whose family has been compelled to emigrate to Athens to find work. Both of these books are available in English, the latter as part of the Kedros publishing house's fine series of contemporary Greek writers in translation, which allows non-Greek speakers to sample the fruits of the country's literature.

It is no problem at all to find translations of the works of the one writer whose name epitomizes 20th-century Greek literature for many foreigners: Nikos Kazantzakis. Nearly every island, it seems, has some connection to him. He went to school for a few years on Náxos; he lived on the island of Égina while working on his classic *Zorba the Greek*; but Kazantzákis was Cretan through and through. Zorba's quasi-New Age, know-thyself philosophy has long been warmly embraced by hippies and island-lovers; while the theme from the film score is the standard background accompaniment in countless tavernas.

For music on the islands is an expatriate as well. And not only Western film music: even the quintessentially Greek *rembetiko* was an import from Asia Minor, specifically Smyrna, where this type of long, sad musical narrative punctuated by instrumental solos – a Greek answer to the blues – was prominent in the 19th century. The main instrument of the *rembetiko* band is the *bouzouki*, supported by its smaller cousin, the *baglamas*. Even in island discos, to the rhythms of modern pop music, local kids will break into the traditional *rembetiko* dances: women entwine their wrists above their heads like belly dancers in the *tsifteteli*, while men immerse themselves in the slow, trance-like solo *zeibekikos*, now turning a tight circle, now bending to touch the ground.

FLORA AND FAUNA OF THE GREEK ISLANDS

At first sight, some travelers are somewhat taken aback by the Greek Islands. If images of Caribbean lushness have influenced your picture of an island paradise, this arid summer landscape of rock and sun-baked golden grass takes a little getting used to. Beaches are lined not with tall palm trees, but rather with scruffy brownish tamarisk trees; other trees are twisted and battered by the strong prevailing winds. And yet for all of its aridity, Greece has an incredible wealth and variety of plant life, if you only keep your eyes open to see it.

Because the islands vary considerably in both altitude and location, their climates range from semi-tropical to nearly northern. Some of the Cyclades are little more than lumps of rock; others sport lush green valleys; while the islands in the eastern Aegean have expanses of forest (many badly damaged in fires in the 1980s and 1990s). Among the most common trees of Greece are the Mediterranean cypress, distinctive as a black finger in the landscape, and Aleppo pine.

Another characteristic feature is the olive tree, both wild and cultivated; the latter is especially important on the islands of Corfu and Lésvos. Other orchard trees include oranges, lemons and other citrus fruits. Strictly speaking, these are not indigenous: lemons didn't arrive in the region until Alexander the Great brought them back from his new territories in Asia.

Plenty of other foreign imports – plants originally brought in from other countries – are now characteristic elements of the local vegetation. Agave and cactus, for example, have both flourished in the island climate. Date palms, also found in the southern islands, originally came from Africa. And the ailanthus tree (*Ailanthus altissima*) was originally im-

Above: In spring, the variety of flowering plants on the islands can best be enjoyed. Right: Octopi hung out to dry.

ported to France from China around 1750, and spread from there all around the Mediterranean. Peasants used to call it *vromodendro*, "stink tree," because of the bad smell its leaves gave off when rubbed.

No one arriving in Greece in the spring, when the hillsides are blanketed with a colorful carpet of wildflowers, could overlook the fact that the country boasts more different species of flower than any other country in Europe. In fact, Greece has more than 6,000 plant species; the British Isles, by contrast, has a mere 2,300. Thirty-six species of orchid have been catalogued on Corfu alone, including the *Orchis palustris*, which has only been found around Lake Korissión.

Because of their geographic isolation from the mainland, the islands don't boast many species of animal. Lizards and other reptiles, such as geckoes, dwell here in abundance, sunning themselves on the rocks or hiding out in the corners of a hotel room.

There's also a range of colorful butterflies to complement the bright wildflowers, though the much-touted "butterfly valleys" of Páros, Rhódos, and other islands are the habitats of the tiger moth, *Callimorpha quadripuntaria*, which is rather drab and uninteresting to look at.

In general, marine life represents the most interesting Greek Island fauna. But much of it is growing increasingly difficult to find. The monk seal, for example, is the most endangered species in Europe; there are only about 500 of them left worldwide, 300 of which are in Greece. The country's first National Marine Park, around Alónnisos (Sporades), protects these as well as a range of underwater life. Dolphins, for example, make their home here.

Corfu has some freshwater turtles; but it's Zákinthos, further south in the Ionian chain, that's famous for these animals. Loggerheads (*Caretta caretta*) have traditionally made their home on Zakinthos' southern shore. To protect these animals from the havoc tourism has wrought upon their numbers, environmental activists fought for years to create a new national park.

The sea's overall population has shrunk in this century; overfishing has diminished the Aegean's fish stock by about 60 percent, which means the local fish is barely enough to cover the needs of the islanders. You sometimes see a fisherman beating a fresh-caught octopus against the rocks to tenderize it, after which he hangs it out to dry on a line, like a piece of laundry.

There are 422 recorded species of bird in Greece, from owls to seagulls, eagles to the lammergeier. Pelicans, woodcocks, and snipes are just a few of the species that stop off here on their annual migrations. In bird reserves such as Corfu's Lake Korissión, the glossy ibis and the great white egret put in occasional appearances; another endangered species is the pygmy cormorant. This lake is also the habitat of otters.

SAILING THE AEGEAN

He makes the winter wind
carry him across
the gray sea,
through the trough
of towering waves.

In Sophocles' *Antigone*, mastery of the sea heads the list of man's great achievements. So much of Greece is surrounded by water that navigating these waters was to become not only a practical necessity, but also a defining characteristic of the national character: on much on the mainland as on the Greek Islands. It is certainly no accident that Greece's heroes throughout the ages have been seafarers, from the wily Odysseus through to the 20th-century shipping dynasties of Onassis and Niarchos.

Above: For many a dream vacation – sailing from island to island. Right: Eight gods of the wind controlled the fates of ancient mariners (Tower of the Winds, Athens).

The world's first ocean voyage that can be scientifically documented took place in the Aegean Sea around 9000 B.C. Little is known about the nature of the earliest vessels to ply the Aegean, even after it was clear that maritime strength was the key to power in the region. By 1500 B.C., seafaring Phoenician traders from Tyre and Sidon linked the Aegean Islands with ports in the Near East, Africa and Italy. As the trading empire of the Phoenicians reached as far as Mesopotamia in the east, Oriental cultural influences found their way to the Aegean; for the Phoenicians traded not only in silver, dyes and ivory, but also in handicrafts.

In 480 B.C., the *polis* of Athens secured its dominance in the Greek world through its naval superiority. Athens' contribution to naval technology was the trireme, a cross between a galley and a sailing ship; in addition to sails, it had three rows of oarsmen, one above the other, who may have sat upon sliding seats much like modern scullers in a rowing shell. Quick and easy to maneuver, they made short work of the larger, more cumbersome Persian ships in the narrow straits of Salamína. A modern reconstruction, 37 meters in length, achieved speeds of up to 10 knots an hour. Even after the advent of modern steam power and shipping fleets, the scale of the island world continued to dictate a certain modesty in the size of human construction, whether of dwellings or of vessels. Sponge fishermen brought in considerable wealth to Kálimnos and Sími, but they still set off for Africa on journeys of many months' duration in small boats in which dozens of men lived for weeks at a time.

The common name for the Greek islander's utility vessel is *kaiki*, or caique, an all-purpose term that covers a wide variety of hull shapes as a general designation for the colorful fishing vessels that bob at anchor in island harbors. In centuries gone by, kaikis relied on two steering oars to determine their course; today, they have central rudders, and usually sport diesel engines, as well, in addition to a low mast for a sail. One common variant of the kaiki is the double-ended hull known as the *trehandiri*.

In antiquity, small boats were built from the outside in: first, the planking was secured, after which an interior framework was added as additional reinforcement. Today, builders follow the more conventional route of creating a skeleton first and covering it with planks. The most common wood used in boatbuilding remains Sámos pine. The planks have traditionally been caulked with pitch from the island of Zákinthos, although this source is gradually drying up.

Whether chartering a kaiki or a sailboat, sailing alone on a "bareboat" or hiring a crew, holiday sailors are in a better position to explore the Greek Islands than virtually any other traveler. Since the 1960s, the Greek Tourist Board has been systematically improving facilities for yachts and other pleasure craft: the result of which is a string of excellent marinas –

34 of them in all – throughout the country. The kingpin of the network of harbors is Themistocles' ancient port at Piraeus, which, expanded and modernized, is now called Marina Zéa and boasts 950 berths. Other significant island harbors include Corfu's Gouviá Bay and Mandráki, the ancient harbor on the island of Rhódos. Today, Greece has the largest fleet of yachts in the entire Mediterranean.

In antiquity, Greece's winds had names and lived in a cave, according to legend, on Tínos. The winds in Greece still have distinctive names and characters. In the Ionian Sea, the prevalent breeze is known as the *maistros*, a moderate northwest wind which generally blows in the afternoon. In the Aegean, the trade winds are called the *meltemi*. These strong winds reach their maximum force in July and August, blowing cold often out of a clear sky, scouring beach-goers with the sting of hard-driven sand and whipping the seas up into a difficult chop which can be extremely unpleasant to navigate in a small boat, especially for the uninitiated.

METRIC CONVERSION

Metric Unit	US Equivalent
Meter (m)	39.37 in.
Kilometer (km)	0.6241 mi.
Square Meter (sq m)	10.76 sq. ft.
Hectare (ha)	2.471 acres
Square Kilometer (sq km)	0.386 sq. mi.
Kilogram (kg)	2.2 lbs.
Liter (l)	1.05 qt.

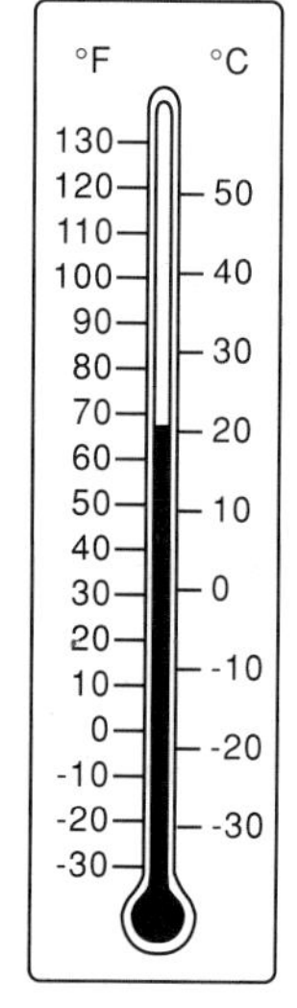

PREPARING FOR YOUR TRIP

When to Go

If you truly want to discover the Greek Islands, go "off season." In July and August (peak season prices!), the islands are overrun with tourists, and local culture and color are almost wholly obscured behind a veil of kiosks selling sunscreen and high-priced cocktail bars. Off-peak, however, in April and May or September and October, you can really get a sense of what life is like here, meeting locals, experiencing a Greek Easter, or simply finding waiters who have time to explain the menu. You also have better weather: warm enough to swim, cool enough to hike. In April and May, the islands are carpeted in a lush green you never see in summer's beating sun, compounded by blankets of wildflowers. In September and October, the effects of the fall sun on the golden hills are more magical than unvarying August light; and you have the insider's sense of staying on after a party, watching everyone pick up after the departed guests and getting back to normal. In October it's still warm enough to swim in the Dodecanese, though it's cooling off up north. Of course, there are no guarantees as to weather, and if you're relying on ferries and are therefore at the mercy of the sea and its moods, allow plenty of time to get where you want to go.

What to Pack

No one going to the Greek Islands will forget to pack a bathing suit; a beach towel is also a good idea. Rubber or plastic thongs, for stony beaches and burning-hot sand (and questionable hotel bathrooms), are useful; women, especially, will want some garment they can slip on over a bathing suit (shorts, a sarong, a T-shirt dress). In the strong sun, people are glad of a sun hat or scarf. Sun tan lotion is available everywhere, but you might want to bring lip block or face block. Insect repellent is also good to have along.

A day pack or bag is extremely useful; bring one that can crumple up to fit in the compartment under a moped seat. Walking shoes or sneakers are essential, even in high summer: anyone who's tried to climb the slippery marble steps of the Acropolis in smooth-soled leather sandals can back this up. Remember that getting to some of the best beaches involves hiking down dirt tracks. A water bottle is useful, although you can buy bottled water everywhere. Bring a pocket knife and corkscrew for impromptu picnics.

If you're going early or late in the season, or plan to rent motorbikes a lot, bring along a light sweater or anorak, or at least a long-sleeved shirt. You may even be glad of a travel umbrella.

Currency

The currency of Greece is the drachma, abbreviated ΔPX (Drs), which comes in coins of 10, 20, 50 and 100 drachmas, and bills of 100, 200, 500, 1,000, 5,000 and 10,000 drachmas. Visitors can bring in as much foreign currency as they like – banknotes exceeding $1,000 have to be declared upon arrival – and up to 100,000 in drachmas. Sums over $1,000 can only be taken out of the country if they were declared at entry; foreign residents may only re-export 20,000 drachmas.

Exchange Rate:

1 US dollar = 305 drachmas

1 pound sterling = 488 drachmas

1 euro = 317 drachmas

Visas and Customs

A valid passport or identity card is required for all citizens of the US, Canada and the EU who want to enter Greece for stays of less than three months. Anyone who wants to stay longer should apply to the Aliens Bureau in Athens (Alexandras 173, tel. 6468103) at least 20 days before the expiration of the three-month period.

Since Greece belongs to the EU economic zone, there is no limit on the import or export of items for personal use from other EU contries. In certain cases, an excessive amount of certain goods will be regarded as commercial and not personal imports. The following goods over the following limits are included here: 400 cigarillos, 800 cigarettes, 1 kilogram of tobacco, 10 liters of spirits, 90 liters of wine, 110 liters of beer. From non-EU countries a person can bring into the country duty-free up to 10 kilograms of foodstuffs and non-alcoholic beverages, 200 cigarettes or 250 grams of tobacco, 1 liter of spirits or 2 liters of wine; and gifts not exceeding a value of 9,000 drachmas.

The same limits apply to goods bought in the duty-free shops (aiprorts; ferries) of a non-EU country. For travelers within the EU free-trade zone – for example, a direct flight from the U.K. to Crete – duty free shopping was discontinued in 19999.

You can only bring works of art (including icons) and antiquities out of the country with written permission from the Greek Archeological Service. In most cases, such exports are not allowed, and violators are faced with severe penalties.

TRAVELING TO GREECE

By Plane

Athens and Thessaloníki are Greece's main international airports. Athens' Elinikon Airport has one terminal for Olympic Airways and one for everyone else. Athens is getting a new, larger airport in Spáta, north of the city, scheduled to open in 2001 in time for the Olympic Games. Thessaloníki is the best place to fly into if you're going to Thásos, Samothráki, or even the Sporades. In season, there are international charter flights from a number of European cities directly to the islands. Rhódos has the third-busiest airport in Greece, and Iráklion, on Crete, is also active; but more and more islands have their own charter-sized airports.

Olympic Airways provides international service to Greece as well as operating an extensive network of domestic links. You can get information through any Greek Tourist Board (EOT) office (see "Addresses"). In the U.S., call 1-800-223-1226 or (212) 838-3600; in the U.K., (0171) 409 3400 (11 Conduit St., London W1R 0LS).As state-run Olympic's monopoly relaxes, new airlines have been starting up. Cronus Airlines offers direct flights from Munich, Frankfurt and London (98 Wigmore Street, London W1H 9DR, tel. 0171-3317090, fax. 3317091).

By Boat

There's frequent car ferry service from **Italy** (Trieste, Venice, Ancona, Ortona, Bari, Brindisi) to Pátras, often stopping in at Corfu. A few ferry lines:

Superfast Ferries, daily service from Ancona, Amalias 30, 10558 Athens, tel. (01) 331-3252, fax. 331-0369; in the

U.S.: 757 Deep Valley Drive, Rolling Hills Estates, CA 90274, tel. (310) 544-3551. Internet: www.superfast.com; e-mail: sffathens@superfast.com.

Strintzis Lines, from Venice, Bari, and Ortona to Pátras (the last two via Corfu) Akti Poseidonos 26, Piraeus, tel. (01) 422-5010, fax. 422-5265. Internet: www.strintzis.gr; e-mail: sales @strintzis.gr.

Ventouris Ferries, from Bari, Pireos 91 and Kithiron 2, 18541 Piraeus, tel. (010) 482-8001, fax. 483-2919.

Minoan Lines, from Venice and Ancona, central office: Leoforos Kifisias 64B, 15125 Maroussi, tel. (01) 689-8340. Internet: www.minoan.gr; e-mail: booking-eta@minoan.gr.

There's also direct service once a week from Haifa, Israel to Piraeus via Crete or Rhódos. Contact **Allalouf and Co. Shipping Ltd.**, 40 Hanamal St., Haifa, Israel, tel. (04) 671743, fax. 679530.

TRAVELING IN GREECE

By Plane

Olympic Airways in Greece (Athens): (01) 926-9111, 936- 9111, fax. 921-9933. Offices at Othonos 6 and Leoforos Syngrou 96, among others. See *Info* section at the end of the appropriate chapter for offices on individual islands. Other new airlines are opening up to claim their share of the market. **Air Greece**, tel. (in Athens) (01) 325-5011/4 or 324-4457/8, fax. 325-5015, has a number of island connections. Another new airline is **Cronus Air**, in Athens, at Othonos 10, Sindágma Square, 10557 Athens, tel. (01) 331-5515, fax. 331-5505.

By Boat

For those who want to travel in comfort and style, a variety of cruises are offered, generally including comprehensive sightseeing programs and guided tours. EOT issues a comprehensive timetable of all the ferry lines' schedules. Unfortunately, this is more a guideline than a gospel: ferry schedules change, especially at the start of high season, which is smack in the middle of the period covered by the book. Check in the harbor before making your plans; there are worse things than having to spend an extra day or two on a Greek island, but it's annoying if you're trying to catch a flight to somewhere else.

Ferry times are clearly posted in the ferry and tourist offices by every island harbor; however, since different offices represent different ferry lines, you may have to ask at several places to get the bigger picture. As for the confusing scene at Piraeus: local papers (including the *Athens News* and the English edition of *I Kathimerini*, in the Greek edition of the *International Herald Tribune*) list the day's and the morrow's departures.

For information on domestic shipping lines in Greece (Athens), call (01) 411-4785 or the Port Authority of Piraeus, (01) 451-11311. For individual ferry lines, see "Traveling to Greece," above. Some of the companies listed on this page also offer connections within Greece during the peak season.

By Flying Dolphin

"Flying Dolphins," the blue-and-yellow hydrofoils, are steadily changing the way people visit islands; it's hard to resist the obvious advantage of getting to your destination in half the time a ferry takes. Of course, the privilege doesn't come cheap, and discount passes aren't valid on the dolphins, neither regular ones nor the larger "Mega Dolphins."

Boats and "dolphins" occupy different spaces in islanders' consciousness. Visitors asking when the next boat leaves the island will be told when the next boat leaves – but not when the next dolphin does. Make sure check with the delphina office as well as the shipping office if you're trying to find out your next chance of getting off the island. Some dolphins leave and arrive at Piraeus; there's an additional *delphina* port on the other side of Piraeus, at Marina Zéa, for departures to the Saronic Islands and some of the Cyclades. Dolphins also run from Ágios Konstandínos and Thessaloníki to the Sporades, and between islands within the Cyclades and Dodecanese archipelagos.

Information on Flying Dolphins: Central bookings: Themistokleos 8, Piraeus, tel. (01) 428-0001/10, fax. 428-3525. Athens office: (01) 324-4600.

By Bus

From Athens, buses to the Peloponnese and the west (including the Ionian Islands), as well as to Thessaloníki and the ferries to Thásos and Samothráki, leave from Terminal A at Kifissou 100; buses to the north (to the ferry ports for the Sporades) leave from Terminal B at Liossion 260, tel. 831-7153 (weekdays).

Once you're on an island, the availability and frequency of buses depends on that island's popularity. Generally, theres at least one bus a day between an island's main centers, which, on larger islands like Mitilíni (Lésvos), can lie two or three hours apart. Tourist offices, travel agencies, and even hotels generally have bus schedules; check times and destinations carefully so you won't get stranded (taxis can get expensive). Bus fares are not high, and the amenities are correspondingly simple; don't expect toilets.

Car and Motorcycle Rental

If you plan to island-hop, don't even think about taking a rented car from island to island; boarding a ferry is stressful enough without having to deal with a vehicle. But once you're on an island, if you really want to explore, it makes a huge difference to have your own set of wheels. Many islands are small enough that a moped is perfectly adequate; but on a larger island, such as Mitilíni (Lésvos), Rhódos or Corfu, the distances are such that a car is the only way to cover an appreciable amount of the territory. The major car rental firms have representatives in large island tourist centers, ports, and at airports; but the legion smaller "mom and pop" type firms often offer more personal service and lower rates.

Many firms are quite specific about what kinds of roads you can attempt: a sensible concern on the islands, where only the main arteries are paved and the rutted tracks to the beaches can wreak havoc on a chassis. It would be foolhardy to try to navigate many of these roads in anything less than a four-wheel-drive vehicle in any case; if you're planning to do some active exploring, rent a jeep. The maps you get at the agencies aren't always accurate: in general, red indicates paved, yellow "secondary" roads, but while some of these "secondary" roads are perfectly respectable, others are little better than goat tracks, partially washed away over the last winter.

If you rent a motorbike, consider a helmet. Of course, it's less fun, and almost no one has one on. But Greece has a higher accident rate than any other European country – precisely because of the carefree driving, narrow roads in poor condition, and lack of helmets.

Gas stations are not plentiful, but are well marked: signs are posted as much as five kilometers away. If you're on a small island, find out where the gas stations are when you rent your vehicle; they may all be located around the main town, which could leave you stranded in a fishing hamlet if you're not careful. Road signs are almost without exception written in both Greek and Roman characters. Sometimes the transliteration follows on a separate sign a bit past the Greek one.

Taxis

There are taxis on most islands. Local rides are metered; there are often fixed rates for between-town trips, but establish what these are before you get in. In general, the cost of a six-to-ten-kilometer trip is not prohibitive. Taxi drivers in Athens are world-famous for their creative pricing: negotiate a fare in advance!

PRACTICAL TIPS FROM A TO Z

Accommodation

Hotels: In high season, it can be extremely difficult to find hotel accommodation; most hotels are booked out months in advance, especially the larger "moderate" hotels which block-book to package tours. Budget travelers can always get a **private room**; ferries are met by a host of locals offering rooms. The quality varies, but is generally at least acceptable. Sleeping on the town beach, once the budget traveler's avenue of last resort, is not popular with the locals. For more information or specific listings, contact the **Hellenic Chamber of Hotels**, Stadiou 24, Athens, fax. (01) 322-5449; branch office at Kar. Servias 2, National Bank of Greece, Athens, tel. (01) 322-9912 (open 8:30 a.m. to 2 p.m. Mon-Sat).

Camping is only allowed in organized campgrounds. For a complete, updated list of Greek campgrounds, "Camping in Greece," contact the Greek Camping Association, Solonos 102, 10680 Athens, tel./fax. (01) 362-1560.

Accommodation in Greece has six different categories: Luxury, and A, B, C, D and E. The lower categories are generally smaller family-run pensions. The classifications in this book are split into three categories:

Luxury ($$$): Establishments that reach at least the internationally-accepted mid-class hotel level. Well-furnished, generally near the sea, with swimming pool, sports facilities, restaurant and bar. A double room with breakfast during peak season, depending upon location, will start at around 25,000 Drs; off-season at around 16,000 Drs.

Moderate ($$): Good tourist hotels. Double room with breakfast from around 15,000 Drs during peak season; 12,000 Drs off-season.

Budget ($): Apartments, pensions and simple tourist hotels. Double room without breakfast from about 7,000 Drs during peak season; 5,000 Drs off-season.

Crime

"Greeks don't steal," said an Englishwoman, leaving her purse lying on a café table when she went off to get something from her house. Still, caution is advisable in tourist centers. As for Athens: keep a tight hold on your purse. Women, the Greeks say, should be especially careful. The late 1990s saw something of a crime wave. Greeks blame it on the huge influx of Albanians who started pouring in when their country's borders opened.

Deportment

While many foreigners regard the Greek Islands as a paradise for nude swimmers, the practice is definitely discouraged by locals, who resent the fact that many Europeans see their islands as playpens for a kind of laxness they'd never allow themselves at home. Other deterrents to nude swimming are increasingly crowded beaches and an increased awareness of the harmful effects of the sun. In the 1980s, there were nude beaches everywhere; in the 90s, you saw more and more bathing suits. In general, topless bathing for women is acceptable, but be circumspect about stripping down – and never on a town beach.

Orthodox churches require visitors to wear proper clothing: shorts, tank tops, and bathing suits are not allowed. Some churches have shawls or cloths by the door that you can wrap around you. Monasteries should not be visited from 1 to 5 p.m.; the time of the afternoon rest.

Smokers and campers should keep in mind that there is a great danger of forest fires during the summer months.

Eating and Drinking

Food: Greeks eat out a lot, but their expectations are quite different from those of European or American diners. They're less interested in the thrill of a new dish or a creative concoction, and meals are more a communal ritual than a gastronomic adventure. Locals choose their menus in animated conversation with the waiter, and select on the basis of what's on hand that day. Fresh food is prepared simply: fish is grilled and served with a slice of lemon, rather than a fancy sauce. And dining is communal; dishes are plunked down in the middle of the table, and everyone helps him- or herself. Separate checks are not the rule in Greece; if you want to pay separately, say "Stó jermanikó trópo," which means "German style."

Hampered by the language barrier, foreign visitors may have trouble at first. For one thing, scanning the menu affords a very poor indication of what's on offer; often, the menu is a standard list, in two or four languages, that appears in restaurants all over Greece. And restaurants that do have special tourist menus, with color photographs of their dishes, are generally less representative of the best of local cuisine. In fact, the quality of a meal is often in inverse relation to the décor: the more tourist frills (such as chair cushions or printed menus), the less interesting the food. Not every visitor enjoys going into a linoleum-tiled, flourescent-lit room crowded with Greeks, but if you're adventurous, and especially if you learn a couple of basic phrases of Greek, you'll often find the freshest fish or most interesting dishes in such places. Don't be shy about going into the kitchen and checking what's on hand; often, the day's specials don't appear on the menu at all.

Of course, deportment depends on what kind of establishment you're in. An **estiatorio**, or restaurant, is, for Europeans, the most conventional option: menus, waiters, wine glasses, the works. More informal is the **taverna**, the kind of place where you sit outside under the grapevines; a common variant of this is a **psarotaverna**, or fish tavern, specializing in seafood. Don't be put off by "snak mpar" signs – sometimes these grace very good tavernas. The bill often includes a small cover charge.

Then there's the **ouzeri**, the plainest in décor; in the row of restaurants along the harbor of an island port, the ouzeri is the one most full of locals, drinking ouzo and eating light snacks: *mezédes*, or starters. Here, you can get a Greek salad (*horiátiki saláta*), *tzatziki* (yogurt-cucumber-garlic dip) and *taramó saláta* (fish roe dip), or fresh fish, such as *márides* (fried anchovies) or *kalamária* (squid), but not prepared dishes like *moussaká* (the layered eggplant and meat dish upon which many visitors subsist during their Greek sojourns) or *stifádo* (meat stew).

There are always a few tourist-oriented cafés along the waterfront offering English breakfasts, ice cream specialties, yogurt and honey (*jaoúrti me méli*), iced coffee (*frapí*), and a few Greek dishes. Spend the day or the night lounging in the comfortable chairs, but go elsewhere for dinner; the food is usually only so-so.

In Greece, breakfast is a meal for the tourists; on the islands, you can find a number of variations on the so-called English, American or Continental breakfast, but locals will just have coffee. Fresh fruit juices are often good. Lunch is the main meal of the day, which, especially in the heat of summer, explains the physical necessity for the long midday siesta that shuts towns up as tight as a drum between about 2 and 5 pm. Dinner might be a few plates of *mezédes*. Much as the Greeks like to deny any kinship with the Turks, the latter dish is one sign of a number of common elements between Greek and Middle Eastern cuisine. Greece's *mezédes* (appetizers) correspond to Middle Eastern *mezze*; other similarities include *gyros*, which you find all over Turkey as *döner* or *iskender kebab*, and *souvláki*, also known as *shish kebab*. One noticeable difference: the Greeks like to use pork. Cinnamon in meat dishes, such as *moussaká*, is a characteristic Turkish touch. Tomatoes stuffed with meat or rice (*domátes jemistés*) appear on tables on both sides of the Aegean. Then there are desserts like *baklavá*, flaky pastry encasing a dense nutty filling, drenched in honey; *khataífi*, a similar filling wrapped in a sort of Shredded Wheat; and *halvah*, the rich nougaty almond confection.

Greeks at a restaurant begin dinner with a range of appetizers, including one Greek salad for the whole table. Note that cucumber-tomato salad, *angouridomáda* is basically a Greek salad without the feta, for considerably less money. In the spring, there might be a plate of *hórta,* boiled local greens, the Greek answer to collard greens or Swiss chard; in summer, this will probably be replaced by zucchini (*kolokidákia*), sometimes prepared as fritters or "zucchini balls" (*kolokidákia keftédes*), served with *skordalia*, a delicious dip of pureed potatoes and garlic (you'll stink for a day afterward, but it's worth it.) Eggplant salad, *melintzáno-saláta*, is also delicious.

Small fried fish, (*márides*), or squid (*kalamária*) are often eaten as an appetizer rather than a main course. Summer is not fishing season in the islands, and much of the seafood that's served then is frozen; the waiter will admit it if you ask, but won't always advertise it. If you're eating alone and want variety, order a *pikília*, a mixed appetizer plate.

The islands do have various culinary specialties, but it's hard to find them on local menus. A perfect example is Ándros' variation on the omelette, the *froutáli*, prepared with local herbs. Mitilíni (Lésvos) offers zucchini blossoms stuffed with feta cheese and vegetarian *moussaká*. On Sérifos, which claims to be a stronghold of Greek cuisine, you can buy a special ceramic pot in which to make *revíthia*; chickpeas stewed in olive oil with onions in a very low oven overnight. A salad of fresh capers will redefine your concept of a caper; you'll never eat the pickled variety in quite the same way again. Rabbit (*kunéli*) and goat (*katsíki*) often appear in island stewpots. Many islands also have their own variants of goat's- or sheep's-milk cheese.

The best snack in Greece is the cheese pie or *tirópitta*, flaky pastry around a feta filling. Another between-meals summer specialty is *lukomádes*. Not to be confused with *lukómes*, the Greek take on Turkish delight, *lukomádes* is a confection of fried dough drizzled with honey or sugar syrup and cinnamon or powdered sugar. Some places translate with the word "doughnut," but the dish is too Greek to be a real cognate. For the Greeks, it's a quintessential expression of lazy summer evenings on the islands.

Drinks: Greeks love their *kafé ellenikó*, the strong mocca served with finely-powdered grounds (never ask for "Turkish coffee"!), which they drink either *skéto* (black), *métrio* (lightly-sugared) or *glikó* (sweet); a double portion is ordered *dipló*. A glass of tap water (*neró*) is usually served with coffee. Coffee is drunk in the *kafeníon*, meeting place of the male world, where the sweet brandy *metaxá* is also frequently enjoyed.

Electricity

Greece's electrical current is the 220 volts standard in Europe; people coming from overseas will need a transformer. In general, the sockets fit standard European plugs (with two round prongs); however, some older places have slightly narrower sockets which the standard plugs don't fit. In a hotel, the reception desk will usually have an adaptor.

Emergency Phone Numbers

First Aid. 166
24-hour medical service
(Athens). 331-0310
Police 100
Fire Department. 199
Breakdown Assistance 104
Forest Fire Center. 191

Tourist Police 171
(24-hour, year-round information in English, German, French and Greek.)
U.S. Citizens Emergency
Aid 721-2951

Handicapped Facilities

Cruise ships and airlines allow wheelchair users access to many Greek islands, although getting up to many archeological sites is difficult if not impossible. For organized tours, contact the **Society for the Advancement of Travel for the Handicapped**, 347 5th Avenue, Suite 610, New York, NY 10016, tel. (212) 447-SATH, fax. 725-8253, or **New Directions**, 5276 Hollister Ave #207, Santa Barbara, CA 93111, tel. (805) 967-2841, fax. 964-7344.

Holidays and Festivals

January 1: New Year's Day.
January 6: Epiphany.
Holy Week and Easter (usually one week later than the Roman Catholic and Protestant holiday).
March 25: Independence Day.
October 28: Ochi Day ("No Day," celebrating Metaxas' refusal to allow Italian troops free passage through the country in World War II).
December 24: Christmas Eve.
December 25: Christmas Day.

The Orthodox calendar studs the islands' year with celebrations. On Epiphany, January 6, an Orthodox priest blesses the waters by throwing a large cross into the wintry gray ocean, to be retrieved by hardy divers. Greek Easter is the highlight of the year; eggs are dyed red (to symbolize the blood of Christ), Easter breads cooked, and wildflowers gathered throughout Holy Week to adorn Christ's bier on Good Friday, although the solemnity of mourning is punctuated by the bangs of firecrackers as local boys practice for the explosion set loose at the announcement of the Resurrection at midnight on Easter Saturday. People are injured in fireworks accidents every year.

Another major holiday is the Assumption of the Virgin (Panagía) on August 15, celebrated with huge church festivals on many of the islands; Tínos' huge pilgrimage church draws hordes from all over the country. Other local saints' days are also marked with festivals: Spiridion in August, Dimitrios in October (Indian summer in Greece is called "the little summer of St. Dimitrios"), Michalis (Michael) and Andreas in November.

These saints' days are not only church festivities; in Greece, people celebrate their name days the way people in other countries celebrate birthdays. The name-day honoree does the inviting, receiving all day visitors conveying congratulations, and often hosting a party.

Hours of Business

Most stores open around 8:30 a.m. Even in Athens, they tend to close between 2 and about 5 or 6 p.m.; on the islands, the towns are dead between these hours. People take their siestas seriously, and really sleep in the heat of the day. Life returns, and stores reopen, in the late afternoon, and are generally open until around 9 p.m. or later. Banks are open weekdays 8 a.m. to 2 p.m.; in tourist areas, some are also open on weekends.

Maps

Local tourist offices generally offer – often, sell – maps of their islands; but even the ones that cost money tend to be rather crude and lacking in detail. The key distinction between paved and dirt roads, for instance, often indicated by lines of different thicknesses or colors, can prove to be misleading, which is something you may not want to discover when you're confronted with an uphill road of scree in the semi-trackless mountains of southern Rhodes. If you plan to do any serious exploring, and especially if you want to hike, it's worth investing in some decent ordinance survey maps, either before you go or in Athens. On islands, streets and roads may not be widely known by their official names, so visitors sometimes encounter blank stares when they're asking directions to a specific address. Addresses in Greece are given with the street name first, the number second. *Odos*, the word for "street," is seldom included in the address.

Money

Cash machines on virtually all the islands of any size accept international cash cards (Visa, Cirrus, Eurocard); still, make sure to take cash if you're going to a really small island. Credit cards are only accepted in big hotels or big-city restaurants, although they're still required by rental car agencies. Travelers' checks are generally accepted. Currency exchanges, unlike banks and post offices, often charge a hefty commission.

Newspapers / Media

A huge selection of international newspapers is par for the course in the beach resorts, reflecting their predominantly foreign clientele. Some islands stock the *Athens News*, an English-language daily published for more than 45 years. In 1998, the Athens edition of the *International Herald Tribune* began including an English-language edition of *I Kathimerini*, "The Daily News," a leading Athens daily. Many of the more expensive resort hotels carry CNN and/or other English-language news stations, such as NBC and Sky Channel. Many Greek television stations show English-language programs with Greek subtitles rather than dubbing.

Sports and Activities

Hiking: Trekking Hellas, Filellinon 7, 10557 Athens, tel. 331-0323/6, e-mail: trekking@compulink.gr; offers organized hiking tours on several of the islands, some of which are combined with travel and accommodation on a traditional fishing boat. They also help organize maps and information for solo hikes.
Windsurfing: Greek Windsurfing Association, Filellinon 7, 10557 Athens, tel. 323-3696 or 323-0068, fax. 322-3251; the body responsible for competitive windsurfing in Greece.
Diving: Aegean Dive Center, Zamanou/ Pandoras 42, Glyfada (near Athens), tel. 894-5409, fax. 898-1120.
Boat Charter / Sailing: Hellenic Yachting Foundation, Akti Navarchou Kountouriti 7, 18534 Piraeus, tel. 413-7351, fax. 413-1191; information on sailing clubs and sailing competitions.
Hellenic Offshore Racing Club, Akti Ath. Dilaveri 3, 18533 Piraeus, tel. 411-3201, fax. 422-7038, also informs about competitions, notably the annual Aegean Sailing Rally through the islands, and can help arrange charter of a racing boat. For information on chartering a boat for cruising purposes, with or without crew, contact the **Hellenic Professional Yacht Owners Association**, Zéa Marina A8, 18536 Piraeus, tel. 428-6393, fax. 452-6335, or the **Greek Yacht Owners Association**, Akti Miaouli 87, 18538 Piraeus, tel. 429-1062, fax. 429-1034. There are also associations on individual islands, such as **Kalymna Yachting** on Kálimnos, which offers both organized trips and individual charter: PO Box 47, 85200 Kálimnos, tel. (0243) 24083, fax. 29125.
Since the 1960s, the Greek National Tourist Organization (EOT) has been investing a lot of money in new yacht harbors; for a listing of these and a wealth of information for sailors, get the EOT brochure "Sailing the Greek Seas."
Running: Long-distance runners can go back to the origins of the marathon in a November event from the village of Marathon to Athens' Olympic Stadium (42.2 kilometers). Contact SEGAS, 137 Sygrou, 17121 Athens, tel. (01) 935-9302.

Telephones and Post

OTE is the Greek telephone office; you can place calls abroad from its offices.

Most pay phones in Greece are card phones, from which you can generally place international calls. You can buy cards at newspaper kiosks with 100 (1,300 Drs), 500 (6,000 Drs) or 1,000 (11,500 Drs) units. Long-distance calls are expensive, especially if made from hotels. Greece's country code is 30; from within Europe, dial 0030; from outside of Europe, your international dialing code plus 30. To call from Greece to the UK, dial 0044; to the US or Canada 001.

There are two mobile phone networks, Panafon and Telestet, so you can use European-based mobile phones with no difficulty. The signal is not equally good on all islands; your signal may go in and out, and on some islands, such as Sími, there's no reception at all. OTE is setting up new antennas to remedy this problem. Even in good hotels, it's difficult to find on-line hookup for computers.

Finding a post office (*tahidromeío*) is no problem; but it's open to question how quickly mail will arrive. Sometimes a postcard or package makes it to Europe in a couple of weeks; but mail sent from the smaller islands in the off season can easily take four to six weeks to arrive.

Time

Greece is one hour later than Central European Time (Paris), 2 hours later than GMT (London); 7 hours later than Eastern Standard Time (the eastern US and Canada); 10 hours later than Pacific Time (California, British Columbia).

Water and Plumbing

Water is scarce on the islands; it often has to be rationed, and many islands have to ship it in. Keep showers short. Take seriously injunctions not to throw anything at all into the toilet; wastebaskets are provided for used paper. Bottled water is available in every kiosk; it's cheap and essential in the summer. Tap water is not always drinkable; ask at your hotel reception desk.

ADDRESSES

Internet

The Foreign Ministry has launched an English-language "news" site with business, political and cultural information, updated daily, at www.cthesis.com. The *Athens News* also updates its site daily: www.athensnews.dolnet.gr.

Embassies and Consulates in Athens

AUSTRALIA: D. Soutsou 37, tel. (01) 644-7303. *CANADA*: I. Genadious 4, tel. (01) 727-3400. *IRELAND*: Vasiléos Konstantinou 7, tel. (01) 723-2771. *NEW ZEALAND*: Xenias 24, tel. (01) 771-0112, 748-6667. *UK*: Ploutarhou 1, tel. (01) 723-6211. *US*: Vassílissis Sofiás 91, Athens, tel. (01) 721-2951, 721-8401.

Greek National Tourist Organization (EOT) Offices Abroad

AUSTRALIA / NEW ZEALAND: 51 Pitt St., Sydney, NSW 2000, tel. (00612) 241-1663, fax. 235-2174. *CANADA:* 1300 Bay St., Toronto, Ontario M5R 3K8, tel. (416) 968-2220, fax. 968-6533; 1233 de la Montagne, Suite 101, Montreal, Quebec H3G 1Z2, tel. (514) 871-1535, fax. 871-1498. *UK AND IRELAND:* 4 Conduit St., London, W1R ODJ, tel. (0171) 4999758, (0181) 734-5997, fax. 287-1369. *US:* 645 Fifth Ave. (Olympic Tower), New York, NY 10022, tel. (212) 421-5777, fax. 826-6940; 168 North Michigan Ave., Suite 600, Chicago, IL 60601, tel. (312) 782-1084, fax. 782-1091; 611 W. 6th St., Suite 2198, Los Angeles, CA 90017, tel. (213) 626-6696, fax. 489-9744.

EOT in Greece

Head Office: Amerikis 2, Athens, tel. (01) 322-3111, fax. 322-2841. Information desks: National Bank of Greece, Sindágma Square, Karageorgi Servias 2, Athens, tel. (01) 322-2545, 323-4130; General Bank of Greece, Ermou 1, Athens, tel. (01) 325-2267.

THE GREEK LANGUAGE

Greek is the oldest spoken language in Europe, although Modern Greek has evolved a long way from Ancient Greek. It's worth your while to pick up at least a few phrases and the alphabet; knowing the latter will give you confidence in dealing with buses, trains and road signs (although the latter are transliterated into Roman characters). And even if your attempts at producing Greek phrases are lamentable, people will be pleased that you're making the effort.

The 24 letters of the Greek alphabet may be difficult, but at least the pronunciation is logical. There are a few "false friends" among the consonants: B and D are pronounced "v" and like a voiced "th," while X is like the "ch" in German "ach," also transliterated as "h." In Greek, a "b" sound is spelled "mp," while an English "d" is "nt." You can see signs for snack bars called "Mpampis": "Bobby's." "G" is usually soft (Gianni is pronounced, as pop fans know, Yanni). Two gs together are "ng"; "angel" derives from the Greek αγγελοσ.

The diphthongs reduce to a relatively limited number of vowel sounds: a is ah (father), e and ai are ay (as in hay), o is oh (clove), and ou is oo (toucan). This leaves ei, h, i, oi, and u, all of which are pronounced ee (as in he).

The Greek Alphabet

Letter		Name	Transliteration
Α	α	**alpha**	*a*
Β	β	**beta**	*b*
Γ	γ	**gamma**	*g*
Δ	δ	**delta**	*d*
Ε	ε	**epsilon**	*e*
Ζ	ζ	**zeta**	*z*
Η	η	**eta**	*e (or long e)*
Θ	θ	**theta**	*th*
Ι	ι	**iota**	*i*
Κ	κ	**kappa**	*k*
Λ	λ	**lamda**	*l*
Μ	μ	**miu**	*m*
Ν	ν	**niu**	*n*
Ξ	ξ	**xi**	*x*
Ο	ο	**omicron**	*o*
Π	π	**pi**	*p*
Ρ	ρ	**rho**	*r*
Σ	σ/ς	**sigma**	*s*
Τ	τ	**tau**	*t*
Υ	υ	**upsilon**	*y*
Φ	φ	**phi**	*f*
Χ	χ	**chi**	*ch, kh*
Ψ	ψ	**psi**	*ps*
Ω	ω	**omega**	*o (or long o)*

The islands have many place names in common. Hóra or Horió (Χορα, Χοριω) means "town"; Paleóhorio (Παλαιο–χοριοω), "old town," is often an area of ruins where the original town once stood. Kástro is a "castle," often Venetian; while Emborió (or Nimborió) was once a "market" (think "emporium"). Vathí (Βαθυ), "deep," is a harbor town; Skála, a harbor or waterside; Pánormos, a bay. Platís Gialós is a "broad beach," while Kamáres means "arches," remnant of an old aqueduct or railway bridge. "Loutras" or Loutraki indicates a spring, as does Pirgí (Πυργι). The ending "aki" is a diminutive (*souvlaki*, a little *souvlos*, or spit).

Glossary

Good day, hello . . . . *Kaliméra*
Good afternoon . . . . *Kalispéra*
Hello (lit. "your health") . . . . *Yássou*
Hello (polite form). . . . . *Yásass*
Excuse me . . . . *Signómi, Oríste*
(the first can be used in the sense of "I'm sorry"; the second, politely to get someone's attention)
Where . . . . *Pú*
Where is . . . . *Pú íne*
When . . . . *Póte*
What time is it? . . . . *Tí óra íne?*
The bus . . . . *To leoforío*
The boat . . . . *To plío*
The beach . . . . *I paralía*
Here, there . . . . *Ethnó, ekí*
Today, tomorrow . . . . *Símera, Áwrijo*
Morning, night . . . . *Proí, Wrádi*
What is . . . . *Tí íne*

How much . . . . *Pósso*
Do you have . . . . *Échete*
I want . . . . *Thélo*
I would like . . . . *Tha íthela*
I don't want . . . . *Then thélo*
That . . . . *Aftó*
A room . . . . *Éna thomátjo*
A glass . . . . *Éna potíri*
Wine . . . . *Krasí*
Water . . . . *Neró*
The check . . . . *O logariasmós*
Do you speak English? . . . .
Omilaté Angliká?
I don't understand . . *Then katalawéno*
What . . . . *Pós*
Please . . . . *Parakaló*
Thank you . . . . *Efcharistó*
One . . . . *Éna, miá*
Two . . . . *Thío*
Three . . . . *Tría*
Four . . . . *Téssera*
Five . . . . *Pénde*
Six . . . . *Éksi*
Seven . . . . *Eftá*
Eight . . . . *Ochtó*
Nine . . . . *Ennjá*
Ten . . . . *Théka*
Twenty . . . . *Íkossi*
One hundred . . . . *Ekató*
Two hundred . . . . *Thiakósses*
One thousand . . . . *Chíljes*
Two thousand . . . . . . *Thío chiljáthes*

AUTHOR

Anne Midgette is a freelance writer on music, art and travel. An opera and art critic for *The Wall Street Journal*, *The New York Times*, *Newsday*, *Opera News*, and *Opern Welt*, she has written or contributed to travel guides to Germany, the U.S., France and the U.K.. for various publishers. She first traveled to the Greek Islands while working toward her degree in Classical Civilizations from Yale University, and has been a devotee of the islands ever since.

The author would like to thank Katerina Agapaki and Stefanos Tschochadzopolous of the Greek Tourist Board in Munich for their exceptional help and patience. Thanks, too, to all the other EOT officers whose assistance made working on this project such a pleasure, especially Dimitra Kaplanelli. And a special thanks to Julia and Michael Koullias for their generous hospitality.

PHOTOGRAPHERS

Amberg, Gunda 22, 228
Archiv für Kunst und Geschichte, Berlin 16, 18, 19, 20, 21, 24, 25, 26, 27, 29, 30, 32, 38, 213
Bärmann, Michael 126
Bersick, Dr. Gerhard 135
Bondzio, Bodo 101
Fischer, Peter 10/11, 12, 44, 97, 128/129, 136, 137, 138, 143, 145, 158, 160, 171, 180, 181, 186, 187, 189, 233, 234
Frangenberg, Johannes 8/9, 64/65, 66, 69, 72, 74, 75, 98, 100, 196/197
Geduldig, Erich (Photo-Press) 108/109, 112, 114
Haafke, Udo 212
Hackenberg, Rainer 15, 23, 31, 33L, 33R, 34, 35, 36/37, 43, 45, 46, 47, 48, 52/53, 54, 59, 61, 110, 130, 133, 146, 148, 149, 152, 153, 156/157, 163, 165, 166, 169, 172, 174, 176, 190, 198, 202, 203, 204, 229, 236, 237
Helms, Bernd 58
Janicke, Volkmar E. 91, 182, 217
Jung, Roland E. 223
Kappelhoff, Marlis 88
Mielke, Harald 89
Rein, Udo 92
Rostiti, Riccardo 118
Skupy-Pesek, Jitka 77
Stadler, Hubert 79, 184
Stankiewicz, Thomas 103, 139, 141
Storck, Manfred 28, 151
Stuffler, Jeanette cover, 206/207, 219, 220, 222, 226
Stuhler, Werner 94, 122, 125
Thiele, Klaus 14, 70, 80, 82, 84, 86, 208, 210, 214, 215, 235
Wothe, Konrad (Silvestris) 116.

A

Aegeus, king 41
Aeschylus 18, 19, 42
Agístri 60
Akrotíri 17, 103
Alexander the Great 17, 21, 27, 93, 179, 234
Alónnisos 114, 115, 121
Alónnisos Town 115
Gérakas 116
Íkos 115
Patitíri 115
Stení Vála 115
Ambelákia 55
Amorgós 96, 107
Agía Triáda 96
Ágios Géorgios Valsamítis, church 96
Arkesíni 96
Egiáli 97
Hozoviótissa, monastery 97
Katápola 96
Mount Kríkelo 97
Anáfi 104, 107
Andíparos 93
Andípaxi 219
Ándros 67, 104
Ágios Pétros, tower 68
Apikía 70
Batsí 68
Gávrio 67, 68
Halikolimniónas 69
Ménites 70
Messariá 70
Órmos Kórthiou 70
Paleópoli 68
Steniés 70
Zagorá 68
Zoodóhou Pigís, convent 68
Ándros Town 69
Archeological Museum 69
Museum of Modern Art 69
Panagía Paltiana, church 69
Áno Koufoníssi 96
Archaic Period 33
Ariadne 41, 93, 113, 201
Arkí 162
Asklipíon 172
Aspronissi 101
Astipálea 169, 170, 193
Análipsis 170
Drakospiliá, cave 170
Schinóntas 170
Astipálea Town 169
Kástro 169
Megali Panagía, church 169
Panagía Portaítissa, church 170
Athena, goddess 34, 41, 42, 48, 202, 223, 224
Athens 13, 15, 18, 19, 20, 27, 29, 33, 34, 39, 40, 41, 42, 43, 44, 45, 46, 48, 49, 50, 55, 57, 77, 123, 141, 199, 201, 228, 232, 236
Academy of Athens 46
Acropolis 19, 39, 40
Acropolis Museum 42
Ágios Elefthérios (Little Mitrópolis), church 45
Ágios Mitrópolis, church 45
Agorá 42, 43
Agorá Museum 43
Arch of Hadrian 47
Areopagus 42
Benáki Museum 47
Boulevard Athínas 45
Byzantine Museum 47
Central Market (Kentrikí Agorá) 45
Children's Museum 44
Erechthion 42
Historical Museum 47
Kanellopulos Museum 44
Kapnikaréa, church 45
Kolonáki 48
Library of Hadrian 43
Likavitós Hill 48
Monastiráki 45
Museum of Cycladic Art 47
Museum of Greek Folk Art 44
Museum of Greek Folk Music Instruments 44
National Archeological Museum 46
National Gallery 48
National Gardens (Voulí) 47
National Library 46
Odeion of Herodes Atticus 42
Olympieion 47
Omónia Square 45
Parliament Building (Sindágma) 46
Parthenon 34, 41, 42
Pláka 44, 45
Pnyx 42
Propylaea 41
Roman Agorá 43
Sindágma Square 46, 47
Stoá of Attalos 43
Temple of Athena Nike 34, 41
Temple of Hephaistos 43
Theater of Dionysus 42
Tomb of the Unknown Soldier 47
Tower of the Winds 44
University 46
Vassílissis Sofías Boulevard 47
War Museum 48
Záppeion 47

B

Balkan Wars 27, 200
Battle of Navarino 26
Byron, George Gordon, Lord 26, 93
Byzantine Empire 22, 23, 24, 25, 47, 179
Byzantine Era 34
Byzantium 22, 23, 24, 35, 220

C

Chíos, see Híos 26
Classical Period 33
Colossus of Rhodes 125, 179
Constantine, emperor 22, 91
Constantinople 22, 23, 24, 25, 27, 28, 91, 212
Corfu (Kérkira) 210, 211, 212, 213, 214, 215, 216, 217, 230
Ágii Déka 215
Ágios Márkos 216
Ágios Matthéos 216
Ahillío (Achilleon) 214
Benítses 215
Ermónes 216
Gardíki 216
Gouviá 216
Kaiser's Throne 216
Kalámi 217
Kassiópi 217
Korissíon, lake 216
Kulúra 217
Lákones 215
Paleokastrítsa 215
Panagía Theotókos, monastery 215
Pandokrátoras, mountain 216
Pélekas 216
Períthia 217
Pondikoníssi 214
Sidári 218
Vlahérna 214
Corfu Town 211, 212, 213
Ágios Iássonas ke Sosípatros, church 214
Ágios Spirídon, church 213
Archeological Museum 213
Byzantine Museum 213
Esplanade (Spianáda) 212
Listón 212
Mitrópolis, cathedral 213
Monrepos, villa 214

New Fortress 212
Old Fortress 212
Platitéra, monastery 213
Town Hall 213
Corinthian Order 34
Crete 14, 199, 200, 201, 202, 203, 204
Agía Tríada 202
Ágios Nikólaos 202
Amári Valley 204
Arkádi, monastery 204
Festós 201
Gourniá 203
Haniá 204, 205
Ierápetra 203
Iráklio 200, 205
Káto Zákros 203
Knossós 200
Kritsá 203
Lasíthi 202, 205
Lasíthi Plain 202
Liménas Hersónisos 201
Mália 201
Mátala 202
Mount Díkti 202
Préveli Beach 204
Préveli, monastery 204
Psiloritis 201
Réthimno 203, 205
Samariá Gorge 204
Sitía 203
Vái 203
Cronus, god 201
Crusaders 24, 25, 179
Cyclades 14, 67
Cycladic Art 32
Cycladic Culture 17
Cyprus 30, 167

D

Dafní Monastery 49
Darius, king 18, 40, 57
Delian League 20, 78
Delos, see Dílos 20
Delta, Penelope 232
Demotiki, language 27, 232
Dílos (Delos) 22, 77, 78, 105
Diocletian, emperor 22
Dionysus, god 42, 70, 93, 113, 147, 148
Dodecanese 13, 159
Donoúsa 96
Doric Order 34
Dörpfeld, Wilhelm 221
Durrell, Gerald 211
Durrell, Lawrence 211, 215, 217, 232

E

Égina (Aegina) 18, 57, 63
Agía Marína 59
Ágios Nektários, monastery 58
Faneroméni, church 57
Hrisoleóntissa, convent 59
Marathónas 59
Mount Óros 59
Ómorfi Ekklesía, church 57
Paleohóra 59
Pérdika 60
Souvála 59
Égina Town 57
Agía Tríada, church 58
Ágios Nikólaos, chapel 57
Archeological Museum 58
Hill of Kolóna 58
Pírgos Markéllou 58
Temple of Aphaéa 58
Town Hall 58
El Greco (Doménikos Theotokópoulos) 79
Elgin, Thomas, Lord 42
Elizabeth of Austria, Empress 214
Erimonissa 95
Ermoúpoli (Síros) 78
Anastásis, church 79
Áno Síros 79
Archeological Museum 78
Kimisis, church 79
Teatron Apollon 79
Town Hall 78
Euboeia, see Évia 13
Evans, Sir Arthur 17, 200
Évia (Euboeia) 13, 116, 117, 118, 119, 121
Artemísio 119
Édipsos 119
Erétria 117
Halkída 116
Istiéa 119
Káristos 118
Kími 117
Límni 119
Mount Dírfis 117
Mount Óhi 118
Oreí 119
Prokópi 118
Evrípou Channel 116

F

Fakinou, Evgenia 233
Filérimos (Ialissós) 183
Fíra (Thíra Town) 102
Flora and Fauna 234, 235
Folégandros 98, 99
Áno Meriá 99
Folégandros Town 98
Hrisospiliá, cave 98
Karavostásis 98
Foúrni 148

G

Geometric Period 33
Gialí 175
Giúra 115

H

Hálki 183
Halkída (Évia) 116
Agía Paraskeví, basilica 116
Archeological Museum 117
Karababa, fortress 117
Kástro 117
Mosque 117
Haniá (Crete) 204, 205
Hatzimihaílis, Theófilos 135
Hearn, Lefkadio 220
Hellenistic Period 34
Hephaistos, god 132
Hera, goddess 13, 77, 119, 151, 209, 224
Híos (Chíos) 35, 140, 141, 142, 143, 144, 154
Agía Markéllas, church 144
Ágio Gála 144
Anávatos 144
Kámbos 142
Kardámila 144
Kárfas 143
Mávra Vólia, beach 143
Melánios 144
Mestá 143
Néa Moní 144
Olímbi 143
Pirgí 143
Pitioús 144
Volissós 144
Vrondádos 144
Híos Town 142, 154
Byzantine Museum 142
Ethnographic Museum 142
Justiani Tower 142
Kástro 142
Korais Library 142
Hippocrates 171
Homer 17, 101, 119, 132, 133, 144, 187, 211, 219, 222, 232
Hozoviótissa, monastery (Amorgós) 97
Hydra, see Ídra 60

I

Ídra (Hydra) 60, 63
Agía Efpraxía, convent 62
Ídra Town 61
Kamíni 62
Limoniza Bay 62
Mandráki 62
Mólos 62
Profítas Ilías 62
Vlihós 62
Ikaría 145, 146, 147, 148, 155
Agíos Kírikos 146
Armenistís 148
Drákanos 147
Évdilos 147
Gialiskári 148
Hristós 148
Kámbos 148
Koskínas 148
Messahti, beach 148
Nás, beach 148
Theokístis, monastery 148
Thérma 147
Inoússes 144
Io 209
Ionian Islands 13, 209
Ionic Order 34
Íos 100, 107
Agía Theodótis 100
Gialós 100
Íos Town 100
Manganári 101
Milopótamos 100
Plakatós 100
Iráklia 95
Iráklio (Crete) 200, 205
Archeological Museum 200
Koules, fortress 200
Ithaca, see Itháki 222
Itháki (Ithaca) 222, 223, 224, 231
Aëtós, mountain 223
Ágios Andréou 223
Anogí 224
Argostóli 224
Ássos 224
Drongaráti 224
Ellinikó 223
Fiskárdo 224
Fountain of Arethoúsa 223
Fríkes 224
Grotto of Melissáni 224
Itháki Town (Vathí) 223
Kióni 224
Kounópetra 226
Kráni 225
Lake Ávithos 225
Lixoúri 226
Loizos Cave 224
Marble Cave 223
Markópoulou 225
Mírto 224
Mount Énos 224, 225
Pelikáta Hill 224
Sámi 224
Skála 225
Stavrós 223, 224

K

Kálimnos 167, 168, 193
Daskalió, cave 169
Emborió 168
Horió 168
Hristós tís Jerousalím, basilica 168
Péra Kástro 168
Plátanos 169
Vathís 168
Kálimnos Town 167
Archeological Museum 168
Sponge Museum 168
Kapodístrias, Ioánnis 27, 213
Karamanlis, Constantine 30, 31
Kárpathos 189, 190, 191, 195
Arkása 191
Kárpathos Town (Pigádia) 190
Menetés 190
Ólimbos 189, 191
Óthos 191
Kásos 191, 195
Agía Marína 192
Frí 191
Kastellóriso 192, 195
Kastellóriso Town 192
Seal Grotto 192
Katharévusa, language 27, 232
Káto Koufoníssi 96
Kazantzakis, Nikos 57, 233
Kéa 80, 81, 105
Agía Iríni 81
Agía Marína, monastery 81
Karthéa 82
Kéa Town (Ioulís) 81
Korissía (Livádi) 81
Panagía Kastrianís, monastery 81
Vourkári 81
Kéa Town (Ioulís) 81
Archeological Museum 81
Lion of Kéa 81
Kefaloniá 224, 225, 231
Kérkira, see Corfu 210
Kéros 95
Kímolos 87, 88, 106
Ellinikó 88
Kímolos Town 88
Prássa 88
Kirá Panagía 114
Kíthira 228, 229, 231
Agía Pelagía 230
Agía Sofía, church 229
Kapsáli 229
Káto Hóra 229
Livádi 229
Milopótamos 229
Moní Mirtidió, monastery 229
Paleohóra 230
Paléopolis 229
Kíthnos 82, 83, 106
Driopís 83
Kanála 83
Kástro Orías 83
Kíthnos Town 83
Loutrá 83
Mérihas 82
Vriókastro 82
Kleobolos, tyrant 18
Knossós (Crete) 200, 201, 202
Kós 170, 171, 172, 193
Alikés 173
Andimáhia 173
Asklipíon 172
Embrós Thermá 172
Kardámena 173
Kástro 173
Kéfalos 173
Zía 172
Kós Town 171, 193
Agorá 171
Castle of the Knights of St. John 171
Hippocrates' Plane Tree 171
Museum 171
Platía Eleftherías 171
Kouros 33
Krokalia 35

L

Lasíthi (Crete) 202, 205
Lear, Edward 211
Lefkáda (Lefkás) 219, 220, 221, 222, 231
Ágios Nikítas 222
Cape Leukádas 222
Faneroméni, convent 221
Kariá 222
Leukas 221
Nídri 221
Pórto Katsíki 222
Santa Maura, fortress 220
Vlihó Bay 221

Lefkáda Town 221
Archeological Museum 221
Icon Museum 221
Lefkás, see Lefkáda 219
Léros 163, 164, 166, 193
Álinda 166
Blefoúti 166
Gourná 166
Lakkí 164
Mount Klidí 166
Panagía Kavourádena, cave church 164
Parthéni 166
Plátanos 164
Xirókambos 164
Lésbos, see Lésvos 134
Lesser Eastern Cyclades (Erimoníssa) 95
Lésvos (Lésbos) 134, 135, 140, 154
Agía Paraskeví 136
Agiásos 140
Ágios Fokás, basilica 139
Ágios Isídoros, beach 140
Ágios Rafaíl, monastery 136
Evthtaloús 138
Ipsiloú, monastery 139
Kalloní 137
Lafiónas 137
Lepéthimnos, mountains 138
Limónos, monastery 137
Mandamádos 138
Melínda 139
Mirsiniótissas, nunnery 137
Míthimna (Mólivos) 138
Mitilíni Town 135
Mória 136
Perivólis, monastery 139
Pétra 137
Petrified Forest 139
Polhinítos 139
Sígri 139
Skála Eresoú 139
Skála Sikaminéas 138
Taxiárhis Mihaílis, monastery 138
Thermís 136
Variá 135
Vaterá 139
Límnos 131, 132, 133, 154
Gomáti 134
Íféstia 133
Kabírion 133
Kamínia 133
Katálakko 134
Kókkino, fortress 133
Kondiás 132
Mírina 132
Moúdrou Bay 133
Néa Koútali 133
Paleókastro 132
Pláka 133
Polióhni 133
Thános 132
Líndos (Rhódos) 185
Acropolis 185, 186
Panagía, church 185
Lipsí 162, 163, 192
Loggerhead Turtles 227, 235

M

Macedonian Wars 22
Macedonia 21, 124
Makarios, Archbishop 30, 31
Márathi 162
Marathon 19, 40
Mastic 140, 141
Mastichochoría 141, 143
Meganíssi 221
Megísti, see Kastellóriso 192
Mehmet Ali 26
Mestá (Híos) 143
Metaxas, Joannes 29
Míkonos 73, 75, 105
Agía Ánna Kalafátis 75
Ágios Stéfanos 77
Áno Méra 75
Kalafáti 75
Kaló Livádi 75
Panórmou Bay 75
Paradise Beach 75
Super Paradise, beach 75
Míkonos Town 73, 74
Archeological Museum 74
Ethnographic Museum 74
Lena's House 74
Maritime Museum 74
Paraportianí, church 74
Windmills 74
Miller, Henry 211, 232
Mílos 88, 89, 90, 106
Adámas 89
Apollónia 90
Filakopí 90
Kléftiko 90
Klíma 90
Mélos 89
Papafrángas 90
Pláka 89
Sarakíniko 90
Tripití 89
Zefiría 90
Minoan Culture 17, 32
Minos, king 17, 146, 201
Minotaur 17, 41, 93, 201
Mírina (Límnos) 132
Archeological Museum 132
Metropolitan Mansion 132
Mirivílis, Stratís 135, 233
Míthimna (Mólivos) 138, 154
Archeological Museum 138
Art Museum 138
Kástro 138
Mitilíni Town (Lésvos) 135, 136, 154
Ágios Therapón, church 135
Ancient Theater 135
Archeological Museum 135
Kástro 135
Municipal Art Gallery 136
Mitilíni, see Lésvos 134
Mólivos, see Míthima 138
Monastery of St. John (Pátmos) 161
Moní 60
Monk Seals 114, 235
Mycenaean Age 17
Mycenaean Culture 32

N

Néa Kaiméni 101
Náxos 93, 107
Ágios Mámas, church 94
Apírados 94
Apollón 93, 94
Filóti 95
Halkí 94
Hrisostómou, convent 94
Mount Zás 95
Náxos Town 93
Archeological Museum 94
Kástro 94
Mitrópolis Zoodóhou Pigís, cathedral 94
Paláteia 93
Portára 93
Néa Moní, monastery (Híos) 35, 144
Nike (Winged Victory) 125
Nikouriá 97
Nísiros 173, 174, 175, 194
Emborió 175
Mandráki 174
Nikiá 175
Paleókastro 175
Páli 175
Panagía to Spilianí, monastery 174
Stéfanos, crater 176
Nissiópi 139
Northeast Aegean Islands 13, 131

O

Oía (Thíra) 102
Otto I, king 27, 44, 45, 47
Ottoman Empire 24, 25, 27, 232
Ottomans 14, 25, 27

P

Paleá Kaiméni 101
Papadiamántis, Aléxandros 232
Papandreou, Andreas 31
Papandreou, George 30
Parikía (Páros) 90
Archeological Museum 91
Crusader Castle 91
Ekatontapilianí, church 91
Páros 90, 106
Driós 92
Hrisí Aktí, beach 92
Léfkes 92
Maráthio 91
Márpissa 92
Náousa 91
Parikía 90
Petaloúdes 92
Pródromos 92
Pátmos 159, 160, 161, 162, 192
Apokálipsis, convent 160
Cave of Saint John 160
Grígos 162
Kámbos 162
Monastery of St. John 161
Panagía Koumana, church 162
Pátmos Town 161
Skála 160
Paxí 218, 219, 231
Gáios 218
Ipapánti, cave 219
Lákka 219
Panagía, monastery 219
Peloponnesian War 20, 34, 41, 57, 189, 211
Pericles 20, 41
Peristéra 114
Persians 13, 18, 19, 20, 21, 33, 40, 41, 55, 57, 77, 123
Pétra (Lésvos) 137
Ágios Nikólaos, church 137
Panagía Glikfoúsa, church 137
Women's Agricultural Cooperative 137
Phidias 19, 34, 41, 42
Pipéri 114
Piraeus (Pireas) 49, 50, 51
Archeological Museum 50
Kastela 50
Marina Zéa 50
Maritime Museum 50
Mikró Límano 50
Municipal Theater 50
Pirgí (Híos) 143
Pithagório (Sámos) 150
Polis 18
Polycrates 18, 150, 151
Póros 60, 63
Kalavreias, beach 60
Temple of Poseidon 60
Zoodóhou Pigís, monastery 60
Poseidon, god 41, 42, 60, 77, 126, 174, 190, 214
Psará 155
Psathoúra 115
Pythagoras 150

R

Rembetiko 233
Réthimno (Crete) 203, 205
Rhodes, see Rhódos 25
Rhódos (Rhodes) 25, 177, 179, 180, 181, 182, 183, 184, 185, 194
Afándou 185
Ágios Isídoros 183
Apóllona 183
Arhángelos 185
Émbonas 183
Eptá Pigés 185
Faliráki 185
Feráklos 185
Filérimos 183
Kallithéas 184
Kámiros 183
Kámiros Skála 183
Koskinoú 184
Kritinia 183
Líndos 185
Monólithos 184
Mount Attáviros 183
Pávlou Bay 187
Petaloúdes 183
Prasoníssi 184
Profítis Ilías, mountain 183
Thári, monastery 184
Triánda 182
Tsambíka, monastery 185
Rhódos Town 177, 179, 180, 181, 182, 194
Aquarium 180
Archeological Museum 181
Byzantine Museum 181
City Wall 182
Evangelismós, church 180
Governor's Palace 179
Ipotón 181
Mandráki Harbor 180
Monte Smith, hill 179
Museum of Decorative Arts 181
Néa Agorá, market hall 180
Our Lady of Victory, church 182
Palace of the Grand Masters 181
Platiá Martíron Evríon 182
Rodini Park 182
Synagogue 182
Roman Empire 22, 23
Romans 21, 34, 77, 90, 136, 170, 172, 199, 217, 220, 223

S

Sailing 236, 237
Salamína (Salamis) 19, 55
Faneroméni, convent 55
Kakí Vígla 55
Peristéria 55
Salamis, see Salamína 40
Samiopoúla 152
Sámos 149, 150, 153, 155
Ancient Theater 151
Heraéon 151
Iréo 152
Karlóvasi 153
Kokkári 152
Kosmádei 153
Koumaradéi 152
Manolátes 153
Megalí Panagías, monastery 152
Mitilíni 150
Mount Lazaros 153
Panagía Spilianí, monastery 151
Panagía Vrondá, monastery 152
Pithagório 150
Platanákia 153
Pnáka 153
Pótami 153
Tunnel of Eupálinos 151
Sámos Town 149, 155
Áno Vathí 149
Archeological Museum 149
Samothráki 125, 126, 127
Gréa Váthra 126
Kamariótisa 126
Mount Fengari 126
Paleópoli 125
Samothráki Town 126
Sanctuary of the Great Gods 125
Santorin, see Thíra 101
Sappho 134, 135, 139
Saría 191
Saronic Gulf 55
Saronic Gulf Islands 13
Schliemann, Heinrich 17, 133, 221, 222, 223

Sérifos 83, 84, 106
Livádi 83
Mégalo Horió 84
Moní Taxiarhón, monastery 84
Sérifos Town 84
Sesklío Islands 189
Shinoússa 95
Sífnos 84, 85, 86, 87, 106
Apollonía 85
Artemón 86
Exámbela 86
Herónissos 87
Hrisopigí, monastery 87
Kamáres 85
Kástro 86
Kíria Vrisiánis, monastery 86
Platís Gialós 87
Profítis Ilías, mountain 86
Vathí 87
Sikelianos, Angelos 220
Síkinos 99, 107
Aloprónia 99
Episkopí 99
Síkinos Town 99
Sími 187, 188, 189, 195
Gialós 187
Horió 188
Kalí Stráta 188
Nimborió 188
Panormítis, monastery 189
Pédi 188
Roukoniótis, monastery 189
Síros 78, 105
Ahládi 80
Azólimnos 80
Ermoúpoli 78
Fanéromeni, church 80
Fínikas 80
Galissás 80
Grámmata 80
Hroúsa 80
Kastrí 80
Posidonía 80
Skiáthos 111, 112, 113, 120
Evangelístria, monastery 113
Kástro 113
Koukounariés, beach 112
Kounístra, convent 112
Lalária 113
Skíathos Town 111
Fortress 111
Papadiamántis House 112
Skíros 119, 120, 121
Linariá 120
Skíros Town 120
Skópelos 113, 114, 120
Ágios Ioánnis 114
Agnóndas 113
Glóssa 114
Loutráki 114
Metamórfosis, monastery 113
Moní Evangelismoú, monastery 113
Panórmos Bay 114
Prodómou, monastery 113
Stáfilos Bay 113
Skópelos Town 113
Ágios Athanásios, church 113
Ethnographic Museum 113
Hrísto, church 113
Kástro 113
Panagía Elefthería, church 113
Skorpiós 221
Solomós, Dionísios 227, 232
Sparta 20, 57, 211
Spétses 62, 63
Agía Anárgiri 62
Agía Paraskeví 62
Bekíri Cave 62
Profítis Ilías, mountain 62
Spétses Town 62
Sporades 13, 111
St. John (Ioánnis Theólogos), evangelist 159, 232
Storace, Patricia 232

T

Télendos 168
Temple of Aphaéa (Égina) 58
Tériade (Stratís Eleftheriádis) 135
Thásos 123, 124, 127
Alikí 124
Kástro 124
Limenária 124
Mariés 125
Mount Ipsário 124
Panaghía 124
Potamiá 124
Thásos Town (Liménas) 123
Acropolis 124
Agorá 124
Archeological Museum 123
Herakleion 124
Makrí Ámmos 124
Theseus 41, 93, 113, 201
Thíra (Santorin) 17, 101, 102, 103, 107
Akrotíri 17, 103
Archaia Thíra 103
Athiniós 102
Fíra (Thíra) 102
Imerovígli 102
Méssa Goniá 103
Messariá 102
Oía (Ía) 102
Pírgos 102
Profítis Ilías, mountain and monastery 103
Thirasía 101
Thracian Islands 123
Tílos 176, 177, 194
Ágios Pandaleímon, monastery 177
Harkadió, grotto 177
Livádia 177
Megálo Horió 177
Tínos 71, 104
Exóbourgo 72
Istérnia 73
Kardianí 72
Kehrovouníou, convent 72
Loutrá 72
Marlás 73
Pánormou Bay 73
Pírgos 71, 73
Vólax 71
Tínos Town 71
Archeological Museum 72
Panagía Evangelístria, church 71
Tunnel of Eupálinos 151
Turks 25, 28, 40, 45, 48, 61, 62, 70, 114, 118, 140, 141, 142, 144, 145, 150, 165, 179, 187, 192, 199, 204, 209, 212, 217, 220

V

Venizélos, Elefthérios 27, 199
Venus de Milo 89

X

Xerxes, King 19, 40

Z

Zákinthos 226, 227, 228, 231
Blue Grotto (Kianó Spiliá) 228
Kíthira Town 228
Laganás 227
Shipwreck Beach 228
Tar Pits 227
Xingiá Cave 228
Zákinthos Town 226
Ágios Dionísios, church 227
Ágios Nikólaos tou Molou, church 227
Kiría tou Angélon, church 227
Museum of Byzantine Art 227
Strata Marina 227
Zeus, god 13, 77, 119, 123, 132, 201, 202, 209, 228

Explore the World

AVAILABLE TITLES

Australia
Bali / Lombok
Berlin and Potsdam
Brazil
Brittany
Burma → *Myanmar*
California
Las Vegas, Reno, Baja California
Cambodia / Laos
Canada
Ontario, Québec, Atlantic Provinces
Canada
Pacific Coast, the Rockies, Prairie Provinces, and the Territories
Canary Islands
Caribbean
The Greater Antilles, Bermuda, Bahamas
Caribbean
The Lesser Antilles
China – Hong Kong
Corsica
Costa Rica
Crete
Croatia – *Adriatic Coast*
Cyprus
Egypt
Florida
Greece – *The Mainland*
Greek Islands
Hawai'i
Hungary
India
Northern, Northeastern and Central India
India – *Southern India*
Indonesia
Sumatra, Java, Bali, Lombok, Sulawesi
Ireland
Israel - *with Excursions to Jordan*
Kenya
London, England and Wales
Malaysia - Singapore - Brunei
Maldives
Mexico
Morocco
Moscow / St. Petersburg
Munich
Excursions to Castles, Lakes & Mountains
Myanmar (Burma)
Nepal
New York – *City and State*
New Zealand
Norway
Paris
Philippines
Portugal
Prague / Czech Republic
Provence
Rome
Scotland
South Africa
South Pacific Islands
Spain – *Pyrenees, Atlantic Coast, Central Spain*
Spain
Mediterranean Coast, Southern Spain, Balearic Islands
Sri Lanka
Syria – Lebanon
Tanzania
Thailand
Turkey
Tuscany
U.S.A.
The East, Midwest and South
U.S.A.
The West, Rockies and Texas
Vietnam

FORTHCOMING

Poland
Sweden

Nelles Guides – authoritative, informed and informative. Always up-to-date, extensively illustrated, and with first-rate relief maps. 256 pages, approx. 150 color photos, approx. 25 maps.